SCM STUDYGUIDE TO RELIGIOUS AND SPIRITUAL EXPERIENCE

SCM STUDYGUIDE TO RELIGIOUS AND SPIRITUAL EXPERIENCE

Jeff Astley

© Jeff Astley 2020

Published in 2020 by SCM Press
Editorial office
3rd Floor, Invicta House,
108–114 Golden Lane,
London EC1Y 0TG, UK
www.scmpress.co.uk

SCM Press is an imprint of Hymns Ancient & Modern Ltd (a registered charity)

Hymns Ancient & Modern® is a registered trademark of
Hymns Ancient & Modern Ltd
13A Hellesdon Park Road, Norwich,
Norfolk NR6 5DR, UK

All rights reserved. No part of this publication may be reproduced,
stored in a retrieval system, or transmitted,
in any form or by any means, electronic, mechanical,
photocopying or otherwise, without the prior permission of
the publisher, SCM Press.

The Author has asserted their right under the Copyright, Designs and Patents Act 1988
to be identified as the Author of this Work

Scripture quotations are from New Revised Standard Version Bible: Anglicized Edition,
copyright © 1989, 1995 National Council of the Churches of Christ in the United States of
America. Used by permission. All rights reserved worldwide.
Acknowledgement is made for use of Figure 3.9 from Wesley J. Wildman, 2011,
Religious and Spiritual Experiences, New York: Cambridge University Press.
Reproduced by permission of the licensor through PLSClear.
British Library Cataloguing in Publication data

A catalogue record for this book is available
from the British Library

978-0334-05796-3

Contents

Introduction vii

Acknowledgements xiii

Part 1 Definitions 1

1 Defining the Terms: Experience, Religious Experience, Spiritual Experience 3

Part 2 Data 17

2 The Characterization, Classification and Reporting of Religious and Spiritual Experiences 19

3 Qualitative and Quantitative Research 27

4 Categories of Religious and Spiritual Experiences: From Mysticism to NDEs 37

Part 3 Debates 55

5 Experience and Experiences 57

6 Triggers and Facilitators 67

7 Experience and Fruits 75

8 Experience and Interpretation 83

9 Objectivity and Veridicality	103
10 Evidence and Argument	115
11 Challenges of Diversity and Naturalistic Explanations	123
12 Religious Experience and Religious Language	135
13 Religious Experience and Revelation	148
14 Gender Issues	162

Part 4 Disciplines, Doubters and Defenders — 169

15 The Psychology of Religious and Spiritual Experience	171
16 Religious and Spiritual Experience in Scripture	179
17 Religious and Spiritual Experience in the Christian Tradition	193
18 The Theology of Religious and Spiritual Experience	205
19 The Philosophy of Religious and Spiritual Experience	216
20 The Anthropology and Sociology of Religious and Spiritual Experience	226

Appendix: Religious and Spiritual Experiences and Neuroscience	244
References	247
Index of Subjects	273
Index of Names	299

Introduction

Guided Study

The SCM Studyguides provide introductions to the study of a specific topic and are aimed at undergraduates and other readers with a serious interest in learning. The *SCM Studyguide to Religious and Spiritual Experience* is not intended as a popular presentation of religious and spiritual experience, or as an *apologia* (argument for or defence or commendation of them). Nor is it an anthology of such experiences, of which there are many available, although it offers some examples drawn from an assortment of sources. Rather, this book is a *guide to studying* these phenomena, their implications and the many debates to which they give rise.

Like other guides, the intention of a study guide is to help people 'find their way about' some area, region, territory or landscape. In this case, the ground that needs to be explored is vast, for religious and spiritual experiences are widespread and enormously varied phenomena, even though some have argued for deep connections and commonalities between them. They are also reported by people across widely diverse cultures, religions, philosophies and worldviews. To make the student's task even more difficult, these experiences have been studied by, and discussed within, a number of very different academic disciplines: in the humanities (e.g. philosophy), the social sciences (e.g. anthropology) and even the natural sciences (e.g. neurophysiology). Hence, the literature on this topic is very diverse and extensive, and sometimes rather demanding – especially in those areas that the student is exploring for the first time.

Inevitably, then, this guide has had to be *selective*. In particular, it is selective in emphasizing religious and spiritual experiences in the Hebrew Bible, the New

Testament and the Christian tradition, and the issues and debates that they raise, rather than attempting to range right across all the scriptural, historical and traditional sources available in the world's religions. This is an appropriate focus for a work published by a Christian publisher. Nevertheless, the greater part of this book deals with debates and disciplines that are also relevant to the study of religious and spiritual experiences within other religious faiths – and those experienced by people who stand outside all religions.

The author realizes that many who read this book will also do so selectively. Not every reader is going to be interested in every kind of religious and spiritual experience, every problem or argument within this extensive region, or every perspective from which it has been surveyed. But perhaps every reader, whatever their particular focus of interest, needs to acknowledge the wider context in which their focus is set; if only because, if they should trespass beyond the limits of their own concerns, they are likely to come across some idea, debate or insight that will help them better to understand the contours of their home territory.

But I must be realistic. This guide is bound to be treated by some readers as they routinely treat other travel guides: as a reference book in which to 'look up' a particular phenomenon, issue, debate or author. To help with this function, I have provided many cross-references to other chapters in the book and fairly extensive index entries. Additionally, in Part 4, 'Disciplines, Doubters and Defenders', I have added some glossaries of key terms and brief overviews of the ideas of some significant contributors to the debates over religious experience.

My hope, of course, is that many readers will want to read through the whole book, and that if they do so they will feel that this task is worth the extra time and energy. I also hope that they will judge that I have at least attempted to report fairly on and provided pertinent quotations of the different positions that have been taken in the study of and debates over religious and spiritual experiences. In the end, however, the teacher (and, therefore, the textbook writer) has to leave the student to decide for themselves the strengths and weaknesses of the arguments of others, and the plausibility and coherence of their concepts. It is right, therefore, to conclude every topic with a (normally implicit) question, 'So, what do *you* think about this, and why?' On the other hand, even teachers hold their own views and values; and mine will doubtless become apparent in the text from time to time. I trust, however, that my own views won't get in the way of your finding your own way around this fascinating, influential, disturbing – and, at times, exasperating – topic.

Fields, Disciplines and Studies of Religious and Spiritual Experience

The different categories of religious and spiritual experiences (RSEs) may be said to represent different (if overlapping) 'fields' or 'areas' of human experience. These experiences are the phenomena that are available for study by scholars and researchers, mainly through their expression in words and other behaviour. This study involves the application of different approaches and methodologies: that is, 'disciplines' or forms of knowledge, each of which has its own distinctive concepts, theories, testing procedures and forms of argument (cf. Hood, 1995b, parts II–V; Schmidt, 2016b). The raw material that constitutes the basis of the resulting analyses and other species of reasoning, represents the main reference of people's talk about the *'facts'* (in terms of the 'empirical facts') or *'data'* of RSEs.

A respected critical investigation into one particular type of explicitly religious experience (visions of Christ) concludes with the claim that one of its greatest challenges had been that 'their study touches on many disciplines', including (in this case) biblical, historical, psychological, theological and philosophical studies. 'The extensive bodies of literature belonging to [these] disciplinary domains … makes the task of interpreting these experiences difficult' (Wiebe, 1997, p. 220). But a multidisciplinary approach, which makes at least *some attempt* to sample 'the vast range of approaches' that are relevant to the study of religious and spiritual experiences (Schmidt, 2016b, p. 9), is increasingly recognized as essential to understanding these phenomena. This also applies to the related field of the study of religious emotions, where it is similarly true that 'the reductionism that we see in some accounts' of such occurrences is 'almost always a result of disciplinary chauvinism and the resulting ignorance' (Roberts, 2008, p. 502).

So, Part 4 offers an attempt at such a multidisciplinary approach, with chapters introducing the following disciplinary perspectives on the field:

- *Psychological* perspectives (Chapter 15).
- *Theological* perspectives (Chapter 18).
- *Philosophical* perspectives (Chapter 19).
- *Anthropological* and *sociological* perspectives (Chapter 20).

- *History* and *historical theology* (Chapter 17) also represent a distinct form of scholarly discipline, whereas *biblical studies* (Chapter 16) covers a range of discrete studies of the languages, sources, forms, structures, contexts and meanings of the material within the Bible.

By contrast with the data studied in the other chapters, Chapters 16 and 17 explore more classical examples of the phenomenon of spiritual and religious experiences, focusing on the specific area of the historical Judeo-Christian tradition.

One significant perspective not included in the above list is that of *neuroscience*, one of the 'natural sciences' that even some of the earlier overviews took seriously, alongside the approaches of the humanities and the social sciences (cf. Staal, 1975, pp. 9–10, 17, 109–12, and chs 11, 12). This is a discipline in which there have recently been considerable technical advances, so that nowadays, in some cases at least, changes in the brain may be identified and recorded through neuroimaging techniques as these experiences happen. My main excuse for largely passing over such fast-developing and significant research is that it requires more specialist knowledge of the anatomy and physiology of the human brain, and the methods of investigating it, than most readers studying humanities or social sciences possess. (Or textbook authors, for that matter.) I have, however, highlighted some of the *conceptual issues* raised by these studies for the philosophy and theology of religious and spiritual experiences in Chapter 11 and various other places in the book,[1] and included a select bibliography on the subject for those who wish to explore it further in the Appendix.

Exercises and References

Many of the Exercises in the book carry the subtitle 'Among the Articles'. These contain a reference and brief introduction to one or more journal articles (or book chapters, essays or published lectures), together with the suggestion that it be read and critically assessed.[2]

Such compositions can be peculiarly valuable resources for students, even at an introductory level, as they provide a succinct argument and/or presentation of data compressed into a relatively limited extent. (Furthermore, journal articles are also normally subject to peer review by other experts in the field.) The articles and other pieces cited in these Exercises have been selected from around 5,000 relevant items, from which a long list of the most promising 1,000 items were chosen for more careful assessment. After drawing on the advice of experts in a range of disciplines and fields, the 40 or so articles that appear in the book were selected. The selection process did not only weigh the importance and quality of their arguments or empirical data, it also assessed them against educational criteria relevant to their use as aids to teaching or study – such as their brevity and clarity of argument and expression, and their potential for generating interest and debate in the context of teaching or discussion.

University students should be able to *access copies* of most of these articles through their institutions' libraries. I recognize, however, that independent students will normally not be able to do this without payment. I hope that this situation may eventually change, and in any case more recent articles are often available online without charge as 'preprints', from 'open access' journals or from the authors' own websites, as an Internet search using the article's title and author should reveal.

I have adopted the convention of ordering series of 'in-text' references in date rather than alphabetical order, as this is more relevant to the development of a debate. *ET* indicates an English translation; and the date of a source's first edition (often in its original language) – or, in some cases, earlier editions – is included in the References section, and sometimes within the text, in square brackets after the date of the edition I have used: e.g. 'James, 1960 [1902]'.

Notes

1 To be dealt with adequately, however, even these conceptual implications would require an analysis of such substantive topics as the nature of human consciousness and of God's relationship to creation, and of the strengths and weaknesses of 'neurotheology' (a field that seeks to explain the relationship between neural processes, theology and RSEs), which lies beyond the scope of an introductory textbook.

2 Here, of course, 'criticism' involves an analysis of the merits and faults of something, and is not necessarily negative.

Acknowledgements

I have learned a great deal about the study of religious and spiritual experiences from many scholars and researchers across different disciplines and universities. It would be invidious to name individuals and may tempt the reader to assume that they are in part to blame for any of my own errors that have crept into this book. Nevertheless, I am most grateful for the help I have had from all these academics, and from the library services of Durham University and the University of Warwick. I should also express particular thanks, first to the Alister Hardy Trust, which has enabled my study of the literature on religious and spiritual experiences by funding part-time appointments as 'Alister Hardy Professor of Religious and Spiritual Experience' at Glyndŵr University and the University of Warwick; and secondly to the Templeton Foundation for project funding for my current post at Bishop Grosseteste University, Lincoln.

I also formally acknowledge my thanks to Cambridge University Press for permission to reproduce the Figure from Wildman (2011, p. 101); to the St Mary's Centre in partnership with St Peter's Saltley Trust for permission to reuse some of my material previously published in their online journal, *Challenging Religious Issues*; and for permission to quote from reports of experiences held in the Archive of the Alister Hardy Religious Experience Research Centre, University of Wales Trinity Saint David, Lampeter, UK.

Part 1

Definitions

1

Defining the Terms: Experience, Religious Experience, Spiritual Experience

This Studyguide aims to provide an overview of the main elements in the study of religious and spiritual experience, and of many of the debates associated with them. We must begin first, however, with a 'naming of parts'.

Spiritual, religious, sacred, supernatural, transcendent or mystical experiences are terms used for human experiences that appear to the person undergoing them (or to others) to convey or imply some sort of contact with or knowledge about a power, presence or reality *beyond themselves and their sense experience*, and frequently beyond the realm of Nature, the physical or whatever is located in space and time. Research has shown that these forms of awareness of 'something beyond' or 'something more' are of considerable significance in the ordinary lives of very many people, as well as being elements of signal importance in the origin and development of the religions. Among other effects, they often evoke or deepen characteristically spiritual, religious or moral attitudes, emotions, beliefs, values and practices, as well as impacting on people's fundamental orientation of life and their quest for meaning.

> **Exercise**
>
> Before reading further, try to write down your own definition of the terms 'religious experience' and 'spiritual experience'.

Experience

In our context, the most significant dictionary definition of the core meaning of the noun *experience* is that of an event, activity or occurrence that leaves a lasting impression. Some would add as defining characteristics its being 'roughly datable' and 'private', and that its subject be 'aware' of the experience (Franks Davis, 1989, pp. 19–22). Employed as a verb, *to experience* means to 'encounter or undergo' this happening, incident or phenomenon (and, as a related sub-sense, 'to feel' it).

The meaning and significance of this broad term is discussed in *theoretical* academic domains such as philosophy (particularly in the philosophy of mind and the theory of knowledge, but also in aesthetic and moral philosophy); and the phenomena to which the term refers represent the fundamental subject matter of the explorations undertaken by the *empirical* studies that constitute the foundations of the natural and social sciences.

One problem with the term experience is that, in non-philosophical usage, it is employed in such a variety of ways. So we may say that we have experience of emotional states, people, things, work, play, music and so on (cf. Miles, 1972, pp. 13–14, 33). More significantly, the word is also ambiguous between:

- 'the sense in which it refers only to what the subject is undergoing' and how this appears to the subject, 'specifically disowning all implications for what may or may not be the case in any objective and external world'; and
- 'a sense in which it implies that there must be an actual object as well' (Flew, 1966, pp. 125–6; 1979, p. 108; cf. Proudfoot, 1985, p. 229).

This distinction is often expressed as discriminating between two types of experience:

1 *Subjective experiences* are normally understood as purely psychological phenomena. That is, they are 'internal experiences' consisting of *merely* 'private' changes in a subject's consciousness (their feeling, thinking, willing or other species of 'mental states' or 'mental events' that 'make up the conscious life of an individual': Blackburn, 1996, p. 238).
2 *Objective experiences*[1] are understood as truthful ('veridical') perceptions *of* 'externally existing objects': that is, of realities that exist independently of the experiencing subjects and the experiences they undergo, and are causally related to them (Smart, 1979, p. 12; Gaskin, 1984, ch. 4).[2]

Although 'subjective' is in this way sometimes *opposed* to 'objective', especially where the latter means true and the former false, these adjectives can also be used for two *complementary* aspects of a single experience: in the sense of 'relating to the subject' and 'relating to the object' (Staal, 1975, p. 62).

A distinction is often made between the *character* of an experience ('that it *feels* a certain way – that there is something that it is like to have it') and its representational *content*, which in many cases is related to its character while remaining 'irreducibly different' (Pendlebury, 1992). Character and content may be said to be related, for example, in the numinous experience (see Chapter 4), which has been described as 'an experience that "has" the experient, rather than the other way around' (Hunt, 2000, p. 354).[3]

Religious Experience

What It Is

When we turn to discussions within religion, we find that many – although by no means all – theologians and students of religion would argue for a central place for the category of experience. At the very least, it has been argued that religious and spiritual experiences 'play vital roles in the formation of religious and spiritual beliefs' (Wildman, 2011, p. 147). Some would even claim that 'if there were no distinctively religious experiences, it is doubtful if religions would exist' (Ward, 2008, p. 162); that 'religious experiences provide the foundation for most of the major religious systems' (Connolly, 2019, p. 1, cf. 18); or even that having a religious experience is 'being in a conscious state that is *soteriologically essential*' within a religious system (Yandell, 1997, p. 367).[4] Ninian Smart included the 'experiential or emotional' as a broad, major dimension of all religions (Smart, 1997, pp. 10–11), although he sometimes interpreted this dimension more narrowly, as involving 'some kind of "perception" of the *invisible* world' or as the view that some visible person or thing is 'a manifestation' of that world (Smart, 1971, p. 28). It is this narrower conceptualization that is our main concern in this book.

But what *is* religious experience? It has been defined in a variety of ways, but remains a rather vague, even an elusive concept – as many who have attempted to define it have acknowledged. Like the term 'religion' itself, the expression is a relatively recent one. Although 'religious experience' is said to have been coined in Europe among Calvinists and Pietists in the seventeenth century, the modern use of the phrase is often traced back to the American psychologist and philosopher, William James (cf. Chapter 19, below), whose *Varieties of Religious Experience* was published in 1902. James wrote there, in a manner reminiscent of the eighteenth-century Protestant theologian, Friedrich Schleiermacher (Schleiermacher, 1958; cf. Chapter 18, below), of the 'inferiority of the rationalistic level in founding [religious] belief' by contrast with the 'unreasoned and immediate assurance' of one who 'feels the presence of a living God' (James, 1960, p. 88).

Among recent philosophers, William Alston avoids the phrase 'religious experience', preferring the term 'mystical perception' (and 'mystical experience' understood as a perception).[5] Alston understands these phrases as inclusive terms that cover any experience that is a 'putative [that is, 'supposed' or 'reputed'] direct experiential awareness of God' (Alston, 1991, p. 35). Richard Swinburne's definition also limits religious experience to objective experiences that seem to the subject 'to be an experience of God (either of his just being there, or of saying or bringing about something) or of some other supernatural being' (Swinburne, 2004, p. 295).

But such supposed *perceptions of an external transcendent presence*, understood in this particular way, do not exhaust the range of religious experiences. For the term appears to be wide enough to embrace not only more purely *subjective experiences* of inner religious transformation (including those that are not explicitly acknowledged as religious, cf. Hunt, 2000), but also *other distinctive and specific objective experiences of unity with or absorption in a greater reality* that transcends oneself. This 'greater reality' may be described in theistic terms,[6] or it may be thought of as an impersonal Absolute (or Brahman) that is identical with the self. In some religious traditions, the object of experience is thought of as *a truth* or fact about reality (e.g. a truth about the nature of the self or the universe) that one receives or sees in a *revelation* or an *enlightenment*, and which may often free one of delusions.

Some philosophers have recently argued for a much wider usage that includes *a range of other experiences*, including those that are 'not so much a revelation of supernatural entities as a heightening, an intensification, that transforms the way in which we experience the world', in a 'natural' transcending experience that may be 'a sudden irradiation that discloses a beauty and goodness, a meaning, that was before occluded' or a self-transcending response to central moral values (Cottingham, 2014, pp. 61–3). This more general 'heightening' or 'intensification' relates to what we might call a *distinction between experience and experiences* (cf. Chapter 5, below). It may be illustrated in Alister Hardy's taxonomy, where some of the largest subcategories identified in the Alister Hardy Archive seem to imply *enduring or extended forms of experience* – e.g. the 'sense of security, protection, peace' and 'joy, happiness and well-being', experiences of prayer (answered prayer characterizes more than 30% of his sample of reports) and consequential changes in a 'sense of purpose or new meaning to life' and in 'attitude to others' (Hardy, 1979, pp. 25–9, chs 4–6; see also Chapter 7, below). When people argue, very reasonably, that there is 'more to religion than religious experience', one possible reply is that much of this 'more' comprises these broad areas of spirituality and morality: that is, moral and spiritual, even aesthetic, attitudes and dispositions, feelings and emotions, and their expressions in behaviour. Rightly or wrongly, a great deal of research on religious and spiritual experience includes such 'subjective experiences', along with more 'objective' – and often particular – experiences of encounter or union.

Drawing attention to these enduring experiences also helps in answering another criticism: the danger of focusing solely on the extraordinary and unusual – and, frequently, the more unruly and therefore memorable – experiences, and ignoring what we might describe as *more everyday religious experience*.[7]

Why It Is

There is quite widespread agreement that in order to merit the designation, a religious experience must be identified, 'from the perspective of the one who has that experience' (and not just, or perhaps not at all, by others), as 'an experience that the subject apprehends as religious' – in the sense that she or he takes it 'to have religious significance or import' (Proudfoot, 1985, pp. 181–2; cf. Davis, 1997, p. 122). This reflects William James's classic identification of religious feelings, acts and experiences in terms of their subjects' apprehending themselves 'to stand in relation to whatever they may consider the divine' (James, 1960, p. 50).

Caroline Franks Davis, while confessing that the quest for a precise definition of religious experience is 'fruitless', wishes to limit the application of the phrase to 'auto-descriptions' by the subjects of the experience, although she quickly extends this rule to cover experiences that subjects may refuse to count as religious solely because of their own restriction of the concept *religious* to some narrow institutional or doctrinal understanding. In such cases, she insists, their experiences may be counted as religious experiences if they are thought to be 'intrinsically religious' by reference to 'other-worldly' factors that make it 'impossible for this type of experience not to be religious' (Franks Davis, 1989, pp. 30–1).[8] Others have similarly widened the application of the term 'religious experience' to include third-party 'hetero-descriptions' that interpret someone else's experience as being 'a type of experience which is commonly given a religious interpretation' (Hay, 1987, pp. 166–7).

Ann Taves, who highlights the 'specialness' of these experiences (understood in terms of their being deemed significant), routinely employs the descriptive phrase 'experiences deemed religious' (Taves, 2009, pp. 12, 15, ch. 1; see Chapter 20, below). This brings to the centre of the stage questions about 'who does the deeming' (either by 'ascription' or 'attribution'),[9] under what conditions and on what criteria, and therefore 'what objects or events are likely candidates for being deemed religious' (Taves, 2009, p. 143; Proudfoot, 2010, p. 308). As noted above, on Proudfoot's view religious experience must ideally be 'identified under a description that can be plausible ascribed to the subject ... it must employ only concepts in the subject's repertoire'; but he, too, recognizes that people seldom explicitly describe their experiences as religious, and observes that these 'are our terms; we must ... decide how they are going to be used', while emphasizing that explanation is itself central to the experience as well as to its study (Proudfoot, 1985, pp. 181, 184, 186, 223).

Nevertheless, the focus here is clearly on the understanding held by 'some individual or group' who undergoes the experience 'on the ground'; hence this is – in anthropological/sociological terminology – an *emic* approach, which refers to the language and perspectives of those being studied and what has meaning for them, and not an *etic* approach, which refers to the language and perspectives of scholars and what *they* regard as important (Taves, 2009, pp. 8, 10, 22–6).[10] Obviously, an observer's identification of another person's religious experience does not imply that the observer endorses any claims assumed by its subject about the accuracy of the experience, or the existence of any outside object of the experience (claims that may 'constitute' that experience – see Chapter 8, below; Proudfoot, 1985, p. 179).

Wesley Wildman uses 'religious experiences' to refer to 'the experiences people have by virtue of being religious or being involved in religious groups', which he claims 'reflects common usage' (Wildman, 2011, pp. 78, 268). Others have cast the net even more widely, to include experiences that confirm the tenets of a religious tradition; those that merely 'conform' to such tenets; and those that simply take place during religious observance or practice, or are the results of some lengthy training or discipline (Rankin, 2008, pp. 11–13). A less specific, but in some ways even broader, account defines a religious experience as 'any experience having content or significance appropriate to a religious context or that has a "religious" flavor' (Gellman, 2005, p. 140; 2018). Surprisingly, the Anglican theologian and ecclesiastic, F. W. Dillistone, defined it yet more broadly, as 'a state of mind or feeling induced by factors beyond ordinary explanation' (Dillistone, 1983, p. 205).

Spiritual Experience

If anything, the term 'spiritual experience' is even more difficult to pin down than is 'religious experience', and not only because it is a category that is often used in a way that includes many experiences that are unlikely to be branded as 'objective' (cf. Holder, 2011). In general, language about the *spiritual* is widely recognized as easy to use but difficult to define. Dictionary entries that define the adjective as 'relating to or affecting the human spirit' (or 'higher moral categories' or 'higher faculties of the mind'), as being 'opposed to material or physical things' or even (*very* unhelpfully!) as being 'religious' or 'devout', are evidently contentious.

In the fourth century, Latin translations and authors in the Christian tradition first used the phrase *sensus spiritualis* ('spiritual sense') essentially to denote a form of direct cognitive contact with God 'analogous to but not reducible to ordinary sense-perception' (Gavrilyuk and Coakley, 2012, p. 3). The term was later used more systematically in Western medieval theology and became foundational in Protestantism in Puritan writers, being especially salient for the eighteenth-century American theologian Jonathan Edwards (for whom spiritual understanding and faith requires a 'new spiritual sense' or 'sense of the heart': Edwards, 1961 [1746], pp. 195–201) and his contemporary, the British theologian John Wesley. In the twentieth century, the 'doctrine of the spiritual senses' was highly significant in the work of the Roman Catholic theologians, Karl Rahner and Hans Urs von Balthasar (see Chapter 18, below, and Mark J. McInroy, in Gavrilyuk and Coakley, 2012, ch. 15). In this tradition, of course, it is God that is the object of spiritual perception.

Most analysts, whether theists or not, agree that *spiritual experiences* represent a broader domain than religious experiences. Wildman notes that some authors use the term to refer to aesthetic, moral or other experiences 'that seem pregnant with existential and ontological significance', but which are not obviously connected with organized religion. In amplifying this, however, he points out that religious people apply this phrase *in addition* to 'dimensions of what they also naturally call religious experiences' – that is, they do not use the term to distinguish these experiences from those that express, reflect or are generated by specifically religious beliefs or practices. Wildman, therefore, allows the category of 'spiritual experience' to cover (a) all 'ultimacy experiences' (see Chapter 4, below) and (b) both those religious experiences that are ultimacy experiences, and some religious experiences that are *not* of ultimate significance to people (Wildman, 2011, pp. 77–82, 268; 2013).

Spirituality itself is another contested term. Nevertheless, it is increasingly recognized as important precisely because it denotes a wide area of human experience, belief and behaviour that includes but extends beyond – often well beyond – the explicitly religious (when that adjective is narrowly defined as relating to, believing in or practising a religion) (see Zinnbauer and Pargament,

1997; King, 1997, pp. 7–12; 2009, pp. 3–4; Heelas and Woodhead, 2005; Oman, 2013; Altmeyer and Klein, 2015).

For many, spirituality has more positive connotations than 'religion', which is a word that is often popularly regarded as 'too thing-ish, too static, too exterior and institutional'. Spirituality, by comparison, is used to denote not only the inner dimension of religious life, but to label – in an evaluative fashion – '"real religiousness" or "religion that really means something"' (Eck, 1993, p. 150).[11] This is close, perhaps, to what others have described as the 'lived experience of faith' (Albrecht and Howard, 2014, p. 235).

My preferred definition of spirituality covers the beliefs and teachings, but more importantly the practices, capacities – and (particularly)[12] – feelings, attitudes (including dispositions and values) and experiences that express what a person takes to be ultimate for her or him. These elements may be said to constitute the 'human faith' commitments in which (all) people trust and in which they find meaning for their lives. In this sense, these commitments may be said to be 'salvific' (that is, saving, redemptive or healing) for people, enabling them to live and flourish, and to relate to other persons and things at a deep level (cf. Fowler, 1981, chs 2, 3; Astley, 1991, pp. 4–5).

This is the sense in which 'our spirituality is "what makes us tick"', determining our motives and behaviour and shaping our character (Wakefield, 2001, p. 1), for it comprises those attitudes, beliefs and practices that 'animate people's lives' (Wakefield, 1983, p. 361). It represents what we may perhaps call the 'human–*horizontal*' dimension, or axis, of a person's spirituality, being concerned with their own spiritual health and sense of meaning, and their relationships with Nature, other individuals and the wider society.

But Wakefield's definition continues by maintaining that these attitudes, beliefs and practices also help people 'to reach out to [any] super-sensible realities' (cf. 'predispose a given community to notice or respond to the Spirit of God': Albrecht and Howard, 2014, p. 236). In another definition, one's 'spiritual core' has been labelled 'the deepest center of the person', and the assertion is made that 'it is here that the person is open to the transcendent dimension; it is here that the person experiences ultimate reality' (McGinn and Meyendorff, with Leclerq, 1993, p. xiii). Spiritual beliefs, practices, attitudes and experiences are often said, then, to be oriented to the values and the 'gods' in which people believe, and to which they 'give their hearts'.[13] These are the things, people, ideas, institutions, etc., that people take to be *ultimate*. They are their 'ultimate concerns', which may or may not correspond to the God/gods/ultimate realities, standards and virtues of the religions. We could describe them as located on the 'transcendent–*vertical*' dimension or axis of a person's spirituality, which links them to transcendent (personal or impersonal) being(s)/realities, to ultimate transcend*ing* values and concerns, or to both; and does so in ways that orientate people to what lies 'beyond' the purely worldly and temporal (cf. Astley, 2003, pp. 141–3).[14]

Thus, Donald Evans describes spirituality (I would say 'horizontally') in terms of a 'moral-spiritual transformation' (which he regards as broadly religious), in which our inherent narcissism is overcome and which is 'the ultimate in human fulfilment'. This allows us ('vertically'?) to surrender our whole selves 'into the Mystery out of which everything continually arises' and makes it possible 'for God to live *as us*' (Evans, 1993, pp. 3–4, 176–7, 195, 250–1, cf. 91–2, 217). John Hick has written of human spirituality as a 'fifth dimension of our nature which enables us to respond to a fifth dimension of the universe': 'the transcendent within us' that answers to 'the transcendent without'. For him, too, spiritual transformation is 'from sinful and/or deluded self-centredness to a radically new orientation centred in the Divine, the Transcendent, the Ultimate', freeing 'the image of God within us' (Hick, 1999, pp. 2, 8). For the theist, this 'vertical', transcendent dimension always provides a pointer to and human pole of a relationship with the divine (for the *Christian*, this is to and with God, Christ or Spirit), as well as to and with other supernatural entities, perhaps, and the 'things of God'.

Religious and Spiritual Experiences

The previous two categories may be grouped together as 'religious and spiritual experiences' (RSEs), as in Wildman, 2011. I sometimes use that phrase or its abbreviation in this book.

Suggestions for Further Reading

Introductory

Aden, Ross, 2013, *Religion Today: A Critical Thinking Approach to Religious Studies*, Lanham, MD: Rowman & Littlefield, pp. 206–15, 217–27.
Gellman, Jerome, 2018 [2004], 'Mysticism', *Stanford Encyclopedia of Philosophy*, available at https://plato.stanford.edu/entries/mysticism/, §8.7.1.
Webb, Mark, 2017 [2011], 'Religious Experience', *Stanford Encyclopedia of Philosophy*, available at https://plato.stanford.edu/entries/religious-experience/.

Advanced

Swinburne, Richard, 2004, *The Existence of God*, Oxford: Clarendon, pp. 293–303.
Wildman, Wesley J., 2011, *Religious and Spiritual Experiences*, New York: Cambridge University Press, ch. 3 (pp. 69–103).

Notes

1 The temptation to call these *public experiences* (of 'public objects') should be resisted, as this would limit such experiences either to the five 'external senses' or to 'qualified observers under specifiable conditions' – conditions that may be difficult to define for some forms of experience (cf. Edwards, 1972, pp. 316–22). The limitation of the sense of 'objective' to 'its ordinary sense, confirmation by seeing, touching or using a tape-recorder' (or inference from what can be so confirmed) underlies many criticisms of religious experience (see Miles, 1972, pp. 30–2). However, if what makes sense experience public is that 'verbal reports of different persons [experiencing something] can be compared', this same criterion may be argued to apply to reports of people having *religious* experiences; and it may be argued *not* to apply across some possible wider community of perceivers – e.g. aliens with different senses (Kwan, 2012, pp. 506, 523).

2 It is, however, also natural to refer to 'the object of an experience' in the lesser sense of *what the experience presents*, without implying that this exists beyond the experience and the person undergoing the experience. Philosophers therefore often speak, in general, of *'intentional objects'* to which mental states are directed, again without implying that these have any existence outside such states of mind (e.g. George Mavrodes, in Katz, 1978, pp. 236–8). The claim that mystical experience is *neither* subjective *nor* objective is considered below in Chapter 12.

3 Philosophers call the experiencing subject – i.e. the person who undergoes an experience – either the *experient* or the *experiencer*. Neither word appears to be in common usage outside philosophy, but the latter does exist in standard dictionaries.

4 Here 'soteriologically' means 'with relation to a person's salvation'.

5 Alston is here applying the adjective 'mystical' *in a broad sense* 'in which it is not restricted to experiences in which all distinctions are blotted out' (Alston, 1994a, p. 863). Alston calls the *narrower* designation of the term (which I outline below in Chapter 4) 'extreme mystical experience' at Alston, 2005, p. 199. According to Jerome Gellman, however, the wider definition of mystical experience as a perception of the transcendent that goes beyond sense experience and introspection reflects 'a more general usage' than does this 'narrow sense' that denotes only unitive experiences (Gellman, 2005, pp. 139–40; 2018).

6 *Theism* is a belief in the existence of a 'personal' God or gods. In 'monotheism' there is only one God, and this deity is normally specified as creating and sustaining the universe and (for many theists) 'intervening' in it.

7 In some instances, such problems may be an artefact of the wording of survey questions (see Chapter 3). One study framed the question in an explicitly episodic way, by adding the explanation, 'that is, a moment of sudden religious awakening or insight' (Back and Bourque, 1970). Analysing recent research in which secondary (high) school students were asked the Greer question ('Have you ever had an experience of God, e.g. his presence or his help or anything else'), it was noticed that some respondents explicitly denied that they had experienced such *particular* occasions, while acknowledging a more general, *continuing experience* (cf. Astley, 2017b). The wording of the question in the Hardy research tradition describes the object of religious experience as being 'different from their everyday selves' (Hay and Morisy, 1978, pp. 255, 257; Hay, 1987, pp. 114, 118). While this wording raises questions about the transcendence and immanence of the object of religious experience (cf. Hardy, 1975, pp. 229–30), the formulation could be construed by a careless reader as referring to a *non-everyday experience*, rather than to a *reality*, that transcends their everyday selves.

8 Many researchers agree that 'one rarely finds the *word* "religious" in auto-descriptions' (Franks Davis, 1989, p. 31). Wainwright argued that for an account to be an auto-account all that is necessary is that the religious experiencer 'endorse it' as an accurate account of their experience, not that they be the *author* of it (Wainwright, 1981, p. 50 n. 63). Franks Davis would probably say 'really ought to endorse it'.

9 Taves defines 'ascription' as 'the assignment of a quality or characteristic to some thing'; whereas she identifies 'attributions' in terms of 'the commonsense causal explanations that people offer for why things happen as they do' (Taves, 2009, p. 181; cf. pp. 10 n. 6, 19, 41, 46, 156–7). ('Attribution theory' labels the psychological explanations of the attempts people make to understand human experience and behaviour by attributing causes to them. See Proudfoot and Shaver, 1975; Spilka and McIntosh, 1995; Taves, 2010; Proudfoot, 2010; and Chapter 15, below.)

10 The meaning of these two terms has been incorrectly transposed in the Glossary to Taves's 2009 book.

11 Diana Eck adds, 'when I use the term spirituality, I mean the disciplined nurturing of inner spiritual life' (p. 151).

12 Empirical studies show that, in general, increased spirituality is related to increased affective (feeling) processes but not increased cognitive (thinking, believing) processes (e.g. Johnstone and Wildman, 2018).

13 'Whatever is (are) the irreducible, energizing center(s) of value and source(s) of meaning in our lives is (are) our gods'. In this broad sense, 'a god is what we worship': for it is that to which we ascribe supreme worth (Tilley, 2010, pp. 34–5).

14 According to some scholars, spiritual values are 'strong evaluations' that may be regarded as broader, deeper and more fundamental, than – and, in this sense too, 'transcending' – moral values (see Taylor, 1989, ch. 1; cf. Donald Evans's account of basic trust and seven other fundamental 'attitude-virtues' that are the main constituents of both religion and morality, in Evans, 1979).

Part 2

Data

2

The Characterization, Classification and Reporting of Religious and Spiritual Experiences

Describing and Categorizing the Experiences

Within the defining characteristics outlined in Chapter 1, many attempts have been made to categorize different types or aspects of spiritual and religious experiences purely conceptually (and, in that sense, 'philosophically', see Chapter 19), theologically, historically or from the standpoints of the various social (and some natural) sciences. Along the way, scholars have also attempted to distinguish the defining characteristics of some of these different category types (e.g. that of mystical experiences).

All such analyses need first to take account of the *phenomenology of these experiences*: that is, how they appear to the recipient, including the qualities that the content or object of the experience 'seems to have' (where 'seems' is used to describe 'how things perceptually seem, whether they are that way or not'). In this general sense, phenomenology is essentially *a descriptive approach* that 'describes the experience "from within" or in terms of how things appear to the subject of the experience as she has the experience' (Yandell, 1993, pp. 16–18;

1999, pp. 215–16). A phenomenological account, therefore, is often said to represent a *non-theoretical* attempt to describe religious experience, rather than to *explain* it (Bettis, 1969, p. 3), at least in principle.[1]

On a more strict and technical understanding of phenomenology, great emphasis is laid on the importance of 'bracketing' (or *epoché*, a Greek word meaning 'to stay away or abstain'). This is the scholarly act of setting aside any presuppositions, explanations, interpretations and (especially) evaluations of what is thought to be perceived, and of the truthfulness or value of the experience – and, thus, of the 'real' existence and nature of its supposed object (cf. Wulff, 1995): 'setting aside those of our voices … that so readily tell us what something is' (Moustakas, 1994, p. 60, cf. 88). Bracketing is a preliminary act in phenomenological analysis, and phenomenology itself is also frequently regarded as 'a mere beginning' in the study of religion, before 'the real task of their evaluation begins' (Staal, 1975, p. 96).

Epoché is rarely totally achieved, of course. An entirely value-free and objective account is simply not realizable. As we shall see in Chapter 8, interpretation will keep creeping in. And in *our reports of other people's reports* of their religious experience, it would be naïve to claim that our own interpretative voice can ever be wholly silenced. These reports will usually be, at least in part and to some extent, our interpretations of their interpretations. In the jargon, they will be inevitably *hermeneutical* (cf. Astley, 2002, pp. 109–14). Even our accounts of what other people take to be significant in their experiences depend on our accepting that they have significance *for them*: that is, that they are expressions of significance – they have a meaning for them. And that, in turn, depends on what *we* understand by something having significance or meaning for someone, especially for ourselves. Clifford Geertz famously wrote of what he called 'interpretive anthropology' (or 'ethnography'), 'What we call our data are really our own constructions of other people's constructions of what they and their compatriots are up to' (Geertz, 1993, p. 9). Our study of the other is inevitably a *translation* of the other's ways of putting things. With hard work and good luck, our accounts *will* display the logic of their ways of putting things, but often (eventually) in language *of our own*.

Nevertheless, we do need to begin with a phenomenological approach: with a genuine looking at the person reporting the experience and a real listening to what she or he has to say about it.

A variety of *classifications of spiritual and religious experiences (or of their*

CHARACTERIZATION, CLASSIFICATION AND REPORTING

different aspects or characteristics) may be found in the literature.² *The data* that represent the raw material for such analyses have in the past been harvested from written religious and spiritual traditions, including sacred texts and the writings of established religious and spiritual authorities who possessed recognized knowledge and expertise in religion and spirituality in general, and/or religious and spiritual experiences in particular.³ These sources were usually recognized as normative within some religious or spiritual tradition, and they also tended to highlight extraordinary, distinctive and exceptional kinds of spiritual and religious experience.

Anthropological studies, however, have been able to supplement these classic accounts with data derived from less elite sources, especially through studies within local and popular, non-Western cultures, societies and traditions (see Chapter 20). Survey studies of the spiritual and religious experiences within the general population of Western societies have further widened the range of the data we now possess in these areas (see Chapter 3).⁴ Both types of empirical study have mined the religious and spiritual experiences of 'ordinary' (lay, non-expert) people, rather than of classic mystics and spiritual virtuosi.

Reports and classifications of wide-ranging, *more or less phenomenological overviews* of RSEs by authors, many of whom include illustrative examples of the different categories they recognize, may be found in the following sources:

- James, 1960 [1902], who draws on Starbuck's data; Paffard, 1973, part II; Goleman, 1977; Hay, 1987, especially chs 9–11; 1990, chs 4, 6; Rawlinson, 1997; Hay, 2006; Connolly, 2019, pp. 104–20.
- Studies of the material in the Alister Hardy Archive including Beardsworth, 1977; Robinson, 1977a; 1978; Hardy, 1979, which includes his summary on pp. 23–30; Maxwell and Tschudin, 1990; Fox, 2003, ch. 6; Hay, 2006, ch. 1; Fox, 2008; 2014.
- In approaches driven by factors additional to their phenomenological perspective: Yao and Badham, 2007; Kwan, 2011, pp. 252–8; 2012, pp. 512–13; Wildman, 2011, ch. 3.

Other classifications are much more explicitly *top-down*, with the classificatory schemes being driven less by the phenomenology of the experiences and more by:

- Empirical, *social-scientific categories* (e.g. Glock and Stark, 1965; Stark, 1965; Paffard, 1976; Aden, 2013, pp. 201–3) or *natural scientific categories* (e.g. Fischer, 1978; Wilber 1993 [1977]).
- More conceptual, *philosophical or theological* distinguishing criteria (e.g. Cohen and Phipps, 1979; Donovan, 1979, ch. 1; Johnson, 1998; Franks Davis, 1989, ch. 2; Yandell, 1993, pp. 21–32; Hick, 2006, ch. 3; Swinburne, 2004, pp. 298–303; Charry, 2007; Kwan, 2011, pp. 271–3; 2012, pp. 516–19; see also the material in Gavrilyuk and Coakley, 2012).[5]

Exercise: Among the Articles

Read and critically assess the following journal article:

Wayne Proudfoot, 1989, 'From Theology to a Science of Religions: Jonathan Edwards and William James on Religious Affections', *The Harvard Theological Review,* **82, 2, pp. 149–68.**

This article offers an interpretative study in the history of the idea of religious experience. Starting from Friedrich Schleiermacher, Wayne Proudfoot traces the shift from an account of the religious affections located within a traditional theological context, to a broadly phenomenological and psychological account as illustrated by the work of Jonathan Edwards and William James. His detailed study of these authors concludes with the claim that it is Edwards's analysis of the 'complexity and the convoluted character of moral appraisal of others and of oneself' that is 'finally more illuminating for the study of religion than James's attempt to find a common nucleus within the varieties of religious experience'.

Reticence and Reporting

In her account of a sudden experience of love at the centre of the universe that was accompanied by a vision of 'golden light', one respondent commented, 'I had a very strong feeling that the vision was not to be chatted about. Indeed, I did not speak of it except to my husband for many years' (4267, Alister Hardy Archive). In a very readable paper that covers in a non-technical and compelling style a lot of issues relating to the question of trusting an apparent religious experience undergone by 'John' (cf. Chapter 9), the author poses this question, 'Does any of this mean that John should or will go about proclaiming to the world his experience with God? Will or should John become overtly evangelical about his experience?' The author then goes on to present his own answer:

> Absolutely not! For him to do so would be as unseemly as going about describing to everyone the great sex he had with his wife the night before. This experience is not a public event and to treat it as such would be desecration. Sharing in a deeply serious and personal way with individuals with whom one is close, however, is quite another matter. (Craighead, 1999, pp. 414–15)

Exercise

Reflect on (and if possible, discuss with others) the significance of, and possible justifications for, Craighead's claim.

In general surveys of religious and spiritual experiences, many respondents indicated that they had previously told no one else about their experience. Figures for such reticence ranging from 28% to 44% of the samples, depending on the particular object of the experience, are given from the Gallup survey reported in Hay and Heald, 1987, p. 22.[6] These authors suggest that 'what appears to be producing the silence is a taboo on revealing the very existence of such a dimension in one's life', lest the respondent 'be thought mad or stupid if they admit it'. The fact that types of experience that are not overtly religiously orthodox are located at the lower end of the frequency range is interpreted by Hay as showing that this *social pressure* is directed most strongly towards traditional religious interpretations of experience (Hay, 1994, pp. 11–12).

In the same article, David Hay reports that inquiries about privacy were included in Hay and Morisy's (1985) interview study of religious experience in Nottingham, with the result that 'approximately one fourth of the positive respondents said they had never told anyone else about their experience, even relatives as close as their husbands or wives. When respondents were asked why they had kept their experiences private, all the replies fell into two categories: (a) fear of being thought mentally unbalanced, or (b) fear of being thought stupid'. Hay adds in a footnote that their replies were 'frequently accompanied by tears and signs of embarrassment' (Hay, 1994, p. 11; cf. 2006, pp. 80–9). Hay also reported in his research that there were 'many signs of reticence' in focus *groups* (especially in the case of men). This contrasted with private research interviews with individuals, where it was 'hardly ever a problem' (Hay, 2006; p. 56, cf. 84).[7]

These factors and figures are certainly relevant to the way we collect data about RSEs. But, bearing in mind Houston Craighead's comments, they perhaps say something about the content of such experiences as well: even, perhaps, something about what it is that makes a religious experience 'religious' and a spiritual experience 'spiritual'?

Suggestions for Further Reading

Introductory

Astley, Jeff, 2017, 'Asking Questions and Analysing Answers about Religious Experience: Developing the Greer Tradition', *Mental Health, Religion & Culture*, 20, 4, pp. 348–58.

Hardy, Alister, 1979, *The Spiritual Nature of Man: A Study of Contemporary Religious Experience*, Oxford: Clarendon, ch. 2 (pp. 17–30).

Hay, David, 1987 [1982], *Exploring Inner Space: Scientists and Religious Experience*, London: Mowbray, chs 9 (pp. 120–34), 14 (pp. 198–211).

Advanced

Craighead, Houston A., 1999, 'William James Be Damned: Is It Evidentially Justifiable to Trust Religious Experience?', *Perspectives in Religious Studies*, 26, 4, pp. 405–15.

Erricker, Clive, 1999, 'Phenomenological Approaches', in Peter Connolly (ed.), *Approaches to the Study of Religion*, London: Cassell, pp. 73–104.

Kwan, Kai-man, 2012, 'The Argument from Religious Experience', in William Lane Craig and J. P. Moreland (eds.), *The Blackwell Companion to Natural Theology*, Oxford: Wiley-Blackwell, ch. 9 (pp. 499–552), pp. 498–501, 512–19.

Notes

1 But see Chapter 8, below.

2 The products of these attempts to impose order on these diverse data or ideas are labelled with a variety of names: including classifications, categorizations, typologies and taxonomies. These terms are often used (and defined by dictionaries) rather loosely and interchangeably, to designate categories, divisions, sets or classes of things that share certain characteristics in common and can be differentiated from other things by reference to these shared features. Because of their connotations in some specialist contexts, however, it is perhaps best to avoid two of these terms. *Typologies* are often associated with classifications into more rigorous and mutually exclusive conceptual types. These may be treated by sociologists as 'ideal (or pure) types', a term that labels mental constructs that are derived from empirical reality but do not conform to it in detail, as certain of their aspects have been selected, accentuated or simplified. *Taxonomies*, by contrast, are rigorous and exclusive classifications that are determined by empirically observable and measurable characteristics, as in the organization of biological specimens into taxa (species, genera, families, orders, classes, phyla and kingdoms) that are specified by their morphology and anatomy, and (especially today) their evolutionary and genetic history. The zoologist, Alister Hardy, when he initially turned his attention to researching the 'natural history' of contemporary religious experience, imagined that he could create 'a hierarchical system like biological specimens' of *types* of religious experience. His data revealed, however, a much more complex situation that required a system capable of distinguishing 'all the different *characteristics* which in varying combinations went to make up the accounts of the experiences rather than being one which attempted to classify the *individual examples* themselves of which hardly two offered exactly the same set of ingredients' (Hardy, 1979, p. 23, italics added). Thus, any one reported experience might exemplify a number of different categories; and, hence, Hardy offers us *a classification of the characteristics of RSEs*, rather than *a classification of the RSEs themselves* (into different types, as is attempted in Chapter 4, below). In 1979, Hardy proposed a provisional classification that listed the features of religious experiences in 12 major divisions (such as 'cognitive and affective elements' and 'antecedents or "triggers" of experience'). Most of these were further subdivided to create an additional one or two levels, giving a total of 92 categories altogether, including these 'subsidiary categories' of characteristics (such as 'awe, reverence, wonder' and 'prayer, meditation'). It has been said that the different

ways in which the cake of religious experience has been sliced says 'more about the intentions of the slicer and the needs of the eater than they do about the cake itself'. This author adds that, 'while it is pointless to find a single unifying characteristic in religious experiences, we can detect "family resemblances" among the different accounts' (Griffith-Dickson, 2000, pp. 89–90; on the notion of family resemblances, see Wittgenstein, 1968, §§66–69, pp. 31–3). The significance and some of the pitfalls of classifications of religious experience are also discussed by Peter Moore, in Katz, 1978, pp. 119–23 and Wainwright, 1981, pp. 38–40.

3 For collections that illustrate these *more elite experiences*, see the references given below and under the categories described in Chapter 4.

4 See the Alister Hardy Archive of religious experiences: http://uwtsd.ac.uk/library/alister-hardy-religious-experience-research-centre/online-archive/, the Mystical Experience Registry: www.bodysoulandspirit.net/mystical_experiences/read/index.shtml, and the Association of Religion Data Archives: www.thearda.com/newsearch.asp?searchterms=%22religious+experience%22&c=ABCDEFGHIJKLMNYZ and www.thearda.com/newsearch.asp?searchterms=%22spiritual+experience%22&c=ABCDEFGHIJKLMNYZ.

5 Note that the research instruments or selection criteria that *gathered the data* organized by such schemes may not necessarily have been driven by these non-phenomenological interests or frameworks.

6 The figures ranging from 61% to 76% cited in Hay, 2011a result from a mistake in transcription from the tables in Hay and Heald, 1987.

7 A reluctance to share experiences that seem to many people so private or particular sometimes appears in survey data, even when they have been elicited by self-administered, anonymous questionnaires. They include intriguing comments such as, 'I can't, it's personal' and 'Not comfortable sharing this information but let's just say …' (Astley, 2017b, p. 354).

3

Qualitative and Quantitative Research

This chapter concentrates on data derived from reports of contemporary religious and spiritual experiences given by the general public, rather than from classic accounts from spiritual masters, and the sacred Scriptures and other traditions of the religions.

Empirical research tracks differences among 'variables'. *Variables* are identifiable elements of a situation or population that show variation, appearing in two or more categories or 'values' (rather than being constant). Sometimes variables may be quantitatively measured, as is the case with numerically coded data: whether these are 'ordinal' (ranked in order, say, of degrees of preference or agreement), 'interval' (ranked in order with a particular distance between each rank, as in IQ scores or reports of annual income) or 'ratio variables' (as interval variables, but with a unique zero point, e.g. age). Numerically coded data is subject to quantitative analysis that often involves the computation of statistical significance.[1] This contrasts with 'non-numerical analysis' of 'nominal variables', such as marital status or occupation, which cannot in the same way be ranked, averaged or numerically analysed.

An adequate empirical study of religious and spiritual experiences will need to employ a range of appropriate research tools from the armoury of the social sciences (for a select bibliography, see the end of this chapter). '*Surveys*', which collect data by questioning a sample of respondents at a particular point in time, usually involve either *self-administered questionnaires* or *interview studies*. In both cases, the questions asked may be either open or closed.[2] *Non-survey data* collection includes experimentation; observational 'field studies' (including 'participant observation', in which the researcher is part of the group being studied); 'ethnomethodology', which gathers data through conversations and observations of both social structures and everyday social explanations; and the study of historical or contemporary documents.

In religious experience research, people are normally asked, prior to any requests for further details, if they 'have ever had' a religious or spiritual experience. While some research traditions use an explicitly religious question here which is often worded in a theistic form, others adopt less limiting phraseology. Examples of a range of such questions may be found in the literature (see Hood and Francis, 2013; cf. Hood, Hill and Spilka, 2009, pp. 344–7). They include the following:

- 'Have you ever as an adult had the feeling that you were somehow in the presence of God?' (the 'Stark question').[3]
- 'Would you say that you have ever had a "religious or mystical experience" – that is, a moment of sudden religious insight or awakening?' (the 'Bourque question').[4]
- 'Have you ever felt as though you were close to a powerful spiritual force that seemed to lift you out of yourself?' (the 'Greeley question').[5]
- 'Have you ever felt you were in close contact with something sacred?' (the 'Wuthnow question').[6]
- 'Have you ever been aware of or influenced by a presence or power, whether you call it God or not, which is different from your everyday self?' (the 'Hardy question').[7]
- 'Have you ever had an experience of God, e.g., his presence or his help or anything else?' (the 'Greer question').[8]

Figures for positive responses to these questions among surveys of the general adult population usually range between 20% and 50%, with the statistic varying with the different questions, the contexts in which they are asked, the nature of the sample, and the date and location of the survey. In some surveys using the Hardy question, the Yes response has risen above 65% (Hay and Morisy, 1978; Hay, 1994; 2006, p. 11; Hay and Hunt, 2000, pp. 9, 32; Aden, 2013, p. 201, cf. 204).

The qualitative research techniques of participant observation and (particularly) unstructured or semi-structured interviewing[9] are central to *ethnographic research* – conceived, broadly, as the study of a culture. At their best, such qualitative research methods should provide a rich and detailed description and an

QUALITATIVE AND QUANTITATIVE RESEARCH

'in-depth' understanding of experiences. However, the gathering and analysis of such data is so time-consuming that very often the research can only draw on comparatively small samples of individuals and groups. These analyses therefore focus on particulars rather than generalities and are typically non-statistical (although some broad numerical patterns are sometimes reported, as illustrated below). The strength of an anthropological approach lies especially in its small-scale focus, which enables the researcher to get to know a particular group of people and their culture in depth. See Chapter 20, below.

Exercise: Among the Articles

Qualitative Research

Read and critically assess the following articles:

Rodney Stark, 1965, 'A Taxonomy of Religious Experience', *Journal for the Scientific Study of Religion,* **5, 1, pp. 97–116.**

Rodney Stark's classic article is a good one with which to start, as it offers a wide-ranging definition, classification and characterization of religious experience. Stark's conceptual analysis is informed by answers to an open-ended question about religious experience answered by 3,000 American church members, from which Stark quotes passages to illustrate four categories of religious experience (which may exist in either divine or diabolic forms): confirming, responsive, ecstatic and revelational. (This taxonomy was tested by Currie, Klug and McCombs, whose study is to be found in the next block of Exercises.)

David Hay, 1979, 'Religious Experience Amongst a Group of Post-Graduate Students: A Qualitative Study', *Journal for the Scientific Study of Religion,* **18, 2, pp. 164–82.**

David Hay's study reports data from interviews with 100 postgraduate students in the UK, 65% of whom claimed that they had at some time 'been aware of or influenced by a presence or a power, whether you call it God or not, which is different from [their] everyday self' (the 'Hardy question'). Their descriptions of these experiences fell into eight broad categories: awareness of a controlling and guiding power; awareness of the presence of God; awareness of a presence in Nature; answered prayer; experience of a unity with Nature; a category comprising extra-sensory perception, out-of-the-body experiences, visions, etc.; awareness of evil; and conversion. The study also asked questions about the content, frequency and other aspects of the experiences.

Lorelie J. Farmer, 1992, 'Religious Experience in Childhood: A Study of Adult Perspectives on Early Spiritual Awareness', *Religious Education,* **87, 2, pp. 259–68.**

The next article draws on ten semi-structured interviews with adults from the USA, exploring spiritual experiences they had had as children.[10] Lorelie Farmer concludes that an increased understanding and compassion for others as adults had resulted from these respondents' 'willingness to be faithful to the truths that they perceived in early transcendent experiences'.

Mark J. Cartledge, 1995, 'Charismatic Prophecy', *Journal of Empirical Theology,* **8, 1, pp. 71–88.**

The Pentecostal and charismatic movements within Christianity are largely predicated on an experience ascribed to the work of the Holy Spirit. This has two major elements: an inner transformation ('baptism in the Spirit' or 'outpouring of the Spirit') and an external manifestation in the exercise of special gifts (*charisms*) of the Spirit, which may include prophecy, healing and the gifts of tongues (*glossolalia*) and their interpretation (see Chapter 4, below). Mark Cartledge's article presents a qualitative study, mainly conducted through semi-structured interviews, of the 'prophetic experiences' of a sample of over 30 Anglican charismatics in the UK.

> **Simon Dein and Christopher C. H. Cook, 2015, 'God Put a Thought into my Mind: The Charismatic Christian Experience of Receiving Communications from God',** *Mental Health, Religion & Culture*, **18, 2, pp. 97–113.**
>
> Charismatic Christian experience is also the subject of the final article in this block, which is another semi-structured interview study. Eight members of a London evangelical church were asked to describe their experiences of God communicating with them. While on occasion God may speak audibly or the experience may be accompanied by supernatural phenomena, in the vast majority of cases such communications come through their own thoughts or impressions. (See also Chapter 16, below.)

Questionnaire surveys, in contrast to interview studies, can work with much larger samples and are more able to provide data that are open to *quantitative* statistical analysis. These questionnaires typically employ closed-ended or fixed-response questions. This approach allows the researcher to discover generalizations and regularities in the data (that is, patterns, associations and correlations) through the computation of statistical measures and tests of significance. Quantitative analysis thus enables the research to test hypotheses about the relative influence of different variables and *possible* causal relationships between them (see note 1). The 'survey instruments' of quantitative research are also more easily assessed in terms of their *reliability* (the extent to which they are consistent measures, yielding repeatable results) and *validity* (the extent to which they are actually measuring what they purport to measure).

Exercise: Among the Articles

Quantitative Research

Read and critically assess the following articles and essays:

Raymond Currie, Leo F. Klug and Charles R. McCombs, 1982, 'Intimacy and Saliency: Dimensions for Ordering Religious Experiences', *Review of Religious Research,* **24, 1, pp. 19–32.**

Rodney Stark's taxonomy of religious experiences (see above) ranked such experiences according to the degree of intimacy they claimed between the human and the divine. In the first article in this block of more quantitative studies, a team of researchers attempts to *operationalize* Stark's religious experience types: that is, to make his abstract concepts ('constructs') concrete so that they can be empirically studied and measured, in this case by specific questions. This enabled the authors to test hypotheses derived from Stark's taxonomy against the responses from around 700 young adults in Canada.

Ralph W. Hood and W. Paul Williamson, 2000, 'An Empirical Test of the Unity Thesis: The Structure of Mystical Descriptors in Various Faith Samples', *Journal of Psychology and Christianity,* **19, 3, pp. 232–44.**

More sophisticated quantitative 'instruments' of operationalized concepts use a battery of question items that together constitute a *scale, measure, inventory* or *index,* whose items are (conceptually) derived from a concept and (empirically) generate responses that correlate closely with one another. Ralph Hood's well-known *Mysticism Scale* draws on items derived from Walter Stace's classic conceptual study of the topic (Stace, 1961). Hood and Williamson employed this scale with a sample of 500 respondents. Their study empirically tested and supported Stace's view that there is a 'common core' to mystical experience which may be separated from its various interpretations (see Chapter 8, below), as well as determining that Hood's scale could identify different factors in mysticism across different faith traditions.

Michael Argyle and Peter Hills, 2000, 'Religious Experiences and their Relations with Happiness and Personality', *The International Journal for the Psychology of Religion,* **10, 3, pp. 157–72.**

This next questionnaire study reports an empirical examination of the mystical experiences of 364 'ordinary people' in Britain, giving details of their intensity, frequency and duration, and how these experiences correlated with measures of personality and happiness. It uses the Eysenck Personality Questionnaire and a new scale to measure 'religious affect', along with other scales.

Leslie J. Francis, 2006, 'The God Experience (Who Has It and Why?): Perspectives from Empirical Theology', *Modern Believing,* **47, 1, pp. 4–21.**

Leslie Francis has developed a number of datasets based on questionnaire surveys of children, adolescents and adults in the UK. In this article, he draws on these data to assess the extent to which characteristics such as age, sex and religious practice can predict religious experience; and whether there are any indications that religious experiences are associated with (a) positive or negative psychological functioning, (b) aspects of psychopathology and (c) different personality types.

Ralph W. Hood and Leslie J. Francis, 2013, 'Mystical Experience: Conceptualization, Measurement and Correlates', in Kenneth I. Pargament (ed.), *Handbook of the Psychology of Religion and Spirituality,* **vol. 1,** *Context, Theory, and Research,* **Washington, DC: American Psychological Association, pp. 391–405.**

In the final essay in this block, Hood and Francis join forces to provide a comprehensive summary overview of the findings of a wide range of measurement-based literature on mystical experience.

Where qualitative research adopts what has been described as an 'inner perspective' on the phenomena being studied, quantitative research facilitates a more 'outer perspective'. Each approach has its own contribution to make in the study of religious and spiritual experiences.

Anthropologists and sociologists, and to a lesser extent psychologists, often produce wide-ranging theories that may serve as illuminating explanatory insights, but which do not lend themselves well to testing against empirical evidence: either on account of their generality or their lack of falsifiable empirical predictions. However, empirical qualitative and particularly quantitative studies may be employed that help to clarify and/or serve to test many of these theories, using results that have been painstakingly gathered from questionnaire- or interview-based social surveys, especially of statistically representative samples.

Suggestions for Further Reading

Qualitative Studies

Introductory

Beardsworth, Timothy, 2009 [1977], *A Sense of Presence: The Phenomenology of Certain Kinds of Visionary and Ecstatic Experiences, Based on a Thousand Contemporary First-Hand Accounts*, Oxford: Religious Experience Research Unit; Lampeter: Religious Experience Research Centre.

Maxwell, Meg and Tschudin, Verena (eds), 1990, *Seeing the Invisible: Modern Religious and Other Transcendent Experiences*, London: Penguin.

Advanced

Fox, Mark, 2008, *Spiritual Encounters with Unusual Light Phenomena: Lightforms*, Cardiff: University of Wales Press.

Wiebe, Phillip H., 1997, *Visions of Jesus: Direct Encounters from the New Testament to Today*, New York: Oxford University Press, chs 2, 3.

Quantitative Studies

Introductory

Francis, Leslie J., 2013, 'Psychology and Mysticism: An Empirical Approach', *Challenging Religious Issues*, 2, 9–16. Available at http://www.st-marys-centre.org.uk/resources/challengingreligiousissues/Issue%202_ChallengingReligiousIssues.pdf.
Hay, David, 1988, 'Asking Questions about Religious Experience', *Religion*, 18, 3, pp. 217–29.
Hay, David, 1990, *Religious Experience Today: Studying the Facts*, London: Mowbray, pp. 79–85.

Advanced

Francis, Leslie J. and Louden, Stephen H., 2000, 'The Francis-Louden Mystical Orientation Scale (MOS): A Study among Catholic Priests', *Research in the Social Scientific Study of Religion*, 11, pp. 99–116.
Hood, Ralph W.; Hill, Peter C. and Spilka, Bernard, 2009, *The Psychology of Religion: Empirical Approaches*, New York: Guilford, ch. 11 (pp. 331–80).

A Select Bibliography of Research Methods

Bailey, Kenneth D., 2008, *Methods of Social Research*, fourth edition, New York: Free Press, especially part two.
Cohen, Louis, Manion, Lawrence and Morrison, Keith, 2017, *Research Methods in Education*, eighth edition, Abingdon: Routledge, parts 3 and 4.
Ely, Margot et al., 1991, *Doing Qualitative Research: Circles within Circles*, London: Falmer.
Gillham, Bill, 2000, *The Research Interview*, London: Continuum.
Gillham, Bill, 2000, *Developing a Questionnaire*, London: Continuum.
King, Nigel, Horrocks, Christine and Brooks, Joanna, 2018, *Interviews in Qualitative Research*, second edition, London: Sage.
Oppenheim, A. N., 1992, *Questionnaire Design, Interviewing and Attitude Measurement*, London: Pinter.

Seidman, Irving, 2019, *Interviewing as Qualitative Research: A Guide for Researchers in Education and the Social Sciences*, fifth edition, New York: Teachers College Press.

Tolmie, Andy, Muijs, Daniel and McAteer, Erica, 2011, *Quantitative Methods in Educational and Social Research using SPSS*, Maidenhead: Open University Press.

Notes

1 Quantitative analyses often distinguish 'dependent variables' (or 'outcome variables'), the value of which depends on one or more 'independent variables' whose effect may vary with the researchers' model or experimental procedure. 'Controlled variables' are kept constant, and 'background variables' have no effect on the outcome of a situation.

2 'Open' (or open-ended) questions allow respondents to answer in their own words, whereas 'closed' (closed-ended) questions offer a limited number of carefully formulated responses from which respondents must choose (although an 'other' response category is sometimes added, together with space for free input).

3 Glock and Stark, 1965, p. 157, Table 8–1.

4 Back and Bourque, 1970, p. 489.

5 Greeley, 1974.

6 Wuthnow, 1976.

7 Hardy, 1979, p. 20; Hay, 1987, pp. 114, 117–18; Franklin, 2014, pp. 7–8.

8 Greer, 1981, 1982.

9 Interviews that do not follow any plan or even do not refer to a research topic (wholly 'unstructured') are rare; but completely structured interviews are usually replaced by (cheaper) self-administered questionnaires. Semi-structured interviews follow a plan decided in advance but leave some leeway to the interviewer in deciding what to ask, what 'prompts' to add and the categories of answer that will be used.

10 See also Robinson, 1977a and 1978.

Quantitative Studies

Introductory

Francis, Leslie J., 2013, 'Psychology and Mysticism: An Empirical Approach', *Challenging Religious Issues*, 2, 9–16. Available at http://www.st-marys-centre.org.uk/resources/challengingreligiousissues/Issue%202_ChallengingReligiousIssues.pdf.
Hay, David, 1988, 'Asking Questions about Religious Experience', *Religion*, 18, 3, pp. 217–29.
Hay, David, 1990, *Religious Experience Today: Studying the Facts*, London: Mowbray, pp. 79–85.

Advanced

Francis, Leslie J. and Louden, Stephen H., 2000, 'The Francis-Louden Mystical Orientation Scale (MOS): A Study among Catholic Priests', *Research in the Social Scientific Study of Religion*, 11, pp. 99–116.
Hood, Ralph W.; Hill, Peter C. and Spilka, Bernard, 2009, *The Psychology of Religion: Empirical Approaches*, New York: Guilford, ch. 11 (pp. 331–80).

A Select Bibliography of Research Methods

Bailey, Kenneth D., 2008, *Methods of Social Research*, fourth edition, New York: Free Press, especially part two.
Cohen, Louis, Manion, Lawrence and Morrison, Keith, 2017, *Research Methods in Education*, eighth edition, Abingdon: Routledge, parts 3 and 4.
Ely, Margot et al., 1991, *Doing Qualitative Research: Circles within Circles*, London: Falmer.
Gillham, Bill, 2000, *The Research Interview*, London: Continuum.
Gillham, Bill, 2000, *Developing a Questionnaire*, London: Continuum.
King, Nigel, Horrocks, Christine and Brooks, Joanna, 2018, *Interviews in Qualitative Research*, second edition, London: Sage.
Oppenheim, A. N., 1992, *Questionnaire Design, Interviewing and Attitude Measurement*, London: Pinter.

Seidman, Irving, 2019, *Interviewing as Qualitative Research: A Guide for Researchers in Education and the Social Sciences*, fifth edition, New York: Teachers College Press.

Tolmie, Andy, Muijs, Daniel and McAteer, Erica, 2011, *Quantitative Methods in Educational and Social Research using SPSS*, Maidenhead: Open University Press.

Notes

1 Quantitative analyses often distinguish 'dependent variables' (or 'outcome variables'), the value of which depends on one or more 'independent variables' whose effect may vary with the researchers' model or experimental procedure. 'Controlled variables' are kept constant, and 'background variables' have no effect on the outcome of a situation.

2 'Open' (or open-ended) questions allow respondents to answer in their own words, whereas 'closed' (closed-ended) questions offer a limited number of carefully formulated responses from which respondents must choose (although an 'other' response category is sometimes added, together with space for free input).

3 Glock and Stark, 1965, p. 157, Table 8-1.

4 Back and Bourque, 1970, p. 489.

5 Greeley, 1974.

6 Wuthnow, 1976.

7 Hardy, 1979, p. 20; Hay, 1987, pp. 114, 117–18; Franklin, 2014, pp. 7–8.

8 Greer, 1981, 1982.

9 Interviews that do not follow any plan or even do not refer to a research topic (wholly 'unstructured') are rare; but completely structured interviews are usually replaced by (cheaper) self-administered questionnaires. Semi-structured interviews follow a plan decided in advance but leave some leeway to the interviewer in deciding what to ask, what 'prompts' to add and the categories of answer that will be used.

10 See also Robinson, 1977a and 1978.

4

Categories of Religious and Spiritual Experiences: From Mysticism to NDEs

Many of the specific types of spiritual or religious experiences detailed in this chapter have generated considerable research, analysis and debate.[1] Patently, those listed below sometimes overlap (see also, e.g., Macquarrie, 2004, especially chs 1, 14, 15).

Mystical Experiences[2]

In its more narrow sense (see Chapter 1) and in contrast to its historical meanings,[3] 'mystical experience' has been regularly understood in recent times as an experience of 'a conscious relation to the Absolute' or God that 'aspires to intimate union with the Divine, to a penetration of the Divine within the soul and to a disappearance of the individuality' of the mystic, who seeks 'to become Being itself' (Margaret Smith, in Woods, 1981, p. 20). On this usage, it is generally assumed that mystical experiences are 'unitary' (or 'unitive') states, in which 'the distinctions which are ordinarily drawn between subject and object, between one object and another, and between different places and times are radically transcended' (see also Chapter 12). Mystical experiences are also commonly thought of as 'intuitive [that is, not derived from conscious reasoning] apprehensions of the (character of) the space-time world as a whole or of something which transcends it' (Wainwright, 1981, p. 1).

Within these broad – and somewhat vague – characterizations, some have identified Christian and some other forms of mysticism as types of *theistic mysticism*, which 'seeks union with God but not identity'.[4] This is then distinguished from *monistic mysticism*, which seeks not communion with God but 'identity with a universal principle' that may or may not be regarded as divine – an identification that may be expressed by such maxims as 'All is One', 'Thou art That', 'I am God' or 'Ātman [a person's soul] is Brahman [the Ultimate Reality]' (Parrinder, 1976, pp. 15, 119–20; cf. Wainwright, 1981, pp. 31–41; Smith, 1992, p. 111).

However, the monistic/theistic distinction has been criticized as over simplistic and is denied by those who argue that Christian mysticism is the same experience as that described as monistic, the only difference being that it is 'interpreted theistically as a seeing of God' (Stace, 1961, p. 94; cf. Smart, 1965 and Chapter 8, below). Stace's argument is that such dualism is 'an undeveloped mysticism' which contradicts the ultimate unity of mystical experience (1961, pp. 231–2). Stace himself distinguished:

- *extrovertive mysticism*, which finds mystical unity as a sacred oneness of all things by looking outward through the physical senses and the multiplicity of the external natural world, perceiving 'the multiplicity of external material objects ... mystically transfigured so that the One, or the Unity, shines through them' (1961, p. 61); and
- a more mature and significant *introvertive mysticism* that shuts off the senses to find unity through turning inward, 'introspectively ... at the bottom of the self, at the bottom of the human personality', as a blissful 'unitary consciousness', 'wholly naked ... [and] devoid of any plurality whatever', where 'all awareness of the world and of multiplicity' is 'completely obliterated' (Stace, 1960, p. 15; 1961, pp. 61–2, 122).[5]

Stace considered theistic mysticism to be a secondary interpretation of this pure introvertive experience.

Robert Forman interprets introvertive mysticism as a *pure consciousness event* ('PCE'), in which the subject empties out all experiential content and concepts, leaving a pure 'wakeful though contentless (nonintentional) consciousness'. A PCE is thus a form of 'knowledge by identity', in which the mystic's consciousness '[encounters] itself through itself' (Forman, 1990, p. 8; 1999, pp. 6–7, 170–1). (Kai-man Kwan argues, however, that the PCE cannot be a *monistic* mystical experience, precisely because it is without *any* conceptual content: Kwan, 2012, pp. 538–9.) On PCEs, see below in this chapter and Chapter 8.

In addition to insisting on a separate class for dualistic God-mysticism, Zaehner formulated two other categories: an extrovertive *nature mysticism*, or *panenhenic ('all-in-one') mysticism* of the unity of all created Nature including one's self; and another form of introvertive experience – a monistic *soul mysticism* – that is based on a sense of the unity of the uncreated soul or spirit, in a state of isolation from matter and the temporal and from all that is other than itself (Zaehner, 1957, pp. 28–9, 100, 151, 165, 167–8, 184, 198–9).

Huston Smith may be read as distinguishing *four types of mystical experiences* (Wildman, 2011, pp. 72–3), classified by the mystics' responses to the four different levels of reality that are said to make up a metaphysical hierarchy (Smith, 1992, pp. ix, 23–5, ch. 3):

- The *terrestrial*, or 'the gross, the material, the sensible, the phenomenal, or the human plane' (oriented to Nature).
- The *intermediate*, or 'the subtle, the animic, or the psychic plane' (oriented to discarnate entities, such as ghosts, departed spirits, angels and demons).
- The *celestial* (oriented to a relationship with a personal deity).
- The *infinite* (oriented to union with 'God in his ultimate nature', or the ineffable God).

William James proposed four *marks of mysticism*. He suggested, as two defining characteristics of mystical states, that they were *ineffable* (defying expression) and *noetic* (states of insight and knowledge, rather than just feeling states). 'Two other qualities', he wrote, 'are less sharply marked, but are usually found' in mysticism: *transience* and *passivity* (James, 1960, pp. 366–8). F. C. Happold extended this list of 'marked characteristics', in a way that narrows James's wide sense of mysticism,[6] by claiming that mystical states are also commonly characterized by 'a consciousness of the *Oneness* of everything' (James's major omission), a 'sense of *timelessness*' and 'the conviction that the familiar *phenomenal ego is not the real I*' (Happold, 1970, pp. 46–8, italics added). Walter Stace had earlier added to James's characterization of mystical states, *feelings of blessedness*, joy, happiness, etc. and *feelings of the sacredness*, holiness or divinity of what is apprehended, as well as noting their *paradoxicality* (Stace, 1961, pp. 79, 110, italics added; cf. Hood, 1975; Smith, 1992, pp. 111–12).

Several *anthologies of mystical writing* cover a range of religious and spiritual traditions, including Stace, 1960; Happold, 1970; Parrinder, 1976; Woods, 1981 and Katz, 2013. Those limited to *Christian sources* include Butler, 1967; Egan, 1996; Dupré and Wiseman, 2001 and McGinn, 2006.

Numinous Experiences

This expression derives from Rudolf Otto, who coined the adjective 'numinous' to describe a category of value and a mental state that was 'perfectly *sui generis* ['of its own kind', 'distinctive'] and irreducible to any other'. This is the characteristic mark of the fundamental sense of 'the Holy', and of the object of that sense: understood as the 'awe-ful'[7] yet entrancing, transcendent, ineffable mystery (*mysterium tremendum et fascinans*) that is 'wholly other' than (that is, different from) the person experiencing it. This numinous object is 'felt as objective and outside the self', and is experienced as an overpowering majesty and urgent energy which results in 'blank wonder, an astonishment that strikes us dumb, amazement absolute' (Otto, 1925, pp. 7, 11, 26, chs IV–VI; see also Chapter 18, below).

Although Otto illustrated the numinous experience from Old (as well as New) Testament Scriptures, and included prophetic experience as an example (Otto, 1925, chs X, XI; 1931, ch. V), he regarded mysticism as itself a form of numinous experience, one that features an '*identification* … of the personal self with the transcendent Reality', and in which 'religious feeling surpasses its rational content, that is, … its hidden, non-rational, numinous elements predominate and determine the emotional life' (Otto, 1925, p. 22; 1932, p. 141). Most scholars today, however, regard these two types of experience as being very different (e.g. Wainwright, 1981, pp. 36–7; Gellman, 2005, pp. 140–1).[8] Thus, Ninian Smart distinguishes the 'outer and thunderous quality' of numinous (which he sometimes calls 'prophetic') experiences from the 'inner visions' of mystical (which he sometimes calls 'contemplative') experiences, describing the latter as experiences that 'refer to those inner visions' that arise from 'practices which are contemplative'. He also includes '"panenhenic" Wordsworthian experiences of a mysterious harmony with nature' in the numinous, rather than the mystical, category (Smart, 1978, p. 13; cf. 1958, pp. 131–4). William Wainwright also distinguishes the unitary state of the mystical experience from the 'sense of absolute otherness, or distance, or difference' that is 'built into the very fabric of numinous experience', arguing that it is only in mystical experiences that 'distances are annihilated and distinctions overcome' (Wainwright, 1981, p. 5). The numinous experience's ontological and moral 'sense of radical separation from God' is generally regarded as a distinctive pointer to God's holy, transcendent otherness (Evans, 1985, p. 80).

Prophetic, Enlightenment and Revelatory Experiences

The experience of receiving, usually while relatively passive, an idea, message or other form of knowledge, or some affective content or impulse, is often recounted in religious traditions (cf. James, 1960, pp. 458–62; Franks Davis, 1989, pp. 39–44). It is described in various ways, as inspiration, revelation, enlightenment and so on. These experiences are generally associated with a sense of authority, and either certainty or very firm conviction, and frequently seem to arrive 'from outside oneself', often without prior reasoning or reflection.

While mysticism is more experience-focused and therefore individualistic, prophecy and enlightenment are more centred on the content or message, and especially its spiritual and moral dimensions, and frequently address matters of historical and social relevance. Although the insight or message may be resistant to expression and its recipient may demur, shrinking from his or her vocation, the prophetic call is insistent and the response to it must be honest and diligent: 'Must I not take care to say what the LORD puts into my mouth?' (Num. 23.12, cf. 24.12; see also Ex. 3.11; 4.10–13; Deut. 18.18; Isa. 6.5; Jer. 1.6; 20.7–9; Amos 3.8; Jonah 4).

In contemporary Pentecostal and charismatic worship, individuals may still offer a prophetic utterance or 'word': a report based on 'an intuitive perception of the activity' of the Spirit (Albrecht and Howard, 2014, p. 239).

(For more on biblical prophecy see Chapter 16, below; for prophecy and propositional revelation, see Chapter 13; for charismatic experiences, see later in this chapter.)

Conversion and Renewal Experiences

This group of experiences is associated with radical redirections (conversions)[9] or regenerations of the mind and heart. They are most often explicitly religious in their content and effects and may be exemplified across the religious traditions. In Christianity, they principally involve turning away from sin and towards God. Transformative conversion experiences may be gradual, but are more often reported when they involve sudden and intense resolutions leading to bursts of feeling, especially of joy and peace, self-surrender and emotional bonding, as well as giving rise to cognitive resolution and social readjustment (see Hardy, 1979, pp. 70–1; Paloutzian, 1981; Malony and Southard, 1992, part III; Iyadurai, 2015). 'Regenerative experiences' of the renewal of a person's faith and spiritual or moral well-being are routinely associated with a sense of salvation, guidance, protection or 'recharging the batteries' (Franks Davis, 1989, pp. 44–8).

Charismatic Experiences

These are particular experiences of Pentecostal and charismatic Christians (although at least some aspects are also shared across cultures; see, e.g., Goodman, 2008). They are, in the main, explicitly religious in their content and effects. As already noted, the theology of Pentecostal and charismatic Christians primarily derives from these experiences, especially the experience of 'baptism in the Holy Spirit' and experiences associated with 'charismatic gifts' (first referenced by Paul in 1 Corinthians 12—14), such as healing, prophecy (see above), and speaking with tongues (or *glossolalia*) and their interpretation. 'Tongues' is a conscious experience of passive, inspired utterance that transcends intelligible language (see Tugwell, 1972, chs 7, 8, 10; Laurentin, 1977, chs 3–5; Robeck, 1985; Johnson, 1998, ch. 4; Kay, 2009, pp. 256–9, cf. p. 30; Cartledge, 2017, chs 2, 3, 4, 10).

For Pentecostal/charismatic Christians, 'spirituality is fundamentally about life in the Holy Spirit' and the language of 'worship' is 'almost synonymous with entering into an experienced sense of the "presence of God"' (Albrecht and Howard, 2014, pp. 235, 241). Further, for these Christians 'experience is vital in knowing the truth, for truth is not merely propositional – it is personal'. They assume that 'Spirit baptism or filling is God's work through the believer' (Land, 1990, pp. 490, 492).

> Pentecostals expect the Holy Spirit to speak to them, to touch their hearts through strong emotions, to reveal something of God to them through ideas and pictures that come to their minds or through dreams, to pray through them in sighs, groans, and in unknown languages, and to transform them ever more closely in holiness to the image of Christ. (Albrecht and Howard, 2014, p. 237)

Trances, Ecstasies, Visions and Auditory Ecstatic Experiences[10]

Such experiences are reported in anthropological studies of non-Western cultures as part of local spiritual traditions. They also characterize a wide variety of historical expressions of Christianity and of other world religions, as well as some contemporary non-institutional Western spiritual experiences and practices.

Vision and apparition experiences, experiences of an auditory nature or other 'quasi-sensory experiences', may be of Christ, Mary, Hindu deities, saints, angels, demons, 'ghostly' experiences of the dead or other entities. They have been classified in a variety of ways (e.g. Hardy, 1979, pp. 26, 31–43; Wiebe, 1997, chs 1, 2); Augustine's distinction between 'corporeal' (bodily) visions, which involve the external senses, and 'imaginative' and 'intellectual' visions, which do not, being particularly useful (cf. Wiebe, 1997, pp. 21, 33). Rare *'theophanies'* (visible manifestations of God/a god) may be included in this category (see Chapter 16).

Ecstatic states are very intense (though often short-lived) euphoric states of consciousness, in which external awareness is reduced or suspended but mental and spiritual awareness expanded. In these states, emotions of excitement, bliss, flow, desire or lightness may be felt, and 'the human ego has the impression that it escapes from itself and "stands outside" itself' (Zaehner, 1957, p. 1; cf. Lewis, 2003; Malinar and Basu, 2008). The experience is commonly expressed in terms of loss and gain or a 'death–rebirth' within the self, and by employing the language of location ('up', 'inside'), light/dark and heat, or enlargement and liquidity ('bubbling', 'melting') (Hunt, 2000, pp. 356–7). In reporting ecstasies or trances, mystics may speak of 'raptures', often regarding them as a deeper form of mystical union. (The terminology is frequently ambiguous.) Teresa of Ávila writes of 'impulses': intense desires enrapturing her from outside that constitute a delectable 'dying for death' which can produce spiritual and physical pain, together with joy and tranquillity.

Some trance-like states are reported as 'transports' or spiritual flights in which the individual's spirit leaves the body and has visions of another world that transcend the experient's imagination ('shamanistic ecstasy': cf. Connolly, 2019, p. 94). Peter Connolly claims that a range of other spiritual experiences (glossolalia, possession, spiritual marriage and certain other mystical states) are in fact varieties of trance experience. The psychological processes involved include the displacement of the conscious mind, which gives free rein to the unconscious. They are, however, shaped by culture and their induction and guidance takes place in ways that are often similar to hypnosis (Connolly, 1998; 2019, pp. 61, 104–20, 180 n. 180).

Although ecstatic states that suspend 'mundane' (worldly) consciousness have been associated with prophecy, biblical scholars frequently emphasize that this element is more pronounced in the earlier prophets whose work is described in the Books of Samuel and Kings, and is less prominent in accounts of prophecy in later epochs (cf. Lindblom, 1962, pp. 4–5, 34–5, 47, 173). Both visions and ecstatic states were reported by the Apostle Paul, but he did not rate the latter as being as significant as his 'thorn in the flesh' (and his prayer for its cure) in evoking religious insight (2 Cor. 12; cf. Sanders, 2016, pp. 251–6). Claims to ecstatic additional revelations (including those arising in charismatic experiences) have sometimes been designated 'enthusiasm', a term that is most often used pejoratively. Christian mystics and commentators on mysticism tend to regard visions, raptures and ecstasies as inadequate and doubtful, 'at best a superficial reflection of an impression which the soul itself was incapable of receiving fully', or even 'a reflex effect of a spiritually immature person' who is overwhelmed by the awareness of God's nearness; and thus 'of no spiritual value' in themselves (Knowles, 1979, pp. 54–5, cf. 97).[11]

Other literature related to this broad category of experience includes Ennis, 1967; Lewis, 2003 [1971]; Greeley, 1974; Kelsey, 1976; Taves, 1999, 2016; Hunter and Luke, 2014; Schmidt, 2016a; Kellenberger, 2017 and Cook, 2018. Phillip Wiebe's study of *visions of Jesus* includes data from 28 interviewees, together with an analysis of a variety of metaphysical, psychological and neurophysiological explanations (Wiebe, 1997).

Spirit Possession

This phenomenon may overlap with the previous category. Possession by a (good or evil) spirit is said to be distinctively marked by features 'such as lack of control, loss of memory, and an awareness of presence' within the body of the person possessed, who is often semi-conscious (Schmidt, 2016b, p. 101; cf. Connolly, 1998; 2019, pp. 29–33, 178–80). Possession by an evil spirit overlaps with the more general 'awareness of an evil presence' frequently reported in surveys (e.g. Hay, 2006, pp. 21–2).

Experiences of God's Grace and Forgiveness, and the 'Internal Testimony' of the Holy Spirit

This broad category employs Christian, especially Protestant, terminology for experiences of:

- conviction about God, the subject's relationship with God or reception of gifts from God (and concerns, in particular, matters of sin, forgiveness and salvation);
- spiritual and moral empowerment and growth, or 'sanctification'; and
- the authoritativeness of Scripture.

Such experiences are usually regarded as the effect of the Spirit's continuing indwelling and revelation. John Wesley described his 'inward impression of the soul' as 'an experience not of a created grace in me, but of God's own love' (*The Witness of the Spirit*, II, 1767, II.6).

Phenomenologically, these experiences are analogous to, and often subsequent to or continuous with, some experience of *conversion* (see above). Thus, what William James describes as an 'affective experience' of 'the state of assurance' – involving peace, a 'sense that all is ultimately well with one', 'the sense of perceiving truths not known before' and a positive perspective on the world (James, 1960, p. 247) – may be placed under either category. The new birth of conversion may be construed as involving an opening of the spiritual senses that should eventually lead to what is variously described as 'a deepening experience of faith', 'growing in grace' or 'sanctification'; and may be regarded as 'a precise experience of the work of the Spirit'. Further 'manifestations of grace' and an experience of 'a positive assurance of new birth' have also been associated with this later stage of becoming Christian (Alan Tippett, in Malony and Southard, 1992, pp. 204–5).

Experiences of Presence

Language about the 'sense of the presence of God' and 'divine–human encounters' is used not only of the experiences listed under the previous heading, but also of numinous and conversion experiences and some others; and even sometimes of theistic mystical awareness. A more general experience of an 'unnamed presence' is also common in general surveys and RSE archives (cf. Hay, 2006, pp. 13–17).

Other Theistic Experiences

Kai-man Kwan (2012, pp. 516–18) has listed various other types of experiences *of God* ('theistic experiences') that do not obviously fall under the categories listed above:

- **Corporate theistic experiences** are undergone within – and contribute to – an experience of community (e.g. experiences in worship, the first disciples' Pentecost experience).

CATEGORIES OF RELIGIOUS AND SPIRITUAL EXPERIENCES

- **Mediated theistic experiences** come through other experiences of Nature, Art, the sense of duty, fellowship, other people, etc. (cf. Chapter 5, below).
- **Interpretive theistic experiences** involve 'a spontaneous interpretation of an event as God's action or message' (e.g. answered prayer, guidance, miracles, healing); presumably these are species of 'experiencing-as', as explored by John Hick (see Chapter 19); for some discussion of the difficulty in categorizing these experiences, see Astley, 2017b, pp. 351–2.
- **Intuitive apprehension of God** is Kwan's name for an unmediated, 'non-sensory awareness or intellectual vision of God in which all phenomenal content is absent' (see Chapter 17, 'Coming to Terms' box under 'beatific vision').

Vivid, Ultimacy, Anomalous and Intense Experiences

These are features of Wesley Wildman's detailed and nuanced explorative mapping of the territory of spiritual and religious experiences (Wildman, 2011, ch. 3; 2013). Wildman claims that his approach is driven by phenomenological, empirical psychological and neurological research. Vivid experiences constitute the basic category ('relatively unusual', typically colourful states of consciousness). These may be either what he calls 'ultimacy experiences' ('defined by subjective judgments of ultimate significance') or 'anomalous experiences' (experiences that are 'unlike whatever we normally experience and expect'). These two categories overlap. Intense experiences are ultimacy experiences that express 'intense existential significance', and which are 'exceptionally information rich' and 'generative of new insights'.[12]

Wildman maps meditation experiences, mystical experiences, spiritual experiences and religious experiences onto this ground plan, as in Figure 1 (Wildman, 2011, p. 101, cf. 81, 268).

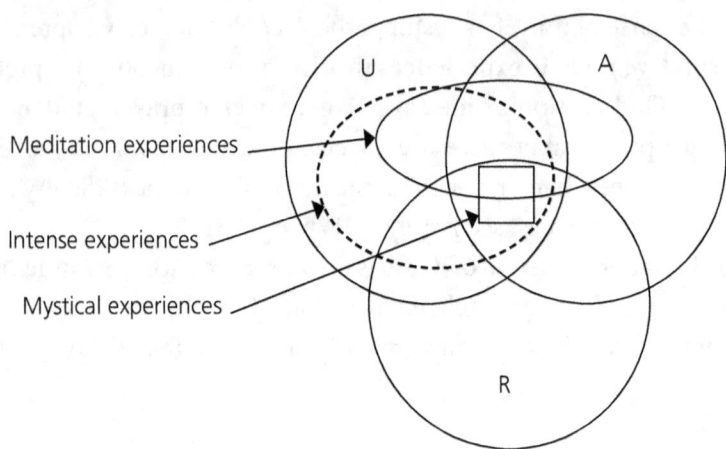

Figure 1: Relationships among all types of experiences discussed: religious (R) experiences, vivid experiences (constituted by ultimacy (U) and anomalous (A) experiences), meditation experiences, and two subclasses of ultimacy experiences: intense experiences and mystical experiences. RSEs are the union of the ultimacy and religious experiences.

Peak Experiences

This phrase was coined by the psychologist Abraham Maslow to refer to deeply fulfilling psychological states of harmony, joy, bliss, 'pure delight', vitality and creativity (see Maslow, 2014, especially Appendix A). He regarded them as eminently life-changing and self-transcending experiences that precipitate an attitude of accepting the world as it is. Maslow viewed mystical experience as a type of peak experience. The radical postmodern and (almost wholly) non-realist theologian, Don Cupitt, has described his blissful peak experiences of 'ecstatic immanence', which is sparked by Nature or language, as the 'mysticism of secondariness' and a 'Revelation of Being' (Cupitt, 1998a, Introduction; 1998b, ch. 1).

Pure Consciousness Events (PCEs)

(These have already been noted under 'Mystical Experiences'.) PCEs are claimed to be pure states of consciousness that include neither a subject nor an intentional object and have no other conceptual content. In them, 'there is no thought, there is no activity, there is no experiencer' (from a report cited in Forman, 1990, p. 28). See also Chapter 8, below.

Experiences of Nirvāna/Nibbāna, Nothingness or No-Self

These are perceptions of Ultimate Reality experienced, in a state of peace, 'super-consciousness' and the highest bliss, as a final release from or extinguishing of unsatisfactory human existence, with its desires, round of rebirths, etc.

Nature Mysticism

This is a joyful, sometimes ecstatic, self-transcending and illuminative awareness of and relationship with the physical universe and biological life. While some vivid experiences of Nature are more akin to numinous experiences (e.g. the awe felt by William Wordsworth before majestic scenery, as expressed in poems such as *The Prelude* and *Tintern Abbey*; cf. Paffard, 1973, chs 4, 5), most of those who have undergone such experiences report them as experiences of a mystical union with Nature (e.g. Paffard, 1976, ch. 4; see above under 'Mystical Experiences'). For theists, the experience and love of Nature are sometimes regarded as moving the recipient towards its creator, experienced in and through, but also beyond the creation: e.g. 'God is placed, not alongside creatures but behind them, as the light which shines through a crystal and lends it whatever lustre it may have. [God] is loved … not apart from but through and in them' (von Hügel, 1923, vol. 2, p. 353).[13]

Experiences of the World's Reliability, Contingency or Design

These are feelings of the dependency or intricate order of Nature and human life that give rise to a mediated sense of an ultimate upholding creator, supreme intelligence or mind behind all things; or of a reliable kinship between ourselves and the natural universe, which is also a creature, made and sustained by God. Some might include here a purported spiritual experience that lies behind what people mean by expressions such as 'wondering at the existence of the world' or 'feeling absolutely safe ... whatever happens' (cf. Wittgenstein, 1965, pp. 8–11). (These may be thought of as a type of interpretive experience or experiencing-as, see above.)

Experiences of a 'Patterning' or Synchronicity of Events

These experiences (which may also be understood as a type of interpretive experience or experiencing-as, and overlap with the previous category) may be understood as perceptions of some kind of general or particular providence, or of karma. They have been described as 'a patterning of events in a person's life that convinces them that in some strange way those events were meant to happen'. They sometimes involve a 'meaningful coincidence' between events that have no observable causal connection, which reveals some form of 'meaningful relationship' between them. The category has been cited as the commonest form of religious and spiritual experience reported in Britain (Hay, 2006, pp. 11–13).

Paranormal Experiences

Some other 'supernatural' or 'transcendent' experiences that are not readily catalogued under the previous heading or the next one may be corralled here. They may be described as 'abnormal', 'exceptional' or 'anomalous' experiences that 'apparently violate the operations of the world' (Wildman, 2011, p. 82). Examples include experiences of telepathy, clairvoyance, some hypnotic states and other 'psi phenomena' that are regarded as parapsychological or psychic (cf. Pike with Kennedy, 1969; Fenwick and Fenwick, 2008; Cardeña, Lynn and Krippner, 2014; Cardeña, Palmer and Marcusson-Clavertz, 2015, parts 6 and 7). Surveys report them as being more widespread than are generally thought (Castro, Burrows and Wooffitt, 2014 found that 37% of British adults reported at least one paranormal experience).

Some of these experiences may be regarded as having 'religious' or 'spiritual' import, under various definitions of those terms.

Out-of-Body and Near-Death Experiences

Such experiences have been the subject of a great deal of interest since the publications of the American physician, Raymond Mooney, in the 1970s. In near-death experiences (NDEs), people who are close to death (or have even been declared clinically dead) take on a different standpoint, as they see themselves 'rise' and 'float' above their physical bodies, on which they can look down and from which they may move away (in an 'out-of-body experience' – 'OBE' or 'OOBE'). Many of them then often feel a release from pain as they 'move through a tunnel' to a 'bright light'. From behind some sort of barrier the patient may then witness, emanating from the light, visions and/or auditory experiences of a holy figure and/or identifiable deceased relatives, which typically give rise to positive feelings; before returning (almost invariantly reluctantly) to their body and its painful condition.

On NDEs, see Zaleski, 1987; Fenwick and Fenwick, 1996, 2008; Fox, 2003; Marsh, 2010; Greyson, 2012; Sartori, 2014; Gregory Shushan, in Schmidt, 2016b, ch. 4 (pp. 71–87), Firth and Wilson, 2019.

Suggestions for Further Reading

Introductory

Hardy, Alister, 1979, *The Spiritual Nature of Man: A Study of Contemporary Religious Experience*, Oxford: Clarendon, chs 3, 4 (pp. 31–67).

James, William, 1960 [1902], *The Varieties of Religious Experience: A Study in Human Nature*, London: Collins, lectures IX, X, XVI, XVII (pp. 194–257, 366–413). (The Random House, New York, 1929 edition of this work is available online at http://web.archive.org/web/20080727010425/http://etext.lib.virginia.edu:80/toc/modeng/public/JamVari.html)

Advanced

Franks Davis, Caroline, 1989, *The Evidential Force of Religious Experience*, Oxford: Clarendon, ch. 2 (pp. 29–65).

Wildman, Wesley J., 2011, *Religious and Spiritual Experiences*, New York: Cambridge University Press, ch. 3 (pp. 69–103).

Notes

1 Some studies of religious and spiritual experiences focus on even more specific categories: e.g. Wiebe, 1997 (apparitions of Christ); Fox, 2008 (light phenomena) and 2014 (experiences of love).

2 It has been claimed that 'mysticism does not refer to any particular kind of system or experience' (Hans Penner, in Katz, 1983, p. 94), that 'there are apparently no reliable dividing lines between religious experience per se and mystical experience' and that efforts to separate them are 'rather inconclusive' (Spilka and McIntosh, 1995, p. 424). According to an empirical study by Ralph Hood, using Walter Stace's criteria of mysticism (Stace, 1961, ch. 2), 'some religious experiences may in fact not be mystical and some mystical experiences may in fact not be interpreted as religious' (Hood, 1975, p. 34).

3 The word comes from the Greek *muein*, meaning 'to close the eyes or lips', and was originally applied to initiation into secret rituals, or to hidden presences, revelations or interpretations. The understanding of mysticism in early philosophers and Christian thinkers, and its change in emphasis in medieval and (especially) post-Enlightenment thought, is succinctly rehearsed by Andrew Louth, in Wakefield, 1983, pp. 272–4.

4 Robert C. Zaehner claimed that Christian mysticism is essentially theistic and therefore *dualistic* (that is, involves two elements). Even though 'the soul feels itself to be united with God by love',

CATEGORIES OF RELIGIOUS AND SPIRITUAL EXPERIENCES

even 'melted away' in God by love, the mystic's individual ego is not annihilated, nor identified with God, only 'transformed and "deified"'. The self 'remains a distinct entity', though 'permeated through and through' with the divine substance. The appropriate analogy that is often appealed to here is that of a close sexual union. *Monistic* mysticism, by contrast, which recognizes only one ultimate reality, is a better fit to the analogy of a drop of water that becomes wholly part of a larger volume of wine (as in identity-union, or 'union without distinction', in which the sense of self has disappeared). (See Zaehner, 1957, pp. 29, 150–2, 204; Lewis, 1970, pp. 269–70; Jantzen, 1989; Pike, 1992, pp. 28–40.) Note, however, that even while describing the union of the soul with God as a 'spiritual marriage', the Christian mystic Teresa of Ávila adds that 'it is as if a tiny streamlet enters the sea, from which it will find no way of separating itself' – although this passage is usually interpreted as an image of an inseparable, not of an undifferentiated, union. It is relevant that Teresa specifically says of 'these comparisons' (i.e. analogies) that 'one makes [them] because there are no other appropriate ones'; and that God and the soul have become *like* 'two who cannot be separated from one another' (*Interior Castle*, VII, ch. II; *ET* www.cheraglibrary.org/christian/teresa/castle.html). Note, too, that Christian mysticism in particular is regarded as dependent on a 'higher capacity' of supernatural perception that is infused by God's free gift of grace, and is only bestowed on a few (Knowles, 1979, p. 19, cf. 84, 97). Theistic mysticism is also found in Sufism, Islam and Jewish Hasidic mysticism, and in some forms of Hinduism.

5 In Gellman, 2005, p. 142, the same distinction is also applied to numinous experiences (see below), but without the references to unity.

6 James depicted 'the more' that transcends sense perception and is the object of transcendent experiences as an 'unseen region' that may be named either as 'the mystical region, or the supernatural region' (James, 1960, pp. 485–92).

7 I have added scare quotes to indicate that this word *should* be spelled 'awful', but that its sense here (marked as 'archaic' in English dictionaries) is that of 'inspiring awe' and *not* its other sense of 'very bad or unpleasant', or its use in adding emphasis.

8 Some use the term numinous to describe any experience of *acquaintance* or *encounter* with the divine, where this is comprehended as a source of wilful (in the sense of intentional, deliberate and free) power.

9 A word based on the Latin *convertere*, 'turn about'.

10 In this book I shall normally refer to 'auditory experiences', rather than using the traditional term 'locution' (cf. Pike, 1986, p. 15 n. 2). I do so because in non-technical language 'locution' refers to an utterance from a source rather than to the recipient's *experience*. The term 'audition' is also sometimes used, although not in the usual dictionary sense.

11 Teresa of Ávila claimed to have received many visions and auditory experiences but came to believe that, for love of the unseen, everything distinctly experienced in this way must be transcended. John of the Cross did not deny the reality of visions and locutions, yet held that 'incomparably greater progress' had been made by those who had known no such experiences and advised that those who had should be directed to move beyond them, voiding the 'desire and spirit of them' (*Ascent of Mount Carmel*, bk. 2, ch. xxii, §19; *ET* https://en.wikisource.org/wiki/Ascent_of_Mount_Carmel/Book_2/Chapter_XXII). Walter Hilton also allowed that the 'spiritual graces' received by beginners in the spiritual life, including experiences of light and feelings of warmth and sweetness, were genuine. But he insisted that such 'exterior signs' reflect the weakness of souls that have not yet experienced inner grace and still rely too much on their feelings and imagination. The invisible God the Holy Spirit is not to be identified with the Pentecostal tongues of fire (Acts 2.3), nor God's interior grace with interior

sensations. Nevertheless, 'until greater grace is given' a person should not 'abandon a good thing until he can discover and use something better' (*The Scale of Perfection*, chs 29–30, in Illtyd Trethowan (ed.), *The Scale of Perfection by Walter Hilton*, London: Geoffrey Chapman, 1975, pp. 94–101).

12 Wildman describes these (likely universal) cognitively and emotionally potent intense experiences in terms of their depth (registered in fear, joy, bliss), horizon (in feelings associated with recognizing difference), scale (in feelings of awe), complexity (feelings of wonder) and mystery (feelings of incomprehension). These core features have both immediate and long-term behavioural consequences, among which Wildman mentions speech and silence, trust, surrender, liturgical acts, compassion, intellectual enquiry and reverence (Wildman, 2011, ch. 4 and pp. 254–7). A number of these elements have been highlighted by other scholars. Thus, Luke Johnson offers a 'working definition of religious experience' that draws on Joachim Wach's four-component description of the phenomenon, portraying it as 'a response to what is perceived as ultimate' that 'involves the whole person', 'is characterized by a peculiar intensity' and 'issues in action' (Johnson, 1998, pp. 60–7; cf. Wach, 1958, pp. 31–7). Wildman characterizes peak, numinous, pure consciousness, absolute dependence, (Mihaly Csíkszentmihalyi's) 'flow' experiences and moral instincts as examples of intense experiences (Wildman, 2011, pp. 105, 122, 222–5).

13 The liberal Catholic writer, Friedrich von Hügel (1852–1925), distinguished the 'exclusive mystic' who embraces the love of God to the *exclusion* of the love of God's creatures – as if God were 'the First of Creatures, competing with the rest for man's love ... alongside them' – from the ('more difficult and rarer conception') of the 'inclusive mysticism' (forming part of a 'larger asceticism') that is described here. (Cf. von Hügel, 1923, vol. 2, pp. 348, 351.)

Part 3

Debates

5

Experience and Experiences

In this next part of the book ('Debates'), we shall explore a number of issues within the study of religious and spiritual experiences that have generated discussion in the literature, beginning here with the debate over the *breadth* of the topic itself.

A Broader View of Experience and Perception?

While some researchers have rightly protested against the narrowing of the concept of experience that results from its being qualified as 'religious' (e.g. Tite, 2013, p. 9), others have commented on the neglect of more 'everyday' religious experiences (and some uncommon extraordinary ones) in the study of SREs (cf. Wildman, 2011, p. 60).

The voices advocating a further broadening include some who espouse orthodox Christian theism. Thus, Kai-man Kwan has expanded the argument from religious experience by arguing for a 'holistic empiricism' that involves what he calls *the rainbow of experience*: that is, the whole of a person's experience, extending beyond religious experience to include experiences of the self and of Nature, and existential, interpersonal, moral, intellectual and aesthetic experience. Together, he claims, these provide 'pointers to both a transcendent realm and a personal God' and 'disprove the alleged superiority of naturalism' (Kwan, 2011, pp. 1, 9–10, 48–51, 94, cf. 137–251).

A similar broadening is found in the work of Keith Ward. While Ward treats religious experience as 'analogous to or even mediated by means of sensory perceptions' (cf. Chapter 9, below), he also writes of a more general 'spiritual sense'. This is something that is mainly concerned with our experience of meaning and of 'objective and intrinsic' value, which he describes as 'seeing things in a certain light', including experiencing 'a moral depth to things'. All these experiences are subspecies, he argues, of *non-scientific knowledge*: that is, knowledge of truths that are not publicly observable, impersonal, dispassionate, mathematically measurable or in accordance with the physical laws of Nature. (Science, after all, is itself an abstraction from the rich-textured, value- and feeling-filled, holistic 'personal perspective' from which we all see and respond to reality.)

Among the facts that are not in this way scientific, Ward includes historical interpretations, facts about human motives and goals, and 'facts disclosed by feelings and communicated by art, music and literature'. One of the attractions of literature, he notes, is that 'it may convey to us ways of seeing the world, of living in it and experiencing it, that are quite new to us'. In fact, all the Arts evoke in us 'a mode of consciousness and apprehension that can enlarge and deepen our way of being in the world'. In this way, they have a clear affinity with and parallel to religion. This, too, helps us to see differently. Ward also affirms this role of those interpretative worlds of meaning of the humanities that convey 'imaginative visions and ideas'. 'In this area, what you see is always a function of what you are. You have to see things in a new way' (Ward, 2008, pp. 163, 167–8, 175, 181–4; 2014, pp. 11, 18, 24).

In making a case for religion, Ward thus widens both the concept of experience and the notion of facts. This strategy chimes with a very broad conception of spiritual envisioning, or spiritual 'visualizing', that finds a special place (among other objects of experience) for *spiritual values*. Their recognition widens not only the concept of spiritual experience but also that of religious experience itself, wherever these values are inextricably linked with religious ideas, objects and practices.

Another British philosopher, John Cottingham, has recently argued for a wider, less rationalistic and 'more humane' understanding of religion. His religious epistemology employs visual metaphors in an articulate and persuasive manner. In *The Spiritual Dimension*, he maintains that 'our religious (and moral and aesthetic) experience' all involve 'transformative ways of perceiving reality', in which 'the whole situation … is reconstituted by the emotional colouring of the supposed facts' (Cottingham, 2005, p. 85). Elsewhere, he writes of 'the illuminations that come from the practice of spirituality', and which cannot be accessed by 'adopting the stance of detached rationality'. Two of these are particularly redolent of accounts of spiritual vision: 'to view life as a precious gift' and 'to see one's own life as … hinging on the choice between good and evil' (Cottingham, 2003, pp. 90–1, 100). In another book, Cottingham is more explicit about this 'epistemology of receptivity and involvement', arguing that being religious is in part 'a project of *formation*, of forming and reforming the self, a process of *askēsis* (training) and *mathēsis* (learning)' (Cottingham, 2014, pp. 23, 68, 148).

To many people, Cottingham confesses, what he identifies here may not count as 'religious experiences', if they mean by that term a specific and explicit revelation of some supernatural entity. By contrast, he describes the experience with which he is concerned as an (imaginative) 'heightening, an intensification, that transforms the way in which we experience the world' – disclosing beauty, goodness and meaning. He adds that these experiences are not 'interruptions into the natural world', describing them rather as 'natural intimations of the transcendent' that are, in fact, 'much more readily available to all' than is either intellectual analysis or '"special" religious experience', and in which 'the ordinary world is "transfigured" and we seem to have glimpses of a deeper and richer reality that calls forth responses of joy, wonder, awe and respect' (Cottingham, 2014, pp. 60–4).[1]

Cottingham also acknowledges a broader understanding of *conversion* that requires 'interior transformations' that include not only 'a reorientation of life to a new set of values', but also a characteristic phenomenology or psychology that involves a new openness 'to new ways of perceiving' (Cottingham, 2014, pp. 176, 157–9). In *How to Believe*, he argues further that the 'transformative vision of reality' that marks the religious worldview (note that visual metaphor) itself changes the way in which the experiencing subject is 'able to see things', and that this is 'inextricably linked' with 'a *moral* change, a change in the character and dispositions of the perceiver' (Cottingham, 2015, pp. 54–5; cf. Dykstra, 1981, pp. 21, 49). Together, these changes change a person's view, so that the world is 'transfigured'.

These changed perceptions, he asserts, are 'disclosures of meaning' in which we see the world 'in its true light', by coming to 'see the truth of what was really there all along' (Cottingham, 2009, pp. 97–8, 123–4). For Cottingham, however, these intimations of the divine presence may only be glimpsed by 'those in an appropriate state of trust and receptivity' who are '*prepared and trained* ... to approach God in humility and awe, to risk the vulnerability of trust and hope' and to express 'thankfulness and praise for the gift of life' (Cottingham, 2007, pp. 36–7, italics added).[2]

It would seem that the moral and spiritual change within the viewer both precedes and follows from the change in the way she sees things. Cottingham also insists that her change in seeing, this 'outlook or vision of reality', is never just a descriptive account of how things are. It is also a 'normative' vision that carries with it the requirement on us to change more than our way of seeing, for it requires us to change *our lives* as we hold them up to the scrutiny of God.

These examples of recent writing by philosophers suggest that the perceptual model of religious experience, with appropriate modifications, may be fruitful for understanding a wider range of spiritual and even moral experience, as well as for explaining the formative role of religious, spiritual and moral learning experiences in aiding these forms of 'seeing' – which includes seeing the things of *this* world differently and acting appropriately. As 'spirituality' is a term that often labels the attitudes, values and dispositions that undergird people's actions and beliefs, such changes may be thought of, fundamentally, as *spiritual changes* (see Chapter 1).

Spiritual Ophthalmology?

The rhetoric of *vision* is, of course, ubiquitous in the spirituality corner of bookshops and the Internet, where references abound to 'seeing the world through spiritual vision', and changing one's perspective and how one should 'view life'. It may also be relevant to note the *general* form and significance attributed to this type of experience, which takes us beyond any specific and particular species of RSE.

This focus could be described as the 'ophthalmic' dimension of spirituality, as I have labelled it elsewhere (Astley, 2007, pp. 4–6, 11, 13, 69, 113–16). It may involve seeing Nature as holy, perhaps; certainly, 'seeing the same things differently', 'more clearly and in more depth' and not superficially; and seeing meaning – 'seeing the point of things'. For theists, it would include learning to see life, the universe and everything more from God's perspective. For

Christians, it would involve seeing with and through the eyes of Jesus: recognizing the signs of the kingdom, seeing the point of the Christ. It is a 'correction of vision', 'a new way of seeing, a reconstruction of sight'. One might then speak of a Christian's personal *theology* as facilitating such a spiritual vision, insofar as it serves as a lens through which Christians try to see their lives, including their suffering and healing, in a Christian sustaining vision. And we may argue, further, that a Christian's Christology is primarily a matter of looking on Jesus *as* the Christ – in a way that is peculiar to (and revelatory of) each individual. The systematic theologian, Mark McIntosh, has written that 'true theologians see everything from this new perspective, from this sharing in the dying and rising of Jesus'; and that Christian revelation comprises 'a network of beliefs ... by means of which Christians seek to think about everything from God's point of view' (McIntosh, 2008, pp. 18, 36).

Religious *faith* itself is sometimes said to include faith as *visio*, as a way of seeing. This is a matter of how we view and interpret the whole of reality, and 'look on' and 'experience it *as*' related to God – seeing things as God's world, God's children, God's gift.[3] Understood like this, faith is a way of seeing 'what is' and of seeing it 'as gracious' (Borg, 2003, pp. 34–6).

This is *not*, therefore, a mere change of subjective perspective; for it is seeing things as they truly are, seeing the truth in things, seeing them *clearly*. Similar visual analogies are also employed within the Christian *ethic*, and with regard to Christian *action*, 'which begins in how we perceive what is going on' with the help of what is given in the Gospels: 'a new set of metaphors and paradigms, new lenses ... Our experience looks different when seen through the lens of the kingdom of God' (Spohn, 1999, p. 71). The Christian claim is that *then* 'reality itself is being perceived from the perspective of God's disposing power'. And 'the reality perceived by faith', which is a 'decidedly greater' reality if it is a *truthful* reality, may then be 'allowed to overflow into the present world, affecting the conditions of life here and now' (Berger, 2003, pp. 194–6).

Implications

If this is part of what spiritual vision is, then what is its status? Is it something that is *innate* to people (to some people, presumably, but not all), and/or can it be acquired, by being – in the broadest sense – *learned*?

If it can be learned, then the requisite 'spiritual learning' would presumably include among its learning outcomes both *learning how to see* in this way (which is a learned skill) and *becoming disposed* to do so (which is a learned dispositional attitude and desire). Stanley Hauerwas and Brian Goldstone relate this sort of perception to formation in their essay, 'Disciplined Seeing', proposing there that 'to "see something *as something*" is, in large measure, already to have been made by it'; and that this is often a consequence of 'pedagogies connected … to "how one sees things" – and, in seeing them, intuiting how properly to live with them' (Hauerwas with Goldstone, 2011, pp. 37, 60).

Spiritual vision surely does form a key outcome of Christian discipleship learning, although it is not always explicitly recognized as such. But then neither is the form of *implicit Christian formation* that facilitates this 'learning to see'. All the same, we may argue that the requisite skill set and dispositions for this task are things that are formed in Christians through a wide range of learning experiences that include many examples, aspects and dimensions of the Church's worship, fellowship and moral action. That is the case, if the Church

> teaches itself to be Christian and inducts new members into its faith primarily through speaking the Christian language and beliefs, expressing the Christian attitudes and affections, and practising the Christian behaviours in its worship, witness and service. (And only secondarily by *talking about* these things, through specific forms of instruction.) (Astley, 2013, p. 51)

Presumably, something similar happens in other religious and spiritual traditions.

There is another area in which the study of religious and spiritual experiences relates to these concerns for a broader view of experience. Those who have researched the prevalence of RSEs among the general public sometimes protest that they have explicitly sought to gather 'accounts of … seemingly more ordinary but deeply felt experiences', rather than just the merely 'remarkable' or the 'strange and striking'; and have sought reports of a 'continuing sense of spiritual awareness' as well as 'the more dramatic isolated experiences' (Hardy, 1979, pp. 18–20; cf. 1975, p. 187).[4] It is significant that Alister Hardy claimed that 'we had said that at first we should not be studying the more ecstatic or mystical states' (Hardy, 1979, p. 29). Even so, a considerable number of the experiences reported to him clearly possessed an extraordinary character. Equally, much of the wider literature on RSEs – including studies of classical mysticism and other experiences from spiritual adepts – does tend to privilege these 'anomalous' accounts (on which, see Taves, 2009, pp. 38–46; Wildman, 2011, pp. 79–84).

For example, nearly 20% of the experiences collected in the Alister Hardy Archive represent what we might call specific and objective (even perhaps 'non-metaphorical') *visions* (Hardy, 1979, pp. 26, 32–4).[5] It may be argued, however, that to be of any lasting value, even that exotic species of experience must lead to *a different and more general form of envisioning that can be applied to everything*, by affecting the way people see things in general. Religious experience must have 'an effect on the way the whole world is perceived, understood, and felt' (Mariña, 2008, pp. 465–6). In other words, 'it must result in a *revision* of everyday experience' (Astley, 2007, p. 5). And at Hardy, 1979, p. 23, the possibility is mooted of a similar 'unexpected' experience leading to the development of just such 'a general sense of spiritual awareness'.[6]

This widening of focus from particular *experiences* to a '*continuing* sense of spiritual awareness', or to other forms of more general spiritual perception, would appear to address a criticism that has frequently been voiced by theologians, that 'religious experience in a wider sense, as something which extends through their whole life' is 'really much more important than any single experience', any 'particular incidents' (Kallistos Ware and Edward Robinson, in Robinson, 1977b, p. 119; cf. Hick, 1999, p. 163). Gwen Griffith-Dickson (2005, pp. 428, 405) even intimates that 'the idea of "An Experience"' may be spiritually 'unhealthy and undesirable' if it represents a form of 'sensation seeking'. Instead, she suggests, religious experience should perhaps be interpreted as being about 'a whole way of life … the epistemological end of personal self-discipline': as a whole-life experience, then, rather than specific experiences. This distinction may be illustrated in even more basic understandings of what constitutes 'ordinary religious experiences', such as those that include the 'sensory religious experiences' that form a core component of religious practice (McGuire, 2016), as well as 'the recognition of the religious meaning of some material context' (Wynn, 2009).

It may be that if the parameters of religious and spiritual experiences are broadened in these ways, the same should happen to the terms of the debate over the veridicality and objectivity of these experiences, and its related perceptual and evidential models, which we shall discuss in Chapter 9. Kwan has adumbrated a number of 'transcendental' *arguments* that point to a transcendental realm. If successful, they would justify claims about the veridicality (Kwan, 2011,

p. 9) of a wide range of RSEs, including experiences of the mystery of the natural world, the self, interpersonal and existential experiences, and central aspects of intellectual, aesthetic and moral experience (Kwan, 2011, chs 9–15). These overlap with other, more traditional debates in philosophy – which are not all supportive, of course – over theistic arguments from reason, consciousness and morality (see, e.g., Swinburne, 2004, ch. 9 and passim; Wainwright, 2005, ch. 4; Craig and Moreland, 2012, chs 5, 6, 7). As some of these authors point out, confidence in such arguments (or widened 'perceptions'?) may be considerably enhanced if they can draw on claims about the objective existence of God – or, to a different extent, some other transcendent reality – that are derived from argument/perception models that employ a narrower view of RSEs, or other sources. On which, see Chapters 9 and 10, below.

> **Exercise: Among the Articles**
>
> *Read and critically assess the following journal article:*
>
> **Mark Wynn, 2009, 'Towards a Broadening of the Concept of Religious Experience: Some Phenomenological Considerations', *Religious Studies*, 45, 2, pp. 147–66.**
>
> Mark Wynn focuses our attention on experiences which, in the first instance, are not of some supernatural entity or devoid of a subject–object structure, but 'where the sense of God is mediated by way of an appreciation of the existential meanings which are presented by a material context'. He hopes in this way to extend the standard philosophical concept of religious experience by taking account of 'phenomenological treatments of sacred place' and 'the materially mediated or sacramental character of much religious experience'.

See also Chapter 18, below, on Karl Rahner, and Chapter 19, below, on John Hick.

Suggestions for Further Reading

Introductory

Astley, Jeff, 2007, *Christ of the Everyday*, London: SPCK, especially chs 1–2 (pp. 1–26), 8 (pp. 112–27).
Cottingham, John, 2009, *Why Believe?* London: Continuum.
Ward, Keith, 2014, *The Evidence for God*, London: Darton, Longman and Todd.

Advanced

Cottingham, John, 2005, *The Spiritual Dimension: Religion, Philosophy and Human Value*, Cambridge: Cambridge University Press, ch. 7 (pp. 127–49).
Ward, Keith, 2008, *The Big Questions in Science and Religion*, West Conshohocken, PA: Templeton Foundation Press, chs 7–8 (pp. 162–215).

Notes

1 This view also seems to map closely onto 'the sort of religious experience' that the pastoral and ascetical theologian, Martin Thornton, designated 'normal': that is to say, 'ordinary experience deepened and enriched' (Thornton, 1974, p. 91).

2 Ward, too, writes of the need 'to cultivate a special sensibility, the spiritual sense' that involves interpreting experiences 'in a special way' (Ward, 2014, p. 11).

3 This is how John Hick interprets religious experience (see Chapter 19). As we have seen in Chapter 4, both Kwan and Franks Davis call this category 'interpretive religious experiences'. While they are ordinary – not unusual in themselves – these experiences are viewed as religious, according to Franks Davis, 'in the light of a prior religious interpretive framework' (Franks Davis, 1989, pp. 33–5, cf. 257); but she makes no reference to Hick's view of religious experience at this point. See also Donovan, 1979, p. 91. The biblical scholar, Johannes Lindblom, writes of 'a special group of visions [elsewhere he places them in the category of 'pseudo-visions'] in which a real object is apprehended by the senses, but linked with an interpretation conceived by the visionary as given him in a revelation'. Lindblom describes these experiences as 'symbolic perceptions', in which 'the object seen is not changed in the apprehension of the observer, but is interpreted in a more or less spontaneous act of reflection' (Lindblom, 1962, pp. 41–2, 137–41).

4 Hardy commented that the very term 'an experience' often signifies 'something exceptional'. He also observed that others had suggested to him that his project would be better named 'the study of

spiritual awareness' (1979, p. 18). (The term 'religious experience' was not at the forefront of Hardy's earliest appeals and does not in fact appear in the 'Hardy question', although it was included in the name of his research unit.)

5 The figure for a sense of (non-human) *presence* was slightly over 20% (p. 27); many of these are likely to be of an out-of-the-ordinary nature. (Remember that Hardy's figures represent percentages of the *reports* of experiences submitted in response to his newspaper and other appeals.) In random sampling in 2000, the percentage of the UK's general *population* who reported having had an awareness of the presence of God is cited as 38%, with figures over 25% listed for each of three other kinds of awareness of presence (Hay, 2006, p. 11). (We should note that neither the Hardy nor the Hay categories are exclusive, as an individual RSE may be described under more than one category.)

6 In Hardy's classification, 'a sense of' a range of cognitive and affective elements is often represented by figures of over 10%, and sometimes over 20%, of all responses. In these cases, many of these responses are likely to be reporting a continuing awareness.

6

Triggers and Facilitators

A significant question for many of those who have received a religious experience (and an even more significant one for those who have not) is, 'What caused it?'

A *cause* is a particular relationship between two events, objects or states of affairs such that one ('the cause') gives rise to – 'brings about' – the other ('the effect', 'result' or 'consequence'). The fundamental nature and necessity of causation eludes physical observation and scientific analysis and has provided a contended topic for the branch of philosophy called 'metaphysics'.[1] But even at the level of observable events, asking about something's 'cause' is ambiguous.

Scientifically, we explain the occurrence of an event by citing past events or states and the laws of their interaction. Yet hearing this claim may properly lead us to respond with an astonished, 'What, *all* of them?' One philosopher, John Stuart Mill, seemed to think so. He argued that the whole cause of an event is the whole set of conditions that are required (are 'sufficient') to produce it. 'In daily life', however, 'we say that scratching the match caused it to light'. In other words:

> Out of the vast variety of conditions that together constitute the sufficient condition [of its combustion],[2] we select one and call it the cause, though they are *all* equally indispensable to the event in question, and all equally parts or components of the sufficient condition. We select the one that we do because (1) it is the last condition to be fulfilled before the event takes place, or (2) it is the condition we believe our hearer does not already know about, or (3) it is the condition whose share in the matter is the most conspicuous. (Hospers, 1967, p. 294)[3]

Nevertheless, there are *many* causes of an event or state of affairs, such as an experience. In Chapters 9 and 10, we shall look at the crucial claim that some transcendent reality, such as 'God', is *the* (or should we now say '*a*'?) cause of religious experiences – a discussion that will take us well beyond everyday or scientific causes. In Chapter 11 (and the Appendix), we touch on 'reductive' or 'naturalistic' explanations that refuse to invoke such transcendent causes. But in this chapter, I want to consider what have been called 'triggers' or 'facilitators' of religious and spiritual experiences: that is, *natural causes* that help to arouse, evoke or precipitate such experiences, or just to deepen, extend or strengthen them. These may be thought of as 'contributory causes', without implying that they are either necessary or (on their own) sufficient to ensure that the experience will happen.

Empirical Studies

In his 1979 study of the first 3,000 reports in the Alister Hardy Archive, Hardy lists 21 categories of 'antecedents or "triggers" of experience'.[4] Four of these categories occurred on average in more than 10% of the records (Hardy, 1979, pp. 28–9, ch. 6 and p. 145):

- 'Natural beauty'.
- 'Participation in religious worship'.
- 'Prayer, meditation'.
- 'Depression, despair'.

Of these, the last category appeared in over 18% of the records. Three other groupings – covering literature, drama, film, music and illness – occurred in between 5% and 10% of the records. Hardy also reported (p. 95) that 'so far' they had 'received surprisingly few accounts of experiences resulting from the taking of drugs' (less than 2% of the records reported drug use).[5]

Ralph Hood's overview of the facilitation of religious experience details only a few of such triggers. He acknowledges the *role of language* not only in facilitating religious or spiritual awareness, but also in providing the 'necessary mediation by which [such] experience becomes reflexively conscious',[6] while denying (against Proudfoot) 'that language and context determine the particularity of emotions'

(Hood, 1995a, pp. 577–9). Hood also reviews the classic experimental study by W. N. Pahnke, which is often designated 'The Marsh Valley Chapel' or '*Good Friday Experiment*', in which seminary students ingested either a psychedelic drug (psilocybin) or a placebo prior to listening to a broadcast of a Good Friday Service. In this experiment, the scores for experiences of unity, transcendence, paradoxicality, joy–blessedness–peace, ineffability and sacredness were rated much higher by the experimental than by the control group (pp. 579–85). Similar studies, including spontaneous reports of religious experiences on the part of those who use psychedelic drugs, have also been reported even among non-religious users (cf. Wainwright, 1981, pp. 55–61). But Hood claims that, unless specifically prompted, the frequency of reports of religious experiences among such users is no more than among those who do not take drugs, and that these may be less highly evaluated than experiences facilitated by prayer.

Emphasis in religious traditions on *private* prayer suggest that religious experiences may be reported after artificial sensory isolation in 'isolation tanks'. Hood's own experimental studies indicated some facilitation of religious imagery with numinous characteristics under these conditions, especially among certain religious individuals (Hood, 1995a, pp. 585–90). Finally, Hood reports his empirical study of *stress* in a natural outdoor setting and its correlation with measures of spontaneous religious experience, and concludes that it is incongruity between the subject's anticipated stress and the actual stress level of the subjects' activities that facilitates such experiences (p. 592).

Drawing on their analogy of religious experience with creative experience and its elements of existential crisis, self-surrender, new vision and new life, Batson, Schoenrade and Ventis surveyed the empirical psychological evidence and possible psychological mechanisms for four 'facilitative techniques' for stimulating religious experience: psychedelic drugs, meditation, religious language and music (Batson, Schoenrade and Ventis, 1993, chs 4, 5). They concluded that, 'although none has the power to *produce* religious experience, each has the power to *facilitate* it', provided that the individual using them does not 'become focused on the facilitator rather than the personal transformation being facilitated', for that psychological state would 'undercut the power of the facilitator to promote transformation and insight' (pp. 151, 154).

In Christianity and some other traditions, the *gift of mystical grace* that is regarded as essential for progress to the higher stages of religious experience is said to be 'normally not given to a soul unprepared', whether by a long process of prayer, meditation, discipline and self-denial, or by an exceptional endowment from an early age (Knowles, 1979, p. 135). Outside theism, the main emphasis is placed on the subject's training in these human practices and spiritual disciplines rather than any outside help, with the exception of the *human* 'facilitation' provided by a qualified spiritual teacher, guru or guide, which most religions deem necessary (cf. Staal, 1975, ch. 10). Among these many disciplines and spiritual pathways, however, most writers on mysticism agree that the apprenticeship of the spirit that constitutes the 'mystical way' is to be regarded as neither certain nor easy. And spiritual masters and their disciples also concur that it is *not for everyone*.

Surveys of the general population reveal, however, that a far wider group undergo religious or spiritual experiences than this analysis would suggest, with relatively few of these respondents referring to any training in meditation or prayer, or the disciplined adoption of other spiritual training such as abstinence, fasting, chanting, breathing, posture or the disciplines of ritual, worship, charity and service; let alone the assistance of a teacher, guru or guide.

Of course, the acknowledgement of a role for divine grace in religious experience rather implies that, in principle, no human effort can be *guaranteed* to produce the experience and even, perhaps, that training may not be needed: claims that might allow greater plausibility to reports of spontaneous experiences in the general population (cf. Staal, 1975, ch. 12). Admittedly, these surveys often tend to elide general and specific experiences (cf. Chapter 5, above), and they are rarely designed to tell us much about any prior instruction or dispositions of the respondents, or even about the elements that facilitated the origin of their experiences. Only when an interview schedule or questionnaire *explicitly* asks about people's character and practices, and the contextual circumstances and formative influences of their experiences, will we know much about the 'triggers and facilitators' in such cases.

The 'Devotional Experiment'

A number of twentieth-century philosophers of religion formulated a form of test that an agnostic might attempt to 'open themselves to the divine', by praying, cultivating the moral and spiritual values advocated by religion, seeking guidance and support from believers, and so on – in order to place themselves in a position (or, rather, condition) to receive some personal form of religious and spiritual experience. These factors may be thought of as particular facilitators for such experiences, in what Caroline Franks Davis has labelled 'a devotional experiment'.

She argues that 'many types of religious experiences could help to confirm' the general hypothesis 'that there is an ultimate, holy, transcendent and benevolent force with which human beings can come into contact, in which they can find their greatest bliss, and without which they cannot be "whole" or live life to its fullest' (Franks Davis, 1986, p. 17; cf. 1989, p. 76). In this account, she draws on Alister Hardy's notion of an 'experimental faith', which revolves around 'a prayer undertaken by an agnostic or an atheist who, having studied the records of experience, is now prepared, with profound sincerity, to attempt the quest …; it might perhaps be a prayer beginning something like this. "God, if there is a God, help me to find you, and having found you, help me to have the strength and courage to do what I feel to be Thy will"' (Hardy, 1979, p. 140). Franks Davis finds justification for such an experiment in faith (albeit one that is entered into without abandoning our critical faculties) even in the writings of the atheist philosopher, John Mackie:

> We shall be intellectually better placed in relation to theism – whether in the end we accept it or reject it – if we have at least once made the experiment of playing along with it, if we have genuinely opened not only the intellectual but also the passional side of our minds to the possibility of conversing with 'the gods', if there are any gods and they are willing to converse with us. (Mackie, 1982, pp. 209–10)

Another Oxford philosopher, Henry Price,[7] formulated a related proposal in the final lecture of Series II of his 1960 Gifford Lectures, revised and published in 1969. He argued there for the important assumption that 'a person's character', their acquired spiritual and moral dispositions to act and feel, can affect their *cognitive* powers so as to enable them 'to be aware of facts [they] could not otherwise be aware of' through certain revelatory experiences. For, 'what a person is capable of being aware of depends in some degree upon the kind of person he is' (Price, 1969, pp. 471–2, 474). This assumption, he argues, is an empirical claim: we have to try it, and see for ourselves 'what effects it has', by developing our spiritual capacities, engaging in (mainly devotional) spiritual practices[8] and seeing whether the evidence is forthcoming. (For Price, the evidence in question is evidence for the basic theistic assertions concerning God and God's relations to ourselves.) Basically, then, the agnostic has to 'entertain the proposition that there is a God … [who] is benevolently disposed to us', rather than to *believe* it. He or she must take it as a hypothesis, and then pray – in what Price describes as an 'imaginative exercise', putting themselves into the shoes of the believer and pray-er, rather as an actor does in playing a role. He calls this 'belief-like' stance, 'assiduous supposing' (pp. 480–6).

In a comparable way, Peter Baelz has depicted a person acting 'on the *assumption* that the basic Christian affirmation concerning the way of God is true', in an 'experiment with life'. While 'it remains more a hope than a belief', it is 'a hope with which ['the half-believer']'[9] is determined to experiment in prayer, reflection and action', and which 'may lead to experiences which chime in with and tend to corroborate belief' (Baelz, 1975, pp. 138–41) – although in this case explicitly supernatural experiences are not so obviously in the author's mind.

That disclaimer may also be relevant to Louis Pojman's later, and apparently independent, construal of an 'experimental faith that is open to new evidence', which depends – not on the belief that God exists – but 'only that one regards such a being as possibly existing' while yet being committed 'to live *as if* such a being does exist', in what Pojman refers to as a 'profound hope' (Pojman, 1986, pp. 224–34).

In William James's famous essay, 'The Will to Believe' (first published in 1896), he offers 'a defence of our right to adopt a believing attitude in religious matters, in spite of the fact that our merely logical intellect may not have been coerced' (James, 1917, p. 100). He was attempting there to give moral permission to someone to believe something on insufficient evidence – or at least to do things that help to self-induce this belief ('such as acting as if we believe'), 'when doing so will help them to bring about something morally desirable' (Richard Gale, in Oppy and Trakakis, 2009b, p. 16). William Wainwright emphasizes that 'James is attempting to show that we are rationally entitled to certain *beliefs* and not just that we are rationally entitled to act *as if* certain beliefs were true or to *cultivate* certain beliefs' (Wainwright, 1995, p. 95).

In the 'devotional experiment', therefore, our working hypothesis involves tentatively thinking that the theistic assumption is true. This, Wainwright argues, is a matter of 'trusting our passional nature'. And that is something we should be permitted to do, because views that ignore or suppress 'our deepest needs and intimations' are not satisfactory, so 'they will not "ring true"' to us (Wainwright, 1995, p. 97). This is not merely an issue of psychology, he insists, but also an issue of rationality.

And it certainly was *for James*, for whom the structure of our minds was in accordance with the nature of reality. If that is the case, then the justification for the experimental faith outlined here would seem to be considerably strengthened.

Those who criticize such an 'experiment' include those for whom it is an experiment 'with a difference' – that is, not *really* an experiment – because 'if commitment is to count as religious it needs to be unconditional, in which case no appeal to consequences is relevant' (Miles, 1972, p. 57, cf. pp. 58–9). Pojman's response to such a claim is likely to be that 'we believe propositions to varying degrees', and that even religious commitments 'are not all-or-nothing states' (Pojman, 1986, pp. 153–5). The nature of religious commitment, religious truths and 'critical openness' in religious believing – not to say the concept and practice of experimentation – requires a more nuanced analysis than Miles allows (cf. Astley, 1994, pp. 94–9, 285–9, and chs 5, 8, 10, more generally; and the literature cited there).

> ### Exercise
>
> Might one argue, then, that one may be rationally justified in facilitating a religious and spiritual experience in this 'experimental' way? If so, why? If not, why not?

Suggestions for Further Reading

Introductory

Baelz, Peter, 1975, *The Forgotten Dream*, London: Mowbrays, ch. 8 (pp. 127–42).
Franks Davis, Caroline, 1986, 'The Devotional Experiment', *Religious Studies*, 22, 1, pp. 15–28.

Advanced

Pojman, Louis, 1986, *Religious Belief and the Will*, London: Routledge & Kegan Paul, ch. XVI (pp. 212–37).

Price, H. H., 1969, *Belief*, London: George Allen & Unwin, series II, lecture 10 (pp. 455–88).

Notes

1 If, indeed, such deep matters apply to causes. David Hume held that they did not, arguing that 'causes' simply represent the regular ('constant') conjunction of two events/things, with one being prior in time to the other.

2 In this example these include the presence of oxygen and combustible material and an increase in the temperature of the match head 'caused by friction', and so on.

3 Hospers refers later to the distinction between *standing conditions* (conditions that are necessary to the event, but occur whether it does or not) and *differential conditions* that make a difference to what would otherwise happen (or not) (p. 302).

4 Hardy writes of 'forms of experience, active or passive, which ... give rise to feelings of a religious kind' (1979, p. 81). The identification of each of these categories as the precipitating cause of a reported RSE seems to have been made by Hardy and his colleagues, rather than by those who reported them; especially where the report of the experience details several other potentially contributory elements.

5 Hardy adds, rather contentiously, 'it should not worry us if it is shown that altered states of consciousness may be produced by chemical means; the chemicals themselves do *not* produce the divine ecstasy, but affect the brain in such a way that a rarely accessible region of the sub-conscious mind becomes available to those who already have, perhaps unknown to them, a mystical streak within them' (p. 97). See Chapter 11 and Appendix, below.

6 Both written and spoken religious language is reported as being employed widely, today as in the past, to effect and affect religious and spiritual experiences, both within and outside the contexts of prayer and worship.

7 Price confessed in secret to friends that he had had a vivid religious experience himself in the mid 1960s – see Hick, 2002, pp. 74–5.

8 Cf. Price, 1966, pp. 17–20.

9 As Baelz calls such a person.

7

Experience and Fruits

A number of scholars have insisted that the justification or genuineness – or at least the value, authenticity or meaning – of spiritual and religious experiences are 'to be assessed in terms, not of their "roots", but of their "fruits"' (Lash, 1988, p. 31; cf. James, 1960, p. 41, cf. 238;[1] Hick, 1989b, p. 309; 1995, pp. 76–81; 1999, pp. 163–7; 2006, pp. 42–3; Wildman, 2011, pp. 146, 152, 155–6, 179, 225, 242; Ward, 2014, pp. 108–10; Tristan Nash, in Schmidt, 2016b, pp. 126–32).

The reference here is to the biblical texts in which Jesus cautions against false prophets, saying that we may 'know them by their fruits' (Matt. 7.16, 20) as 'the tree is known by its fruit' (Matt. 12.33, cf. 7.17–19; Luke 6.44). William James describes this biblical injunction as 'our empiricist criterion'. Hick designates 'the observable spiritual and moral fruits of religious experience in the individual's life' a 'universal criterion, common to all the great traditions, both theistic and non-theistic' (and which is also exemplified by what he calls 'secular' or 'political saints').[2] Wildman writes, 'no matter how RSEs come to us, what they produce in our lives and in our wider social contexts is what matters most'.

While most emphasis is rightly laid on the wider social and moral fruits of such experiences, we should also consider the individual's own *spiritual* fruits (cf. Hick, 1995, p. 77). These fall much closer to the tree, where we may think of their seeds germinating in the form of the growth of spiritual virtues and a 'spiritual vision' in the individual who undergoes the experience: elements that may themselves motivate and direct further, and wider, moral fruiting (see Chapter 5, above).[3] This distinction may be compared with James's own demarcation between (a) 'inner happiness and serviceability', the 'immediate delight' that a state of mind causes; and (b) the 'good consequential fruits for life' to which it subsequently leads (James, 1960, p. 37).[4]

Paul lists a wide range of 'fruit of the Spirit' (rather than of spiritual *experience*): namely, 'love, joy, peace, patience, kindness, generosity, faithfulness, gentleness and self-control' (Gal. 5.22–23). In each of these spiritual and/ or moral fruits we may distinguish elements that represent *both* overt actions and *inner* dispositional virtues, and Paul seems to have intended his phrase to cover both. Overt action is clearly intended by John the Baptist's demand that *his* hearers 'bear fruit worthy of repentance' (Matt. 3.8; Luke 3.8), as it is also intended by Jesus' image of the branches of the 'true vine' (himself) bearing the fruit of mutual love (John 15.1–17). In the New Testament, the metaphor also implies that such outer fruits are expressions or outworkings of inner states such as faith, 'abiding' in Christ or possessing the Holy Spirit, and should not therefore be viewed (solely, or even not at all) as a human 'work' produced by human effort – but as a consequence of the divine presence and activity.[5]

The *inner transformation* described or implied in such accounts may be framed in a less supernatural or theological manner in terms of a shift in a person's character that would normally and naturally result in right actions (and, some would say, morally *ought* to do so). The inner transformation of the self that is reported by mystics[6] and those undergoing more ordinary religious experiences (or even intense aesthetic experiences), in which their view of themselves and the world is 'radically transformed', has been described as 'a consequence and corollary of self-transcendence' and is often associated with self-surrender. Neuroscientists claim that the biological basis underlying these changes is an increased emotional discharge that allows for the formation of new neural connections that results in 'a realignment of one's understanding of one's self and the world in relation to the ... experience' (d'Aquili and Newberg, 1999, pp. 161–2).

But any remarkable experience has the potential to change people. 'Other experiences, other interests, look different after a glorious trip, after torture, after a sublime dive into serenity, etc.' (Smart, in Katz, 1983, p. 126).[7] It is not surprising, then, that many religious and spiritual experiences have been claimed to effect such a transformation (Hay, Reich and Utsch, 2006, pp. 47–8). Although their claims have sometimes been disputed, *the classic mystics* held that their experience – together with, it must be admitted, their 'apprenticeship', nurture and instruction along the way to full mystical union – was associated with a 'high degree of moral and spiritual purity', accompanied by and consequent on their 'escape from self-love' and (in the case of Christian mystics) their identification with Christ in his love for God and humankind, all of which was achieved wholly through the reception of God's unmerited grace (Knowles,

1979, pp. 36, 46–7). In reports of *experiences from more ordinary subjects*, which are mainly collected from respondents who have not explicitly undertaken any similar spiritual training or discipline, we may find many similar accounts of the development of the spiritual and moral fruits of spiritual and religious experiences. These reports particularly mention the disposition for and feeling of 'total love': 'I seemed filled with love for and felt I had to do everything for complete strangers' (838, Alister Hardy Archive). 'I became conscious that at the centre of the Universe, and in my garden, was a great pulsating dynamo that ceaselessly poured out love. This love poured over and through me ... I have no excuse now for unloving behaviour towards another – a gift of grace brings awesome responsibility!' (4267, Alister Hardy Archive). 'I behave better; it touches the conscience' (Hay, 1987, p. 159). Other accounts of religious or spiritual experience bear witness to a changed sense of spiritual meaningfulness in life, or – and often along with – the development of more loving attitudes and behaviour towards other people (cf. Hardy, 1979, pp. 98–103; Fenwick & Fenwick, 1996, p. 4; d'Aquili and Newberg, 1999, p. 143; Fox, 2014).

It is difficult to support some of the assumptions in the literature, however, especially those about the moral fruits of RSEs. Thus, although he argues that 'almost every spiritual experience worthy of consideration must have some effects', Alister Hardy's classification of 'consequences of experience' from the Archive includes only effects on the experiencer's 'sense of purpose or new meaning to life' (mentioned in only 18% of the first 3,000 reports), 'changes in religious belief' (less than 4%) and 'changes in attitude to others' (7%) (Hardy, 1979, pp. 29, 99).[8]

And the literature itself contains some cautionary references. For example, while recognizing that Christianity and some other religious traditions and communities treat a resulting life marked by virtue as a criterion of a genuine religious experience and that, psychologically and socially, 'mysticism often appears to have a positive and beneficial effect on the moral lives of those who are touched by it', William Wainwright also notes:

- Mysticism can also make a person indifferent to moral values (e.g. he claims that classical Advaita Hinduism and Hīnayāna Buddhism advocate a form of non-moral 'ethical egoism' that seeks the private good of release from the cycle of rebirths or enlightenment).

- It is not clear that mysticism teaches any moral truths that are 'not available to us apart from mystical experience', and therefore that 'any moral ideal or norm depends on mystical consciousness for its validity' (Wainwright, 1981, pp. 86–7, 202–8, 225–6; cf. 2005, ch. 11).

Pragmatism

Pragmatism is the view that truth is 'what works'. William James thought of himself as a 'radical empiricist' and pragmatist, for whom truth is to be judged by what works well – 'on the whole' (James, 1912, 1917). 'The pragmatic theory of meaning holds that the whole meaning of a belief or proposition is a set of conditional predictions specifying what experiences one will have in the future if certain actions are performed ... [It] acquires truth when these predictions are actually verified' (e.g. good winning out over evil in the long run would verify the truth of the religious hypothesis, which includes the tenet, according to James's own words, that 'the best things are the more eternal things ... [that] say the final word') (Gale, in Oppy and Trakakis, 2009b, pp. 13–14).[9]

Philosophical reaction to this position has been, on the whole, harsh. In a (sympathetically critical) exposition of James's pragmatism, H. S. Thayer concludes that – although James was 'not espousing a subjective doctrine of truth' – his argument that certain metaphysical and religious beliefs 'could be "justified" by their effects in organizing, stimulating, and adding a sense of value to human life and experience' (in leading to other ideas and experiences) is 'startling' (Thayer, 1964, pp. 451, 453). Other critics have responded more sternly:

- 'The pursuit of *truth* and the pursuit and enhancement of *life* are both fundamental value pursuits, but the pursuit of irreducibly different values, and we cannot count on the first invariably to further the second' (Hepburn, 1992, p. 140).
- 'Granted, true beliefs tend to foster success. But it happens regularly that actions based on true beliefs lead to disaster, while false assumptions, by pure chance, produce wonderful results' (Horwich, 1992, p. 511).
- 'Truth has rights and privileges of its own, and they are not the same as those of utility' (Blackburn, 2005, p. 9).

However, Richard Gale argues that in the *Varieties* (e.g. James, 1960, pp. 322, 364, 394, 485 (+ n. 2), 493–4, 496), 'James is quite explicit that the answer to the "objectivity" question is independent of the biological and psychological benefits that accrue from mystical experiences' (Gale, in Oppy and Trakakis, 2009b, p. 19).

Other Tests of Authenticity

Other tests of the authenticity of religious experiences have been proposed, in addition to their moral and spiritual effects.

In the Judeo-Christian tradition, at least, openness to spiritual experience has always been tempered by a certain wariness. Thus, prophecy in Israelite religion was open to being tested, often against the fulfilment of historical predictions (cf. Isa. 7.10–17) or even occasional 'experimental' tests (cf. 1 Kings 18), but also for coherence with the acknowledged revelation of God's character and acts (cf. Hos. 11.1–9). In the New Testament, Paul listed both prophecy *and* the 'discernment of spirits' among the gifts of the Spirit in 1 Corinthians 12.10.

> *Prophecy*... was uttered in ordinary though probably excited, perhaps ecstatic, speech. It was not for this reason true; hence the necessity for a further gift, which enabled the possessor *to distinguish between spirits*. Here *spirits* signifies the Holy Spirit and other possible sources of ecstatic phenomena. It was necessary (and it required another gift) to know whether the inspired speaker (who is probably to be distinguished from those who uttered a word of wisdom or knowledge) was actuated by the Spirit of God, or by some demonic agency. (Barrett, 1971, p. 286)

Within later Christian tradition, too, mystics and others were often cautious about their own experiences (see Chapter 17). Being religious, and having religious experiences, is not a function of being gullible. Thus, Hildegard was silent about her visions until commanded in a revelation to disclose them. And Teresa of Ávila appears to have worried a great deal about the authenticity of her experiences, concerned about the possibility of their originating in the work of the Devil rather than of God, and she sought advice from her confessors on this point. In her account of the stages of mystical prayer, she references the dangers of the Devil whom she thought was able, at various stages, to 'tempt the soul with his own supernatural effects or … use natural states to his own advantage'. Teresa did offer advice about distinguishing demonic from divine influences, identifying the former with aridity and languor of the soul and the latter with joy and growth of true humility and other virtues. Divine quiet, she believed, also builds confidence in the mercy of God, increases the desire for penance, counters the fear of trials and augments the resolution 'to revile the merely mundane'. Demonic quiet, by contrast, ends in disquiet and, eventually leaves 'neither light in the understanding nor steadfastness in the will'.

Even locutions (see Chapter 4, above) could be demonic or imaginary and must therefore be tested against the teachings of Scripture and the Church; but also as to whether they have power and authority, are etched in the memory, instil confidence and alleviate distress, and bring tranquillity, peace and a sense of deep certainty. Locutions with these effects, and those that are spontaneous and distinct, cannot be induced. In the most convincing cases, God does not use human language. Teresa offers similar tests for visions, which may also mislead – and may, indeed, include visions of the Devil. (See Bagger, 1999, pp. 175, 183–93, quoting Teresa, 'Spiritual Relations Addressed by Saint Teresa of Jesus to Her Confessors', *ET Complete Works of St Teresa*, vol. I, New York: Sheed and Ward, 1957, pp. 321–8; cf. Schreiner, 2011, pp. 310–13.)

It has been pointed out that Teresa's supernatural explanations for religious experiences are essentially explanations of what appear as 'anomalous or seemingly impossible events' that are not brought about by the experiencer's own powers but are consonant with Scripture – including, presumably, its revelations about the character and intentions of God. In these ways, they parallel her explanations for *miracles* (Bagger, 1999, pp. 203–7, 224–8).

This point bears further reflection. The traditional understanding of a miracle is that it is an event that:

(a) cannot be explained by natural causes, and therefore seems inexplicable even as scientific understanding develops; and
(b) evokes religious sentiments such as awe and gratitude, and seems to express the character of a loving God.

Schleiermacher's own definition famously dropped the contentious aspect (a), retaining only the aspect of religious and moral significance. He claimed, therefore, that 'miracle is simply the religious name for event ... The more religious you are, the more miracle would you see everywhere'; and thus that 'all events alike are miracles' (Schleiermacher, 1958, pp. 88, 114; cf. 1928, pp. 183–4).

This essentially 'non-interventionist' theology has informed liberal Christian theology ever since. It is highly relevant to the location of divine causality in, and therefore the nature of, religious experiences: especially in debates as to whether their being anomalous or scientifically inexplicable is a valid test of their authenticity. We shall need to return to some of these claims later (see Chapters 9, 11, 16).

Suggestions for Further Reading

Introductory

Hardy, Alister, 1979, *The Spiritual Nature of Man: A Study of Contemporary Religious Experience*, Oxford: Clarendon, pp. 98–103.
Hay, David, 1987, *Exploring Inner Space: Scientists and Religious Experience*, London: Mowbray, ch. 11 (pp. 153–67).

Advanced

Hick, John, 1985, *Problems of Religious Pluralism*, Basingstoke: Macmillan, chs 5, 6 (pp. 67–95).
Hick, John, 1999, *The Fifth Dimension: An Exploration of the Spiritual Realm*, Oxford Oneworld, ch. 18 (pp. 163–70).
Wildman, Wesley J., 2011, *Religious and Spiritual Experiences*, New York: Cambridge University Press, pp. 124–30, 149–56.

Notes

1 Proudfoot points out that James mistakenly claimed that this view was held by Jonathan Edwards. But 'for Edwards, the chief distinguishing mark of the religious affections is their origin or cause' as supernatural and divine, with the behavioural fruit only serving as reliable evidence of that causal attribution (Proudfoot, 1985, pp. 166–9; cf. Edwards, 1961 [1746], part III, sect. I, cf. XII).

2 For more on Hick's pragmatic criterion, see Chapter 19.

3 However, this distinction might appear to make it even more difficult 'to distinguish between an actual experience and [its] consequences' (Hardy, 1979, p. 98).

4 From an Aristotelian perspective, virtues are constitutive of the human flourishing of the person who possesses them, if that is understood as that person's 'well-being', 'living and doing well' or 'success'. But *Christian* virtues and those encouraged in some other faiths include more self-denying, even self-sacrificial attitudes, values and behaviours that require a more radical interpretation of what constitutes a 'successful' or 'good' life.

5 Jesus speaks of 'evil fruit' as well as 'good fruit', indicating that the term 'fruit' is neutral. But there is a tendency to use the word predominantly of positive products: of ripe, rather than spoiled, fruit. Paul also uses the term to refer to both good and bad consequences, writing of both 'fruit for God' and 'fruit for death' (Rom. 7.4, 5). But Ephesians (5.9–11) distinguishes 'fruit of light' from 'unfruitful works of darkness'; and in Gal. 5.19, 22, Paul contrasts the fruit (Greek *karpos*) of the Spirit with works (*'erga*) of the flesh, perhaps so as to stress that good deeds are the natural – even automatic – result of *God's* agency or presence, rather than a merely *human* work in which the flesh is seen as 'surrendered to its weakness and/or manipulated by sin' (Dunn, 2003, p. 68 n. 76, cf. 65, 124; cf. Sanders, 2016, pp. 274, 497, 559–60). As G. N. Stanton notes, 'the phrase "fruit of the Spirit" ... is evocative: "the fruit" is not the result of the believer's effort, but of the gift of the Spirit' (Stanton, 2001, p. 1164). For these reasons, perhaps, one should exercise caution in using the metaphor of fruits, instead referring more neutrally to the 'effects' or 'consequences' of religious experiences (cf. Hardy, 1979, pp. 29, 98–103; Wildman, 2011, p. 179).

6 According to G. W. Barnard, mystical experience is *defined* as necessarily transformative (Hood, 2006, p. 129).

7 For a very detailed overview of the psychology of transformation in both religious experience and psychosis, see Hunt, 2000.

8 In one survey, around three-quarters of those who had a religious experience felt that it had altered their 'outlook on life', although only 10% said that it had encouraged moral behaviour (Hay, 1987, p. 157). The link between the two is not always made, unless this change of 'outlook' is itself a change in *moral* vision: cf. Chapter 5, above; see also Kwan, 2011, ch. 13 (pp. 208–26); Ward, 2014, ch. 3 (pp. 23–30).

9 But for James, those for whom religious experience works appear to be the *first-hand believers*, who have received their religious experience directly and are frequently regarded as somewhat heretical by second-hand believers and institutional religion, whose sense of inwardness is over and its spring dried up (James, 1960, p. 330).

8

Experience and Interpretation

Essentialism is the broad philosophical view that things have essential, unchanging properties without which they could not exist, and that these properties must be distinguished from their merely 'accidental', non-essential properties (which may vary). Essential or 'built-in' properties define something, making it what it is; they give it its 'essential' or 'determinate' nature. *Contextualism*, or social *constructivism*, by contrast, is the view that nothing can be understood in this abstract way, just 'in itself', but only in its concrete (experiential, historical or cultural) context. This difference in viewpoint has led to profound disagreements over the nature of religious experience.[1]

Essentialists

Essentialists tend to regard religious experiences as extraordinary experiences that are *inherently* religious or mystical: their religiousness is 'built into' the experience. Proponents of this view treat all religious experiences as essentially everywhere the same, or at least as existing in only a few basic forms. Most of the differences between religious experiences are then ascribed to how they are later interpreted ('post-experience'). In this way, essentialists make a *radical distinction between religious experience and its interpretation*.

This 'universalist' or 'ecumenical' thesis gives rise to the idea of a *common core* to mysticism, and sometimes to religious experience in general, whose characteristics are regarded as independent of any specific, culturally bound tradition. Such views may be attributed, for example, to Mircea Eliade, Robert Forman, William James, Abraham Maslow, Rudolf Otto, Ninian Smart, Walter Stace, Huston Smith, Evelyn Underhill and Keith Ward. Smart presents his own summary of the position like this:

> (1) Phenomenologically, mysticism is everywhere the same. (2) Different flavours, however, accrue to the experiences of mystics because of their ways of life and modes of auto-interpretation. (3) The truth of interpretation depends in large measure on factors extrinsic to the mystical experience itself. (Smart, 1965, p. 87)

Claims for a common core are sometimes – although by no means always[2] – expressed in terms of a single, transcultural 'perennialism' or *perennial philosophy of common ideas*, which are thought to underlie the variety of accounts of religious experiences and, indeed, of many religions, theologies and philosophies. A concept that goes back to Leibniz (1646–1716), the *philosophia perennis* was understood by Aldous Huxley (1946, Introduction) to consist primarily of the metaphysical beliefs that everything depends on a hidden transcendent, non-physical ground and source, which to know (and achieve identity with) is the final goal of human life; and that every person has something similar to ('or even identical with') this 'divine Reality' within themselves, which is usually called a 'soul'.

In reality, such highest common factor accounts, or lists of what is 'left behind when the conflicting "interpretations" are strained out' (Franks Davis, 1989, p. 173), are rarely extended beyond mystical experiences. This encourages the criticism that in privileging this one type 'as the standard' for all religious experience, perennial universalism 'turns out to be another form of exclusivism' (Aden, 2013, p. 223). The perennialist claim may be strengthened, however, by its incorporation of numinous experience into what has been called a 'broad theism' (Franks Davis, 1989, pp. 174–5, 190–2).

Some have argued that the cross-cultural similarities are best explained by their being 'biologically structured', having 'their innate basis in qualities intrinsic to human nature' (thus, Michael Winkelman, in Schmidt, 2016b, pp. 43–4, 50).

Constructivists/Contextualists

Constructivists (sometimes called contextualists) hold very different views. They *reject the priority of experience over language* and regard the differing situations in which people undergo experiences as providing these experiences with all their different concepts and interpretations. Hence their claim that there is *no common religious experience* – at any rate, not in any unqualified way. They also argue that we *cannot separate these interpretations from the experiences themselves – denying the distinction between experience and interpretation*. The religious experiencer and his or her culture play a large part in 'constructing' the experience, which doesn't and couldn't exist as independent of them (as the essentialists claim).

On this second view, there are no fundamental, 'essential' characteristics of a religious experience that are to be found below its specific religious and cultural expressions. So, there is *no uninterpreted, contentless, 'pure experience'* or 'pure consciousness', which is 'unmediated' (by concepts, and especially by language) – that is, that is not clothed in and stamped by, perhaps even created by, a person's religious language and beliefs. And it is these *beliefs that determine the sort of experiences* that people undergo.

> *There are* NO *pure (i.e. unmediated) experiences*. Neither mystical nor more ordinary forms of experience give any indication, or any grounds for believing, that they are unmediated. That is to say, *all* experience is processed through, organized by, and makes itself available to us in extremely complex epistemological ways. The notion of unmediated experience seems, if not self-contradictory, at best empty ... because of the sort of beings we are, even with regard to those ultimate objects of concern with which mystics have intercourse, e.g. God, Being, nirvāna, etc. (Katz, 1978, p. 26, italics original)

Therefore, for example, 'the Hindu experience of Brahman and the Christian experience of God are not the same':

> The forms of consciousness which the mystic brings to an experience set structured and limiting parameters on what the experience will be, i.e. on what will be experienced, and rule out in advance what is 'inexperienceable' in the particular, given, concrete context. (Katz, 1983, p. 5, cf. 41–3)

Constructivists, therefore, *reject the idea of any common core* that lies beneath the differing interpretations of mysticism, or of religious experience in general. In this context, religious pluralism is a form of constructivism in which differences in religious concepts mean differences in religious experiences, as a consequence of these *experiences being shaped and conditioned by a religious tradition*. There exists, then, a *true plurality of religious experience*, for there are as many types of different religious experience as there are different concepts and beliefs (leading to different expectations) that interpret them.[3]

On this view, 'no one goes "naked"' even into 'the desert' of solitary religious experience; they all 'carry with them the clothing or baggage of the culture that has produced them, has shaped … the worlds of their experience' (Lash, 1988, p. 59).[4] And *this shaping takes place within the experience* itself, not during the course of the experiencers' reflections after their experience. It takes place 'by shaping or colouring the actual object or content of the experience ("incorporated interpretation")' (Moore, 1973, p. 148) and is the result of 'an internalized residue of an earlier social world … imprinted on us' (McCutcheon, 2012, p. 8). This constructivist/contextualist position is argued for by Matthew Bagger, John Hick, Steven Katz, Nicholas Lash, Russell McCutcheon, Peter Moore, H. P. Owen and Wayne Proudfoot, among others – including many exponents of feminist approaches (see Chapter 14).

The Debate over Constructivism and Perennialism

Inevitably, this debate has largely been a theoretical one. The extent to which the views of those who undergo religious experiences can be *shown empirically* to be relevant to the sorts of experiences that people have depends on the experiencers' self-awareness and their critical reflection on their own beliefs and experiences, which are very difficult matters to assess. Nevertheless, it may be worth citing Michael Walker's follow-up study of just over 100 people who had submitted reports of their experiences to the Alister Hardy Archive, all of whom had indicated a sustained form of experience. Walker's questionnaire asked them, 'Would you say that your experience followed your acceptance of particular beliefs or that your beliefs arose out of experience?' Their answers were distributed across seven categories. (I assume that this was an open question and that it was the researcher who allocated the answers to the categories.) Despite Alister Hardy's comment that 'no clear picture emerged', his report of the research indicates that 42% of the sample regarded belief as primary (mostly 'interacting with experience'), whereas only 26% regarded experience as primary (with a minority indicating that it was 'interacting with belief'). A further 27% of the responses to the question were coded as 'interaction – neither belief nor experience primary'. Hardy noted that those who reported striking, 'out-of-the-blue' experiences tended to regard experience as primary, whereas 'those who looked back to a conversion experience where they heard and accepted particular truths naturally regarded belief as primary' (Hardy, 1979, p. 119). (A more sophisticated empirical study supporting the common core theory is provided by Hood, 2006, and is discussed below. See also Hood and Williamson, 2000, explored in one of the exercises in Chapter 3, above.)

As we have already noted in Chapter 6, there are many triggers or facilitators of RSEs. Do *these* elements provide the interpretations for those experiences? Two of the 'principal modes of preparation' for mystical experience identified in the literature, and which are recognized as not being necessarily exclusive by John E. Smith (in Katz, 1983, p. 254), *do* in fact employ concepts. They are:

1 Rational dialectic, leading the mind by rational steps to grasp what is beyond discursive thought.
2 Moral preparation.

Two others, however, are broadly *non-conceptual*:

1 Disciplining the body through exercises of relaxation or ascetical practices.
2 Drugs and intoxicants.

In debate, some have argued that it is possible – although, admittedly, sometimes difficult – to distinguish *interpretations* of religious experiences from *descriptions* of them (Wainwright, 1981, pp. 27, 46 n. 39). But can we? Wayne Proudfoot thinks that we cannot make that distinction:

Understanding the experience of another requires mastery of the concepts and rules assumed by that experience. An experience is already interpreted and thus is constituted in part by the description under which the subject identifies it. To understand the experience of another or even my own experience requires that I identify it under the appropriate description. When it is said that there is no uninterpreted experience, or one attends to the interpretative component of religious experience, the reference is to the concepts within which the subject has tried to make sense of his experience, and to the tacit theoretical framework he has employed. Interpreting religious experience may include both an understanding of the description under which the experience is identified by the subject or in the culture in which it is embedded, and an attempt to arrive at the best explanation of the experience. (Proudfoot, 1985, p. 71)

Religious beliefs and practices are interpretations of experience in that they are attempts to make sense of and to account for the phenomena and events with which one is confronted ... They are attempts to understand, where understanding can be construed as seeking the best explanation. It is in this sense that there is no uninterpreted experience ... [A]ny perception or experience is already shaped by the concepts and implicit judgments we bring to it. (Proudfoot, 1985, p. 43, cf. 61)

By contrast, Wainwright argues that, as cognitive (in the sense of factual or objective) experiences incorporate judgements and therefore concepts:

of course we cannot describe these data without conceptualising them, but it does not follow that we are unable to abstract the data from the concepts which are incorporated in the experiences which include them ... (To describe the sensa [sense data] involved in an experience of a desk, one need not use the concept of a desk.) (Wainwright, 1981, p. 49 n. 53, cf. 117–22).

Within mysticism, constructivism has been defined as the claim that 'mystical experience is significantly shaped and formed by the subject's beliefs, concepts, and expectations'. It is often argued that this claim derives from the *general view* that 'all experiences ... are in a significant way formed, shaped, mediated, and constructed by the terms, categories, beliefs, and linguistic backgrounds which the subject brings to them' (Forman, 1990, pp. 3, 4). At base, then, constructivism draws on the more general epistemological assumption that *all* ordinary human experience is processed or organized (or, metaphorically speaking, 'filtered' or 'moulded'). Constructivists then apply this claim to mystical experience; it, too, must be 'shaped by concepts' (Katz, 1978, p. 26).[5]

For Proudfoot and many constructivists, the *attribution of causes* is central to the nature of religious experiences: 'beliefs about the causes of one's experience are themselves constitutive of the experience', especially in identifying it as religious. Thus, 'the distinguishing mark of a *religious* experience is not the subject matter but the kind of explanation the subject believes is appropriate' (Proudfoot, 1985, pp. 114, 231, italics added). Similarly, Matthew Bagger writes, 'to express an experience in concepts presupposes that concepts in part compose the experience'; in particular, 'any experience includes an implicit commitment about the best explanation of the experience and this commitment constitutes the experience' (Bagger, 1999, p. 40).[6]

It is hard to deny that an explanatory interpretation – for example, that God is the substantive cause of, and therefore best explanation for, the experience – *does* seem to lie at the heart of many subject's understanding of their religious experience. Nevertheless, 'the constructivist does not address the question as to whether some exterior reality exists' (Bagger, 1999, p. 98).

Mapping Constructivism

Distinctions have been made between different *types of constructivism*.

1 Jerome Gellman calls one species, '*soft*' or '*weak constructivism*', identifying this as the view that 'there is no mystical experience without at least some concepts' (Gellman, 2018, §6; cf. 2005, p. 148). After all, 'even "divinity" and "ultimate reality" are human concepts ... so too is "presence"' (Griffith-Dickson, 2000, p. 95). This position *is* consistent with perennialism, provided that there are some transcultural concepts (and therefore experiences) that are common across mystical traditions. It may also allow that our experience is not *solely* formed by religious beliefs and values and that 'some of the shape of the experience ... is [also] provided by ... sensory input or whatever'. The position, therefore, has also been termed 'incomplete constructivism' (Forman, 1990, p. 13; 1999, p. 41).

2 '*Hard*' or '*complete constructivism*' presents greater difficulties and leads to a stern denial of perennialism. It involves the claim that 'a mystic's cultural background massively constructs – determines, shapes, or influences – the nature of mystical experiences' (Gellman, 2018, §6). Yet, in responses to others, Proudfoot is explicit that his own constructivism does *not* imply that the experience was not 'real' (Taves, 2009, p. 92 n. 1), that 'language is everything' or that experience is 'caused by language, or entirely made up of language' (Kelly, 2002, p. 171). However, Steven Katz (1978) not only famously rejected the distinction between experiences and interpretations; he also unambiguously claimed that religious models (a complex category which, within Christianity, includes the Church, Jesus and 'the imitation of Christ') 'contribute heavily … to the *creation* of experience' (Katz, 1983, p. 51, italics original). Robert Gimello has also sometimes painted a picture of the wholesale construction of religious experience out of religious beliefs and values, in a way that makes this experience comparable to a hallucination, and suggested that these experiences are 'induced' (sometimes as 'deliberately contrived exemplifications of … doctrine') and that it is doctrine that is 'determinative of religious experience' not the other way round. Gimello argues not only that 'what is perhaps mislabeled "interpretation" is actually ingredient in and constitutive of religious experience', but also that these 'structures of meaning' are 'of the essence of mystical experience. They engender it' (Gimello, 1978, p. 193; 1983, p. 62; cf. Forman, 1990, p. 13; 1999, p. 41).

3 A third version, sometimes identified as '*catalytic constructivism*', is the view that certain beliefs and practices 'themselves act as catalysts for mystical experiences' (Forman, 1999, p. 42; cf. 1990, p. 14). Forman uncovers its presence even in the writings of some complete constructivists (see Gimello, 1983, pp. 71–2). This is the mildest and least problematic type of constructivism, and is reminiscent of Ian Ramsey's thesis that one of the main functions of religious language is to help to evoke a disclosure of the divine mystery (Ramsey, 1957, ch. II; 1965, chs I, III; cf. Astley, 2004, pp. 31–2; 2017c). See also Chapter 13, below.

Exercise: Among the Articles

Read and critically assess the following journal articles:

Donald Evans, 1989, 'Can Philosophers Limit What Mystics Can Do? A Critique of Steven Katz', *Religious Studies*, 25, 1, pp. 53–60.

Donald Evans here joins the debate between essentialists and constructivists, arguing on the side of the former group. As Evans points out, reference to the diversity of mystical descriptions, while it illustrates the constructivist thesis, does not *prove* it. Rather, he argues, epistemology may be mistaken in ruling out the possibilities (1) 'that some mystics successfully shed all conceptual and linguistic frameworks and enter a state of pure consciousness' and (2) 'of some element of direct experience when mystics experience spiritual entities'.[7]

Stephen S. Bush, 2012, 'Concepts and Religious Experiences: Wayne Proudfoot on the Cultural Construction of Experiences', *Religious Studies*, 48, 1, pp. 101–17.

Stephen Bush's more recent study highlights three unresolved issues in Wayne Proudfoot's constructivist argument: 'the significance of non-intentional aspects of experience, the distinction between concepts as required for experience and concepts as constituents of experience; and the problematic place that Proudfoot gives to inference to the best explanation in accounting for experiences'. Bush concludes that 'it follows that the debate is far from being exhausted'.

Some Arguments on Both Sides

The fundamental presupposition of constructivism appears to be that there can be no 'pure awareness' because we can only experience with the aid of memory, language, expectations and 'intentionality' (in the sense of an experience being 'about' or 'directed towards' its object) – all of which imply conceptualization. Concepts are therefore 'constitutive of' experience (Proudfoot, 1985, pp. 33, 121–2). This has led many to argue that 'the very idea of an experience that is in no way formulated is impossible', or at least that 'the experience can have no content at all if you can't say *anything* about it' (Taylor, 2002, pp. 26–7; cf. Lash, 1988, pp. 12, 173–4, 242–3). Thus, for example, 'seeming to have been enlightened is not a concept that one can prize off an experience and then find the real experience underneath' (Yandell, 1993, p. 187).

So, because a constructivist like Proudfoot regards religious interpretations as constitutive of religious experiences, he can argue 'as a logical matter' that, for example, 'one cannot attain nirvana by accident' (Proudfoot, 1985, p. 123). But this sounds as if he is legislating for what experiences are possible (cf. Evans, 1989, above). Patently, the constructivist account best fits those situations where disciplinary practices that assume certain doctrines, accompanied by intensive study of and/or explicit direction or instruction (and consequential formation) in the beliefs of a tradition, are designed to engender religious experiences (Proudfoot, 1985, p. 147). But is it true right across the piste of religious experiences?

The following issues have been raised by critics of constructivism.[8] (See also Chapter 6.)

1 William Alston has responded to the view 'that there could be no form of cognition that is not mediated by general concepts and judgment', by labelling it 'a baseless prejudice'. He holds to a notion of *direct awareness*, 'acquaintance' or 'direct apprehension', of some '*presentation, givenness, or appearance*'. This awareness is, he argues, 'a mode of cognition that is essentially independent of any conceptualization, belief, judgment, or any other application of general concepts to the object'; although he does allow that 'it typically exists in close connection' with them (and can be influenced by them). Nevertheless, 'X's looking a certain way' to someone does not consist in that person 'knowing or believing something about it or conceptualizing it in a certain way'. *Adult* perception, he admits, may be 'typically shot through with conceptualization

and belief – but that is a further development'. Against Proudfoot, therefore, Alston argues that the claim that either religious experience or sense experience themselves involve an *interpretation* of (what Alston insists is) 'an essentially subjective experience' that is both non-conceptual and non-judgemental, is 'either a confusion or a gross non-sequitur'. 'From the fact that we use concepts to identify something as of a certain type ..., it does *not* follow that *what* we are identifying "involves" concept and judgments. If it did, we would be unable to classify anything but cognitive psychological states.' To identify a conscious state as a pain, for example, we must employ the concept of pain; but this does not mean that pains 'involves concepts or judgments' (Alston, 1991, pp. 37–9, 41, 187, italics original, cf. 16, 27–8).[9] This sounds like an outright rejection of the central plank of constructivism, which is the claim that *our experience of X as X* ('if so identified by us') 'obviously and necessarily draws on the concept' X (Bagger, 1999, p. 125; in this example, X is a cabbage).

2 In the debates over religious experience, perennialists are often accused of misinterpreting texts and jumping to the conclusion that 'mystical experiences are the same for all mystics'. Their move from the text to the experience that lies behind it is frequently criticized as hermeneutically ('interpretatively') naïve – although exactly the same criticism has been directed against constructivists (cf. Bagger, 1999, p. 107; Forman, 1999, p. 32). Thus, Nelson Pike argues that there are distinct states in a Christian mystic's union with God that are not derived from Christian theology, and which are therefore likely to reflect the experience rather than its doctrinal interpretation; he further argues that there is 'no "*one* supremely great experience" that Christian mystics classify as *the* experience of union' (Pike, 1992, p. 114, italics original). The implication that every concept affects every experience has also been challenged.

3 Some close parallels in different religions between different doctrinal formulations appear to result from their being indebted to the same philosophical tradition (e.g. medieval Jewish, Christian and Sufi mystics are all influenced by Neo-Platonism). But on the constructivist explanation, this should lead to their positing a similarity of experience (cf. Forman, 1990, p. 17). Conversely, as two terms may have different senses but the same referent,[10] 'it may be that

a single *experience* can plausibly be referred to with two different terms' – for example, after conversion to a different religion (Forman, 1990, p. 18).

4 Furthermore, previously acquired concepts are also sometimes *disconfirmed* by religious experience: both neophytes and adepts having found that their religious experience has come as a *surprise* to them. Yet extreme constructivism does not seem to allow for the 'possibility of the Real affecting the mystic's consciousness in any new or creative way' (Stoeber, 1992, p. 111). Franks Davis refers to multiple examples of religious experiences 'at odds with the received tradition' or 'unrelated to the subject's prior religious concepts (if any)' (Franks Davis, 1989, p. 162). Similarities in mystical descriptions across *very different* traditions are also hard to explain on the constructivist thesis (Stoeber, 1992, p. 112).

5 The 'pre-cultural, pre-linguistic origin' of NDEs and OBEs is frequently claimed to be supported by (a) their conflicting with the expectations and cultural backgrounds of the experiencer, (b) their often being spontaneous, and (c) the fact that the experiencers often do not have language to describe them (Shushan, in Schmidt, 2016b, pp. 77–8; cf. Fox, 2003, pp. 134–5). Further, many general surveys of religious experience – including many of the 6,500 reports collected in the Alister Hardy Archive – are not reported by people who make particularly positive references to religious beliefs, or acknowledge any formal nurture in beliefs or instruction in religious practices, as one might expect on a constructivist account. One experient actually reported an inability to 'interpret this experience satisfactorily' until he read 'some months later … Otto's "Das Heilige"'[11] (510, Alister Hardy Archive).

Do such claims cast doubt on the constructivist principle that, for example, 'mystical experience(s) are the *result* of traversing the mystical way(s)' (Katz, 1983, p. 6, cf. pp. 13, 23, 30)? Perhaps *psychology* can help with these issues?

The problem of constructivism is unquestionably exacerbated by the assertion that interpretation, inference and conceptualization can operate *at an unconscious level*. If this is the case, 'because they are unconscious … they seem to us to be part of what is "given", that is simply there rather than part of a mental act of construction' (Griffith-Dickson, 2000, p. 97; cf. Bagger, 1999, pp. 5, 10, 37–40, 47).

Ralph Hood has claimed strong support for a common core hypothesis in empirical psychology. He contends that there is a common experience of unity in mysticism that may be identified in various faith traditions, but which 'simultaneously transcends them'; he adds, however, that this is 'decidedly not a perennial philosophy' (Hood, 2006, p. 126, cf. 127, 135). Hood's research instrument, the M-scale (see Chapter 3), identifies two stable factors in contemporary mystical experience: one with a minimal interpretative element and a second that is heavily interpreted. Later versions of his scale further distinguish between introvertive and extrovertive forms of mysticism. Using this scale in empirical studies across a range of cultures, with question items worded differently to fit different religious traditions, shows 'strong support for the claim that mystical experience is identical as measured across diverse samples', whether it is expressed in neutral or specifically religious language (Hood, 2006, pp. 128–31; cf. Hood and Williamson, 2000). As a consequence, Hood proposes that ('Walter Stace's') common core thesis is supported by contemporary measurement studies.

Once again, however, this is not a wholesale denial of constructivism, for Hood also acknowledges that 'any claim to experience is partly an interpretation' and that 'even if mystical experiences are unmediated,[12] neither their recollection nor their description can be'. Nonetheless, he writes, 'the ability to discount the description of experience in favor of experience itself is essential to any understanding of mysticism and to our support of the common core hypothesis' (Hood, 2006, p. 122).

Pure Consciousness Events

Until recently, constructivism has been in the ascendancy; although – as we have seen – its critics have presented a variety of arguments that might give the student pause, at least before accepting a *comprehensive* constructivism. In the 1990s, however, a new group arose in response to the constructivist thesis. These were the 'psychological perennialists', 'new perennialists' or 'neo-perennialists', led by Robert Forman. They singled out the *pure consciousness event* (PCE) as the paradigm of an underlying experience shared across religious traditions. The PCE, Forman writes, is 'one quite interesting and relatively common form of introvertive mysticism' (Forman, 1999, pp. 6–7; on introvertive mysticism and the PCE, see Chapter 4). He defines it in terms of 'wakeful contentless consciousness' and insists that PCEs 'show signs of being neither constructed nor shaped in ... form, content, or process'.

Such an experience comes, it is argued, through a 'forgetting' or 'emptying out' of language. The only way a PCE 'can be engendered is by ceasing to think – ceasing, in other words, to use language' (Forman, 1990, pp. 21, 25, 42). It thus has, Forman contends, 'no mental or sensory intentional object' (that is, no content or object of consciousness) to be shaped; it is not analogous to sense experience; and it does not involve language. What is being described here is a sort of *knowledge-by-identity*, not knowledge about something or a 'knowledge by acquaintance' with it. '"That" which one knows when knowing one is aware is *all* that is recalled after he or she has continued "void of conceptions"' (Forman, 1999, pp. 95, 125, 171).

This is clearly a *sui generis* form of knowledge. It is characterized as 'prelinguistic', 'nonconceptual' and 'noncognitive'. 'In pure consciousness, there is only consciousness, encountering itself through itself' (Forman, 1999, pp. 77, 132). If PCEs exist, this implies that not *all* experiences are constructed. But on the constructivist framework, 'it does not make much sense to speak of states of "pure consciousness"' (Penner, in Katz, 1983, p. 89).

Forman insists, however, that this experience cannot, on its own, form the ground for a *perennial philosophy*. Nor does he assert the universality of PCEs (1990, p. 39). Nevertheless, PCEs can provide *evidence* of cross-cultural claims, provided that such an experience is found in different cultures. And Forman and others claim to have sourced reports of such experiences in a wide variety of religious and cultural contexts, both through history and in the present day (including the Buddhist philosopher Paramaartha, the Christian mystic Meister Eckhart and Forman himself).

Gellman (2005, p. 147; 2018, §5.2) has summarized current criticisms of PCEs under the following headings.

1 The danger of idealization in their reports.
2 Exaggerating the notion of a complete 'forgetting/emptying out', which is not *central* to Christian mysticism and may only be a *prelude* to contemplating God.

3 Reports of 'emptying out' may refer only to ordinary experiential content being replaced by extraordinary contents.
4 Sometimes experiences are described as *un*conscious states.
5 Conceptual events may be present in the experience but have been repressed, or have been experienced only in nebulous ways, and were therefore not remembered.

At the neurophysiological level, research seems to some extent to confirm that states of 'pure awareness' ('awareness without content') – although rare – do exist and may be generated (in the brain's posterior superior parietal lobules) when ordinary brain activity is cut off from consciousness (d'Aquili and Newberg, 1993; 1999, p. 188). Interestingly, these authors claim that this awareness also eludes the categories of subjectivity and objectivity. But Griffith-Dickson points to the evidence that sensory information (1) goes first to the limbic system of the brain, where it is sorted by pattern matching, and that it (2) arrives more slowly at the neo-cortex, where it is subject to further analysis and elaboration after the perception. 'In a way', she muses, 'this means that both protagonists are right'. For, 'there is an initial act of [non-volitional] pattern matching as well as a potential (but not inevitable) rumination: two different moments and ways where our understanding of our own experience may go wrong or right' (Griffith-Dickson, 2007, p. 688).

Agreeing to Differ?

Intriguingly, at the start of these debates in the 1970s, in response to the claim that experiences are themselves interpreted and contain interpretation within them (and therefore that 'no perception can be quite neutral'), Ninian Smart responded that there are 'different degrees of interpretation'. Yet he still considered that the distinction between experience and doctrinal interpretation remains useful, 'in providing a directive to be as phenomenological as possible about the experiences being reported' (Smart, 1978, p. 14).

So, the debate over constructivism may be sometimes less polarized than some antagonists imply. One constructivist sympathizer asks, 'if concepts and beliefs do not exhaustively constitute experiences, could there be some non-conceptual aspect of experiences that is common across cultures?' But, he adds, 'is it plausible to think that there are experiences that have no object'? (Bush, 2012, p. 114). (Robert Forman and others have responded in the affirmative, as we have seen.)

Keith Yandell regards *both* those scholars who wish to 'prise off the alleged conceptual overlay to see the experience in its native form' *and* their opponents (who hold that nothing would survive this process) as having a point; but both positions also have their limitations. 'No experience lacks features that makes concepts applicable to it', he writes. This is 'an inherent feature of experiences'. All the same, being accessible to concepts in this way is not a 'barrier to an experience being reliable' (Yandell, 1997, pp. 368–9).

According to Ann Taves, 'we need to abandon the constructivist axiom that beliefs and attitudes are always formative of, rather than consequent to, experience in any very strong sense, in favor of a model that takes "bottom-up" or unconscious processing more seriously'. In particular experiences, she avers, there is an *interaction* between the subject's bottom-up (culture insensitive) processing and her context's top-down (culture sensitive) processing (Taves, 2009, p. 93).

Whatever side we take in the constructivist/perennialist debate, we must acknowledge that the distinction between experience and interpretation is not clear-cut, and that 'there is a complex interplay between experience and doctrine' (Peter Moore, in Katz, 1978, p. 110). Perhaps the resolution of this debate is a matter of *both–and rather than either-or*, with the difference between the two positions re-envisioned as a *difference in degree rather than a difference in kind*. In her chapter on 'Experience and Interpretation', Caroline Franks Davis argues that 'one cannot drive a wedge' between the two, and that 'there is no absolute dichotomy between concepts derived from experience and concepts brought to experience, or between "experience" and "interpretation"' (Franks Davis, 1989, p. 165, cf. 154). On this view, which Michael Stoeber calls *experiential-constructivist*, we would have to acknowledge 'a dynamic interchange between the Real and the mystic whereby the mystic is continuously involved in conceptual development and spiritual learning' (Stoeber, 1992, p. 114).

As we have seen, Donald Evans has criticized Katz for dogmatically ruling out the possibility of pure consciousness. Nevertheless, he admits that 'there are many other kinds of mystical experience, and concerning these [Katz's] insistence on differences dictated by traditions is very plausible'. According to Evans, these include examples 'where mystics view transparency as a necessary but subordinate stage on the way to translucency', and types of mystical experience of 'God as Supreme Spiritual Being or of the shekinah or the Virgin Mary'. However, Evans suggests that there may also be different direct experiences even here, as well as differences of framework that shape these experiences, thus articulating another form of a both–and hypothesis (Evans, 1989, pp. 55, 57–60). We have already heard Ninian Smart sounding an irenic note early in this debate. He writes later, 'Though it is quite obvious that interpretation gets so to speak built into experiences – thus making experiences of the same type different in particular ways – it does not follow that there does not exist a type to be identified cross-culturally as "consciousness purity" or as "mystical"' (Smart, in Katz, 1983, p. 125).

The distinction between the essentialist/perennialist position and that of the constructivists/contextualists also maps onto *the theological debate between so-called liberals and postliberals*. The recognition that 'individuals possess different aptitudes/characteristics that can affect experiential processing … is a postliberal, that is, cultural-linguistic, achievement. … In short, all experiences are mediated' (Sears, 2017, p. 15). Theological postliberals such as George Lindbeck understand the theological *liberal* (or '*experiential-expressive*') position as the view that the religions are outward manifestations of a common underlying basic experience, arguing against it that these religions themselves shape these experiences in very diverse ways (Lindbeck, 1984, pp. 16, 37; see below, Chapter 18). While agreeing with this point, the cognitive anthropologist and theologian Robert Sears argues that postliberalism simply ignores experiential similarities or dismisses them as trivial. The idea of a 'common human experience' (and common human environments and conditioning) needs to be reclaimed, he insists. For Sears, *both* the liberal model of cross-cultural invariance at the level of pre-reflective experience *and* a rigid postliberal model that denies the profound similarity between experiences must be transcended (Sears, 2017, p. 17).

I conclude with some final suggestive comments on this long-lived, vexed debate.

> One can distinguish … between situations where I know I am having to do a lot of work to make sense of what I experience, and experiences where identifying or understanding what I experience is straightforward. Whatever the difference between such experiences may be, however, it is not the case

that I am a judge in the first instance and a video camera in the second. The difference between them is not an imagined difference between 'subjective' and 'objective', still less between 'biased' and 'accurate'.

Rather than conceiving of experience and interpretation according to a single model, like a kernel and a husk, our notion of interpretation then ought to be as broad and as varied as possible. In some uses of the term, interpretation is a matter of *bringing something to expression*. Perhaps it is an original, inexpressible, or at least wordless, phenomenon which is then brought into speech as an act of interpretation. The paradigm for this view might be the act of playing a piece of music on an instrument; one speaks of the performer's 'interpretation', but the latter is not merely something added on to the piece. The piece only exists in its being performed and thus [is] inevitably 'interpreted'. 'Interpretation', while not creating the thing, nevertheless is the only manner in which it can exist. The language used to describe experience then – even if it is 'added on later' – does not so much conceal as reveal. This would mirror the experience we often have of not really understanding something until we have talked about it, explained it to someone else. (Griffith-Dickson, 2000, p. 97)

Gwen Griffith-Dickson adds that the term interpretation can also be used of (a) translation (where there may be a variety of correct translations, but 'this does not mean that *any* translation is correct'), and also of (b) understanding what another person says in a conversation, in which we allow for correction. In these cases, she maintains, we expect a dialogue in which language moves back and forth between people, getting 'closer to understanding, and, in fact, to "truth"' (Griffith-Dickson, 2005, p. 403; cf. 2000, p. 98).

Exercise

What do you think are the main issues that this debate has kept alive? How – if at all – may they be resolved?

Suggestions for Further Reading

Introductory

Aden, Ross, 2013, *Religion Today: A Critical Thinking Approach to Religious Studies*, Lanham, MD: Rowman & Littlefield, pp. 206–27.

Griffith-Dickson, Gwen, 2000, *Human and Divine: An Introduction to the Philosophy of Religious Experience*, London: Duckworth, ch. 3 (pp. 81–98).

Advanced

Proudfoot, Wayne, 1985, *Religious Experience*, Berkeley, CA: University of California Press, ch. II (pp. 41–75).

Stoeber, Michael, 1992, 'Constructivist Epistemologies of Mysticism: A Critique and a Revision', *Religious Studies*, 28, 1, pp. 107–16.

Notes

1 Philip Almond's analysis proposes a range of *five different views*, of which (pure?) essentialist and constructivist perspectives represent the extreme ends, 1 and 5 respectively (Poloma, 1995, citing Almond, 1982, p. 128):

1. All mystical experience is the same and there is a unanimity of mystical utterance.
2. All mystical experience is the same, but interpretations differ according to the mystic's religious or philosophical framework.
3. There is one form, divisible into a small number of types of interior mystical experience, which cut across cultural barriers.
4. There are as many different types of mystical experience as there are paradigmatic expressions of them.
5. There are as many different types of mystical experience as there are incorporated interpretations of them. (On 'incorporated interpretations', see elsewhere in this chapter.)

2 See below and e.g. Smart, 1965, pp. 75, 86. (Smart argued that perennial philosophies take us beyond the sameness of experience to a sameness of doctrine, but 'truth of doctrine depends on evidence other than mysticism'.)

3 Thus, 'the catalogue of varieties can never be completed' (Proudfoot, 1985, p. 220) and, for example, 'different mystical languages … represent or express different mystical worlds' (Penner, in Katz, 1983, p. 93).

4 In any case, constructivists ask, as these shaping ideas and understandings (mediated through languages and vocabularies) 'are never those simply of an individual', in what sense do we ever 'really have an individual experience'? (Taylor, 2002, pp. 27–8).

5 An 'epistemological assumption' is one that relates to the theory of knowledge ('epistemology'). This particular assumption is often said to be a *Kantian claim*. Immanuel Kant may be thought of as a constructivist about everyday perceptual experience, in that he argued that the mind plays a part in producing objective knowledge by applying innate 'categories' of the understanding (such as substance, plurality or causality) to sense experience. One might say that these categories are the preconditions of the construction of objects in the mind, and that they synthesize the random data of the senses into intelligible objects. However, Kant viewed these categories as both inescapable and *shared by all humans*, and did not think of them as contributing to the phenomenological content of the experiences they shape. Nor did Kant himself extend this framework to an understanding of mysticism. See Forgie, 1985; Anthony Perovich, in Forman, 1990, pp. 237–53; Eddy, 2002, pp. 94, 178–9.

6 Bagger argues that William James's earlier and more thoroughly psychological works expressed this recognition of 'the conceptual contribution in all forms of experience', so that perception 'fuses thought and sensation' and pure experience is an abstraction or 'unattainable ideal', except for infants. 'James to some extent realizes the close relationship between experience and language', including conceptual judgements such as an inference to the best explanation (Bagger, 1999, pp. 25–30, 37–40). In his later *Varieties*, however, James is less nuanced and adopts the model of sense perception for religious experience, interpreting both forms of experience as pure sensations uninfluenced by concepts and beliefs (p. 42). Cf. below, Chapter 10 n. 8.

7 Donald Evans (1927–2018) was a professional analytical philosopher who, unusually, was much involved in later life as a psychotherapist, spiritual counsellor and in directing meditation 'as part of a Mystic Journey' whose aim was 'eventually to let go into the Source [Ultimate Mystery] to be lived by the Source' (Don Evans, 1998, 'Spiritual Counsellor and Psychotherapist', unpublished MS, p. 4).

8 For other philosophical criticisms of constructivism and/or perennialism, see Barnard, 1992; Bagger 1999, ch. 4; Gellman, 2018, §§4–6.

9 As we have heard from another commentator, 'Proudfoot may very well be right that concepts necessarily are preconditions for and accompaniments to religious experiences, but that doesn't establish them as constituents of the experiences' (Bush, 2012, p. 107).

10 As, e.g., 'morning star' and 'evening star' both refer to the planet Venus.

11 On Otto, see Chapter 18.

12 For Hood, the claim to 'unmediated contact with reality' in the experience is the central defining feature of mysticism (Hood, 2006, p. 122).

9

Objectivity and Veridicality

Perhaps the most significant of the debates over religious experience, particularly for philosophers of religion and theologians but also for many experients themselves, is the question of their veridicality ('truthfulness') or objectivity (whether or not they have a real, actual or 'external' object, whose existence is independent of the person having the experience).[1]

Experiences that include a subjective sense of the presence of – or of a relationship or union with – a divine personal being or impersonal Absolute often seem to be *self-authenticating* to those who have them. Their occurrence alone may then be thought to be sufficient to establish their veridicality and objectivity, as the subjects of the experience are 'not able to help themselves' believing in the truth of the experience and the reality of its putative object (cf. Chapter 19, on John Hick). In such cases, people are unlikely to think that their experience needs any further support by way of argument or evidence.

But this reaction is not as widespread as some critics claim. As has been pointed out, the great Christian mystics were well aware that they 'cannot uncritically accept any old claim to be directly aware of God' (Alston, 1991, p. 210; and see above, Chapter 7). And, more generally, 'few mystics themselves really make a claim for self-authentication; and if they do, it is for the validity of *their experience*; not the entire edifice of Christianity or Islam or Advaita Vedanta, on the grounds of a single experience.' Elsewhere, few claims about the personal significance of one's own experience are regarded as possessing universal validity. Therefore, 'we ought to observe a distinction between the subject's right to take her experience seriously, and the experience's value as evidence for general knowledge and truth-claims that are held to be valid for everyone' (Griffith-Dickson, 2000, p. 86). (See below, under 'Experience and Testimony'.)

Trusting and Checking Experiences

Religious people certainly do claim truthfulness and objectivity for their own experiences, and sometimes for the experiences of others, as well: for example, that God can and has revealed Godself in such experiences (Mavrodes, 1970, p. 77). But the basic challenge facing the proponents of religious experience is, 'How do we know that this is not an *illusion*?'[2]

The main criticism of the claim to objectivity for religious experience is that the normal *criteria of testing for objectivity* that we employ in sense experience are absent in these cases. These tests include checks against other senses[3] and under different 'lighting conditions', the fulfilment of empirical predictions, the discovery of other causal mechanisms that lead to the experience; as well as tests of consistency with other experiences and intersubjective agreement with other 'perceivers'.

Perhaps the fundamental issue, however, is that many (most?) people do *not* experience God or any Ultimate Reality, even when they find themselves in the same situation as those who do. Religious experience is not universal, nor is it continuous and unavoidable, as is sense experience. An initial defence against this criticism may be mounted, however, for it is possible to argue as follows.[4]

1 The *transcendent object* of these experiences has such a nature that it (e.g. God) cannot be expected to be universally available to human experience. Its difference from objects in the (created, spatio-temporal, physical) world means that (a) an object of experience of this nature would not be perceivable by (universal) sense experience; (b) its (general, universal) activity and/or presence would be related to the whole universe, and may therefore not imply any particular and identifiable empirical claims; and (c) a transcendent *agent* (as in the case of the theistic understanding of this transcendent object as a personal God) would be free to give or to withhold particular revelations.

2 *Human experiencers* are limited, fallible and/or sinful receivers and interpreters of religious and spiritual experiences.[5] They may also need to be in some particular cognitive, spiritual or moral condition before they can properly experience the transcendent, so that *the 'faculty' of religious experience may not be possessed by everyone* or not all of the time.[6]

3 Admittedly, religious experience, unlike sense experience, is not 'a common possession' of humankind, and may not be 'continuously and unavoidably present'; but *'why suppose that what happens only occasionally cannot have cognitive value?'* Nor does it matter that mystical experience may seem 'meagre and obscure' in comparison, for certain of our sense experiences (such as taste and smell) also lack the richness and detail of other senses (Alston, 2005, pp. 208–9). The claim that there could not be any sort of faculty of religious experience would be a prescriptive claim, of course, and 'we cannot decide what capacities for experience are possible in an *a priori* manner'[7] (Kwan, 2012, p. 521; cf. Alston, 1994b, p. 893).

Many philosophers would endorse in general terms the claim that *it is rational to trust one's own experience* – that 'what one seems to perceive is probably so' (the so-called *Principle of Credulity*),[8] while agreeing with Richard Swinburne that this is only the case 'in the absence of special considerations'. They may disagree with Swinburne, however, that these and other challenges to ('defeaters' of) claims to veridicality can be resolved in the case of all (or even some) religious and spiritual experiences. According to Swinburne, the *special conditions that can limit the Principle of Credulity* are as follows (see Swinburne, 2004, pp. 303, 310–22; cf. Franks Davis, 1989, chs 4, 5, 8; Gale, 1994b):

1 the conditions of the experience, or the person having it, have been found in the past to be unreliable;
2 similar perceptual claims have been proved false;
3 on background evidence, the object of the experience was probably not present; and
4 the supposed object of the experience was probably not its cause.

Swinburne claims that these conditions *do not normally apply to religious experience*, because:

1 most religious experiences are reported by people who make reliable perceptual claims and are not taking drugs;
2 this has not been proven;
3 God is present everywhere; and
4 if God exists, God sustains all casual processes – and, in that sense, God is among the causes of *whatever* brings about a person's religious experience.

Swinburne therefore concludes that 'a religious experience apparently of God ought to be taken as veridical unless it can be shown on other grounds significantly more probable than not that God does not exist' (Swinburne, 2004, p. 321). Many would say, however, that this claim is too strong, for *any* given example of any experience *always* requires 'supplementation by additional corroborating experiences' (Gutting, 1982, p. 149). Yet, Gary Gutting continues, this proves not to be a problem in this case, for he argues that, if religious experience of God is objective we might expect that: '(1) those who have had such experiences once would be likely to have them again; (2) other individuals will be found to have had similar experiences; (3) those having such experiences will find themselves aided in their endeavors to lead morally better lives.' And all these expectations, he argues, do in fact follow from 'the nature of the experienced being and its concern for us'. Thus, Gutting is willing to argue that 'for some religious experiences, all these expectations are fulfilled to a very high degree' (Gutting, 1982, p. 152; contrast O'Hear, 1984, pp. 47–8).

Evidently, however, the *fulfilment* of Gutting's expectations (1) and (2) are empirical claims that have been contested. Many empirical studies of 'ordinary' religious experiencers do not support (1), and (2) depends on what is considered to be a 'similar' religious experience. The third of Gutting's tests is the *pragmatist's criterion* that what is true may be decided by what 'works' – what leads to the best results. As we have seen, in the case of spiritual and religious experiences, this is very often understood in terms of the 'fruits' in a person's moral and/or spiritual life. Thus, for example, 'the consequences of the experience must be good for the mystic', producing 'such virtues as wisdom, humility and charity' (and possibly 'sanity'). A genuine religious – or, at least, theistic – perception should also lead to 'words, actions and example that build up the community' (Wainwright, 1981, pp. 86–7). But does it? (See also Chapter 7, above.)

Alston's Argument

William Alston's (1921–2009) discussion of this topic was intended to meet the criticism of the dissimilarity between religious experience and sense experience at a more general level.[9] His argument has been described, even by its critics, as a *'tour de force*, exceeding in thoroughness and depth' any in the literature (Gale, 1994a, p. 138) and as 'very nearly sound. It certainly gets a great deal right' (Wildman, 2011, p. 162).

While Swinburne concentrates on the rationality of individual beliefs based on an individual's particular religious experience, Alston provides a more social analysis. Like Swinburne, however, he argues that 'any supposition that one perceives something to be the case ... is *prima facie* ['at first sight', 'on the face of it'] justified ... unless there are strong enough reasons to the contrary' (Alston calls such reasons 'overriders'). Because of this origin, *any* beliefs based on experience 'possess an initial credibility': 'they are innocent until proven guilty.' This view, which Alston asserts is 'widely advocated for sense perception', is 'the only alternative to a thoroughgoing scepticism about experience' (Alston, 1998, p. 67). This is Alston's equivalent of Swinburne's Principle of Credulity (Alston, 2005, p. 205).

Advocates of religious and spiritual experiences often pose the question, 'Why *should* all experience be just like – or even closely analogous to – sense experience?' Alston develops this point, arguing that there is more than one sort of justifiable, socially established, persistent *doxastic practice*, which is his name for a way of forming beliefs and evaluating them (from the Greek *doxa*, understood here as 'opinion' or 'belief'). Sense perception, introspection (awareness of one's own conscious states), memory and various forms of reasoning provide us with other, everyday examples. In all such cases *we cannot help trusting these practices*. We cannot, however, *justify* any of them without circularity; it is only by relying on a doxastic practice that we build up evidence of its reliability (e.g. that our sense experience varies with changes in its objects). In truth, then, 'there is no rational alternative' to engaging in these practices, and the outputs of one practice can only be discredited by the results of another if there is 'a massive and persistent inconsistency' between them (Alston, 1991, p. 171).

Alston's core argument is that *religious experience may be regarded as yet another of these socially established, doxastic practices*.[10] In which case, it should not be disqualified from rational acceptance (Alston, 1991, pp. 149–53, 168–70,

194), for that would be to adopt 'an arbitrary double standard' (Alston, 2005, p. 207). For religious experience, too, is firmly established and interwoven with other practices; and it, too, has 'stood the test of time' by providing a set of beliefs that are sufficiently internally consistent and consistent with beliefs derived from other doxastic practices.[11] Alston goes so far as to accuse the critics of religious experience of the *epistemic imperialism* of 'subjecting the outputs of one belief-forming practice to the requirements of another' (Alston, 1998, p. 69). And he points out that other socially established, persistent doxastic practices, such as introspection, are similar to religious experience in being quite different from sense experience.[12]

With respect to the *demand for further checks*, Alston argues that the practice of religious experience already has its own *overrider system* of 'checking procedures' and 'tests of spiritual receptivity' (cf. Alston, 1991, pp. 209–25). These are not always the same sort of test as is found in other doxastic practices such as sense experience, but – as with sense experience – they are *internal to the practice*: in all such cases, 'the practice supplies both the tester and the testee; it grades its own examinations'. Choosing tests is always an '"inside" job' (p. 217). So, the tests for religious experience that are built into a religious doxastic practice have their origin in religious beliefs, guidelines derived from past religious experiences and so on.[13]

Criticisms of Alston

- Richard Gale contends that every argument he knows for the cognitivity of religious experience is based on an *analogy with sense experience* (Gale, 1991, p. 228; cf. Wainwright, 1981, p. 82). Yet Alston maintains that he is not treating the religious doxastic practice as rational (which is a slightly different claim) because it is analogous to that of sense experience, but solely because it is another socially established doxastic practice (Alston, 1991, p. 223; cf. Gale, 1994a, p. 137). We may reasonably suggest, however, that Alston's argument might, perhaps 'must', 'in the end, appeal intuitively (if not explicitly) to our natural affinities for [such] analogical reasoning' (Griffith-Dickson, 2005, p. 427); and Alston himself admits that the argument trades on 'certain analogies' or 'points of resemblance' between the two practices (Alston, 1991,

p. 224; cf. 1994b, p. 892; Wainwright, 1981, ch. 3). But if so, we still need to ask ourselves, 'Do these analogies hold?'
- Many of Alston's critics emphasize the *disanalogy between RSEs and sense experience* that we touched on earlier in this chapter, often highlighting the fact that the object of RSEs is not a physical object located in time and space – as it is in the case of sense experience (cf. Martin, 1955; 1959, ch. 5; Gale, 1991, ch. 8; 2005). These criticisms include *the absence, in the case of RSEs*, of:
  - an identifiable causal relationship between the experience and its object;
  - relevant repeatable, causal conditions that are independent of the person undergoing the experience;
  - agreement between perceivers; and
  - agreement on what counts as the perceiver's faculty of religious intuition being in 'proper working condition' (Gale, 1991, p. 308).
- As Kwan points out, however, even if critics such as Gale are right about the necessary conditions for veridical *sense* experience, the implications they draw for religious experience are too sweeping, as: (a) physical objects are not the only possible kind of existing thing and (b) sense experience is not the only 'viable kind of experience' (Kwan cites as other examples intellectual and moral intuition, introspection and personal memories) (Kwan, 2012, p. 535).
- The incompatibility of beliefs derived from religious experiences remains a serious objection, but Alston argues that many incompatibilities do not amount to serious conflicts (for example, it is not only God but also human beings that *have both personal and impersonal aspects* to their nature) and that, as with physical things, beliefs are based on how things *appear* to us rather than how they are 'in themselves' (Alston, 2005, pp. 209–13). (For more on this topic, see Chapter 11.)
- According to some critics, Alston's guidelines in his overrider system – because they are derived from historical practices – may be tainted by an androcentric bias, and some would add that they are now scientifically outdated (see Chapters 11, 14, below). Further, they are specific to the religious tradition of which they are constituent parts, so – unlike the case of sense perception – believers cannot appeal to common procedures to adjudicate their disputes (see Chapter 11).
- Others argue that a converted non-Christian could not apply the *Christian* doxastic practice and its internal overrider system to assess her own conversion experience to Christianity. 'In such experiences the subject is not

yet Christian and cannot employ the Christian over-rider [*sic*] system when becoming convinced to accept the Christian practice and its over-rider system' (Gellman, 2018, §8.1).

- Alston may have underestimated the extent that there exists a plurality even of Christian communal doxastic practices, some of which 'would accept far fewer or far more constituents [e.g. authorities and checking procedures] in their overrider systems' (Tilley, 1994, pp. 163–4; cf. Alston, 1994c, pp. 176–7).

(For Alston's responses to Gale and other critics, see Alston, 1994b; 1994c.)

> ### Exercise
>
> What, in your view, are the most significant weaknesses in Alston's position, and why?
> How might Alston defend his position against these criticisms?

Experience and Testimony

Another issue that is very often raised in the debate on this topic is the distinction between first- and third-person (or 'first-' and 'third-hand') justifications: that is, the contrast between the epistemological status of the person who has had a religious experience and that of those others (the majority) who have not.

Many philosophers of religious experience take a view similar to that of William James, who argued that a religious experience provides grounds for the beliefs of the person who experiences it, but not for others.[14] Thus, it is John Hick's view that individuals may rationally trust the veridicality of their own religious experiences, at least if those experiences are 'sufficiently vivid' (Hick, 1974, p. 210). But anyone who doesn't 'experience religiously in any degree whatever' – that is, who is 'absolutely un-mystical' in Hick's phrase – can have no good grounds for religious belief (Hick, 2008, p. 29). Under accounts such as these, in which the authority of an experience for its subject 'carries no obligation for one who has not undergone the experience', the experiences of mystics have been called 'testimonies not to some direct perception but to the beliefs that enter into the identification of the experience'[15] (Proudfoot, 1985, p. 154).

Other philosophers, however, argue that there is no reason why one cannot reasonably hold that other people's experience of God provides one with evidence that God exists (e.g. Yandell, 1999, pp. 234–5).[16] Swinburne has argued, for instance, for a broadly applicable *Principle of Testimony* to complement his Principle of Credulity: that '(in the absence of special considerations) the experiences of others are (probably) as they report them' (Swinburne, 2004, p. 322). He contends that this principle should be extended to embrace religious experience. The appropriate special considerations in this case include evidence of the other person's lying, exaggeration or misremembering. If these factors do *not* apply, a person has good reason to trust other people's experiences as well, although not as good a reason as she has to trust her own experiences – yet, 'in so far as a number of others give similar reports, that greatly increases their credibility' (p. 323). We may agree with Swinburne here that without this additional principle of reasoning, our knowledge in general would be very limited indeed. Alston has argued, in a similar way, that there is no 'sound reason' for our not accepting other people's testimony in the case of religious experience, as we do in sense experience, provided that we think that their doxastic practice of religious experience is 'reliable or rational' (Alston, 1991, pp. 279–84).

One may raise in this context a somewhat different point, one that is more religious (or spiritual or psychological – even, 'liberal') rather than purely philosophical. 'Religiously, why would you want your own experiences to be the ground of someone else's knowledge or faith? Isn't it better to leave them space to have their own experiences and reach their own subsequent conclusions than to consent to your verdicts?' (Griffith-Dickson, 2005, p. 429). In matters of personal concern, we tend to want to decide for ourselves. Religion, we feel, ought to be had and held *at first-hand*. What do you think?

Suggestions for Further Reading

Introductory

Craighead, Houston A., 1999, 'William James be Damned: Is it Evidentially Justifiable to Trust Religious Experience?', *Perspectives in Religious Studies*, 26, 4, pp. 405–15.

Advanced

Alston, William P., 1992, 'The Autonomy of Religious Experience: The Epistemic Status of Religious Belief', *International Journal for Philosophy of Religion*, 31, 2/3, pp. 67–87.
Alston, William P., 1994, 'Review: Précis of Perceiving God' and 'Reply to Commentators', *Philosophy and Phenomenological Research*, 54, 4, pp. 863–8 and pp. 891–9.
Griffith-Dickson, Gwen, 2005, *The Philosophy of Religion*, London: SCM Press, ch. 14 (pp. 411–36).
Swinburne, Richard, 2004, *The Existence of God*, Oxford: Clarendon, ch. 13 (pp. 293–327).

Notes

1 Phillip Wiebe distinguishes an experience being objective ('produced by an object existing externally to the percipient') and being veridical (which he defines, 'imprecisely', in terms of the experience having 'a close (supposed) resemblance' to the object producing it) (Wiebe, 1997, pp. 35–6). Richard Gale distinguishes a religious experience being veridical (which would be shown by its apparent object 'causing the experience in the "right way"') and its being *cognitive* (shown by the experience constituting 'evidence or warrant for believing that the object exists and is as it appears to be in the experience', when that is considered *on its own*). 'Necessarily', however, 'any cognitive perception is a veridical perception of an objective reality'. Gale believes that religious experiences, 'although possibly veridical', could *not* be cognitive because 'we could never know on the basis of these experiences either that this object exists or that the experience is caused in the "right way" by it' (Gale, 1991, p. 287, cf. 326–7, 340, 343). In the end, Gale rejects the possibility of the veridicality of religious experience as well, since God has no objective existence sufficiently analogous to the objects of veridical sense experience.

2 In the philosophy of perception, an *illusion* is an incorrect interpretation that is public and repeatable (for example, a mirage or a stick appearing bent under water), whereas *delusions* are private

perceptual derangements. In the dictionary, however, these senses overlap: illusions are defined as 'false or unreal perceptions' (and, as a subsense, beliefs), whereas delusions are defined as 'idiosyncratic beliefs' that are 'not in accordance with a generally accepted reality'. I shall refer to 'illusions' in both cases (see below, Chapter 11 in the section on Freud).

3 Despite its diversity of content, religious experience is often understood to be a unitary and distinctive 'sense' (unlike the five senses of sense experience, which may be checked against one another). The contrary suggestion should not be too quickly dismissed, however, that 'theistic mystical experiences and numinous experiences' (and perhaps other types of religious and spiritual experiences) may 'support and reinforce one another in the way in which the various kinds of sense experience' do (Wainwright, 1981, p. 104).

4 Cf. Donovan, 1979, ch. 4; Wainwright, 1981, pp. 88–96; Evans, 1985, pp. 92–3; Franks Davis, 1989, ch. 5.

5 As Thomas Hobbes put it in 1651, 'though God Almighty can speak to a man, by Dreams, Visions, Voice, and Inspiration; yet he obliges no man to beleeve he hath so done to him that pretends it; who (being a man) may erre, and (which is more) may lie' (Hobbes, 1914, ch. 32, p. 200).

6 With respect to the cognitive condition, Mavrodes draws analogies from sense perception, arguing that we may only have the relevant experience if (a) we are in what we may describe metaphorically as the 'right location' (cf. 'you can see it from over here') and (b) we possess the correct expectation and concept about what is there to be perceived (cf. 'this is what to look for'). Cf. Mavrodes, 1970, pp. 83–5; Astley, 1981.

7 That is, in a way that is solely theoretical and 'independent of experience'.

8 Kai-man Kwan has sensibly renamed this, the *Principle of Critical Trust* (Kwan, 2011, chs 4, 7; 2012, pp. 507–12, 524–46).

9 The main source is his book-length presentation in Alston, 1991; but Alston's summaries of his argument and briefer reflections on it may also be found in various journal articles and book chapters: e.g. Alston, 1992; 1994a; 1998 and 2005.

10 As discussed in Chapter 1, Alston uses the phrases 'mystical experiences' and 'mystical perceptions', rather than 'religious experiences', but intends these terms to be understood in the same broad way (Alston, 1991, pp. 11, 35–6).

11 Alston described *Alvin Plantinga's position* as a 'close relative' to his own views (Alston, 1991, p. 195). Plantinga criticized the traditional 'foundationalist' view, which justified beliefs *either* because they could not be doubted (as in Descartes' argument for the indubitability of 'I think therefore I am') *or* because they were grounded in other justified beliefs. By contrast, Plantinga (quite reasonably) argued that such an epistemological bar is too high for us to get over, since our beliefs about an external world are *not* justified in this way. Rather, such sensory beliefs must be treated as 'properly basic' and foundational (that is, believed on the basis of no others), and therefore as requiring no further justification. Plantinga then argues that it is equally plausible to extend this status to people's beliefs about God. But some of those beliefs may derive from an experience of God's manifesting Godself to the believer. This would fit one understanding of what John Calvin called our distinct faculty of illumination, our 'sensus divinitatis', that allows us to be aware of God's actions and dispositions towards us (Plantinga, 1981, 1983; cf. Franks Davis, 1989, p. 87). It should be mentioned, however, that some hold that this *sensus* is only a recognition *that* there is a God, not an experience *of* God (Helm, 1997).

12 However, Bagger argues that Alston's account of doxastic practices in general 'pictures them as too unimpeachable and far too isolated from one another in our overall epistemological functioning' (Bagger, 1999, p. 117).

13 'Overriders' may be *rebutters* (which contradict or render a belief improbable) or *underminers* (abnormalities in the experience that render it unreliable, i.e. inadequately justified) (Alston, 1991, pp. 72, 79, 191). An 'overrider system' forms part of most mature doxastic practices, including sense experience (though not, perhaps, introspection); it 'censors', corrects, checks or 'filters out' certain beliefs as incompatible with what we *already* firmly believe. It is made up of relevant facts appropriate to the subject matter, 'together with ways of finding out more when needed'. For sense perception, for example, these facts concern the physical and social environment; but for (theistic) religious experience, the overrider system 'concerns God and His relations to His creation' (p. 167). 'Anything in the doctrinal system of a religion can make a difference to the overrider system' (p. 191), and such 'relevant considerations' can in principle show 'putative perceptions of God ... to be incorrect, or inadequately based' (p. 295).

14 'No authority emanates from them ['mystical states'] which should make it a duty for those who stand outside of them to accept their revelations uncritically' (James, 1960, p. 407, cf. 409–11).

15 This expresses Proudfoot's 'constructivism', on which see Chapter 8, above.

16 Keith Yandell argues that this may be the case even when those other people do not *themselves* accept this belief on the basis of their own experience.

10

Evidence and Argument

As we have seen, philosophers are primarily interested in religious experience as a seemingly objective rather than a purely subjective matter. But this epistemological claim may take one of two forms, and it is helpful to distinguish clearly between (1) the view 'that certain experiences constitute *veridical perceptions* of God', and (2) any form of '*argument from* religious experience' (cf. Alston, 1991, p. 3). These two different approaches, sometimes designated the 'perceptual' and the 'interpretive' views (Sudduth, 2009, p. 222), may be represented as follows.

1 *Religious experience is a perception of God*. It is, therefore, an 'external experience', in the sense of a reliable, direct 'experience of an externally existing object' (Gaskin, 1984, p. 80). William Hasker calls this approach *experientialism*, the view that some religious beliefs are 'directly grounded in religious experience' (Hasker, in Audi, 1995, p. 253) and not on any inference.[1] Crucially, such experiences may provide us with 'experiential evidence that God exists' (Yandell, 1993, p. 274). This assimilation of religious experience to direct acquaintance is resisted by many philosophers, however, who contend that 'experiential beliefs have the character of hypotheses and require supporting reasons for justification' (Bagger, 1999, pp. 199–200, cf. 203 and chs 5, 7 generally; see also, e.g., Proudfoot, 1985, pp. 152–3, 164–5).

   Alston's doxastic practice approach is to be placed in this category (Alston, 1991, pp. 3, 66–7) and is widely regarded as the fullest defence of the claim that experience of God is a genuine experience – a form of direct *perception*.

2 *Religious experience constitutes good grounds* (or evidence) from which we can reason to the existence of *God, as the best explanation of such a phenom-*

enon. This position requires an inferential *argument* in which the existence of the phenomenon of religious experiences serves as a premise.

Although Swinburne views his own position as an inferential 'argument from religious experience' (Swinburne, 2004, ch. 13), Alston is justified in interpreting it as a defence of religious experience as perception, and thus as similar in nature to his own (Alston, 1991, pp. 3 n. 2, 195). For other arguments from religious experience, see Donovan, 1979, pp. 89–95; Franks Davis, 1989, ch. 3; Yandell, 1993, part V; and cf. Kwan, 2012.

A great deal of philosophical debate has centred on approach (1). On that account, knowledge of God (or of any other object of religious experience) is 'not an abstract knowledge, but one that is concrete, intuitive, and without reasoning, analogous to that of the senses' (Albert Farges, 1926, cited by Wainwright, 1981, p. 160). In such discussions, *intuition* is understood as a direct awareness that is not 'discursive', 'reasoned' or 'inferred'. In that sense, it is 'immediate' (not mediated), a mode of knowledge that does 'not admit of further support or reason' (Lewis, 1970, p. 50), being marked by a 'directness of ... thought and judgment'[2] that distinguishes it from inference (Mavrodes, 1970, pp. 65–6).[3]

To most religious people, treating religious experience as a perception of God would seem to establish God's existence more securely, as they are *directly experiencing* the object of their beliefs. This seems greatly preferable to relying on any form of argument, for 'if God has been *present* to one's experience, there is no need to postulate him as part of an explanatory theory to be assured of his existence' (Alston, 2005, p. 198). As John Cook Wilson famously put the distinction, 'If we think of the existence of our friends; it is the "direct knowledge" which we want: merely inferential knowledge seems a poor affair ... We don't want merely inferred friends. Could we possibly be satisfied with an inferred God?' (Wilson, 1926, p. 853). Compare: 'I can infer that my friend loves or forgives me, but I can also experience this love or forgiveness through our personal interactions ... something similar needs to be said about the human-divine relationship'; 'inferring that God forgives or loves me is fundamentally different from experiencing divine forgiveness or love itself' (Sudduth, 2009, p. 231).

On the other hand, considering the existence of God as the best explanation for the phenomenon of religious experience has other advantages, as approach (2) treats religious experience as something that demands to be interpreted and explained by the belief-system of theism. Further, while approach (1) seems to apply most readily to a person's own religious experience, approach (2) may be used to give an account of *other people's* religious experiences and therefore be used by anyone (see Chapter 9, above, under 'Experience and Testimony').

However, a bald inductive argument that swiftly moves from the existence of religious experiences to God as the best explanation for them (sometimes called an 'abductive argument') will seem too simplistic to many philosophers and theologians. Peter Donovan has outlined a more nuanced argument along the following lines.

(a) If God (as described in belief-system S) exists, then experiences open to interpretation under S will be likely to occur. (For example, if S is Christianity, there are likely to be experiences of prophetic revelation, a holy or numinous presence, answered prayers, the sense of forgiveness after confession of sins, renewed lives following acts of faith and so on.)
(b) Experiences interpreted under S do occur.
(c) No better ways of explaining the occurrence of those particular experiences are known.
(d) Therefore it is reasonable to conclude that God exists.

(Donovan, 1998, p. 166 [1979, p. 91])

Significantly, Donovan points out that, as a consequence, 'the truth or falsity of an interpretation is not to be found by looking merely at the experience involved. It is necessary as well to examine the whole theological system in terms of which the interpretation of that experience is made' (1979, p. 35); for 'one's estimate of the value of any particular experience will depend on how one evaluates the total belief-system in terms of which that experience is thought to be significant' (1979, p. 72).[4] And that seems to offer us a third position that lies between religious experience as direct perception and religious experience as the premise of an inferential argument.

A Middle Way?

Mavrodes, having distinguished inference rather sharply from direct experience, as the basis for belief, admits that this binary categorization will probably fit 'only a few cases'. Mostly, the reasons for a belief 'are likely to form a web woven of experience, inference, and testimony (and perhaps other factors also)'. Therefore, 'the whole apparatus of theology' may serve us as 'an extensive conceptual framework which exhibits the meaning of the particular experience, or at least provides a place for it' (Mavrodes, 1970, pp. 86–9).

This 'both-and position' has been well developed by Basil Mitchell (1973, ch. 6). Mitchell reasoned that the choice between God as an uncertain, inferred, explanatory hypothesis and God as an experienced reality of which we can be certain is not an exclusive one. He offers an analogy. A sailor's claim to see a lighthouse through a storm can only be judged in the light of other reports, the calculations of map positions and so on. We cannot decide about the objectivity of his seeming to see the lighthouse *simply on his report alone*. 'The question whether there was a lighthouse there and the question whether the officer of the watch saw it or saw something else, or just imagined that he saw it, can only be answered in relation to some overall appraisal of the situation.' Note, however, that this does not make the lighthouse 'merely an inferred entity and not an experienced reality'. It is rather that *direct experience often needs the support of indirect reasoning* in order to justify a claim to knowledge by observation (Mitchell, 1973, p. 113). And, as others would argue, 'to allow this background of related experience in sensory perception but not in religious experience constitutes a double standard' (Peterson, Hasker, Reichenbach and Basinger, 1991, p. 50). Mitchell concludes his argument:

> It is assumed that claims to direct awareness of God must be either self-authenticating or disguised inferences. Since they are clearly not self-authenticating they must be disguised inferences. I suggest a third possibility: that they are what they purport to be, cases of direct awareness, but that the claim that this is what they are relies upon there being a theory or conceptual scheme in terms of which the claim can be adequately defended. (Mitchell, 1973, p. 115)

In the case of claims about the existence of God, therefore, whether 'seeming to experience God' is sufficient for supposing that one *does* experience God will depend in part on *just how probable or improbable is the existence of God, as judged by background evidence and argument*. In other words, on this view, religious experience can never be sufficient on its own. 'Theistic religious experience, *all by itself* does *not* constitute evidence for the existence of God – 'other things need to be true before a report of a religious experience can be considered veridical' (Davis, 1997, p. 135).[5]

Hence, the claims that people make that they have had an experience of God (or of some other Ultimate Reality) need to be supported by a coherent framework of defensible beliefs: that is, by a worldview that includes a coherent, plausible theology or metaphysics. *Claims to religious experience cannot stand alone.* Further, Mitchell's example shows

> that a perceptual claim in need of verification may form part of the evidence in its own favour, without the least hint of vicious circularity, and – the other side of the coin – that an experience may be 'interpreted' in terms of the very doctrines (e.g. 'the ship is near land') for which it constitutes part of the evidence. It is not necessary first to show that God probably exists, only then accepting some claims to have experienced him directly; religious experiences can work *in conjunction with* other types of evidence for religious claims.[6] (Franks Davis, 1989, p. 144; cf. Alston, 1991, pp. 292–307)

In this way, certain religious experiences may provide evidence for religious beliefs within a *cumulative argument* (e.g. 'a cumulative case for theism': Franks Davis, 1989, ch. 9). Therefore, 'it is reasonable to believe that religious experiences are genuine only if the religious system within which they are understood is itself found to be plausible' (Griffith-Dickson, 2000, p. 119). Here is Alston's account of the argument.

> Putative perceptions of God are not 'self-authenticating', but instead are in principle subject to being shown to be incorrect, or inadequately based, by relevant considerations, that is, 'overridden'. But this is possible only if we have a stock of knowledge or justified belief concerning the matters in question, in this case concerning God, His nature, purposes, and activities. Thus mystical perception can function as a source of justification for M-beliefs

[= beliefs that God is doing something to the subject or has some perceivable property] only against the background of a system of epistemically justified beliefs concerning [God] ... Such a system is built up at least partly on the basis of mystical perception itself.[7] (Alston, 1991, p. 295)

This is one place where Christian theology is *required*, then, with respect to Christian religious experience (and where other belief-systems become relevant for other religious experiences). 'Dogmatic theology (along with natural theology) provides significant input to the larger belief framework in which religious experiences are situated and over against which their deliverances may be tested' (Sudduth, 2009, p. 228; cf. Taliaferro, 2012, p. 18).

But should the theologians necessarily have the last word? Matthew Bagger is an example of one philosopher who has robustly criticized the perception model of religious experience, collapsing it into an argument to a best explanation. He contends that all experience is 'something that includes inference (of a sort) from previous beliefs and commitments, something which we need not take at face value and which we can critique in light of our wider cultural values' (Bagger, 1999, p. 11). However, he argues, our cultural values today include *the principle of unrestricted naturalistic explanation*. In the constructivist style (see Chapter 8, above), Bagger asserts that the fact 'that an experience *feels* immediate to someone does not necessarily mean that beliefs or concepts did not in some fashion influence the experience' (p. 28), and that *any* experience 'includes an implicit commitment about the best explanation of the experience and this commitment constitutes the experience' (p. 40). Specifically, therefore, religious experiences *include*, as a response to some stimulus, 'a tacit commitment to a religious explanation' that 'exhibits the logic of an inference to the best explanation' of such experiences (p. 47).[8] We cannot, therefore, avoid making this explanatory justification explicit, and then assessing its force.

In discussing the veridicality of religious experience, therefore, especially in arguments from religious experience, the strength and extent of the initial evidence must be taken into account; but so also should the strength and extent of other favourable evidence *and* of any counter evidence or rational considerations. As Wesley Wildman puts it, in his own rich account, we must certainly honour, 'take proper account of' and take 'with due seriousness' what he calls the *cognitive immediacy criterion*, which includes the sense that religious experiences seem to be self-interpreting, self-evident and self-confirming. He requires, however, that we must *also* honour five other criteria (Wildman, 2011, pp. 153–6):

- 'we experience in ways that reflect our culture and religious formation';
- our belief formation is socially transmitted by traditions;
- beliefs arising from religious and spiritual experiences need to cohere with beliefs that have been created by 'disciplined rational reflection';
- the cognitive content of RSEs is 'richly symbolic', as it refers to ultimate concerns that transcend us; and
- these experiences are 'value-laden' and 'value-suffused'.

Suggestions for Further Reading

Introductory

Donovan, Peter, 1998 [1979], *Interpreting Religious Experience*, Oxford: The Religious Experience Research Centre [London: Sheldon], ch. 5 (pp. 95–124 [73–97]).

Gaskin, J. C. A., 1984, *The Quest for Eternity: An Outline of the Philosophy of Religion*, Harmondsworth: Penguin, ch. 4 (pp. 78–103).

Advanced

Franks Davis, Caroline, 1989, *The Evidential Force of Religious Experience*, Oxford: Clarendon, ch. 4 (pp. 93–114).

Mitchell, Basil, 1973, *The Justification of Religious Belief*, London: Macmillan, ch. 6 (pp. 99–116).

Notes

1 Hasker defines an *evidentialist* programme as one that is based on the view that 'religious beliefs can be rationally accepted only if they are supported by one's "total evidence", understood to mean all the other propositions one knows or justifiably believes to be true'. Unfortunately, this position may be adopted by either of these approaches to religious experience, as we shall see.

2 George Mavrodes does not say that *experience*, as such, is without thought and judgement (as is our sensory input); indeed, he writes, 'experiencing something is a cognitive activity involving a conscious judgment ... if there is no judgment at all there is no experience' (Mavrodes, 1970, p. 62).

3 This awareness may sometimes come *through* something else, however, and *in that sense* it may be said to be *mediated*. In these cases it is often mediated through spatio-temporal objects or events within Nature, Jesus' life and death or the history of salvation; or through 'concepts, language, symbols' that represent these sensible realities (Smith, 1968, pp. 52, 71n, 79–80). Such 'media' or 'mediators' of an experience of God may include 'any object or event in the natural world', as a consequence of the relationship between God the creator and the whole of creation (Mavrodes, 1970, p. 69), and for some the category includes human language that represents these media (cf. Ramsey, 1974, pp. 120–40). Alston, however, although he grudgingly allows for what he calls an 'indirect perceptual recognition' of God through 'direct awareness of something in creation' (Alston, 1991, p. 28), *focuses in his argument on religious experience that is a 'direct' perception* in the sense that it is 'unmediated' (and thus not 'indirect', as it would be if seen through images) – and therefore also 'non-sensory' (2005, pp. 201–2). A number of other defenders of the perceptual model, however, argue that *most* religious experiences are *'direct, though mediated'* experiences, because of their related 'complex causal chain' that always includes the operation of our central nervous system, and in some instances an external medium such as those listed above – or other people, music and so on (Evans, 1985, pp. 86–8). See also Chapters 13, 19, below.

4 Donovan also adds that the under-interpretation of an experience can be as bad as over-interpreting it, because we risk missing its true significance (1979, p. 28).

5 Cf. 'a religious experience apparently of God ought to be taken as veridical unless it can be shown on other grounds significantly more probable than not that God does not exist' (Swinburne, 2004, p. 321).

6 And, we may add, with any inferential arguments that also support religious knowledge claims (cf. Franks Davis, 1989, p. 241).

7 Alston calls this position 'modest foundationalism' (1991, pp. 299–300).

8 We may recall that Bagger argues that this was also William James's earlier (and 'more fully articulated and carefully defended') view of experience, from which he resiled by treating religious experiences as analogous to sense experience in the *Varieties*. See Bagger, 1999, ch. 2; and above, Chapter 8 n. 6.

11

Challenges of Diversity and Naturalistic Explanations

Perhaps the two most challenging criticisms faced by the claims to veridicality/objectivity of religious experience that we explored in Chapter 9 are (a) the fact that accounts of different religious experiences often disagree markedly and give rise to incompatible beliefs; and (b) the assertion that there are naturalistic explanations for such experience that do not require it to have any real supernatural object as an additional cause.

Diversity

When incompatible beliefs within religious traditions are based on religious experience, they are frequently said to undermine the veridicality of such experience. There are, however, a *range of defences* against this criticism.

- These varied experiences could all be *genuine experiences of different aspects of one transcendent reality*. John Hick's 'pluralistic hypothesis', for example, makes such a claim for the many symbolic 'masks', 'faces' or 'maps' (whether personal 'personae' or impersonal 'impersonae') of the one ultimate, 'trans-categorial'[1] and transcendent 'Real', as this is *experienced in different ways* by different people and traditions (Hick, 1985, chs 3, 6; 1989, ch. 14; 2006, ch. 16; see also Chapter 19, below).

- There may be *only one sort – or only a few sorts – of religious experience*, or *a common core* to all the different experiences *that different cultures and individuals interpret differently*. Such a common core may be said to be *core* in focusing on 'the most central and important element of religious belief' (expressing the nature of what is supremely Real, a similar awareness of separation from it and of a 'fitful awareness of a closer union with it'), and *common* in so far as there is 'an overlapping identity of description of the Real' across differing religious traditions – whose doctrines are inherently flexible and thus allow 'many varieties of interpretation' that talk about 'recognizably similar topics' (Ward, 2005, pp. 4, 6, 8; a similar view is taken by Franks Davis, 1989, pp. 190–2 and Kwan, 2012, p. 537; see also Chapter 8, above).
- Provided that religious experience is not regarded as infallible, some of these incompatible beliefs may be *errors based on non-veridical experiences*, or *misperceptions or misinterpretations* (intentional or unintentional) by free human beings of the one, true object of the experience. Or, in Alston's terms, one religious doxastic practice may be 'more reliable' – perhaps also more fruitful? – than alternative religious doxastic practices (Alston, 1991, ch. 7).
- God may *'accommodate' revelation to the limitations of human understanding*, even perhaps revealing information or Godself 'progressively' by conferring religious experiences in accordance with the capacity and culture of those who receive them.[2]
- According to Swinburne, as a consequence of other evidence *some religious experiences may have a 'lower evidential worth' than others* – as may be the case with 'apparent experiences of supernatural beings and things other than God' and 'more specific religious experiences' (Swinburne, 2004, pp. 324–5).
- Although *consensus has not yet been achieved* in religious experiences, consensus was only slowly achieved in other areas of human knowledge, even in the natural sciences (Alston, 1986).
- Disagreements between reports of religious experiences may be partly explained by the language that they employ:
  (a) *either* because of the use of *underspecified analogies* (similarities that are expressed in terms that are stretched beyond their normal, mundane range of use) and *metaphors* (figures of speech, which – unlike analogies – do not literally apply but suggest images and generate cognitive insight);
  (b) *or* because of the use of *apparently descriptive language 'non-cognitively'*,

so as to express or evoke attitudes, emotions or even experiences rather than to make (or perhaps even imply) cognitive claims (See Astley, 2004, chs 4, 5, 8, especially pp. 54–6; and Chapter 12, below.)

> **Exercise: Among the Articles**
>
> *Read and critically assess the following journal article:*
>
> **Heim, S. Mark, 2000, 'Saving the Particulars: Religious Experience and Religious Ends', *Religious Studies*, 36, 4, pp. 435–53.**
>
> This article reflects on the diversity of religious experiences in an exercise in the theology of religions (that is, the interpretation and evaluation of the divergent truth-claims and views of salvation that are asserted or implied by different religious traditions). Mark Heim contends that, 'although liberal and conservative theological extremes share a largely undefended assumption that there is and can be only one religious end, one actual religious fulfilment', *if diverse religious ends were to be acknowledged* apparently 'conflicting' testimony – including that of religious experience – may be regarded as 'essentially valid description of different conditions of religious fulfilment'.

Kwan has argued that the degree of conflicts among religious experiences is 'grossly overestimated'. In Kwan, 2012 (pp. 536–46), he reclassifies religious experiences according to the extent to which they are 'compatible', 'incompatible', 'friendly', 'unfriendly' or 'neutral' with respect to *theism*. Thus, he contends that structureless 'pure consciousness experiences' are theism-neutral (because they have no content), as is nature mysticism (because it can be interpreted either theistically or monistically, reflecting the unity of all things either in God or in an impersonal Absolute). Peak experiences, NDEs and experiences of evil spirits, angels or the departed (including saints) may be interpreted theistically (and are therefore 'theism-friendly'). Experiences of contingency or design also 'point somewhat in the direction of a transcendent Creator-Designer'.

Experiences of other deities are designated *'theism-unfriendly'* (presumably unfriendly to *mono*theism). This group may yet be accommodated theologically, however, as Scripture itself does in those Old Testament references to *created* supernatural beings in 'the court of Yahweh' and New Testament references to principalities and powers. For Kwan, the prime example of *theism-incompatible experiences* are monistic mysticism and experiences of Nirvāna. Monistic experiences can only be accommodated to theism by claiming that 'the Personal Ultimate can manifest itself in a nonpersonal way' (something, we may observe, that human persons routinely do). Kwan criticizes interpretations of Nirvāna or the Absolute as wholly structureless because this makes these realities utterly ineffable and experiences of them by discrete individual subjects completely impossible.[3]

As a whole, Kwan concludes, religious experiences 'still support theism more than naturalism' and a case may be made that those experiences that are 'pro-theism' have 'greater weight' than those that are 'anti-theism' (Kwan, 2012, p. 547).

> ### Exercise
>
> In your view, how much of a problem for religious experience is the 'problem of diversity'?

Naturalistic Explanations

The other most challenging criticism faced by claims of the veridicality of religious experience is that there are naturalistic (mainly sociological, psychological or neuroscientific) explanations for such an experience that do not require it to have any real supernatural object as an additional cause. This charge is briefly considered here, but see also Chapters 15, 20 and the literature cited in the Appendix.

Critics of religious experience frequently quote Bertrand Russell's quip:

From a scientific point of view, we can make no distinction between the man who eats little and sees heaven and the man who drinks much and sees snakes. Each is in an abnormal physical condition, and therefore has abnormal perceptions. (Russell, 1935, p. 188)

But can religious and spiritual experiences be 'explained away' by – and thus 'reduced to' – any natural causes? According to Proudfoot, *descriptive reductionism*, which is 'the failure to identify an ... experience under the description by which the subject identifies it' is unacceptable: it misidentifies that experience, even if it is an RSE. *Explanatory reductionism*, however, which consists in 'offering an explanation of an experience in terms that are not those of the subject and that might not meet with his approval', is 'perfectly justifiable'. In point of fact, he claims that it is normal procedure (Proudfoot, 1985, pp. 196–7). Some may also agree with Proudfoot that 'it would be strange for someone to report a religious experience and to subscribe to a psychoanalytic or sociological explanation' as a *complete* and *exhaustive* account of it. Others, however, might think that religious experience (including mystical experience) are terms that *may* properly be used – as they increasingly seem to be used – in a way that construes them as a 'simple description of certain mental and/or physiological states', rather than as including an explanatory commitment that these states 'could not be accounted for in naturalistic terms' (Proudfoot, 1985, pp. 138–9, 187; cf. Gale, 1991, p. 315).

Various reductionist psychological and sociological explanations have been given for religious or spiritual experiences (cf. Franks Davis, 1989, chs 6, 8; Wulff, 2000, pp. 410–12, 416–27). *Pathological explanations* have included hyper-suggestibility, severe deprivation or maladjustment (including sexual frustration, intense fear of death and infantile regression), mental illness and abnormal psychological states. *Non-pathological explanations* include the claim that religious experiences can be completely explained by reference to the subject's '*set*' (beliefs, expectations, cultural background, etc.) or '*setting*' (context). Thus, sociological explanations have proposed, to take one example, that mystical experiences occur primarily in disenfranchised and other marginalized groups, and among aspirants to a higher status who are seeking greater access to social or political power.

Sigmund Freud's general dismissal of religion asserted that it was an obsessional 'universal neurosis' that took the form of a wish-fulfilment (Freud, 1928

[1927]; see below, Chapter 15). This *projection*, which transformed the human super-ego into God, was caused by psychological, though socially shared, processes: individual human wishes that included repressed desires and defence mechanisms. These were rooted in childhood experiences that gave rise to psychodynamic tensions. A longing for this *false illusion*[4] may, for some, create psychotic hallucinations.

Parallels and overlaps have been widely noted between the experiences and transformations of the self in religious and spiritual experiences and those in psychosis (defined as 'a severe mental disorder in which thought and emotions are so impaired that contact is lost with external reality'). These include emotions of bliss, dread and crisis; trance-like or 'blank' states (comparable to temporal lobe seizures); losses/gains of meaning; extremes of physiological arousal (both high and low); growth, healing, transformation and self-actualization; and peak experiences. Harry Hunt notes that there is 'growth and even spiritual potential within some psychoses, and a potential for psychotic-like crisis within some spiritual experiences'. After a detailed review of the issues, he concludes:

> that mysticism can have psychotic features and vice versa without thereby being identical; that a cognitive-affective account of the abstract imagistic bases of transpersonal experience does not rule out a physiology of arousal; that adult developmental features of mystical experiences do not prevent them from embodying the thematics of early childhood experience; and that 'positive' and 'negative' forms of numinous experience meet in a common crisis whose resulting 'fruits' can be dynamic or static. (Hunt, 2000, pp. 360, 390)

Karl Marx's critique of institutional religion is predicated on a more *social* projection and illusion. For Marx (1818–83), ideas are formed and explained by social practice. Religion is to be viewed both as an expression of suffering and a protest against it; but it is always an *alienating* false consciousness – a false resolution of the class conflicts and injustices that really arise out of materialistic (economic) forces (Marx and Engels, 1957, pp. 37–8, 66, 131). It is, perhaps, relevant that the positive healing effect of RSEs is regarded by some commentators as a factor in the success of evangelical and Pentecostal outreach in those social groups and historical periods where economic hardship and dislocating change are to the fore.

However, regardless of what other data may show about the relationship between people's social and psychological status and their religious beliefs, practices and social groupings, *empirical results from hypothesis testing using quantitative data* drawn from those who have undergone *religious and spiritual experiences* show that neither the Freudian nor the Marxian challenges are supported by empirical evidence. In fact, these data indicate that such experiences:

1 appear to be less common among those who are less psychologically adequate (Francis et al., 2015), are positively correlated with positive affect (Hay and Morisy, 1978; Hay, 1994) or display no correlation with measures of psychopathology (Francis, 2013; Hood and Francis, 2013);[5] and
2 seem to be less common among those who suffer more economic stress (e.g. Hay, 1987, pp. 174, 178–80, 203–4; 2011a).

Still, this does not answer the more general question, 'Can socio-scientific evidence in general undermine claims to the objectivity of RSEs?'

As naturalistic explanations of religious *belief* are now so widespread, we may take a moment to address this more general form of the issue. It is arguable that such explanations can only 'work' if they can claim that psychological or sociological factors, or whatever, are not only (in some cases) *sufficient* to explain religious belief, but that they are also always (and therefore in all cases) *necessary* conditions for them: that is, that the belief cannot occur without such factors. But this would be to assume that there is *no* sound basis for religious belief, and that is a very sweeping assertion that would require a great deal of argument. In fact, the broader naturalistic claim is by no means obvious and the debate over it remains far from settled. Thus, while theories of projection might, and probably should, make people suspicious of their own religious beliefs; unless 'there could not be adequate reasons' for religious belief (including, perhaps, reasons based on religious experiences), these criticisms represent 'a hollow triumph'. In particular, 'Why should I abandon what I can see to be sound reason for the belief just because it has been shown that many other people hold the belief without having any such grounds?' (Alston, 1966, pp. 91–2).

Swinburne defines a religious experience as 'an experience that seems (epistemically) to the subject to be an experience of God'.[6] He argues that such an experience is *really* an experience of God if and only if its seeming to a person that God is present 'is in fact caused by God being present' (Swinburne, 2004, pp. 295–6). However, theism understands God to be the supernatural cause that not only *brings the universe into existence*, but also sustains it and its autonomous causal powers in being. For God wills the incessant act of 'continuous creation' that *keeps all things in the universe in existence*, together with the laws of their interaction that God has determined. (God is, here, the 'primary cause' that enables all natural 'secondary causality'.) So theists may hold that even 'a match will not burst into flame unless God wills that it does so' (Wainwright, 1981, p. 75; cf. Matt. 10.29?). As such, a creating-and-preserving God will *always* be among the causes of human experience, and even 'naturalistic' or 'psychological' explanations of religious experience need not defeat its claim to objectivity.

Of course, the question is often posed in other terms, which assume that a more discrete and particular action is required on God's part for there to be a religious experience. This might be an act of *particular providence* that operates within the limits of natural causation (including its quantum fluctuations), or it may be understood to be a *miraculous* act that goes beyond these limits.[7] As we might expect, psychological and social influences are normally regarded as competitors with any theist's claim to divine intervention behind religious experiences (Fales, 1996a, 1996b). However, 'religious experience need not be miraculous' (Kwan, 2011, p. 90). But, in any case:

> The mere fact that a religious experience apparently of God was brought about by natural processes has no tendency to show that it was not veridical. To show this, you need to know that God did not cause these processes. That can be attained only by showing that there is no God – for, if he exists as defined, clearly he is responsible both for the normal operation of natural laws and for any occasional violation. (Swinburne, 2004, p. 320)[8]

In his own day, William James criticized the unfalsifiable 'medical materialism' that reduced claims to objective religious experience to supposed disorders of the body, whether these were events in the brain's occipital cortex (causing Paul's vision on the Damascus road) or in the colon (causing George Fox's pining for spiritual veracity) (James, 1960, p. 35). Today, the most radically reductionist explanations of religious experiences are based on experimental neurophysiological studies of the brain, which appear to 'explain away' these experiences as the effect of *neurological states* (see the literature cited in the Appendix, below). Strictly speaking, however, these studies may be regarded only as *evidence for correlation*,[9] *not of causation*; and, besides, a creator, providential and/or interventionist God would be most likely to cause religious experiences precisely *by* affecting our brain and/or our related psychological states. The psychologist, Ralph Hood therefore comments:

> One cannot discount the reality of the experience as genuinely mystical because it was facilitated by a chemical or any other proximate [that is, closest] cause ... Furthermore, identifying triggers of an experience cannot be used to reduce the experience to a causal claim that it was the trigger that caused the experience.[10] (Hood, 2006, p. 123)

A similar point may be made from a philosophical perspective:

> A psychological explanation can affect our estimation of the veridicality of an experience ... However, the sheer fact of providing a psychological explanation that satisfies our curiosity on a certain point and thus seems adequate for a certain purpose, does not exclude the possibility that an experience or some moment in it is nevertheless veridical. (Griffith-Dickson, 2000, p. 115)

In the end, all reductionist debates will inevitably resolve into what is essentially a *philosophical debate*, either over the plausibility of understanding spiritual and religious experiences as *reliable perceptions* of God/Ultimate Reality or of divine action *as their best explanation*, in the face of rival naturalistic claims based on neurological, psychological or sociological factors alone.

Many critics, however, *have* rejected supernaturalist explanations for religious experience. Such a position was exemplified in the 1970s by T. R. Miles (a psychologist who declared himself a Quaker), who argued that religious belief required no '"non-material" story' (Miles, 1972, p. 22, cf. 2–3, 5, 27, 49–51) and by Frits Staal, who took the view that mystical experience has 'nothing to do with gods' or belief in God (Staal, 1975, pp. 179, 184). Similar positions continue to be held today, as the following examples confirm.

- Matthew Bagger insists that the once live option of supernaturalism has become 'explanatorily otiose' (i.e. it serves no useful purpose) and has no legitimate application to 'particular events in the mundane order', such as religious experiences (1999, p. 16, cf. 14–17, 56–7, 131, 197–8, 203–6, 219–21, 225–8).

- Wesley Wildman who, while admitting the potentially positive personal and social effects of spiritual and religious experiences, advocates 'a religiously positive form of naturalism' that rejects both disembodied and divine personal beings (Wildman, 2011, pp. xii, 73, 242, 264–5, 266).[11]
- Peter Connolly is doubtful that any RSE can be said to be superior to any other because of its 'fruits', but in any case regards them all as human fabrications 'rooted in common psychological processes', none of which are 'experiences of reality as such'. They are just 'believed-in imaginings' or 'illusions' (Connolly, 2019, pp. 7–8, 29, 116, 126, 131–2, 142, 150–1).

Suggestions for Further Reading

Diversity

Introductory

Hick, John, 1985, *Problems of Religious Pluralism*, Basingstoke: Macmillan, chs 6, 7 (pp. 88–109).

Advanced

Alston, William P., 1991, *Perceiving God: The Epistemology of Religious Experience*, Ithaca, NY: Cornell University Press, ch. 7 (pp. 255–85).

Franks Davis, Caroline, 1989, *The Evidential Force of Religious Experience*, Oxford: Clarendon, ch. VII (pp. 166–92).

Naturalistic Explanations

Introductory

Franks Davis, Caroline, 1989, *The Evidential Force of Religious Experience*, Oxford: Clarendon, ch. 8 (pp. 193–238).
Hay, David, 2006, *Something There: The Biology of the Human Spirit*, London: Darton, Longman and Todd, ch. 8 (pp. 165–87).
Peterson, Michael, Hasker, William, Reichenbach, Bruce and Basinger, David, 2013, *Reason and Religious Belief: An Introduction to the Philosophy of Religion*, New York: Oxford University Press, ch. 13 (pp. 291–318).

Advanced

Hick, John, 2006, *The New Frontier of Religion and Science: Religious Experience, Neuroscience and the Transcendent*, Basingstoke: Palgrave Macmillan, Part II (pp. 55–123).
Wildman, Wesley J., 2011, *Religious and Spiritual Experiences*, New York: Cambridge University Press, ch. 2 (pp. 31–68).

See also the literature on neuroscience and RSEs listed in the Appendix.

Notes

1 That is, going beyond all categories.

2 Cf. Davis, 2009, pp. 39–41. Admittedly, the notion of a 'progressive revelation' – at least in its liberal redaction – more usually locates the progression within human understanding rather than God's initiative; see Stiver, 2009, pp. 91–2.

3 Cf. the 'Christian' and 'Muslim' protestations in Ninian Smart's constructed 'dialogue of religions': 'While theism can convincingly absorb and enrich the mystical path without detriment to the latter, the mystical path cannot absorb theistic belief without relegating it to second place' (Smart, 1960, p. 72; cf. Stoeber, 1992, pp. 115–16).

4 Note that, for Freud, a 'delusion' is a *false* illusion caused by a psychological state. On his view, it was generated by complex wishes that include unconscious desires (Adolf Grünbaum, in Oppy and Trakakis, 2009a, pp. 267–77; cf. Chapter 9 n. 2, above).

5 Hood and Francis, 2013 report a 1993 study which suggested that dimensions of their personality was the factor that sets psychotics apart in the data, with psychotic mystics exhibiting resistance and rigidity and 'normal' mystics exhibiting openness and fluidity.

6 By this *epistemic sense* of 'seems', Swinburne is referring to 'what the subject is inclined to believe' on the basis of his/her present experience.

7 For this distinction, see Astley, 2010, pp. 161–8; cf. Langford, 1981, pp. 5–24. See also Swinburne, 1970; Ward, 1990, chs 5–10; Corner, 2005.

8 The difficulty remains, however, as some critics claim and Swinburne himself notes (2004, p. 321) that on this view there cannot be *any perceptions of the absence of God*. But the nature both of God and of experience may imply that we really do not know what 'experiencing God's absence' would amount to, anyway, other than not – or not any longer – experiencing God. Perhaps the phrase should be interpreted as an *entirely subjective feeling* of loss, feeling bereft or not being cared for. But in interpersonal relationships these experiences are quite compatible with the perception of and continued existence of the other person, and even of their active supporting presence with us (even, exceptionally, of their continuing feelings and acts of love and care towards us). (Compare two true lovers, each of whom claims of the other that 'you no longer love me' – for each one *feels* that the other no longer loves them, although each is wrong.)

9 The reference here is to the *scientific* use of correlation, defined in terms of one variable fluctuating in parallel with another ('positive correlation') or in the opposite direction ('negative correlation'). In the humanities, as in more general usage, 'correlation' means a 'mutual relationship' and 'to correlate' is to link or relate two things (e.g. science and religion).

10 Nor that it *alone* caused it. On triggers, see above, Chapter 6. Note that a transcendent cause of religious experience could not literally be said to be at *any* distance from the brain, as by its nature it is: either (a) 'outside' the created spatiotemporal universe, in the sense of having no spatial location or extension itself and, perhaps, having no temporal parameters – being 'timeless', yet nevertheless being intimately associated with this universe through the continuous act of keeping it in existence (in the case of God); or (b) united with all of the spatiotemporal universe and somehow inclusive of it (in the case of an impersonal Ultimate Reality).

11 Wildman is a 'religious naturalist' who argues that, although we *may* still maintain that supernatural agents 'spark RSEs' through the brain's causal mechanisms, such a hypothesis 'comes to seem increasingly exorbitant and implausible when it is repeatedly shown to be superfluous for explaining the meaning and value of RSEs' (Wildman, 2011, p. 243, cf. 248–9, 261–2).

12

Religious Experience and Religious Language

Descriptive Language

It is a commonplace that the nature of religious experience itself, as well as its supposed object, transcends language, straining the descriptive resources of any person who takes on the task of reporting this experience. Even religious emotions – including the 'longing' and 'yearning' of the soul for God – can 'far outpass the power of human telling', as the late medieval hymn, 'Come Down O Love Divine', puts it. The insufficiency of human language to describe religious experience and its transcendent object(s) is as frequent a topic of regret in the writings of mystics as it is among their commentators and critics. But it is also a fundamental axiom in practically all Christian theology, as in most religions.

It is especially in mystical and numinous experience, however, that both the experience and its object are routinely described as too great, too extreme, too 'awe-ful' or too sacred, to be adequately expressed in words. They are therefore both commonly characterized as 'indescribable', 'unutterable' or 'ineffable' (from the Latin *effari*, 'to utter').[1] John of the Cross (see Chapter 17) writes that, even when mystical wisdom is communicated to the mystic 'most clearly':

> it is still so secret that the soul cannot speak of it and give it a name whereby it may be called; for, apart from the fact that the soul has no desire to speak of it, it can find no suitable way or manner or similitude by which it may be able to describe such lofty understanding and such delicate spiritual feeling. And thus, even though the soul might have a great desire to express it

and might find many ways in which to describe it, it would still be secret and remain undescribed. For, as that inward wisdom is so simple, so general and so spiritual that it has not entered into the understanding enwrapped or cloaked in any form or image subject to sense, it follows that sense and imagination (as it has not entered through them nor has taken their form and colour) cannot account for it or imagine it, so as to say anything concerning it, although the soul be clearly aware that it is experiencing and partaking of that rare and delectable wisdom. It is like one who sees something never seen before, whereof he has not even seen the like; although he might understand its nature and have experience of it, he would be unable to give it a name, or say what it is, however much he tried to do so, and this in spite of its being a thing which he had perceived with the senses. How much less, then, could he describe a thing that has not entered through the senses! For the language of God has this characteristic that, since it is very intimate and spiritual in its relations with the soul, it transcends every sense and at once makes all harmony and capacity of the outward and inward senses to cease and be dumb. (John of the Cross, *Dark Night of the Soul*, bk. II, ch. XVII, §3; *ET* 1959, pp. 83–4; www.carmelitemonks.org/Vocation/DarkNight-StJohnoftheCross.pdf)

Exercise

Read Isaiah 6.1–8; Mark 9.2–8.

In these famous passages, note the relation between human language and religious experience at two levels:

1 in the verbal responses made by the prophet or disciple;
2 in the narrator's account of the setting and the overall experience.

How is the language being used here?

Clearly, many of those who have known the most extreme forms of religious experience *have* attempted to convey some sense of it in human words, even mystics such as John of the Cross.

Analogical and Figurative Language

Total mystery would be beyond all words, and therefore all theology. It would result in a total form of agnosticism, of not knowing *anything* about the object of religious experience. It is not surprising, therefore, that most theologians and reflective religious writers prefer to tread a more 'affirmative' or 'positive' path, rejecting total silence, complete negation and 'pure equivocation' (that is, the practice of applying language to God with a completely different meaning from the meaning it has when applied to humans or other creatures). They normally achieve this:

- *either* by using human words *analogically*, with a stretched or shifted meaning appropriate to God's different nature (as we routinely do in everyday life by stretching words in the opposite direction, when we say, for example, that a dog is 'intelligent' or 'cunning'): so that God may be said *really* to be wise, loving, powerful, etc., but only *in God's own way*;
- *or* by using human words figuratively, especially *metaphorically*, 'speaking about one thing in terms that are seen to be suggestive of another' (Soskice, 1985, p. 15) by carrying over words applied to humans or other created things in order to apply them to God, of whom we may then speak in more imaginative and illuminating, ways: so that God is declared to be – 'but *not* literally' – a father, mother, king, shepherd, friend; even a lion, a fortress or a rock.

In 'describing human experiences which few have had and for which, consequently, there is no established set of literal terms', mystics like other religious writers and theologians are apt to appeal to metaphors in order to find words adequate to the experience. This figurative language is often very striking: language such as 'the dark night of the soul', 'spiritual marriage' or entering 'the cloud of unknowing' (Soskice, 1985, pp. 96, 151). So are the analogies that are also employed. Thus, Teresa of Ávila writes that the soul is 'like a bee' who leaves its hive and is 'constantly flying about from flower to flower', so the soul should sometimes cease thinking of itself and, instead, 'soar aloft in meditation upon the greatness and the majesty of its God' (*Interior Castle*, The First Mansions, ch. II; *ET*, www.cheraglibrary.org/christian/teresa/castle.html). But it is also 'like an infant still feeding at its mother's breast', who feeds her baby without its having to move its own lips (*Way of Perfection*, ch. xxxi; *ET Complete Works*, vol. II, London: Burns & Oates, 2002 [1991], p. 130). Elsewhere, Teresa uses the analogy of a small fluttering bird that has been 'trying with its understanding and its will and all its strength to find God and please Him; and now He is pleased to give it its reward in this life', and so 'puts it into the nest where it may be quiet' (Teresa of Ávila, *Life*, ch. 18; *ET* quoted in Happold, 1970, pp. 352–3).

Teresa writes that her experiences transcend both understanding and precise description: 'these visions and many other things impossible to describe, are revealed by some wonderful intuition that I cannot explain. Perhaps those who have experienced this favour and possess more ability than myself may be able to describe it, although it seems to me a most difficult task' (*The Interior Castle*, The Sixth Mansions, ch. V, 9, cf. ch. IV, 5, ch. X, 2; *ET*, 1921, p. 90, cf. pp. 84, 109, www.documentacatholicaomnia.eu/03d/1515-1582,_Teresa_d%27Avila,_The_Interior_Castle_Of_The_Mansions,_EN.pdf).

Human language is bound to seem inadequate coinage for descriptions and interpretations of the divine/Ultimate Reality. But if all those who claim to have had any experience of God, or of any other transcendent reality, were to choose inarticulate silence as their only response, the rest of us would not benefit much from their silence. In order for that to happen, there must be *communication*, especially communication about the non-contemporary and personal experiences of other people. We do and must rely on the medium of language.

Non-Cognitive Language

Taking a more extreme position,[2] some contend that the function of at least certain mystical expressions is not to describe reality at all, but 'to evoke the knowledge of *how* to live freely' and 'to recondition the expectations about the subjective factors in one's experience' (Frederick Streng, in Katz, 1978, pp. 153–4; see also Miles, 1972). Ian Ramsey, a liberal philosophical theologian and Anglican bishop, argued that *many forms of religious language have the power to evoke a religious experience* (what he called a 'discernment') and revelation ('disclosure') of the divine mystery. Ramsey even held that certain words for God, such as 'immutable' and 'impassible', had as their 'main merit' the ability 'to give a kind of technique for meditation' that evokes a religious disclosure (Ramsey, 1957, p. 53; cf. 1965, pp. 66–71). But he *also* insisted that the mystery so discovered can be represented by these same words, which serve as 'models' (sustained and systematically employed metaphors) for God, provided that they are suitably 'qualified' and not taken literally.[3]

Much of the language of prayer and worship, he argued, seems to operate in an evocative way, as this religious language takes us into 'a moment of vision, a moment of silence where God discloses himself' (Ramsey, 1971, p. 21), without giving up its function of articulating the mystery of that which is disclosed there.[4] According to Ramsey, the same may be said of the narratives, poetry and reflections within Scripture, of Christian hymnody – and even of doctrinal theology. All theology, he argued, is anchored in 'a characteristically religious situation – one of worship, wonder, awe' (Ramsey, 1957, p. 89).

Language of Intimate Union

Different types of mysticism employ different linguistic imagery. As we saw earlier, in theistic mysticism, although 'the soul feels itself to be united with God by love', it is not annihilated by, nor wholly identified with, God; only transformed and 'deified'. The analogy or metaphor of a close sexual union is hinted at by some of the mystics themselves, with the soul being said to be 'enveloped' in or 'penetrated' by God (Zaehner, 1957, pp. 29, 150–2). But Christian mystics employ a whole dictionary of imagery of union with the divine, elements of which may tempt us to construe this experience in more monistic terms. Teresa, for instance, writes of the Lord telling her that the soul 'dissolves utterly, my daughter, to rest more and more in Me. It is no longer itself that lives; it is I.' She adds, however, that 'as it cannot comprehend what it understands, it understands by not understanding'; and that this union 'cannot be expressed more clearly, since all that happens is so obscure. I can only say that the soul conceives itself to be near God' (from Teresa of Ávila, *Life*, ch. 18; *ET* quoted in Happold, 1970, p. 354).

This language of direct intimate contact with God may be contrasted with claims of a *total* identification with God or absorption into God, ideas that are much more common in Eastern religions. These monistic experiences are even more difficult to describe; and because they are said to transcend the duality of the subject–object distinction, 'experience' may not even be an appropriate word. Here are some expressions of this extreme form of mystical union, from the Hindu Scriptures, the *Upanishads*:

> The Self is the lord of all; inhabitant of the hearts of all. He is the source of all; creator and dissolver of beings. There is nothing He does not know. He is not knowable by perception, turned inward or outward, nor by both combined. He is neither that which is known, nor that which is not known, nor is He the sum of all that might be known. He cannot be seen, grasped, bargained with. He is undefinable, unthinkable, indescribable. The only proof of His existence is union with Him. The world disappears in Him. He is the peaceful, the good, the one without a second. (*Māndookya-Upanishad*; ET *The Ten Principal Upanishads*, VI, London: Faber and Faber, 1937, p. 60)

> In the beginning there was Spirit. It knew itself as Spirit; from that knowledge everything sprang up. Whosoever among gods, sages and men, got that knowledge, became Spirit itself. ... Even today he who knows that he is Spirit, becomes Spirit, becomes everything; neither gods nor men can prevent him, for he has become themselves ...
> 'For as long as there is duality, one sees the other, one smells the other, one hears the other, one speaks to the other; one thinks of the other, one knows the other; but when everything is one Self, who can see another, how can he see another; who can smell another, how can he smell another; who can hear another, how can he hear another; who can speak to another, how can he speak to another; who can think of another, how can he think of another; who can know another, how can he know another? ... How can the knower be known?' (*Brihadāranyaka-Upanishad*; ET *The Ten Principal Upanishads*, X, London: Faber and Faber, 1937, bk. I, pp. 121–2, bk. IV, pp. 151–2)

Even in Christian devotion, contemplative prayer is regarded as being at the limit of all linguistic activity. Here every attempt either to use sensory imagery to picture God, or to communicate with God by means of the intellect, are seen to have broken down. Some Christian writers have called this the highest union with God in 'pure prayer', without words, images or any consciousness of anything except God. The fifth-century Denys/Pseudo-Dionysius (see Chapter 17) distinguished *cataphatic theology* (which uses positive names for God, such as 'Life' and 'Being') from *apophasis*, which asserts that the divine is 'a most incomprehensible absolute mystery' about which we can only say *what it is not*. In this case, God is 'not, in fact, any of the things he is called' (Roberta Bondi, in Richardson and Bowden, 1983, p. 32). So, the 'true initiate' is plunged:

> unto the Darkness of Unknowing wherein he renounces all the apprehensions of his understanding and is enwrapped in that which is wholly intangible and invisible, ... and being by the passive stillness of all his reasoning powers united by his highest faculty to Him that is wholly Unknowable, of whom thus by a rejection of all knowledge he possesses a knowledge that exceeds his understanding ... Ascending yet higher we maintain that It is not soul, or mind, ... nor can the reason attain to It to name It or to know It. (Pseudo-Dionysius, *Mystical Theology*, chs 1, 5; ET London: SPCK, 1940, pp. 194, 200–1)

But even such 'infinite unsaying' (denying) of claims about God in 'negative' or 'apophatic' theology,[5] which is achieved by stripping all human or finite images from language about God, is *not wholly non-descriptive*. For to say what God is not does seem to say *something* about God.

Suspending all human language and activity in a silent waiting upon God is often regarded as a catalyst for a most potent religious experience, with spiritual writers claiming that it is into this silent waiting that the mystery of the God, who is beyond words, may break. While words may 'frame' and lead into the silence, they maintain that it is only in the silence that God is truly evoked, met and 'realized'. It may be argued, both theologically and psychologically, that the more strongly we are convinced of the 'mysterious, infinite, and transcendent character of God', the more likely we are to treat any words about this God as being 'so inadequate to be worthless – or even blasphemous' (Wiles, 1976, p. 58).

Ineffability

William James records this quality as one of the distinctive marks of the mystical experience. As 'no adequate report of its contents can be given in words', he writes, mysticism 'defies expression'. Its quality cannot therefore be imparted to others. This is a position that James described as being similar to the one faced in communicating with those who lack 'the heart or ear' for music, or for being in love, when one tries to make those experiences clear to them (James, 1960, p. 367).

Ineffability may refer to the experience itself or to its object, and is often applied to both. Even if the religious experiencer does encounter God/the divine/ Ultimate Reality, many would argue that what she or he comes to know in this way must be strictly incommunicable, as its content surpasses human thought. In particular, whatever the mystic puts into words is 'at best a translation, a paraphrase, of what he has seen'. As they move into what is called the cloud of unknowing, language fails them: 'the last trace of thought or of humanly exercised love ceases and the ineffable enters in' (Knowles, 1979, pp. 73, 99, cf. 19).

Yet much of this seems to be a question of what has been called *definitional ineffability*, 'which holds that since the "object" [or content] of religion (and presumably of religious experience) is infinite … and since what is infinite is not definable, nothing can be said about this "object"' (Yandell, 1975, p. 167). If this is what ineffable means, however, there is a logical problem with the application of the term either to a religious experience or to its object; as it would seem to create a contradiction in terms. As Augustine put it, 'if that is ineffable which cannot be spoken, then that is not ineffable which is called ineffable' – as, once again, 'when this is said something is said' about God (*On Christian Doctrine*, bk. I, ch. 6; *ET* Indianapolis, IN: Bobbs-Merrill, 1958, pp. 10–11). But, surely, neither God/the Absolute, or any experience of the same, is *totally* indescribable. Hence, Yandell further argues that there can be 'no totally aconceptual ineffable experiences'; although he also goes on to conclude – after a detailed technical argument – that 'there seems to be no good reason to accept the ineffability theme in any of its versions' (Yandell, 1993, part II, p. 115).

We might prefer to retain the word, however, while thinking in terms of *degrees of 'effability'* (as we might speak of degrees of closeness, or aptness, of different analogies to something) – with 'totally ineffable' at one end or limit of the scale.

Proudfoot also observes that ineffability is a relative term. 'Nothing can be either effable or ineffable *tout court* [simply]', he explains, but only with respect to a particular language system (Proudfoot, 1985, pp. 125–6). This is unquestionably true, but it is not perhaps very helpful. He further argues, more contentiously, that in this context ineffability language is used as a *grammatical rule*, a 'criterion for the identification of an experience as mystical' (1985, p. 127).

In this role, it precludes the possibility that the experience being related could be captured ('wholly captured'?) in words, or in any language system prescribed for it: thus maintaining, or creating, a sense of mystery in the hearer or reader.

Others have suggested a similar, *second-order status* for the language of ineffability, as telling us how to use and interpret the language of the mystics and other religious experiencers.

- Richard Gale submits that the term is merely an honorific title marking the value and intensity of an experience. 'I believe that the real reason for the mystic's claiming some sort of unique ineffability for his experience is to be found in the inestimable significance and value which the experience has for him. It seems that the more highly we prize some experience the more we shun applying concepts to it.' In effect, then, the mystic is telling us that 'it is the direct experience itself which counts and that language is a very poor substitute' (Gale, 1960, p. 474).
- Arguing along similar lines, Ninian Smart reminds us that the language of ineffability/indescribability is not unique to religious experience and should not to be taken in an absolute way. Smart suggests that such terms have the function of a 'special sort of intensifier' that 'both concedes and yet mitigates the failure in expression' (Smart, 1958, p. 70). Again, these terms express the inadequacy of our descriptive language, as well as marking a superlative description (cf. the more everyday phrase, 'I simply cannot say how grateful I am') (Smart, 1978, pp. 17–20; cf. Smart, in Katz, 1983, pp. 120–1).
- According to a yet more extreme suggestion, 'to say of an experience that it is ineffable is not a statement of the impossibility of expressing it, but a way of expressing it, to wit, a way of saying that it is non-linguistic' (Short, 1995, p. 667). This would be to treat this sort of language, when used to report on the object of a religious experience, as *non-cognitive*: in the sense of not fact-asserting or fact-denying, not information imparting, *not descriptive* – and, therefore, as not having any factual meaning (see above).

There are problems as well as possibilities with describing the transcendent in either analogies or metaphors (see above; cf. Astley, 2004, chs 4, 5; 2010, ch. 3); but both forms of language implicitly acknowledge the difficulty of describing any ultimate mystery in the nature of God, or Ultimate Reality: something that could be fully captured by *no* human descriptions. But they do this without giving up the task of theology altogether, and without playing the stop card of total ineffability – preferring what has been called a 'limited and provisional ineffability' (Kwan, 2011, p. 55).

Walter Stace and, more recently, Robert Forman have suggested that ineffability applies to an experience *while it is being experienced*. On Forman's view, as the mystic is engaged in meditative procedures that decrease her or his cognitive activity, during that mystical experience '*all* language, is forgotten'. Thus 'any language used to describe or report on that experience is *not* language which was employed in the primary event' (Forman, 1990, p. 41). (Forman has called this the 'forgetting model'.)

It may be argued, however, that this practical reason for the mystic's incapacity to formulate a description should not prevent this taking place after the experience is over.

Paradoxicality

Claims to ineffability are often associated with the idea of *paradoxes*, linguistic expressions that are normally understood as *apparent contradictions* and therefore defined as 'seemingly absurd or self-contradictory' propositions 'that may in fact be true'. It is undeniable that religious language, like the religious experience itself, is often 'out of the ordinary'; and the employment of paradoxical language can be one way of pointing to this claim. The P-word may be used, then, on occasions and in part, simply for rhetorical effect, or as another way to cope with the difficulty of describing the experience or its object (see above; cf. Gellman, 2005, p. 144). But *actual logical absurdity* is rarely defended. Most writers on religious experience prefer to honour Aristotle's law of non-contradiction, which states that an attribute cannot both belong and not belong to the same subject in the same respect.

The main exception to this policy was Walter Stace. His argument was that mystical paradoxes are accurate descriptions of an *experience that is literally self-contradictory* (Stace, 1961, ch. 5). He believed that 'the laws of logic do not apply to mystical experience' and was therefore willing to claim that mystical paradoxes reflect paradoxical experience – 'the language correctly mirrors the experience' (pp. 304–5). On this view, when logical contradictions are spotted in the language of mystics, we should assume that they are intended. (Stace also claimed that this is why mystics – understandably but mistakenly – assert that their experience is 'ineffable'.) All attempts to explain away mystical paradoxes fail, Stace argues. They cannot be explained as rhetoric, metaphor or as ambiguous language. 'In my view', he wrote, 'the mystical experience is inherently beyond the logical understanding, not merely *apparently* so' (Stace, 1961, p. 175, italics original). Notoriously, Stace argued for all of the following paradoxical claims (1961, ch. 3):

1 mystical experiences are neither subjective nor objective;
2 the laws of logic do not apply to statements about mystical experience or its object;
3 all Pure Selves are the same and the same as the World Self; and
4 the mystical One both is and is not identical with the physical universe.

Claim (1) that mystical experiences transcends the duality of the subject–object distinction that underlies most veridical experience (Stace, 1961, pp. 218, 231–2) has been criticized on the grounds that mystical experience is an experience *of something*, and therefore is in some sense an objective claim. The 'contradiction theory' (2) holds that the laws of logic are 'the necessary rules for thinking of and dealing with a *multiplicity* of separate items', but that 'in the One there are no separate items to be kept distinct, and therefore logic has no meaning for it' (Stace, 1961, pp. 270–1). However, the principle that beliefs should not be self-contradictory appears to be a formal criterion of rationality, without which no further discussion can take place. As self-contradictions say nothing, they cannot serve a descriptive purpose. Wainwright (1981, pp. 138–59) also argues that Stace's philosophical arguments against dualism and monism are flawed; and – against (3) and (4) – that he has 'failed to establish that the world, individual selves and the One both are and are not the same' (p. 159). He contends, therefore, against Stace, that mystical experience is 'not alogical [i.e. *non*-logical] and does not transcend subjectivity and objectivity' (p. 232). Wainwright concludes that at least some paradoxes can 'either be explained as metaphors, or instances of rhetorical exaggeration, or resolved by ambiguation'; while other paradoxes are simply false, where they are clearly logically impossible (1981, pp. 148, 154).

Stace does seem to have adopted a highly unconventional account of religious language. Ian Ramsey declared himself 'surprised that Stace, after his vigorous campaign against literalism in the higher reaches, takes this word "unity" so "literally" as to suppose that the experience which it characterises must be necessarily a uniform blank. On such a view the best theology will be negative indeed; so negative as to say nothing whatever' (Ramsey, 1955, p. 122). Hywel D. Lewis agreed that Stace's position creates an 'extraordinary' paradox, the perplexing consequence of an 'unsound' and 'presumptuous' understanding of transcendence (Lewis, 1969, pp. 310–19). The list goes on. Peter Moore, describing Stace's view as 'somewhat eccentric', argues that such paradoxes *are* more often found in rhetorical or figurative, theological or liturgical contexts, rather than as descriptions of experience (Moore, in Katz, 1978, pp. 106–7).

Ninian Smart concurs with other critics that paradoxes are often rhetorical, 'constructive Irishisms as it were … intelligible challenges to assumptions', although some are analogies:[6] neither category should be regarded as contradictions. He argues that even the so-called 'dialectical paradoxes', 'do not work unless the principle of non-contradiction holds' (Smart, in Katz, 1983, pp. 121–2). John E. Smith regards mystical insights articulated in a dialectical fashion as designed primarily to evoke a sympathetic and receptive mind, or as pointing to 'the path that the meditator is to follow' (Smith, in Katz, 1983, pp. 264–5). And Proudfoot treats paradoxicality rather like ineffability (see above); it is a feature of the 'rules governing the identification of an experience as mystical', which serves the function of shaping 'the expectations of seekers' (Proudfoot, 1985, pp. 135–6).

Suggestions for Further Reading

Introductory

Astley, Jeff, 2004, *Exploring God-Talk: Using Language in Religion*, London: Darton, Longman and Todd.
Gellman, Jerome, 2018 [2004], 'Mysticism', *Stanford Encyclopedia of Philosophy*, available at https://plato.stanford.edu/entries/mysticism/, § 3.

Advanced

Blum, Jason, 2012, 'Radical Empiricism and the Unremarkable Nature of Mystic Ineffability', *Method and Theory in the Study of Religion*, 24, pp. 201–19.
Soskice, Janet Martin, 1985, *Metaphor and Religious Language*, Oxford: Clarendon, ch. VIII (pp. 142–61).

Notes

1 The opposite adjective, 'effable' (meaning 'describable in words') is now rarely used. 'Eff' and 'effing', alas, have rather different meanings …

2 The radical non-realist, Don Cupitt, interprets the supposed 'experiences' themselves as 'the product of a process of unconscious religious thought' that merely says 'something important and interesting about *the experient*' (Cupitt, 2001, p. 79, italics original). But in this case the language is still descriptive and therefore cognitive (fact-asserting).

3 Models such as 'father', 'rock', 'good', 'wise' are qualified by the adjectives or adverbs 'infinite(ly)', 'heavenly', 'eternal', etc., or by juxtaposing a variety of models (thus, God is 'shepherd' *but also* 'judge', 'husband', 'mother', 'king', 'wind' and so on).

4 Ramsey insisted on speaking of this as religious language's 'representative' function, reserving the term 'description' for literal accounts of mundane objects.

5 This is sometimes described as following the *via negativa* or 'negative way', which is much emphasized in Eastern Orthodox theology. For a much more careful analysis of the precise meaning of these terms, see Coakley, 2009, p. 281 n. 3.

6 Smart treated the difference between analogy and metaphor as one of degree rather than of kind; whereas for Thomas Aquinas and his followers, *analogy is a literal usage* in which words can be literally applied to God but only with a 'stretched' or 'extended' meaning, although not one that has been stretched so far as to become figurative.

13

Religious Experience and Revelation

There is no doubt that, 'on the whole, theologians tend to be ambivalent about "religious experience"'. This is largely because Christian theology wishes to prioritize, not human experience, but the doctrines (literally 'teachings') of the Christian faith. At least on the surface, then, 'theology is not the introspective exploration of the human condition, but the attempt to understand what it means to have been subject to God's address in the history of a particular nation (Israel) and the life, teaching, death and resurrection of a particular person (Jesus)' (Robert Pope, in Schmidt, 2016b, pp. 105, 109).[1]

> **Exercise: Among the Articles**
>
> *Read and critically assess this essay:*
>
> **Pope, Robert, 2016, 'Immediate Revelation or the Basest Idolatry? Theology and Religious Experience',** in Bettina E. Schmidt (ed.), ***The Study of Religious Experience: Approaches and Methodologies***, **Sheffield: Equinox, pp. 105–24.**
>
> The theologians' ambivalence about religious experience results from its advocates' concern (a) for the person who receives a religious experience, (b) for 'religion' rather than specifically for '"the religions" (or one of them)', and especially (c) for elevating religious experience

> over divine revelation. However, even within a traditional theological framework, Pope argues, the concept of tacit knowledge may permit religious experiences to 'retain a place in helping to form our patterns of knowing, ... as an aspect ... of faith seeking understanding' or 'theological reflection'.

Revelation versus Religious Experience?

In theological debate, the main issue over religious experience is undoubtedly its apparent conflict with the theological doctrine of revelation. The word 'revelation' is from the late Latin, *revelare*, to 'lay bare'. Revelation is understood as the disclosure or 'unveiling' of God or, more usually, of God's word, character or will. In Christianity and some other religions (especially Islam), the authority of revelation has held precedence from their beginnings.

For the eighteenth-century Protestant theologian, Fredrich Schleiermacher (see Chapter 18), religion was viewed essentially as *piety*. This was, in turn, understood as a 'feeling', an 'intuition', a 'sense and taste for the infinite', a 'feeling of absolute dependence' or 'God-consciousness'. God is directly known in this religious experience. Although he believed that religious experience was shaped by belief and practice, doctrine for Schleiermacher was regarded as something secondary to and derivative from this experience: so much so, in fact, that he characterized Christian doctrines as 'accounts of the Christian religious affections set forth in speech' (Schleiermacher, 1928, p. 76).

Schleiermacher has therefore been interpreted by many as engaged in 'theology from below up' – a subjective method of doing theology in which humans find out about God by introspection, rather than by listening to God, and therefore create an anthropocentric theology or a psychologizing of revelation.

This elevation of religious experiences to a primordial and primary role, and its close companion of a liberal[2] understanding of doctrine that views it solely as a (partial and inevitably inadequate) expression of religious experiences and emotions, has inevitably been criticized for displacing divine revelation 'as the real locus of authority' (Livingstone, 1971, p. 110). In doing so, it is argued, it also removes concern for the truth about, and the truth that *is* God from the centre of Christianity. 'For Schleiermacher', the great twentieth-century theologian Karl Barth wrote, 'proclaiming God means proclaiming one's own piety', not announcing the objective reality and Word of the transcendent (Barth, 1972, p. 454). Schleiermacher's viewpoint, therefore, is in radical contrast with Barth's 'downward theological method', in which God is the subject of the act of revelation rather than the object of religious experience. Barth wrote:

> the Reformers propagated the teaching of the Word of God in its correlation with faith as the work of the Holy Spirit in man.
> Schleiermacher reversed the order of this thought. What interests him is the question of man's action in regard to God. (Barth, 1972, p. 459)[3]

For Barth and others, therefore, knowledge of God comes exclusively from the activity and initiative of God, routed through the incarnation of Christ; and not through a general religious experience grounded in God's creative relationship with all humankind.

Barth famously insisted that the 'only antidote to the weakness he observed in liberal Protestantism was the vigorous exclusion from the principles of theology of any kind of independent status for human rationality or potentiality' (Sykes, 1979, p. 46). *Human reason* is therefore severely put in its (limited and subordinate) place in the account of religious truth and religious knowing given by Barth and his followers. *Religious experience* was also rejected, because it was regarded as falling into the same category as unaided, universal human reason, when treated as a source of religious knowledge (in 'natural theology'). They must both be rejected *for theological reasons*, as these phenomena represent fallen humanity 'writ large'. Neither reason nor religious experience can deliver what they pretend to offer – a 'natural' way from the human to the divine. And that is because God, the transcendent creator, can only be known 'through God': the human reception of such revelation being understood as a matter of God's inspiring grace and our response of obedience, *not* in terms of our autonomous religious experience or reasoning (e.g. Barth, 1957a, ch. V, sect. 26; 1957b, pp. 715, 727–40; 1962, pp. 846–50). Theologians who take this line argue that, 'while there is clearly talk of religious experience in the Christian tradition, its significance in theological reflection is secondary to the revelation of God in Christ' (Pope, in Schmidt, 2016b, p. 116).

But in the view of the psychologist, Rodney Stark, *phenomenologically speak-*

ing revelations 'are merely the most intense and intimate form of religious or mystical experiences – those episodes involving perceptions and sensations which are interpreted as communication or contact, however, slight, with the divine' (Stark, 1999, p. 291). In revelation, 'the divine has not only taken the person to his bosom, but into his confidence', as 'the recipient is given a message concerning divine wishes or intentions' (although, admittedly, this is the least common form of religious experience reported in Stark's survey of 3,000 American subjects: see Stark, 1965, pp. 107–11).

Is experience a denial of revelation? Not if 'experience understood as encounter is always disclosure of reality transcending the one who experiences' (Smith, 1968, p. 49); and not if 'a revelation is an experience that is brought about deliberately by its object and, at least in part, for the sake of the knowledge which the experiencing subject is to gain' (Mavrodes, 1970, p. 53). In order for there to be any revelation, God must presumably have to be and to do something; but as a matter of logic, *human beings must also experience this 'unveiling'*. Hence, 'To disclose oneself one has to make oneself apparent ... at the heart of revelation there lies religious experience' (Smart, 1969, p. 119). In fact, Schleiermacher himself claimed that 'every intuition and every original feeling proceeds from revelation' (Schleiermacher, 1958, p. 89).

Religious experiences may be God-given if revelation is God's gift, but these experiences also 'belong' to those who receive them. And, certainly, their descriptions and interpretations do; so that at least in terms of *human acceptance and reception*, theologians may claim that revelation is 'nothing apart from human apprehension of it' (Tanner, 1997, p. 266). If God were wholly to take over the cognitive and interpretative faculties of human beings, the reports of biblical authors would be inerrant ('incapable of error'), as biblical fundamentalists insist. And in that case, religious experience would seem to lose its independent status. But biblical scholarship has recognized since the eighteenth century that the biblical texts are the products of human, and therefore fallible and sinful, recipients of God's message, activity or encounter; and have therefore interpreted the Scriptures as including fallible human interpretations in response to God's revelation.

God gives, then; but humans must be open to *receive* what God gives, or there will be no communication, and nothing will ever be revealed. More generally, 'the Christian faith cannot be apprehended as true until the experience of the believer appropriates it as true' (Inbody, 2005, p. 52). 'Revelation, to be revelation, has to be in principle, subjectively effective. It has to be such that it can find its [way] into the life of the individuals and communities to which it is directed' (William Abraham, in Avis, 1997, p. 213).[4] Even those who take the highest view of revelation claim that this affirmative response is crucial in the process of revelation, although they often insist that it is only by a further divine act of enlightenment, or *inward testimony of the Holy Spirit* (cf. Chapter 4), that humans can become convinced that this revelation came to us, as the Reformer John Calvin put it, 'by the instrumentality of men, from the very mouth of God'.

Before leaving this point, however, we may reflect on one of William James's defining characteristics of religious (or, at least, of 'mystical') experience, that is *passivity* (James, 1960, p. 368; cf. Clarke, 1981, pp. 521–2). Hood and Francis (2013, p. 394) claim that this element 'emphasizes both the experience of being controlled by a superior power and the undeserved, gratuitous nature of the mystical experience'. This is surely also a feature of any revelation. While the human will may be engaged in preparation for or the facilitation of such experiences, and to some extent in their later interpretation, the activity of the Other in *bestowing* an experience or revelation is an essential element, at least in theistic religious traditions.

This characteristic is also often reported in experiences captured in the wider and more democratic net of surveys and invited testimonies about religious experience: 'it came from the outside and unasked' (356, Alister Hardy Archive; Hardy, 1979, p. 77); 'the experience has never been forgotten … [But] it was quite unsought' (2848, Alister Hardy Archive; Maxwell and Tschudin, 1990, p. 52). It is hard for the Christian theologian *not* to find parallels here with many traditional accounts of the nature of God's *grace*, which is normally defined as the free, forgiving love and acceptance that God bestows, regardless of a person's intellectual, moral, spiritual, religious or other merit, and is so central to Christian theology as to have been described as 'theological shorthand for God's continual engagement with us' (Gorringe, 1989, p. 169).

A tradition that celebrates such gratuitous activity on the part of God need not feel particularly uneasy about the unpredictable – and therefore disruptive – examples of religious experience in the empirical literature. For Joshua is not applauded for his concern that God's Spirit may be at work too widely, causing the wrong people to prophesy in the wrong places (Num. 11.24–30); nor is Bishop Butler much commended – not even by Anglicans – for assuming that the Spirit would not rest on the wrong people, in this case those who are not episcopally authorized.[5] *To pneuma* – the wind or Spirit – 'blows where it wills', as Jesus is reported to have said to Nicodemus (John 3.8).

None of this means, however, that each and every apparently revelatory religious experience should be given exactly the same authority. For what *counts as* divine revelation will be judged by a range of criteria, including moral, spiritual and theological evaluations of its *content*, and of its *reception* and *effects* also (see also Chapter 7).

Religious Experience versus Theology?

In an early and wide-ranging review of the relevant writings of Alister Hardy and the first publications of the Religious Experience Research Unit, which extended over many issues of the journal *New Blackfriars*, the Dominican theologian Simon Tugwell argued that 'one very sad consequence of this anti-doctrinal, emotional picture of religion is that it leaves no room' for what he called 'the gnostic, [noetic] element',[6] and therefore for 'any truth which can fascinate and fulfil the mind' (Tugwell, 1979, p. 72). This is a serious claim, and those who wish to hold together religious experience and theological reflection need to respond to it.

In 1273, an earlier Dominican, Thomas Aquinas, now regarded as the pre-eminent Christian theologian of the Middle Ages, responded to a mystical vision that he received during mass by giving up work on his massive treatise, the *Summa Theologiae*. Afterwards, he told his secretary, Brother Reginald, 'All that I have written appears to be as so much straw after the things that have been revealed to me.' However, few would seriously interpret this story to mean that we should no longer bother with that treatise or any of Aquinas' other books, or *anything* from the vast libraries of theological reflection that have been written down the centuries. While most theologians would not want to deny some value to religious experience, even fewer would really want to deny truth-claims based on reflective, systematic and even dogmatic or speculative theology, either.

There is increasing support for the view adumbrated above (in Chapter 10) that, whether religious or spiritual experience is an experience of some sort of transcendent reality or not cannot solely be judged by the fact that someone undergoes that experience. Experiences are not 'self-authenticating' in that sense. They cannot stand alone. That is why what Scripture and doctrine teaches, and what philosophers and theologians debate, remains highly relevant to claims to religious experience; as what others say is, too, of course, including psychologists and sociologists, historians and (now) experimental neuroscientists. They all have a right to have their say.

But 'having a say' is not always a matter of 'having the last word'. Nor is it to be thought of as having the *only* word. At least, that is the view taken by those who regard religious experience claims at all seriously.

Swimming rather against the theological tide, Michael Sudduth has recently gone so far as to argue that *'religious experiences have made dogmatic theology possible'*, partly because 'dogmatic theology involves a systematic reflection on the data of scripture, but scripture is in large part a record of religious experiences ostensibly involving the communication of divine truths' (see Chapter 16). But Sudduth adds a further reason, that 'religious experience and its data *confirm some of the content of dogmatic theology'* – most generally with regard to beliefs about 'the personal nature of God and the fact of divine-human interaction' (Sudduth, 2009, p. 229, italics added, cf. 231).

Religious experience may also contribute to a *natural* theology that seeks to develop a knowledge of God independently of biblical revelation (cf. Taliaferro, 2012, p. 18; Kwan, 2012). While famously rejected by some Reformed (Calvinist) Christian theologians, such as Barth, natural theology has historically been widely endorsed by both Protestant and Catholic traditions. Sudduth (2009, pp. 224–5) lists the contribution of religious experience to natural theology in:

- the argument from religious experience to certain theistic beliefs;
- the grounding of beliefs in particular divine actions towards particular recipients; and
- increasing the antecedent probability of theism, strengthening the conclusions of natural theology.

Propositional and Non-Propositional Revelation

The concept of revelation has been analysed in two main ways.

1. On the understanding of a *propositional* or *verbal revelation*, God tells people about Godself by revealing a *set of truths or statements* about God's nature or intention. However it is conveyed to its recipients, this is a form of religious communication that arrives already expressed in words, although (as noted earlier) God may 'adjust' and 'descend' to our capacities, 'accommodating' this revelation to our limited understanding (cf. Stiver, 2009, p. 92; Davis, 2009, pp. 39–40).

2. On what is sometimes called the *non-propositional* view of revelation, however, what is revealed are not any words or truths about God but *God's own nature, activity or presence* (cf. Hick, 1983, pp. 68–75). Thus, for example, God is revealed as the God of judgement and love in and through events of the 'salvation history' of the Old and New Testaments – in the exodus from Egypt, the struggles for justice for the poor within Israel, and pre-eminently in Jesus. Such events reveal the activity and the character of God (Baillie, 1964, ch. IV) as people 'saw in them' – or 'looked on' them, or 'saw them *as*' – the grace and demand of the Almighty. More radically, God may also become known more directly as an encountered reality, and something of God's character and intentions inferred from that experience.[7] On these non-propositional views, the theology that clothes these revelations is not itself God's direct word. It is, rather, composed from human reflections on the events, including descriptions of the kind of God whom people 'perceived' as acting behind and within these historical events and personal encounters.[8]

Yet, 'even if one holds that it is God who is revealed, and not propositions about God, this cannot be rendered intelligible in a form which does not entail that the person to whom God is revealed is thereby made aware of some critical truths about God' (Penelhum, 1971, p. 92). Regardless of the form that a revelation may take, therefore, *in order for there to be knowledge (or belief) about it the revelatory experience needs to be transcribed into truths.* Only then can it count as a revelatory experience of God.[9] On the model of non-propositional revelation, it is most obvious that it is human beings who give this revelation its words. But even within propositional revelation, experience plays its part, as does human reflection and, therefore, 'insight'.

Interestingly, these two interpretations of revelation seem to imply two different analogies for the underlying 'revelation experience' undergone by those who receive them.

- Propositional revelation best fits an *auditory model*, with revelation regarded as a sort of 'hearing', although it involves some 'inner sense' instead of our ordinary sense organs (and is sometimes 'seen' – cf. Isa. 1.1; 2.1). On this model, God 'speaks' the 'word of the LORD' and humans 'hear' and remember God's self-revelation, a divine message that they then have to record and interpret.
- Non-propositional revelation seems to imply, by contrast, a *visual model*, in which humans 'see' God's 'acts' (in, say, history, Nature or Jesus), and occasional disclosures of God's presence and nature (or, say, Christ's status). They or others may then describe, interpret/record these events, but their main contribution will be *what they infer from these experiences* about the divine character and intentions, and afterwards report or proclaim.

Exercise

Which of these two interpretations, do you think:

1 is closer to the biblical understanding?
2 is more defensible, theologically or philosophically?
3 provides the better fit with reports across the spectrum of religious and spiritual experiences?
4 provides the better fit with the understanding of revelation in particular religious traditions?
5 offers the most defensible *analogy* for religious experience?

And why?

On the face of it, prophetic religious experience would seem to suggest a propositional analysis. 'The word of the LORD came to me saying …' is how the Old Testament prophets spoke of the revelatory event (e.g. Jer. 1.1–10; 2.1–3; Ezek. 6.1, etc.; cf. Isa. 20.2–4). Paul sometimes seems to be saying something similar (e.g. 1 Cor. 7.10; 11.23). Although biblical scholars now seem reluctant to endorse this once-popular view (see below, Chapter 16), other authors have declared that 'it seems absurd to deny that God reveals words' (Davis, 2009, p. 35). Outside Scripture, similar experiences have been claimed by Pentecostal/charismatic Christians and others who receive 'words of revelation', as well as by classical mystics, etc.[10] The model is often criticized as a type of 'divine dictation theory', in which God ensures that his words are infallibly recorded in Scripture or Church tradition; but there is no need to insist that the divine words that enter the minds of the human recipients of revelation (possibly through some form of telepathic communication) are received, understood or recorded by them without any human contribution or error creeping in.

The non-propositional analysis is now by far the more popular, and widely considered to be the most plausible account of how historical events are interpreted as revelatory by the authors and traditions of Scripture. While many theologians adopt this position, it is still most strongly represented by liberal scholars, some of whom have even argued that '"God speaking" is a myth for "the development of human insights in response to Divine guidance"' (Ward, 1994, p. 129; cf. Maurice Wiles, in Avis, 1997, pp. 103–10). Nevertheless, it has to be admitted that the 'analogical base' of divine revelation – its analogy with *human* revealing – suggests a wider range of meanings and authorizes no straightforward relation to agency (as admitted by Wiles, in Avis, 1997, p. 102).

Some authors object to the *disparagement of propositions* in many discussions concerning the concept of revelation, regarding the reasoning behind this as tendentious. In the history of doctrine, even among medieval theologians, 'doctrinal affirmations are to be recognized as perceptions, not total descriptions, pointing beyond themselves … [as] reliable, yet incomplete, descriptions of reality' (McGrath, 1997, p. 17). Nor is propositional revelation *unduly intellectualist*, and it should not be understood as *made up of abstract and existentially irrelevant knowledge or static truths*, 'inscribed in stone', that are unsuited to the dynamics of changing lives and cultures (Gunton, 1995, ch. 1).

In fact, theologians may agree that 'propositions are secondary and therefore dependent for their truth on the personal presence of God to the world which is revelation; and … upon the gift of the Spirit who mediates the revelation in words appropriate to different historical contexts'. But they may also stress that these propositions are also *intrinsically related* to what they articulate, 'the revelatory action of God in Christ'; and insist that *that* wisdom 'had to be given cognitive form if it was [to be] worthy of belief' and to become communicable to others. Revelation, therefore, one may argue yet again, *has to become propositional* (Gunton, 1995, pp. 9, 100–1, 106).

Novelty, Variety and Openness

The liberal approach to religious experience and revelation espoused by Schleiermacher and later, mainly Protestant, theologians was almost invariably associated with a striking emphasis on openness and provisionality in religious belief. Because experience prioritizes the human psyche, and the theologizing which engages with it is regarded as a very human activity, *liberal Christianity* stands in marked contrast to all 'theologies of obedience' that view human frailty and wilful sinfulness as inevitably victorious, corrupting factors. It also opposes the more extreme, fundamentalist accounts that believe that God has immunized divine revelation from any sort of error.

Liberal openness may, in principle, include a positive attitude to the great diversity of different religious and spiritual experiences that exist, which itself tends to disrupt any attempt to narrow and fix the limits of theology.[11] Christian doctrine itself comprehends a great variety of positions – much more than many non-theologians realize (see Astley, 2010, pp. 17–18). The liberal may well regard this diversity as a good thing; as diversity is so perceived elsewhere: as one engine of evolution within populations of living things that need to adapt to better fit changing environments, for instance; and as a significant expression of individuality within human societies.

Yet many regard the variety of religious experience as suspect, just because of its variety; often extending their disquiet to claims about how widely it is spread.[12]

While some versions of Christianity adopt a strong view of revelation that confines it to the canon of *Scripture*, others – especially Catholic and Orthodox Christians – recognize a '*tradition*' alongside the Bible that derives from the transmitted teachings and practices of the Christian faith and represents another – however subservient – medium of revelation, within a Church that is seen as permeated and guided by God's Spirit. Inevitably, however, the more traditional the tradition, the better; and it is the most ancient crystallizations and deposits of this twenty-century long tradition that are most esteemed. Hence, traditional Protestant Churches took over much of this non-controversial tradition (in particular, its ancient creeds and doctrinal definitions) and in some cases adopted or respected its liturgical forms and the theological reflections of the early 'church fathers', while in principle testing these traditions – and all later novelties of doctrine and practice – in terms of their 'conformity to Scripture'.[13]

Still, the tension between the *conservation* and the *development* of Christian belief has been a recurrent concern throughout Christian history, especially where these beliefs were understood as part of God's continuing inspiration and revelation, which might even produce creative insights that enabled the records of Christianity's 'original events or words to be read in a new way' (Brown, 1994, p. 128). In principle if not always in practice, the Pentecostal and charismatic movements within the contemporary Church accept an even more radical notion of new revelation that is given through the charismatic gifts of prophecy and interpretation of 'tongues' (glossolalia), which are patently grounded in *contemporary religious experiences*.

Whatever theological principles they appeal to, Christians do well to recognize that their faith itself soon developed as a challenge to another faith (developing Judaism), and that they look to a Lord who was extremely disruptive of many settled religious, moral and spiritual convictions. And there can be no doubt that, down the subsequent centuries, Christianity has certainly changed considerably from its origins. While Christianity may claim *continuity despite these changes*, and although radical change *is* compatible with a continuing identity (as our own life histories show), markedly new and different beliefs and novel religious and moral practices have developed within the faith, notwithstanding its tests of 'conformity'. Perhaps the Churches need to be more honest about the many ways in which Christianity has in the past and still continues to 'change its mind'. Contemporary religious experience, it may be argued, merely adds something else into this mix. And it by no means the most novel or the most disruptive ingredient.

It is only fair to point out, however, that those who value the elements discussed here will be able to find similar claims to variety, openness and novelty in other traditions within Christianity and Christian theology that do *not* so clearly foreground religious experiences. Thus, the fact of the development of Christian doctrine was strenuously argued by the nineteenth-century Anglo-Catholic (but soon to be converted to a Roman Catholic) theologian, John Henry Newman (Newman, 1975 [1845]). And variety, openness and novelty today may be explained in terms of changes in interpretation of Christian Scriptures and traditions, sometimes amounting to claims to a *continuing revelation* through further imaginative reflection on biblical texts (cf. Brown, 1999, 2000), or with reference to a 'generosity' and *'openness to dialogue' now regarded as implicit* in the Christian faith, even in some of its apparently conservative understandings (cf. Franke, 2005; Fodor, 2005, pp. 244–5).

Suggestions for Further Reading

Introductory

Avis, Paul (ed.), 1997, *Divine Revelation*, London: Darton, Longman and Todd.
Gunton, Colin E., 1995, *A Brief Theology of Revelation*, Edinburgh: T. & T. Clark.
Land, Steven J., 1990, 'Pentecostal Spirituality: Living in the Spirit', in Louis Dupré and Don E. Saliers, with John Meyendorff (eds), *Christian Spirituality: Post-Reformation and Modern*, London: SCM Press, ch. 17 (pp. 479–99).

Advanced

Brown, David, 1994, 'Did Revelation Cease?', in Alan G. Padgett (ed.), *Reason and the Christian Religion*, Oxford: Clarendon, ch. 6 (pp. 121–41).
Davis, Stephen T., 2009, 'Revelation and Inspiration', in Thomas P. Flint and Michael C. Rea (eds), *The Oxford Handbook of Philosophical Theology*, Oxford: Oxford University Press, ch. 2 (pp. 30–53).
Dulles, Avery, SJ, 1983, *Models of Revelation*, Dublin: Gill and Macmillan.
Ward, Keith, 1994, *Religion and Revelation: A Theology of Revelation in the World's Religions*, Oxford: Oxford University Press.

Notes

1 We should register the emphasis here on the *particularity* of revelation.

2 Or, to use George Lindbeck's term, 'experiential-expressive' (Lindbeck, 1984; see Chapter 18, below).

3 Ellen Charry has argued that 'Schleiermacher has stated the case backward' in a different sense, in that it is Christian doctrines that shape religious feelings into attitudes, 'even unselfconsciously so' (Charry, 2007, pp. 421–2).

4 More philosophically, reveal is a 'success' or 'achievement verb', rather than a task verb. But to limit the achievement to one 'in principle' (as Abraham does here) goes against the spirit of this distinction, and Gilbert Ryle's rule that 'in applying an achievement verb we are asserting that some state of affairs obtains over and above that which consists in the performance, if any, of the subservient task activity' (Ryle, 1963, pp. 143–4).

5 Joseph Butler, while Bishop of Bristol, had a famous encounter with John Wesley, in which they disagreed on Wesley's right to preach without a license.

6 The text actually reads 'neotic'.

7 In Avery Dulles's subtle analysis, 'revelation as doctrine' (the propositional view) is distinguished from four types of broadly non-propositional forms of revelation that interpret revelation 'as history', 'as inner experience', as 'dialectical presence' (gracious encounter through God's word) and 'as new awareness' in an expansion of consciousness (Dulles, 1983, part one).

8 On yet another view of revelation, God may be said simply to supervise or authorize a person's actual writing or speaking, for this gives their words – which are the creation of human beings – a divine authority and function as 'God's words'. The analogy here is with a senior official or manager signing a letter or issuing a report that has been written 'in his/her name' by others. See Wolterstorff, 1995, especially pp. 51–4, 186–7.

9 Some would argue further – in a manner that might have both expressivists and constructivists applauding, although at different points – that 'like poetry, visionary and prophetic language is not the expression of an experience *by means* of language but an experience in language' and 'whatever contact God, the Absolute, the Transcendental ... had with the prophet it was by way of language and the images and meanings and insights it generates' (Barrett, 1990, pp. 213, 219, italics original).

10 Thus, the famous American Cistercian Trappist monk, Thomas Merton (1915–68), reported hearing an inner voice telling him to 'Go to mass' and on another occasion, 'You know what you ought to do. Why don't you do it?' (Merton, 1948, pp. 206, 248).

11 It should be clear that, even despite any recognition of a common core to the traditions of the world's religions, they remain astonishingly *diverse*.

12 Even though few of these critics would praise the attempts of Joshua or eighteen-century bishops to limit the spread of the Spirit, as noted earlier.

13 Although this sometimes meant no more than checking that they didn't contradict Scripture.

14

Gender Issues

If, as feminist theory would claim, all experience is *gendered*, we should expect that this will be true of religious and spiritual experiences also. Jerome Gellman (2018, §9) lists three main feminist criticisms of a perceived androcentric bias[1] within mysticism and its philosophical treatment.

- It is largely treated as a private psychological episode of a solitary person (as William James interpreted it), rather than being studied in its socio-political ramifications and through its current practices.
- At times it has ignored or marginalized women's mysticism. This is partly as a consequence of the fact that, historically, females were considered more vulnerable to demonic possession than men and their reports of religious experience were therefore treated with more suspicion.
- 'The traditional male construction of God has determined the way male philosophers think of theistic experience.'

> **Exercise: Among the Articles**
>
> *Read and critically assess the following journal article:*
>
> **Jantzen, Grace M., 1994, 'Feminists, Philosophers, and Mystics',** *Hypatia***, 9, 4, pp. 186–206.**
>
> This article provides a sociological perspective on the theological, historical and philosophical debates concerning religious experience. Grace Jantzen challenges the widely held view that mysticism is essentially characterized by intense, ineffable, subjective experiences.

> Actually, she writes, it 'has undergone a series of social constructions, which were never innocent of gendered struggles for power' (Jantzen, 1994, p. 186; see also Chapter 20, below). This social construction of mysticism must not be allowed to remove mysticism and women from their involvement with political and social justice.[2]

Jantzen has elsewhere argued that the tendency to interpret mysticism as monism by many, predominantly male, theologians and philosophers – even in the case of Christian mystics such as Bernard of Clairvaux, Meister Eckhart and John of the Cross – may be due to the scholarly assumption that the sexual imagery used by mystics to describe the union of God with 'the soul' implies a loss of self on behalf of the soul (which was always spoken of as feminine) as it is submerged by God (always spoken of as male).[3] But this reading of the images is not only 'simplistic' but also incorrect, as Jantzen shows. Reading the mystics properly and thus taking them seriously would, she suggests, 'radically undermine patriarchal ideas of sexuality and power' (Jantzen, 1989, pp. 163, 166).

Nonetheless, in her own feminist assessment of the notion of 'epistemic transformation' and of Teresa of Ávila, Sarah Coakley appeals to a recognition of the significance of a mystical union that goes beyond the normal limits of 'reason' and 'perception'. It is one in which 'we do not so much grasp or "perceive" God' (in what feminist philosophers call 'perception at a distance'), but 'more truly God grasps *us*' (as in our 'knowing and loving of another' person), in a 'fostered ... special epistemic passivity that is the condition for the possibility of this graced contemplative occurrence' (Coakley, 2009, pp. 300, 307–8). (The emphasis, presumably, should be on 'special' here.)

Elsewhere, Carole Rayburn maintains that 'too often and too unfairly, females have been seen as having a passive, receptive-only role in erotic experiences with males', and that this is a consequence of their having been 'socialized to fear ownership of their assertive actions' (Rayburn, 1995, p. 490). Interestingly, one empirical study (Hood and Hall, 1980, p. 195) reported that 'females used receptive language to describe both erotic and mystical experiences'; but in the case of males, although they 'used agentive [action] language to describe erotic experiences, they did not use agentive language to describe mystical experiences', employing receptive terms just as frequently as did the women. These authors argue that 'for males to speak of union with God has always been problematic, given the sexual or erotic descriptions that apply only to opposites' (p. 204).

The feminist scholar, Melissa Raphael, contends that Rudolf Otto's account of numinous experience, in particular (see Chapter 18), is 'mediated and constituted by the androcentrism of Otto's own world-view'; and that the rich variety of female religious experience goes well beyond the numinous experience alone. In addition to his male construct of God, as the Other to whom we must submit, Otto's emphasis on the *themes of separation, transcendence and the sacredness of spirit* is said to encourage a disparagement of women's spiritual experience and its own *themes of intimacy, immanence and the this-worldly*. For women, Raphael argues, the sacred is found within the created world and human embodied existence, and the material world is not regarded as a barrier to religious experience. The *lowliness and 'creature-feeling'*, identified by Otto as central to the experience of the sacred, are particularly problematic for women in a society dominated by men (Raphael, 1994, pp. 513, 518–22; and cf., more generally, Daly, 1973).

Mary Jo Neitz also criticizes the Batson, Schoenrade and Ventis model of dramatic, life-changing religious experience (1993, ch. 4, summarized on p. 115), which proposes a four-stage sequence of existential crisis (precipitated by the experience), self-surrender, a new vision and a new life. Neitz argues that a feminist reading would submit 'that this sequence of events is likely to have a profoundly different meaning for women than men'. The 'surrender of the self', for example, has very different connotations and implications for the two sexes. Above all, 'a feminist perspective forces us to ask whether a story that assumes autonomy as the starting point and then suggests that the outcome of religious experience is a wholeness that comes from pursuing a kind of disciplining of the will is equally appropriate for males and females in our culture' (Neitz, 1995, p. 523). (Let alone earlier cultures, one might add.) *Autonomy* is stereotypically and (to a large degree) empirically associated more with males than with females, even today; and relationships and 'connectedness' remain more typical attributes of females than of males. 'Rather than seeing the autonomous individual as unrealistically isolated from others', Neitz offers as a *preferable model* of autonomy 'the actions of a mother and child', in which we may 'see a form of autonomy that develops through relationships' – as well as a 'model of nurturing power' (p. 532).[4]

As one religion scholar has summarized the debate:

> Feminism accepts the principle that culture constructs the world of human beings and their beliefs, morals, ways of life, relationships, roles, and practices. Yet it adds the insight that men are the ones who do this social constructing of reality and that they do it to their own advantage. Within the frame of reference of feminism, male domination, therefore, is the distinctive characteristic of the religious experience of women. (Aden, 2013, p. 219)

In patriarchal societies, therefore, religion itself can be co-opted to enforce this domination. Feminists in general support both constructivism and anti-essentialism (see Chapter 8), as well as appreciating a wider diversity of religious experience. But Aden argues that a consistent anti-essentialist stance *undermines* the possibility of a collective political voice for women; and that 'any definition of a common core of women's experience across cultures' might seem to commit the same sin as the patriarchal position, by privileging 'a *certain type* of women's experience among the diversity' (Aden, 2013, p. 226, italics added). Further, historians of mysticism have not always welcomed a feminist critique that accuses them of sidelining the contribution of women mystics; although others have welcomed it. Thus, Bernard McGinn has commented on 'the entry of women into the once-patriarchal realm of theology', especially in this area, as 'helping to overcome, at least in a gradual and not yet final way, one of the most disastrous wrong-turns in the history of Western theology: the divorce sundering spiritual teaching from academic theology that became evident at least as early as the fourteenth century' (McGinn, 2013, p. 18).

An Appropriate Analogy?

Gwen Griffith-Dickson's 'telling analogy'[5] for religious experience may also be relevant in a chapter on gender issues, as the phenomenon she describes is more common in women than men. The analogy is introduced with the story of 'Prudence', who – having never had one – is 'a sceptic about orgasms'. Prudence consults her friends, and even her brothers, who report a variety of such experiences (some of them incompatible), despite their agreeing in warning her that, 'You cannot really describe it … You just have to experience it for yourself.' Later in life, Prudence undergoes scientific training and even conducts experiments on this experience with several volunteers under the gaze of 'impartial witnesses'. Sadly, all 'fail to achieve their aim under these laboratory conditions' (all, that is, except her 'indefatigable younger brother', who produces the desired effect even in a laboratory …).

Orgasms are, apparently, like religious experiences, in that:

- not everyone has one;
- those who do often give conflicting descriptions while frequently regarding their different experiences as examples of the same thing; and
- perfectly good naturalistic explanations exist for them without capturing 'how it felt'.

In these respects, we might agree that this is a very illuminating analogy. Griffith-Dickson concludes, however, that we have here 'a model of how something can be experienced "in oneself", "of oneself", while it still makes sense to speak of the intrinsic participation of another' (Griffith-Dickson, 2000, pp. 133–6, 139). Yet, the author's unpacking of the analogy quite explicitly states that these events don't always rely on the presence of another. But 'intrinsic' means 'essential', 'belonging naturally together'. One could argue, then, that *another* is 'natural' to the orgasmic event as an intrinsic contributory 'accompaniment' to our anatomy and physiology, and that of most other animals, and to the evolution of sexual reproduction – and (theists would, therefore, add) part of the intention of their creator. Even so, we can still distinguish in the analogy between experiences that are wholly subjective and those subjective experiences created by an objective other, existing outside ourselves.[6]

Perhaps Griffith-Dickson is merely making the point (as she explicitly does on p. 140) that, in this second case, 'this particular experience "of another" can only be experienced through oneself'; and that, although it can be understood in psychological and physiological terms, this does not mean that there might not also be *another* cause of the experience.

Before we leave this analogy, we should note that its proposer also uses it to claim other pertinent similarities between these two experiences (pp. 141–2).

1 It 'suggests that a rigid distinction between experience and interpretation is misguided; not least because the interpretation is *part of* the experience'.
2 In both the religious and the sexual experience, the absence of experience – the failure to experience something when others claim to do so – 'may be down to the quality of the relationship or experience'.

This second point chimes with a common criticism of much analysis of religious experience – which is a concern that is consistent with one of the major themes of feminism – that it *underplays the significance of religious experience as a relationship* (Griffith-Dickson, 2000, pp. 138–9, 143; cf. Coakley, 2009, p. 294). As Griffith-Dickson has commented:

> We would be more successful in our analysis if we do not view religious experiences as an analogy with sensory experience or information-gathering in the sciences ... Arguably religious experiences are more like experiences of a relationship than perceptions of a material object ... Many personal experiences, especially those that occur within a relationship, cannot be experienced by another exactly as we do. We can encourage others to have their versions of such experiences, perhaps by describing how we did it, but we must then recognize that their experiences would be unique and personal; and above all, subject also to the will of the other party whom one wishes to experience. (Griffith-Dickson, 2007, p. 686)

Suggestions for Further Reading

Introductory

Griffith-Dickson, Gwen, 2000, *Human and Divine: An Introduction to the Philosophy of Religious Experience*, London: Duckworth, ch. 6 (pp. 133–44).

Reed, Esther, 1997, 'Revelation in Feminist Philosophy and Theology', in Paul Avis (ed.), *Divine Revelation*, London: Darton, Longman and Todd, ch. 9 (pp. 156–73).

Advanced

Jacobs, Janet Liebman, 1992, 'Religious Experience among Women and Men: A Gender Perspective on Mystical Phenomena', *Research in the Social Scientific Study of Religion*, 4, pp. 261–79.

Sjørup, Lene, 1997, 'Mysticism and Gender', *Journal of Feminist Studies in Religion*, 13, 2, pp. 45–68.

Notes

1 That is, of focusing on the male.

2 It should perhaps also be pointed out, however, that – for whatever reasons – historically, female mystics often saw their work as supporting the dominant role of males within the Church (cf. Bagger, 1999, p. 155).

3 The image of mystical union as a 'spiritual marriage' is used by both male and female classical mystics, and some commentators have treated the theology of John of the Cross as an attempt 'to feminize the soul' in light of the male imagery used for God.

4 One might compare Paul Moser's account of *filial* knowledge of God's reality (that is, knowledge that relates to or is due from a *son or daughter*), which goes beyond knowing that God exists to include a humble voluntary submission to God as Parent and Lord, entrusting ourselves to God, attuning ourselves with God, and being transformed by God. This 'personifying evidence of God' is given in a personal response to God, who is known best in relationship (Moser, 2010, pp. 172, 210–16).

5 She apologizes for any offence it may cause, as do I, but comments that she failed to find a more prosaic one (Griffith-Dickson, 2000, p. 133). After reading Griffith-Dickson's account, students may wish to reflect further on Craighead's comment in Chapter 2, above (under 'Referencing and Reporting').

6 Interestingly, Richard Gale calls an orgasm 'a paradigm of a subjective experience', and uses it as an analogy to critique Gary Gutting's tests for the objectivity of God experiences: that they are likely to be repeated in the same individual, that others have similar experiences and that experients are aided in their endeavours to lead better lives. For orgasms also satisfy all three of Gutting's criteria – provided that the third is understood as aiding 'sexually' rather than 'morally' better lives (Gale, 1991, pp. 311–12; cf. Gutting, 1982, p. 152 and Chapter 9, above).

Part 4

Disciplines, Doubters and Defenders

15

The Psychology of Religious and Spiritual Experience

Psychology is the scientific study of the human mind and its functions (*psyche* is Greek for 'breath, spirit, soul'), including the experiences, thoughts and behaviour of individuals and groups. It covers a very wide field and embraces many theoretical and empirical disciplines, approaches, schools of thought, research methods and themes. A number of these have been applied to the study of religious and spiritual experiences.[1]

In this chapter, psychology is construed broadly as a social science. However, evolutionary psychology and neuropsychology (see Appendix), much cognitive psychology and some other forms of psychology are more accurately categorized as *natural* sciences, in that they deal with the study of the physical world in the form of the human brain.

> **Focusing on ...**
>
> *Freudian Theory* is notorious for developing a radical critique of religion, based on Feuerbach's theory of projection (see Chapter 20). **Sigmund Freud (1856–1939)** was a positivist, committed to the view that truth could come only from the evidence of science or the inferences of reason. God was to be understood, therefore, as nothing more than an illusory projection of the human mind. Drawing on early anthropologists, Freud speculated on the

> origin of civilization and religion by positing an early tribe's murder of its tyrannical father, who was loved but also hated as a rival to their mother's affections. The guilt for this act was assuaged by the sacrifice of a totem animal that represented the murdered father,[2] who thus becomes the tribe's god: one that is made in the image of a stern but benevolent father, who meets our needs but is also our rival, preventing us fulfilling our secret desires. Freud's key idea was 'that the evolutionary stages of the development of religion in the human race were the same stages as the psychological development of the individual' (Aden, 2013, p. 49).
>
> Hence, religion was essentially the cultural expression of a universal obsessional and irrational neurosis, which originating in the child's helplessness and need for a father's protection. Freud thought of the adult as one who now recognizes his own father as 'a being of narrowly restricted power, and not equipped with every excellence', and who therefore harks back to the 'image of the father whom in his childhood he so greatly overrated' and exalts this figure 'into a deity', making it into 'something contemporary and real' for the adult (Freud, 1973 [1933], pp. 198–9).
>
> This situation could transmute into a religious experience based on wish-fulfilment. In fact, though, 'individual religious experience … took a back seat to Freud's critique of culture'. He was also limited by the psychology he invented, with his limitation lying in 'the narrowly conceived catalogue of meaning for religious experience posited by drive theory' (the theory of psychological needs and their satisfactions) (Shafranske, 1995, pp. 220, 224).

Post-Freudian psychoanalysis has sometimes focused on *Object Relations Theory*, which concentrates on the self's relation to others and their internal representations, especially that of the mother. Some have used this theory to interpret religious experiences of yearning and union in terms of the infant's relationship with her mother. John Bowlby's *Theory of Attachment* (which is much used as an explanatory model in the sociology of religion) suggests that God is an 'attachment figure', such that 'in times of distress, the experience of God as a safe haven gives rise to the same feelings of comfort and security provided by secure human attachments'. In contrast to Freud, however, there is nothing in the perspective of Bowlby's attachment theory that assumes that religious belief is 'inherently pathological, infantile, or regressive' (Kirkpatrick, 1995, pp. 455, 467).

Exercise: Among the Articles

Read and critically assess the following journal article:

Meissner, W. W., 2005, 'On Putting a Cloud in a Bottle: Psychoanalytic Perspectives on Mysticism', *Psychoanalytic Quarterly*, LXXIV, pp. 507–59.

William Meissner's article addresses the psychoanalytic understanding of mystical phenomena and mystical ecstatic states, with particular reference to descriptions found in the anonymous medieval classic, *The Cloud of Unknowing*. Some common psychoanalytic views of mystical phenomena are discussed and criticized, and the author seeks to formulate an approach to the understanding of these extraordinary mental and spiritual states that is both more congruent with accounts of authentic mystics and more consistent with psychoanalytic principles.

Focusing on ...

Carl Gustav Jung (1875–1961) was more kindly disposed to religion than Freud (e.g. Jung, 1933, p. 137). Thus, while Freud was antipathetic to the 'dark' phenomena of mysticism, Jung was much more sympathetic. So much so, indeed, that some modern accounts of mysticism have taken up his terminology of – and his postulation of the existence of – a *collective unconscious* that is responsible for the spontaneous production of myths, visions, dreams and religious ideas, with its realm of *archetypes* (primordial images or ideas of symbolic significance) (cf. Jung, 1983, parts 3, 4, 7, 8). Jung also extensively cited the concept of the numinous and insisted that 'the soul possesses by nature a religious function' (Jung, 1983, pp. 239, 262).

> The idea of an all-powerful divine Being is present everywhere, unconsciously if not consciously, because it is an archetype. There is in the psyche some superior power, and if it is not consciously a god, it is the 'belly' at least, in St. Paul's words. I therefore consider it wiser to acknowledge the

> idea of God consciously, for, if we do not, something else is made God, usually something quite inappropriate and stupid such as only an 'enlightened' intellect could hatch forth. (*Collected Works of C.G. Jung, Volume 7: Two Essays in Analytical Psychology*, ET Princeton, NJ: Princeton University Press, 2014 [1967], p. 71)
>
> The seat of faith, however, is not consciousness but spontaneous religious experience, which brings the individual's faith into immediate relation with God. Here we must ask: Have I any religious experience and immediate relation to God, and hence that certainty which will keep me, as an individual, from dissolving in the crowd? (*The Undiscovered Self*, ET Boston: Little, Brown, 1958, p. 85)
>
> Jung believed that people could learn about themselves by interpreting their mystical experiences. He emphasized the union of opposites and the concept of spiritual marriage, and saw religious experience in terms of a progressive psychospiritual integration, in which 'all facets of the soul are first differentiated and then integrated' (Halligan, 1995, p. 249). Jung also referred to many cases of synchronicity or 'meaningful coincidence' between parallel, causally unconnected events, which he believed were caused by activated archetypes.

The reconciliation of opposites is a key element in the research programme into non-ordinary conscious states that is labelled *Transpersonal Psychology*. This claims to integrate the spiritual and transcendent aspects of human experience with the framework of modern psychology. It developed from the perspective of *Humanistic Psychology*, which reacted both against (a) what came to be seen as a pessimistic and narrow view of human beings within Freudian psychoanalysis, and (b) the focus on overt behaviour within *Behaviourism*, by adopting a more holistic, 'whole person', view of persons and their creativity, free will and positive potential. Humanistic psychology acknowledged spiritual aspiration as an integral part of the self, and incorporated Maslow's focus on 'self-actualization' and 'self-transcendence'. Transpersonal psychology encompasses the study of many elements of spiritual and religious experiences, especially spiritual practices, trances, peak experiences, mystical awareness and conversion. A number of publications by its proponents have attempted detailed models or maps of spiritual development and experience (e.g. Wilber, 1993 [1977]; Washburn, 2003). Some of these are very ambitious, incorporating insights from Eastern spirituality and disciplines, as well as research on psychedelic drugs.

Transpersonal psychology is often criticized for a lack of scientific rigour, particularly by *Empirical Psychology*, which is defined by the American Psychological Association as an approach to the study and explanation of psychological phenomena that emphasizes objective observation and experimental method as the source of information about the phenomena under consideration. It focuses on data gathering and model building, and thus is often also contrasted with the approach of *Rational Psychology*, which accentuates philosophy, logic and deductive reason as sources of insight into the principles that underlie the mind and that make experience possible. (Perhaps now best exemplified in 'philosophical psychology'.)

Psychologists engaged in qualitative and (especially) quantitative and experimental studies often distinguish their own 'scientific' or 'objective' approach from what they discern as more 'armchair' or 'broad brush' forms of psychological theorizing. The material on RSEs in Chapter 3 of this book illustrates the methods of empirical psychology, as do the following studies.

Exercise: Among the Articles

Read and critically assess the following papers:

Hay, David, 1994, '"The Biology of God": What is the Current Status of Hardy's Hypothesis?', *The International Journal for the Psychology of Religion*, 4, 1, pp. 1–23.

David Hay's article outlines Alister Hardy's hypothesis that religious experience involves a kind of awareness that has evolved through natural selection because of its survival value to the individual. A description is given of attempts to test this view in comparison with competing hypotheses about religious experience that derive it from religious distress, social effervescence and neurosis. Along the way, Hay presents a useful summary of the Hardy tradition of research into the character of religious experience, and some of its implications.

Argyle, Michael, 1997, 2009, 'The Psychological Perspective on Religious Experience', RERC Second Series Occasional Paper 8, first published April 1997, second edition October 2009, Lampeter: Religious Experience Research Centre.

(Currently available without charge from: https://repository.uwtsd.ac.uk/367/)

Michael Argyle's paper provides a more consistently psychological overview of work on the variety of religious experience, its methods of arousal (referencing both traditional methods and experimental procedures using drugs) and its relation to personality factors, effects, proposed psychological explanations and social aspects.

Azari, Nina P. and Birnbacher, Dieter, 2004, 'The Role of Cognition and Feeling in Religious Experience', *Zygon*, **39, 4, pp. 901–18.**

This article analyses the role of emotion and cognition in religious experience, as well as the complex nature of emotions. The authors argue that religious experience cannot be reduced to pure feeling or pure thought, but may be interpreted as 'thinking that feels like something'.

Hood, Ralph W., 2013, 'Theory and Methods in the Psychological Study of Mysticism', *The International Journal for the Psychology of Religion*, **23, 4, pp. 294–306.**

Ralph Hood's lively article explores theory-driven empirical research into mystical experience, as championed by Bernie Spilka. Hood's broad survey of the psychological literature ranges from William James, through attribution theory, conversion and the experience/interpretation disjunction, to quasi-experimental studies of triggers of religious experience.

Batson, Schoenrade and Ventis (1993, pp. 87–115) argue that the psychological process involved in religious experiences may be understood best by analogy with another reality-transforming set of experiences – *human creativity*, an analogy that its authors believe is consistent with or positively supported by empirical psychological evidence. These researchers define creative thought as 'the process whereby one's cognitive structures are changed towards greater flexibility and adaptability through greater differentiation and integration'. 'In a creative change, the old reality is not denied but is transcended; it is seen for what it is, one way of looking at the world that has only a limited range of application', by contrast with 'the new insight or illumination' (pp. 94, 95, 101). The authors note the similarity of creativity with the stages of what William James called 'uniform deliverance' in religion and religious experience, where 'uneasiness' is followed by 'solution' (James, 1960, p. 484) and elements of crisis, self-surrender, new vision and new life are displayed. 'Religious experience involves cognitive restructuring in an attempt to deal with one or more existential questions' (Batson, Schoenrade and Ventis, 1993, p. 106). For other claims about a *sequence of stages* within religious experiences, see also Boyatzis, 2001; Edwards and Lowis, 2001 and cf. Tamminen, 1994.

Suggestions for Further Reading

Introductory

Argyle, Michael, 1990, 'The Psychological Explanation of Religious Experience', *Psyke & Logos*, 11, pp. 267–74.
Paloutzian, Raymond F. and Park, Crystal L. (eds), 2013, *Handbook of Psychology of Religion and Spirituality*, New York: Guilford, chs 11, 21 (pp. 215–33, 422–40).

Advanced

Batson, C. Daniel, Schoenrade, Patricia and Ventis, W. Larry, 1993, *Religion and the Individual: A Socio-Psychological Perspective*, New York: Oxford University Press, chs 4, 5 (pp. 81–154).

Hood, Ralph W. (ed.), 1995, *Handbook of Religious Experience*, Birmingham, AL: Religious Education Press, parts III, IV, V and ch. 21 (pp. 200–475, 494–519).

Hood, Ralph W., Hill, Peter C. and Spilka, Bernard, 2018, *The Psychology of Religion: An Empirical Approach*, New York: Guilford, chs 10, 11 (pp. 309–403).

Meissner, W. W., 1984, *Psychoanalysis and Religious Experience*, New Haven, CT: Yale University Press.

Wulff, David M., 1997, *Psychology of Religion: Classic and Contemporary Views*, New York: Wiley, chs 3, 5, 8, 11, 12 (pp. 49–111, 169–204, 320–70, 472–581).

Notes

1 For overviews of a range of psychological theories and approaches in relation to religious experience, see Hood, 1995b, chs 9, 10–19, 21.

2 It is from this fact, Freud believed, that the sacrifice of the mass was derived.

16

Religious and Spiritual Experience in Scripture

Among other elements, the sacred Scriptures of many religions contain accounts of:

- primordial experiences of encounter or union with the divine or the Absolute, or with lesser supernatural entities;
- revelations of God's (or the gods') presence, character or instruction;[1] and
- other moments or extended periods of heightened awareness, insight or changes in people's attitudes, beliefs, emotions and commitments.

The Hebrew Bible/Old Testament and the Christian New Testament include occasional references to even more anomalous experiences: for example, mysterious and partial theophanies (e.g. Ex. 33.18–23; Isa. 6), visions of mundane or extraordinary scenes (e.g. Ex. 3.1–6; Jer. 3.11–13; Ezek. 1.1–28, 37.1–14; Amos 7.1–7, 8.1–3) and experiences of angels;[2] and vivid narratives about Jesus' transfiguration and resurrection appearances.

The focus of much recent biblical scholarship, however, has been on theological, sociological, literary and 'hermeneutical' matters (issues of interpretation), and has tended to include little consideration of any transcendent experience that might lie behind the oral and written traditions that resulted in the present biblical narratives.

Prophecy

In the Old Testament, the *role of the prophets* is key, and in the New Testament, prophecy is a well-regarded spiritual gift (1 Cor. 14.1). The experience of prophetic inspiration is articulated in a variety of metaphors of God's Spirit (or sometimes 'hand') 'descending', 'falling on', 'resting on' or 'coming over' the prophet; or 'laying hold of him', 'possessing him', being poured onto him, put on him or bearing him away (e.g. 1 Sam. 10.9–13; 2 Chron. 24.20; Isa. 11.2; Ezek. 3.4, 22; 11.5; Joel 2.28). The prophet not only speaks 'the word of the LORD' but may also on occasion express God's message through actions ('acted prophecy': e.g. Jer. 32.6–15, 36–44; Ezek. 4; Hos. 1). The danger of false prophecy, and therefore the necessity of forms of moral and spiritual evaluation ('discernment'), are recognized in both Testaments (cf. 1 Kings 22.19–23; Jer. 23.11–15, 21–2; 28.5–17; 1 Cor. 12.3; 14.29; 1 Thess. 5.19–22; 1 John 4.1; see Moberly, 2006).

In his magisterial 1962 study, *Prophecy in Ancient Israel*, Johannes Lindblom devotes his third chapter to 'The Supernormal Experiences and General Activities of the Classical Prophets'. He argues there that the term 'audition' (an auditory perception or hearing with the 'inward ear' within an ecstatic experience) may be correctly applied to some of these experiences, especially in the inaugural visions of the prophets. But these represent only a small minority of cases. In most contexts where Yahweh speaks to the prophet and the prophet hears God's voice, 'there can be no talk of auditions in the strict sense'. Rather,

> the idea of hearing is only a means of describing the inspiration by which the high ideas emerged in the soul of the prophet, and is used because of the conviction that all that was given to the prophet, was given him from God and did not originate in the man himself ...
>
> Numbers of the so-called 'auditions' in the prophetic revelations are exalted poetry, or even fictitious literary productions and nothing else. In other cases they are expressions of an inner awareness that the prophet stands under Yahweh's command and is an object of divine impulses. A small minority are real auditions, i.e., auditions received in ecstatic experience. (Lindblom, 1962, pp. 121, 137)

Instead, Lindblom concentrates on *'the revelatory state of mind' of the prophets*. Although he portrays this as including 'the consciousness of hearing words and seeing visions which do not come from the self', he describes it as also having – as 'perhaps the most constant element' – 'the feeling of being under an influence external to the self, a divine power'. But Lindblom regards this feeling as being 'analogous to the poetic experience of inspiration', characterizing such experiences as (pp. 173, 179, 181, 197):

- 'mostly emotional and imaginative, not intellectual';
- not induced but spontaneous (in the later prophets) – although there were some predisposing conditions; and
- reflective rather than destructive of the prophet's personality.

The prophet's message, it would appear, is a recalling of the true Mosaic faith – 'in accordance with true Yahwism, but opposed to the popular way of thinking' (p. 315). But the message is applied by the prophets in new ways and in new circumstances.

This sort of account would allow a prophet's oracles to be construed as (a) non-propositional rather than (b) propositional revelation: that is, as (a) theological interpretations provided by the prophet of historical events that are 'seen-as' acts of God, and of God's inferred intention, nature and character; rather than as (b) statements and commands received directly from the mind of God and 'heard-as' God's message (see above, Chapter 13). What Lindblom writes elsewhere about revelation and inspiration (e.g. pp. 23, 35–6, 114, 122, 310–11, 321) seems to confirm that these categories could be understood on the model of seeing as much as that of hearing. Lindblom writes that 'the deepest source of [the prophets'] knowledge of God was history, above all the history of the chosen people' (p. 311). 'History was to the prophets the field of divine action' (p. 323).

Yet, biblical revelation has been traditionally understood more in the propositional mode 'as inspired speech: as the uttering of words crafted not by human artifice but coming to and through the mind unbidden' (James Dunn, in Avis, 1997, p. 11). On that view, *the prophets' words* also come from an outside source; they are *not* speaking 'visions of their own minds, not from the mouth of the LORD' (Jer. 23.16) or prophesying 'out of their own imagination' (Ezek. 13.2).[3]

> Morning by morning he wakens –
>   wakens my ear
>   to listen as those who are taught.
> The LORD God has opened my ear … (Isa. 50.4b–5a)

Elsewhere in the 1960s, however, we find scholars who seem to accept the assumption of the derivation of prophetic oracles from 'genuine visionary or auditory experiences' (von Rad, 1968, p. 46). While acknowledging that in these ancient prophetic texts much is left unsaid, both about the prophet's self-consciousness and the processes of disclosure and discernment involved, Gerhard von Rad claimed that 'there is universal agreement that visions and auditions came to the prophets from outside themselves' (p. 39). 'As far as we can see', he writes, 'the prophets of the eight and seventh centuries [BC/BCE] received their call through God's direct and quite personal address to them' (p. 36).

And even today, God's role in the prophetic experience is still modelled by some in propositional terms, with the prophetic medium being normally understood as God's *word* and the prophetic spiritual 'sense organ' that of 'hearing', although the view is much less common. Another recent commentator writes that 'it appears that the prophets went into a trance and believed themselves possessed by the Spirit of the LORD' (Barker, 2003, p. 491). But it is also argued that, unlike ecstatic trances, the prophet seems normally to be fully conscious with his mind engaged (Dunn, in Avis, 1997, p. 12).[4] This contrasts with a dream (cf. 1 Sam. 28.6; Jer. 23.25), although the biblical God can also reveal himself or his message in dreams, as is clear from other passages (e.g. Gen 28.10–17; 31.24; 1 Sam. 28.6; 1 Kings 3.5; Matt. 2.12).

But these days the alternative, non-propositional and non-interventionist view of prophecy seems to be very widely assumed, underplaying the supernatural element in the reported experiences of ancient Israelite religion. Now, of course, contemporary scholars who read and interpret the Hebrew Bible/Old Testament know what they are doing. They are self-aware and self-critical and do not just follow the crowd in their scholarly methodology. Interestingly, one such scholar (Walter Moberly) accepts that his own view on prophecy may reflect both (a) what he regards as a more up-to-date *theological* position, which is non-interventionist and even less supernaturalist, and (b) a *textual* scholarly claim that the key biblical passages on prophecy and discernment do not *themselves* show any 'interest in, or appeal to, unusual psychological states, or practices that might induce or accompany them'. Indeed, reviewing the case of Paul's account of his own glossolalia and his experience of being taken up into the 'third heaven' (2 Cor. 12.1–4), Moberly plausibly claims that the Apostle mentions these things 'only in order to downplay their significance and to direct attention elsewhere for the truly significant marks of spiritual authenticity' (Moberly, 2006, pp. 35–8, 221–3, 229).

One might also argue, of course, with or without any such underplaying in the texts, that the theological, moral and spiritual *message* of the Old Testament prophets has an authenticity and truth that is, in principle, independent of the manner in which it was 'received' and formulated; in the same way that much Judeo-Christian moral and spiritual teaching is independent of the more interventionist, extraordinary or otherwise intellectually challenging elements in the Books of Law and the Gospel narratives. But that *would* be to take a particular theological position, and one that still remains controversial.

Prophecy must be categorized as a form of *communication*, however, and scholars such as Martti Nissinen (2017, pp. 21–2) often insist on its status as a 'form of social communication', stressing (quite correctly) that 'the prophetic performance happens within a community that ultimately makes prophecy functional by acknowledging its value, veracity, and applicability'. This *social dimension of prophecy* tends to shift the scholarly focus from the individual prophet 'who mediates the divine message' (and from whatever experience – if any – lies behind it), and on to 'the human recipient(s) of the divine message' to whom the prophet speaks, and also to later recipients who receive this message in written rather than oral form. (We may note that the prophet himself is not here designated as a 'recipient', as he was by von Rad, 1968, pp. 38–9.)

This scenario is undeniably parallel to the more general theological claim that a revelation does not *become* a revelation for anyone until it is accepted as such or, to use the theological jargon, 'received' as such: *reception* being defined as a community's authentic reception of a teaching through an act of interpretation that allows that teaching to become effective.[5] Yet, Nissinen continues, 'the recognition of the performance as prophecy presupposes a shared belief in the superhuman … deity or deities whose words are being mediated, and the shared conviction … of the capacity of the person in question of acting as a prophet. This conviction often arises from the patterned public behavior of the prophet.' Elsewhere, in a chapter on 'Prophecy and Ecstasy', the 'shared scholarly consensus' is rehearsed that 'prophetic performance is typically associated with a specific state of mind variably called ecstasy, trance, or possession' (p. 171), but this 'point of view of the performer' is (again correctly) balanced by 'the point of view of the audience'.

This shift of focus is all very illuminating and shows proper scholarly impartiality. But *from the point of view of the student of religious and spiritual experiences*, the prominence given in the conceptual construction of prophecy to these social categories of reception, response, audience and public 'performance' may be frustrating, for it inevitably makes it easier to ignore the role of these experiences within prophecy and to bypass questions about their true origins.

The New Testament

What do we find in New Testament studies? Klaus Berger's study of 'identity and experience' in the New Testament illustrates a similar bias towards a sociological and functional perspective. Under the heading, 'The Causes and Conditions for Specific Experiences and Modes of Perception', Berger writes that 'seeking to account for such experiences … does not mean providing some sort of rationalistic explanation', rather 'it means attempting to locate them in a religious, social, or historical context such that we can understand the function of such experiences within their cultural milieu'. Later, he describes the alternative assessment of texts of visions as either 'scholarly fictions' or 'actual experiences' as 'more apparent than real', although he admits that any 'purely artificial provenance' is less probable because a text that is 'purely the product of the writing desk' has yet to be found (Berger, 2003, pp. 10, 113; cf. 16, 101–2, 121). These are sensibly cautious comments for any historian to make; but they once again leave concerns about the veridicality of these experiences unaddressed.

Yet, the New Testament scholar James Dunn, in his study of *Baptism in the Holy Spirit*, claimed that the evidence from the New Testament is overwhelming that 'the Spirit, and particularly the gift of the Spirit, was a fact of experience', and that it was 'the most significant element and focal point of conversion-initiation' and was inseparable from it. For according to the New Testament, it is the gift of the Holy Spirit that makes a person a Christian (Dunn, 1970, pp. 227–9).

Focusing on ...

Jesus

Claims about Jesus' spirituality or other aspects of his self-understanding[6] are risky to make, as the history of the various 'quests of the historical Jesus' underscores (cf. Thiessen and Merz, 1998, ch. 1 (pp. 1–15)). This is partly because all our knowledge of Jesus is mediated through an oral and written tradition that conveyed its accounts 'from faith to faith'.[7] But mainly it is because that tradition does not seem to have been interested in the biographical and psychological perspectives that contemporary readers would expect to be matters of central concern.

> The gospels provide us no window into the inner life of Jesus; although biography-like, they are not biographies in the usual sense of the word ... [in them] Jesus does not expose himself to us in such a way as to enable us to penetrate into his consciousness. We have no access to what he is thinking about himself and his mission except indirectly through what he says and does, and in his reaction to what others say of him. (Hagner, 2010, pp. 324–5)

Even so, while New Testament scholarship once shied away from this task, disavowing nineteenth-century reconstructions of Jesus' self-understanding (including that of Schleiermacher), scholars who espouse a more reflexive and chastened *quest of the historical Jesus* today may attempt to 'speak of Jesus' experience with a fair degree of confidence', at least when drawing on the Synoptic Gospels[8] (James D. G. Dunn, in Wakefield, 1983, p. 221).

We have noted how sociology has been very influential in modern biblical scholarship. The sociological understanding of 'charismatic authority', defined by Max Weber as a quality in an individual by which he is seen as extraordinary and endowed with exceptional – even supernatural – powers, has long been applied to Jesus. But this designation seems to have been bestowed on him by scholars largely with respect to his social relationships, but with little reference to his own religious experience, see Thiessen and Merz, 1998, ch. 8 (pp. 185–239). While accepting that Jesus did have 'one or two experiences which could be called ecstatic', even James Dunn claims that 'he was charismatic in the sense that he manifested a power and authority which was not his own ... but was given him, his by virtue of the Spirit/power of God upon him'. Dunn does add, however, that 'Jesus' consciousness of Spirit is the eschatological dimension to Jesus' ministry', and that this is a matter of his 'distinctive and even unique' experience of God (Dunn, 1975, pp. 87, 90).[9]

Holy Spirit

In English Bibles, the noun 'spirit' translates the Hebrew *ruach* and the Greek *pneuma*. Both words are also used for:

- a beneficial or destructive 'wind', often construed as a dynamic force or mysterious power that is thought of as an instrument of God;
- good or bad (created) immaterial spirits;
- the vital 'breath' of life created by God; and, therefore,
- the seat of human intelligence and emotion, our inner life, 'soul' or heart', which is an aspect of the person (but not one that is so intrinsically constituted that it may continue in separation from the material body).[10]

More significantly, the Spirit or 'Spirit of God' is the living energy of the personal God who is acknowledged as the Lord of Israel and eventually as the creator of all. The Spirit's operation extends to the creation, God's activity in history, human artistic endeavours, wisdom and judgements (and, therefore, rulers), and, supremely, the inspiration of prophets (see above). It is noteworthy that the classical prophets speak less about the Spirit (which is not mentioned in Amos or Jeremiah), perhaps because Yahweh speaks to them directly so 'they had no need of an intermediary power such as the spirit' (Lindblom, 1962, p. 178).

In the New Testament, the Spirit is associated with the coming, baptism and temptations, and the inspiration, healing and teaching ministry of Jesus. But predominantly – as 'the Spirit of Jesus' – it is referred to as a new, particular activity of the Spirit given to and acting in:

- the first disciples after Pentecost;
- all later disciples from their conversion/baptism, both as the Spirit and in 'gifts of the Spirit'; and
- the fellowship and worship of the 'Body of Christ', which is the Church.

> It is in the New Testament that the phrase the 'Holy Spirit' (*hagion pneuma*) begins to be used of God's Spirit.
>
> ## Human Spirit
>
> The word *pneuma* is also used in the New Testament about 40 times to refer to the dimension of a human being, the human spirit, that is open to a relationship with God (cf. Rom. 1.9; 8.16; 1 Cor. 2.11; 6.17); just as *sarx*, 'flesh', is the aspect of humans that is open to sin (as in Rom. 7.18, 25; 8.6; Gal. 5.16–17; 19–23).[11] This *continuity, though not identity*, between God's Spirit and the human spirit seems to be accepted throughout the Christian Scriptures (cf. Ps. 51.6–12; 139.1–18).
> (Cf. Dunn, in Wakefield, 1983, pp. 357–8.)

Luke Timothy Johnson also claims that the New Testament writings 'emerged from powerful religious experiences' as a 'secondary reflection on primary experiences that are now inaccessible to us' (Johnson, 2010, pp. 3–4, 84, cf. 6, 9–10, 13–14, 93, 95–107). Johnson's influential study, *Religious Experience in Earliest Christianity* (1998), is subtitled, 'A Missing Dimension in New Testament Studies'. What is missing, he complains there, is the recognition that 'the world evoked by the texts of the New Testament is literally a spirit-filled world'.

As in Old Testament studies, the historical-critical method that dominates the academic study of these texts is primarily a history of theological ideas or social institutions, for which 'the language of religious experience appears overly subjective and elusive to serve the cause of historical reconstruction' – and is therefore often 'demystified as camouflage for political position-taking within religious traditions' (Johnson, 1998, pp. 9, 13, 25, cf. 184–5). To ignore this language, however, is 'to neglect the specific historical character of this movement and thereby to make its historical continuation and success all the more difficult to understand' (p. 36). Johnson therefore wishes to complement the historical study of the New Testament with a sort of phenomenological approach to these experiences, in an attempt to see them more adequately – while suspending judgement about the existence or non-existence of their 'extramental' dimension (pp. 44–5, 57). He argues that this is not a 'surreptitious form of theology', but rather 'a way of seeing ... that begins with the assumption that religious language and religious experience are actually about something and deserving of attention in their own right' – a perspective that can make 'as vigorous use of historical, sociological, psychological, and anthropological perspectives as any reductionist approach', but without eliminating the phenomenon in the process (pp. 182, 183).

Many studies of the cultural context of the New Testament writings have also drawn convincing links with Jewish mystical and apocalyptic traditions, but without denying 'actual experiences on the part of individual visionaries' (Williams, in Schmidt, 2016b, pp. 139). In her own research, Catrin Williams argues that aspects of *John's Gospel*, as well as other New Testament passages, may have been 'intended as an experience-inducing text' (p. 141). She illustrates the relationship between text and experience for the author of John's Gospel, by means of four examples:

- the claim in the Prologue (John 1.1–18) that 'the children of God', unlike the world, have 'seen' (with the eyes of faith – that is, 'perceived') Jesus as the embodiment of God's glory;
- the fact that certain characters also see Jesus during his ministry in both the physical *and* the spiritual sense (e.g. 1.29, 32–4, 35–51; 3.2, 11–12; 4.29; 9.25; 12.46);
- that Abraham (e.g. 8.56) and Isaiah (12.38–40) are also said to have (correctly) seen Jesus; and
- that through his resurrection the disciples see Jesus and will do so once more (14.18–19; 16.22; 17.24; 20.25, 28–29).

As with the rest of biblical studies, however, students of the New Testament tend to be more influenced by sociology than psychology. Perhaps it is not surprising, therefore, that Johnson's focus on the 'irreducibly individual', because somatic and psychosomatic, understanding of religious experience (Johnson, 1998, pp. 47–8) was later blurred by attempts to understand the 'social facilitation' of these experiences: that is, how they are shaped by social forces and understood in community settings. Hence the proposal advocated by the social historian Philip Tite (2013) to focus, 'not on the phenomenal encounter of an individual, but rather on the social facilitation of experiential moments, specifically, in how these moments are enabled ... both individually and corporately', while recognizing that in dealing with the past 'the historian only has access to remnants', that is, texts and other artefacts, which underscores his claim that attempts at 'getting at the internal psychology of ancient individuals' are futile (pp. 10, 11, 15).

At the same time, other scholars have widened the understanding of religious experience in the New Testament to include less extraordinary and particular experiences, including studies in the Society of Biblical Literature's/Brill's recent *Experientia* Project (published out of Williston, VT, 2008, 2012).

Exercise: Among the Articles

Read and critically assess:

Hurtado, L. W., 2000, 'Religious Experience and Religious Innovation in the New Testament', *The Journal of Religion,* **80, 2, pp. 183–205.**

While New Testament scholars have for many years shown 'a widespread reluctance to attribute much causative significance to religious experiences in the innovations that mark the development of early Christianity', Larry Hurtado relates a revival of interest in recent decades in religious experience, stimulated in part by the attention devoted by Pentecostals and other charismatics to the experience of the Holy Spirit recorded in the New Testament. This article sets this discussion in the context of social-scientific views on religious experience and highlights the significance of revelatory experiences in generating one particular, remarkable innovation in early Christianity – the cultic veneration of Jesus Christ.

Ashton, John, 2003, 'The Religious Experience of Jesus', *Harvard Divinity Bulletin,* **32, 1, pp. 17–20.**

John Ashton's article explores the references to Jesus' own religious experience, as recounted in the Gospel traditions about Jesus' baptism, temptations, the experiences associated with his healing ministry and his understanding of God, and his sharing of his own mystical experience with his most intimate disciples on the Mount of Transfiguration.

> **Kourie, Celia, 2009, 'A Mystical Reading of Paul',** *Scriptura*, **101, pp. 235–45.**
>
> In this article, Celia Kourie argues that 'Paul the mystic, not Paul the moralist, or organizer of the early Christian communities' is the revealer of God's secret wisdom. Paul makes known a mystical union with the risen Jesus, expressed in his expression *in-Christ*, 'which can be seen as the major leit-motif of Pauline thought'.
>
> **Batluck, Mark, 2011, 'Religious Experience in New Testament Research',** *Currents in Biblical Research*, **9, 3, pp. 339–63.**
>
> Mark Batluck's article reviews recent research on religious experience in the New Testament through four distinct streams: as mystical/revelatory experiences; encounters of the Holy Spirit; through its historical dimensions in the Gospels; and 'categorically, trying to account for the grand scope and effect of religious experience recorded in the writings of the New Testament'.

Suggestions for Further Reading

Introductory

Holder, Arthur (ed.), 2011, *The Blackwell Companion to Christian Spirituality*, Oxford: Wiley-Blackwell, part II (pp. 35–70).
Rad, Gerhard von, 1968 [1967], 'The Prophets' Call and Reception of Revelation', in Gerhard von Rad, *The Message of the Prophets*, ET London: SCM Press, pp. 33–49.
Wiebe, Phillip H., 1997, *Visions of Jesus: Direct Encounters from the New Testament to Today*, New York: Oxford University Press, ch. 4 (pp. 111–49).
Williams, Catrin H., 2016, 'Text and Experience: Reflections on "Seeing" in the Gospel of John', in Bettina E. Schmidt (ed.), *The Study of Religious Experience: Approaches and Methodologies*, Sheffield: Equinox, ch. 8 (pp. 135–50).

Advanced

Berger, Klaus, 2003, *Identity and Experience in the New Testament*, ET Minneapolis, MN: Fortress, chs 1, 6, 9 (pp. 1–25, 82–127, 186–218).
Dunn, James D. G., 1975, *Jesus and the Spirit: A Study of the Religious and Charismatic Experience of Jesus and the First Christians as Reflected in the New Testament*, London: SCM Press.
Johnson, Luke Timothy, 1998, *Religious Experience in Earliest Christianity: A Missing Dimension in New Testament Studies*, Minneapolis, MN: Fortress.
Moberly, R. W. L., 2006, *Prophecy and Discernment*, Cambridge: Cambridge University Press.

Notes

1 These include frequent claims to prophetic revelation (routinely prefaced by phrases such as 'the word of the LORD came to me', 'the LORD said to me', 'thus says the LORD', etc.).

2 Note, however, that in the Old Testament 'the angel of the LORD' is often indistinguishable from the LORD – that is, 'Yahweh' – himself.

3 In the splendid ancient story about the prophet Micaiah, however, God does agree to send a deceitful *outside source* to the prophets, in the form of a 'lying spirit'. Although, in this case, the language is perhaps most readily interpreted as metaphorical (1 Kings 22.1–40), the story does reveal a recognition that the appeal to the prophets' confidence, their numbers or even their 'outside' inspiration is not necessarily a guarantee of truth.

4 And, yet, perhaps 'in a strange way detached from himself and his own personal likes and dislikes' and 'drawn into the emotions of the deity', as well as learning God's designs (von Rad, 1968, pp. 40–2)?

5 See Chapter 13, above.

6 Such as Schleiermacher's assertion of Jesus' perfect God-consciousness (Schleiermacher, 1958, pp. 385–90; 1928, pp. 385–9; see also Chapter 18, below).

7 Cf. John 20.31: 'These things are written that you may come to believe that Jesus is the Messiah, the Son of God, and that through believing you may have life in his name'.

8 That is, Matthew, Mark and Luke.

9 Dunn, we may note, describes Paul as 'both more of a charismatic and less of a charismatic than Jesus', experiencing more 'in the way of visions and ecstasy' than Jesus, but with a ministry less characterized by healings and exorcisms, and with much less self-conscious authority, but who placed more emphasis on prophecy. Paul's religious experience, however, was marked 'by a dependency on Jesus as Lord' and an experience of the grace of Christ and the Spirit of Christ; his experience, therefore, was 'experience of Jesus, consciousness of Christ, that is, the recognition of the impress of Christ's character in Paul's experience'. Dunn concludes, 'the religious experience of the Christian is not merely

experience like that of Jesus, it is experience which ... is derived from Jesus the Lord, and which only makes sense when this derivative and dependent character is recognized' (Dunn, 1975, pp. 258, 342).

10 A worthwhile life after death, belief in which develops very late in Israelite religion (and therefore only appears in a couple of Old Testament texts), is envisaged as a re-creation or 'resurrection' of the psycho-physical, intimate unity of the body and its embodied soul that together comprised the person in this life.

11 Whereas *soma*, 'body', is regarded as morally neutral.

17

Religious and Spiritual Experience in the Christian Tradition

The importance of paying serious attention to the historical context of religious experiences and the scholarly study of the particular texts that report them, cannot be overestimated. Philosophers and theologians, in particular, have often been accused of highly selective, abstract, simplistic or otherwise misleading accounts of the, often occasional, convoluted and unsystematic writings of exponents of Christian and other traditions of mysticism (cf. Bagger, 1999, pp. 3–4, 137–8).[1] The sheer amount and complexity of the primary sources that represent the historians' raw material makes errors on the part of those who do not know this material well particularly likely.

Studies in church history, historical theology and the history of Christian ideas provide a very rich resource of accounts of spiritual and religious experiences down the two millennia of Christian history and thought. This is a vast field, covering innumerable historical sources and a multiplicity of contemporary interpreters of them. So, once again, this chapter can do little more than scrape its surface.

Exercise: Among the Articles

Bernard McGinn's reputation as a student of the history of Christian mysticism justifies choosing three of his articles for this exercise, which together provide a historical overview that explores the accounts, contexts and interpretations of mystical experience in the early church fathers, early and late medieval Catholic writers, and the Protestant Reformers.

You are, therefore, encouraged *to read and critically reflect on the following journal articles:*

McGinn, Bernard, 1996, 'The Changing Shape of Late Medieval Mysticism', *Church History,* **65, 2, pp. 197–219.**

McGinn, Bernard, 2001, 'The Language of Inner Experience in Christian Mysticism', *Spiritus: A Journal of Christian Spirituality,* **1, 2, pp. 156–71.**

McGinn, Bernard, 2015, 'Mysticism and the Reformation: A Brief Survey', *Acta Theologica,* **35, 2, pp. 50–65.**

Focusing on ...

Augustine (354–430)

Augustine, who was Bishop of Hippo in North Africa, has become a pivotal figure in Christian thought, especially in the West where themes from his copious output have been very influential among both Catholic and Protestant theologians.

For Augustine, 'the soul's quest for God is mediated neither by the bodily senses nor through language but is accessible to the spiritual senses' (Matthew R. Lootens, in Gavrilyuk and Coakley, 2012, p. 63). These are exercised by an inner self (*homo interior*) and are capable of perceiving God as well as God's activity: God may be directly experienced through these five spiritual senses. Although marred by sin, our spiritual senses may be restored by God's grace and their eventual goal is the 'beatific vision', which Augustine believed was possible in a limited and fragmented way even within this life (see below).

Augustine uses the language of spiritual perception, principally of vision, both metaphorically and more literally (but still allusively). In his later writings, he distinguished a person's eyes in their head from the 'eyes in the heart' that are their organs of moral perception. Augustine's visions at Milan (including a vision of God's light and voice) and Ostia (a vision shared by his mother) are reported in bk. VII, 10 and bk. IX, 10 of his *Confessions* (written 397–8). He also recounts there his conversion, which he viewed as God's grace acting on all his spiritual senses:

> You called me; you cried aloud to me; you broke my barrier of deafness. You shone upon me; your radiance enveloped me; you put my blindness to flight. You shed your fragrance about me; I drew breath and now I gasp for your sweet odour. I tasted you, and now I hunger and thirst for you. You touched me, and I am inflamed with love of your peace. (Augustine, *Confessions*, bk. X, 27, *ET* London: Penguin, 1961, p. 232)[2]

Some claim that Augustine is a great mystic, but others deny him the designation altogether. There are, certainly, elements of mysticism in his writings. For example, his encounter with God is an interior journey, involving purging the mind of sensual images. But Augustine's spirituality always includes an *intellectual element*. 'Despite the primacy of love in Augustine's theology, the ascent to God is a mental, as well as an affective and emotional, journey' (Gerald Bonner, in Wakefield, 1983, p. 33). His spirituality is also both personal and Christocentric.

Coming to Terms with Christian Mysticism

Asceticism: This term (from the Greek *askesis*, 'discipline' or 'training') is used to label pathways to self-knowledge, and knowledge of the transcendent, that are often associated with deprivations of some sort; and whose ends are regarded in Christian spirituality as the true meaning of life.

Beatific Vision: This is the traditional name for the vision of God's essence itself and is regarded as the supreme human fulfilment. It has usually been thought of as possible only 'in heaven', as the perpetual and immediate (not mediated) spiritual perception of God from the experiencer's resurrection body. But some have held that it was also exceptionally bestowed on a few favoured individuals (e.g. Moses and Paul) during their lifetime on earth.

Contemplation: In the Christian tradition, the word has been used ambiguously to denote either (a) the highest employment of the mind reaching into the depths of Christian truth, or (b) an advanced type of (perhaps) effortless and God-given prayer. On this latter understanding, it has been said to begin with what Teresa of Ávila called 'the prayer of quiet' and to lead to the *state* of contemplation. In this state, the mystic is infused by God's special grace with supernatural knowledge and love of God, in a transforming 'prayer of union' with God that itself may ultimately lead to spiritual 'betrothal' and 'marriage' (cf. Knowles, 1979, pp. 29–30, 84, 87–8).

In some writers, contemplative prayer is also used of some more ordinary forms of prayer (cf. Harton, 1933, pp. 263, 272) that serve as a bridge to this mystical 'infused prayer' or 'supernatural prayer'. These earlier stages of prayer might include simple attention[3] (the 'prayer of simplicity'), prayers of 'active recollection' ('active' because the soul's own effort is crucial and controlling) and the prayer of 'passive' (supernatural) recollection, which is involuntary and involves God's own action upon the soul.

The term contemplation is often contrasted with **meditation**, a spiritual practice that employs words, images and symbols. In 'contemplative', 'interior', 'mystical' or 'mental' prayer the soul bypasses such symbols and media, and thus transcends discursive thought so as to realize direct contact with God.

Stages of the Spiritual Journey: Using the analogy of a journey, spiritual 'progression' is sometimes said to include several stages. Teresa writes of a journey into and through an 'interior castle' that passes through seven chambers, to meet God in the innermost mansion (see also below). Some have identified three overarching stages of the spiritual journey.

1. In the *purgative* stage, the soul turns from sin to virtue. This is the 'active' part of the journey, where the soul is conscious of its own effort, although supported by grace, to overcome sin and draw closer to God; whereas the next two stages are regarded as the 'passive' part of the journey, in which the soul becomes aware of God's action towards it and the related religious experiences 'will not come except God bestows' them.[4]
2. In the *illuminative* stage, the soul enters into supernatural prayer.
3. In the *unitive* stage of the journey, the soul enters first spiritual betrothal and then **'spiritual marriage'**.

Dark Night of the Soul:[5] As used in Walter Hilton's *The Scale of Perfection* and, especially, John of the Cross's *The Dark Night of the Soul* and *The Ascent of Mount Carmel*, this term covers distressing experiences of 'darkness' and 'night' within the spiritual journey, which arise because its transcendent end is necessarily cloaked in unknowability. This situation is made worse by human spiritual blindness. The soul must be drawn away from its attachment to the things of the world and the desires of the senses, an experience sometimes known as the 'night of the senses'. Only then – in a rarer experience of more intense suffering – is it further purified and spiritually reoriented towards God (in the 'night of the spirit').[6] Then God's illumination dawns, the transforming union with God is granted and the darkness escaped.

The darkness through which the true mystic travels is regarded as 'in fact the rejection, for love's sake, of everything that is not God' (Knowles, 1979, p. 136).

Focusing on ...

Denys (or Dionysius) the (Pseudo-)Areopagite

This is the supposed author of a body of work, including the *Divine Names* and *Mystical Theology*, which were supposed to be written by a convert of Paul but in fact appeared first in the sixth century from the pen of someone deeply influenced by later Platonism. The aim expressed in these texts is that of an ultimate union of the whole creation with God, through its perfection or 'divinization'. This union is the final stage of the 'three ways' of the mystical tradition: purification, illumination and union.

Denys's writings are rich in light-related imagery, which he uses to describe the process of spiritual perception and illumination that is initiated in baptism. He denies that God can be perceived by the physical senses, only by 'super-cosmic eyes' (and, presumably, other analogous spiritual sense organs), and insists that all affirmations fall short of describing God in words or symbols. ('Everything may be ascribed to Him [God] at one and the same time, and yet he is none of these things.') For Denys, the ultimate reality 'transcends all affirmation by being the perfect and unique Cause of all things, and transcends all negation by the pre-eminence of His simple and absolute nature – free from all limitation and beyond them all' (*Mystical Theology*, ch. V, *ET* London: SPCK, 1920, p. 201). 'God is in no way like the things that have being and we have no knowledge at all of His incomprehensible and ineffable transcendence and invisibility' (*Celestial Hierarchy*, 141A, *ET* Mahwah, NJ: Paulist Press, 1987, p. 150).

Denys's theology of negation (his 'apophatic theology') describes the soul ascending and passing beyond knowledge or perception into God's darkness and being reduced to 'complete speechlessness' as, in utter submission and ecstasy, it unites with 'God who is completely unknowable'. Then the soul 'knows by not knowing in a manner that transcends understanding' (*Mystical Theology*, 1.3, *ET* Oxford: Oxford University Press, 1981, p. 173); and, as Andrew Louth puts it, 'the soul in its love for God knows God's love for itself and is united with him' in an 'unknowing union' of love (Louth, in Wakefield, 1983, p. 109).

Meister (Johannes) Eckhart (1260–1327)

Eckhart was a German Dominican mystic who studied and taught in Paris. Despite being elected a Dominican Provincial, he was accused of heresy in the last year of his life. Eckhart has had a considerable influence both outside and within the Church, through writings focused on a cosmic mysticism of the Godhead (influenced by Neo-Platonism) and a creation-centred, politically conscious and profoundly intellectual spirituality of compassion and justice-making. God keeps giving new being, and our own creativity reveals our divinity in our kinship with God. 'The creature is like the mirror image before the original; if the one pulls back, then the other disappears'; 'the image is able to exist only in the return into its original' (Haas, 1988, pp. 148–9). Eckhart describes this as 'God giving birth to God in the soul'. Then God dwells in the innermost highest dimension of the soul, where 'these two are one' and God timelessly creates the entire cosmos within Godself. 'If my life is God's being then God's existence must be my existence and God's isness is my isness' (*The Essential Commentaries, Sermons, Treatises and Defence*, ET London: SPCK, 1985, p. 288).

Eckhart advocated an experience of God found through detachment, letting go and letting be. 'Where clinging ends is where God begins to be'; 'True detachment is nothing else than for the spirit to stand immovable against whatever may chance to it.' God is experienced as 'One not-God, One not-spirit, One not-person, One not-image'; and is 'the denial of all names, the nameless nothingness and superessential darkness' (*Sermon 83*, ET London: SPCK, 1981, p. 208).

The Carmelite Experience

Carmelites are a Christian religious order of monks and (later) nuns founded in the twelfth century. Traditionally, Carmelite affective spirituality was sceptical about supernatural experiences and emphasized the mystical journey in humility towards union with God beyond all sensory perceptions and images. Its most famous representative writers are the two reforming Spanish Carmelite saints, Teresa and John of the Cross.

- **Teresa of Ávila (1515–82)** underwent supernatural experiences early in life and a series of intense visions from 1555, including one of an angel piercing her heart with a spear[7] and an experience of 'spiritual marriage' (experienced beyond a stage of spiritual affliction, and represented as the culmination of the life of prayer). Her *Interior Castle* (1577) presents the fullest formulation of spiritual marriage in mystical writing. The whole plan of the book was revealed in a vision of 'a beautiful crystal globe like a castle', whose 'inhabitants enjoyed more light the nearer they were to the centre'. This is where the King of Glory resides, who can be reached through six other 'dwelling places' (*The Interior Castle, ET* London: SPCK, 1979, p. 26). (See https://catholicstrength.com/2017/03/23/the-souls-journey-to-god-a-concise-summary-of-saint-teresa-of-avilas-interior-castle/ and Bagger, 1999, ch. 6.)
- **John of the Cross (1542–91)** was influenced by Teresa. He wrote poems and mystical treatises, including writing on the topic of spiritual marriage. John developed from Denys the symbolism of the dark night of the soul, in which the soul itself (in 'active nights') and God alone ('passive nights') prepares it for union with God. 'The passive night of the spirit, in which the absence of God is most grievously experienced, becomes nonetheless the threshold of union, the darkest part of the night which precedes the dawn' (Colin Thompson, in Wakefield, 1983, p. 232). With regard to visions and auditory experiences, however, John warns that 'the private experiences of individual mystics have no value whatsoever as sources of information ... [and] to treat them as such is to risk a variety of pitfalls of considerable threat to the spiritual life' (Pike, 1986, p. 16; n. 5 gives references from John's *The Ascent of Mount Carmel*). The problem with 'locutions' would seem to be that God's utterances use words in extraordinary senses, and the problem with God's symbolic visions is that there is no way of being sure what the intended meaning is; hence, for John, these two types of mystic apprehension 'cannot be taken as a source of propositional knowledge' (Pike, 1986, pp. 21, 36). (See also above, Chapters 4, 12, 13.)

The English Mystics

This title is given to a group of fourteenth-century English contemplatives who wrote on personal spirituality. Affectivity is a prominent feature in their writings. They also highlighted the bestowal and reception of God's grace in contemplative prayer and mystical experience, which was often focused on (though eventually transcended) the humanity – and especially the passion – of Christ.

- **Richard Rolle (c.1300–49)**, a hermit, was an exponent of affective mysticism who used the imagery of the senses to depict experiences of the spirit. He described his love for Christ as 'warmth, song and sweetness' (*The Fire of Love*, ch. 14, ET London: Penguin, 1971, p. 88) and declared this experience a foretaste of God that could only be fully enjoyed in heaven. His best-known book was *The Mending of Life*.
- The anonymous **author of the *Cloud of Unknowing*** – an influential text that expounded apophatic theology – wrote *Prive Counselling*, which also glorifies experience over knowledge, and other texts. In the *Cloud*, negation is regarded as the way to contemplative perfection. Separating oneself from the world of the senses (which are left behind, covered up in a 'thick cloud of forgetting') and even from the self, through the agency of meditating on one's sins and Christ's passion, the contemplative can come to God. This involves, however, penetrating – although not dispersing – the thick cloud of unknowing by striking it with 'the sharp dart of longing love', which is ultimately the gracious gift of God. For the author of the *Cloud*, God 'may well be loved, but not thought. By love he can be caught and held, but by thinking never' (*Cloud of Unknowing*, chs 6, 8, Modern ET London: Penguin, 1961, pp. 60, 65).
- **Walter Hilton (died 1396)** was a hermit and later an Augustinian canon and theologian, whose most famous work is *The Scale* [or *Ladder*] *of Perfection*. He writes there about his own experience of God through contemplative prayer, from which knowledge comes love. Although union with God is everyone's goal, there are degrees of union to which some are called but not others. But when God's grace is received, 'the eyes of the soul turn to God and contemplate him clearly, and it knows with certainty that it knows and sees him ... [not] as he is in the fullness of his Godhead,

but ... to whatever extent he wills to reveal himself to a pure soul in this mortal life, according to the measure of its purity'. 'Every experience of grace is an experience of God himself, and may be called God' (*The Scale of Perfection*, ch. 42, Modern ET London: Geoffrey Chapman, 1975 [1957], p. 138).

- **(Mother or Lady or Dame) Julian of Norwich (c.1342–c.1420)** became an anchoress (a female recluse who resided in a cell often attached to a church – in this case, St Julian's Church in Conisford at Norwich). Although she said that she had never sought 'a physical vision or revelation from God' (*Revelations of Divine Love*, ch. 3, Modern ET Harmondsworth: Penguin, 1966, p. 66), in 1373, at a time of severe illness over a night and day, Julian experienced a series of 16 visions or 'shewings' that included not only visions of Christ's passion but also lively everyday imagery that Julian reflected on later in her *Revelations*.

  Julian stressed the necessity of humility and patience, as well as the courtesy and homeliness of God, employing the image of motherhood for both God and Christ. 'God is our Father and our Mother and our spouse'; 'Jesus is our true Mother ... from whom true motherhood begins, with all the sweet protection which endlessly follows' (*Revelations of Divine Love*, chs 58–60, Modern ET London: SPCK, 1987, p. 295). Although sin is inevitable, in the end 'all shall be well and all shall be well, and all manner of thing shall be well' (*Revelations of Divine Love*, ch. 27, thirteenth revelation, Modern ET New York: Doubleday, 1997, pp. 54–5, cf. 124). In other words, 'sin separates us from God, but, from the viewpoint of divine love, the pain that sin causes in us is a necessary part of the purgative process of falling and rising that we undergo throughout this life' (McGinn, 1988, p. 204). For Julian, prayer was basically a longing for God. She was told that the meaning and content of her revelations was Love, revealed by Love, for Love.

- **Margery Kempe (c.1373–c.1440)**, in marked contrast to Julian, was the mother of 14 children and much-travelled in later life. She is known for her strong compassion for sin and her tears of anguish at suffering. For long periods she was conscious of a close communion with Christ; her devotional life was also 'enriched with considerable erotic imagery' (McGinn, 1988, p. 205). *The Book of Margery Kempe* was the first autobiography in English.

Hildegard of Bingen (1098–1179)

Hildegard was a German Benedictine nun, elected in 1136 to lead her community. She is widely recognized today as a prolific composer, philosopher, author, natural historian, theologian and general polymath, in addition to being famous for her visionary and mystical writings. At first she kept her many visions and auditory experiences secret, refusing to write for a long time 'through doubt and bad opinion and the diversity of human words, not with stubbornness but in the exercise of humility' (*Scivias, ET* New York: Paulist Press, 1990, p. 60). Later, however, she was the recipient of a divine command to disclose their contents, 26 of which are detailed in *Scivias* (1142–51). These experiences started at the age of three and continued throughout her life. Hildegard's *Book of Divine Works* (c.1163) details cosmic and mystical visions. Her religious experiences were received, 'not in dreams, nor in ecstasy', but 'with the inner eyes of my spirit and heard with my ears, in heavenly mysteries' (*Divine Works*, Foreword; *ET* New York: Crossroads, 1990).

Suggestions for Further Reading

Introductory

Holder, Arthur (ed.), 2011, *The Blackwell Companion to Christian Spirituality*, Oxford: Wiley-Blackwell, part III (pp. 71–174).
Hollywood, Amy and Beckman, Patricia Z. (eds), 2012, *The Cambridge Companion to Christian Mysticism*, New York: Cambridge University Press, especially part I (pp. 37–136).
McGrath, Alister E., 1999, *Christian Spirituality: An Introduction*, Oxford: Wiley-Blackwell.
Wiebe, Phillip H., 1997, *Visions of Jesus: Direct Encounters from the New Testament to Today*, New York: Oxford University Press, ch. 1 (pp. 15–39).

Advanced

Dupré, Louis and Saliers, Don E. with John Meyendorff (eds), 1990, *Christian Spirituality: Post-Reformation and Modern*, London: SCM Press.

McGinn, Bernard (ed.), 2006, *The Essential Writings of Christian Mysticism*, New York: Random House.

McGinn, Bernard and Meyendorff, John, with Leclerq, Jean (eds), 1993, *Christian Spirituality: Origins to the Twelfth Century*, New York: Crossroad.

Raitt, Jill with Bernard McGinn and John Meyendorff (eds), 1988, *Christian Spirituality: High Middle Ages and Reformation*, London: SCM Press.

Notes

1 It should be noted that these days historical study – like the work of the biblical scholar – often adopts a sociological perspective, using sociological categories of power, status and social pressure to illuminate the context, and even the content, of religious and spiritual experiences (e.g. Bagger, 1999, ch. 6 (pp. 135–96)).

2 Mystics such as Teresa of Ávila 'use the senses, like taste and touch, for the deepest states, which require contact between God and the mystic' (Bagger, 1999, p. 176 n. 51). According to Nelson Pike, 'the spatial picture that goes with the taste of God is, very specifically, God inside, that is, God in the most intimate contact-relation with me'; hence, 'spiritual sight gets nothing like the attention given to spiritual touch and to spiritual taste in the literature on Full Union' in mysticism (Pike, 1992, pp. 55, 56).

3 'One-pointedness' is said to be the equivalent in Hindu thought (Thouless, 1971, pp. 123–4).

4 Teresa of Ávila, 'Spiritual Relations Addressed by Saint Teresa of Jesus to Her Confessors', *ET Complete Works of St Teresa*, vol. I, New York: Sheed and Ward, 1957, p. 331.

5 Although in origin (and still primarily) a Christian conception, the language of the 'dark night' has been applied to similar experiences from Jewish, Muslim, Pagan and Buddhist sources. It is also sometimes treated as synonymous with psychological constructs such as 'psychic death' or 'ego death'.

6 In which it is 'stripped even of any remaining spiritual gratification and of every consoling image of itself' (Rowan Williams, in Wakefield, 1983, p. 104).

7 'The pain was so great, that it made me moan; and yet so surpassing was the sweetness of this excessive pain, that I could not wish to be rid of it. The soul is satisfied now with nothing less than God' (Teresa's *Autobiography*, ch. XXIX, part 17, *ET* Baltimore, MD: John B. Piet & Co., 1882).

18

The Theology of Religious and Spiritual Experience

The term 'theology' is often used in educational institutions to label a range of 'Christian studies' that together offer *a multidisciplinary study of the field* of the Christian religion, and especially of its Scriptures, history, teachings, practices, institutions, divisions and debates. This chapter, however, is concerned with the *discipline* of theology, which is the particular form of structured reflection on Christian beliefs that is most clearly exemplified by systematic, dogmatic and philosophical theology – although often in concert with studies in historical theology.

> **Focusing on …**
>
> **Friedrich Daniel Ernst Schleiermacher (1768–1834)**
>
> Schleiermacher was a German Lutheran theologian who is often credited, although within Christian theology as often criticized (cf. Chapter 13, above), for his 'turn to the subject' and for the pre-eminence he gave to religious experience. Despite its long history of contemplative and mystical traditions, he has been described as 'the first most important thinker in the Christian tradition who shifted attention from text and doctrine to religious experience' (Smart and Konstantine, 1991, p. 133; cf. Mariña, 2008, p. 461). Dubbed 'the father of liberal theology' (at the age of 18 he was disowned by his father for his liberal doctrinal views), Schleiermacher attempted to free Christian doctrine and practice from dependence on intellectual (especially

metaphysical) speculation and ecclesiastical tradition and authority, treating Christianity as a particular stream of religious consciousness in history. Along the way, he became the standard-bearer for all those who criticize objective, dispassionate doctrine in the name of a personal, felt religion that must originate within oneself (Schleiermacher, 1958, p. 47).

In his *On Religion: Speeches to its Cultured Despisers* (1799), Schleiermacher asked his readers 'to reimagine religion from an experience within the human condition' (Kelly, 2002, p. 14). He identified the essential spirit of religion with 'piety', understood as religious consciousness, rather than with its intellectual and moral dimensions as emphasized during the Enlightenment. (He argued that piety 'cannot be an instinct craving for a mess of metaphysical and ethical crumbs'.) Emotion is more characteristic of religion than actions or beliefs, and the essence of religion is the autonomous *human experience* of God that occurs within the subject: which he variously described as 'immediate feeling', 'a revelation of' or 'sense and taste for' the Infinite, or 'the unity of intuition and feeling' (Schleiermacher, 1958, pp. 31, 36, 39–40) and (later) as the 'feeling of absolute dependence' (Schleiermacher, 1928, p. 17). Dogmas and doctrines are all the result of contemplation, reflection and comparison based on this experience. They are, therefore, 'nothing but general expressions for definite feelings' (1958, p. 87); they represent – as he later came to express it in his magisterial *The Christian Faith* – 'the religious affections set forth in speech' (1928, p. 76).

Despite the range and ambiguity of this language, it is clear that Schleiermacher understood religious experience mainly as a direct experience *of* God, as in prophetic and mystical encounters with the divine, rather than as a set of 'subjective experiences' or feelings (such as confidence, acceptance and joy) *from which* the existence and action of God may be inferred (as Otto seemed to understand him; see below and Chapter 10). His intention appears always to have been to speak of an objective *apprehension* or emotional *perception* of the spiritual. God is directly known in religious experience. 'To feel oneself absolutely dependent and to be conscious of being in relation with God are one and the same thing', he wrote. In this sense, 'God is given to us in feeling' (Schleiermacher, 1928, p. 17). Thus, for Schleiermacher, intuition is an 'immediate perception' of the infinite in us, which results in certain feelings. Together, they distinguish an experience that transcends language – it is 'indescribable' and 'lost for my speech'. The predominant feeling state that is associated with this experience is that 'feeling of absolute dependence' that is the essence of piety. For Schleiermacher, 'this experience is not only prior to language but is prior even to the subject/object differentiation. Furthermore, [it] is universal: it is accessible to every human being'. It is this religious self-consciousness that is the test against which, in the end, 'all Christian doctrine is ultimately measured' (Kelly, 2002, pp. 24, 46).[1]

Rudolf Otto (1869–1937)

Although disowned by many contemporary theologians, Rudolf Otto was in his day an influential German Lutheran theologian as well as a pioneer in the phenomenology of religion. He was greatly influenced by Friedrich Schleiermacher's emphasis both on piety and on the secondary, derivative status of religious beliefs (see Otto, 1931, ch. VIII; and above). He criticized Schleiermacher, however, for relying (as Otto mistakenly thought) on an inference to God as the cause of religious experience, rather than interpreting this experience as a direct intuitive perception.

Unlike many other religion scholars, Otto himself underwent what he took to be the human experience that lies at the heart of all religion and is *potentially* virtually universal. He also held that it was futile to discuss religious experience with people who had never had such an experience, asserting only a few pages into his classic work, *Das Heilige* (1917; translated as *The Idea of the Holy*, third impression, 1925), that whoever cannot direct their mind 'to a moment of deeply felt religious experience ... whoever knows no such moments ... is requested to read no further' (Otto, 1925, p. 8).

In this book, Otto coined the adjective 'numinous' to mark the non-rational experience of otherness and mystery in the presence of the 'unnamed Something' that is its object (which he also designated as 'numinous' or the 'numen'). Otto stressed that this feeling response is itself ethically neutral, but focused on the '"extra" in the meaning of "holy" above and beyond the meaning of goodness' (Otto, 1925, pp. 6–7).

> Let us consider the deepest and most fundamental element in all strong and sincerely felt religious emotion ... we are dealing with something for which there is only one appropriate expression, *mysterium tremendum*. The feeling of it may at times come sweeping like a gentle tide, pervading the mind with a tranquil mood of deepest worship. It may pass over into a more set and lasting attitude of the soul, continuing, as it were, thrillingly

vibrant and resonant, until at last it dies away and the soul resumes its 'profane', non-religious mood of everyday experience. It may burst in sudden eruption up from the depths of the soul with spasms and convulsions, or lead to the strangest excitements, to intoxicated frenzy, to transport, and to ecstasy. It has its wild and demonic forms and can sink to an almost grisly horror and shuddering. It has its crude, barbaric antecedents and early manifestations, and again it may be developed into something beautiful and pure and glorious. It may become the hushed, trembling, and speechless humility of the creature in the presence of – whom or what? In the presence of that which is a *Mystery* inexpressible and above all creatures.

...

The qualitative *content* of the numinous experience, to which 'the mysterious' stands as *form*, is in one of its aspects the element of daunting 'awefulness' [sic] and 'majesty', ... but it is clear that it has at the same time another aspect, in which it shows itself as something uniquely attractive and *fascinating* ... The daemonic-divine object may appear to the mind an object of horror and dread, but at the same time it is no less something that allures with a potent charm, and the creature, who trembles before it, utterly cowed and cast down, has always at the same time the impulse to turn to it, nay even to make it somehow his own. The 'mystery' is for him not merely something to be wondered at but something that entrances him; and beside that in it which bewilders and confounds, he feels a something that captivates and transports him with a strange ravishment, rising often enough to the pitch of dizzy intoxication. (Otto, 1925, pp. 12–13, 31)

In addition to the feeling of dependence or 'creature-consciousness',[2] therefore, the numinous is also experienced in two very different ways:

- as *tremendum*, which contains three related 'moments' of emotion: *a sense of awe-fulness* (its unapproachability giving rise to a feeling of dread), of *overpowering might* and of absolute *reality and worth* (over against one's own impotence and unworthiness), and *of 'urgency or energy'* that conveys the sense of passion and will in the numinous object as the living God (Otto, 1925, pp. 13–21); and
- as *fascinans*, that is, fascinating (Otto, 1925, ch. V) – for the numinous is experienced also 'as an object of search, desire, and longing ... for only it will quench the deepest desires of the soul', and 'the source of unspeakable bliss ... beyond comparison with any earthly joys' (Mariña, 2008, p. 469).

The element of fascination combines with the feeling of awefulness in what Otto called 'a strange harmony of contrasts'. Together, they constitute the 'dual character of the numinous consciousness', which captivates and entrances as well as provoking wonder, bewilderment and holy terror (p. 31). On p. 28 n. 1, Otto references Augustine's words, which 'very strikingly' suggest the 'benumbing element of the "wholly other" and its contrast'.[3] The element of attraction may be rationalized and expressed in religious analogies such as God's 'goodness', 'love', 'mercy', 'pity' or 'comfort' (Otto, 1925, chs IV–VI).

Although the experience itself is *non*-rational (note, not 'irrational') – and unmediated by language and tradition – it becomes articulated and expressed ('*schematized*'[4]) in various ways through such analogical religious language and beliefs. Thus, the element of *tremendum* is expressed in terms of a daunting, overpowering awefulness and dread (as in biblical references to the 'wrath of God'); and *mysterium* marks that which is 'beyond our apprehension and comprehension'. The *mysterium tremendum* therefore gives rise to talk of the 'transcendence' (otherness) of God.

For Otto, this religious experience is a unique species of experience: 'perfectly *sui generis* and irreducible to any other'. It is an experience so distinctive that it can only be understood by being reproduced in the reader. Therefore, it 'cannot, strictly speaking, be taught, it can only be evoked, awakened in the mind' (1925, p. 7). Nevertheless, there are different levels to the experience, and secular analogies as well – including the 'uncanny' and 'spooky', and the horror and 'shudder' evoked by stories of ghosts.

As discussed above (Chapter 4), Otto regarded mysticism as an extreme form of numinous experience. For most scholars, however, the numinous describes the 'outer and thunderous quality' of an intense, external *encounter* (sometimes regarded as 'prophetic') with the divine, or even with Nature; in marked contrast with the serene 'inner visions' of mystical *unity* that arise from contemplative practices.

The sense of the numinous itself is said to be without moral and rational components. In thus transcending concepts, it represents the sort of account of religious experience that is rejected by constructivists (see Proudfoot, 1985, p. 88). For Otto, numinous experience is a natural capacity of human beings, who undergo a common core of experience that is broadly identical across cultures, although it is expressed in different ways (this is 'perennialism' – on constructivism and perennialism, see Chapter 8, above).

Otto was especially influential on the psychologist Carl Jung (see Chapter 15), the phenomenologist Mircea Eliade (cf. 1959, pp. 8–10; 1968, pp. 123–4) and the philosopher Ninian Smart (cf. Sarbacker, 2016). Students will find chapters I to VI of Otto's *Idea of the Holy* fairly non-technical, as are chapters X and XI, in which he traces examples of numinous experiences in the Old and New Testaments. Other accessible examples may be found in his Appendixes to this book (1925, pp. 183–234).[5]

Karl Rahner (1904–84)

Rahner was a German Jesuit and the pre-eminent Catholic theologian of the twentieth century.[6] In Rahner's view, religious experience is not some particular experience *among* others. Rather, Christian claims *fit with ordinary experience*. He viewed all human experience as the key to theological meaning, asserting that everyone (even those who claim to be atheists) is on some level aware of God and that everyone also has experience of the offer of God's grace. This is our basic, original, irrevocable orientation to God – our 'transcendental orientation towards mystery' (Rahner, 1978, p. 52). For, 'when the mind knows some particular object, or wills some finite value, it never merely knows or chooses the particular but is always at the same time reaching beyond it, towards the whole of being, and therefore towards God' (Kilby, 2007, p. 97). So, also, 'in the act of loving one's neighbor a person has an experience of God at least implicitly' (Rahner, 1978, p. 456).

This experience involves a pre-apprehension (*Vorgriff*) of infinite being, which is built into our human nature as the 'horizon' for all our knowing, or the 'light' which illuminates all the objects our intellects can grasp. It is a condition of the possibility of our experience, without which we shouldn't be who we are. Further, God's grace is 'an ever-present gift offered to us at such a fundamental and central level that it affects all we are, and know, and do', and takes us beyond our nature. Both elements (awareness of God and experience of grace) are not separate from our experience of the concrete and finite, but *given in it* – in a way that we can recognize, although only ambiguously (Kilby, 2007, p. 98–9). When we 'let ourselves go', in our commitment to and experience of human values such as forgiveness, obedience, sacrifice and love (and the struggle and emptiness that commitment can bring when we 'no longer belong to ourselves'), *then* 'we begin to live in the world of God himself' and to taste 'the pure wine of the spirit'. This is the *experience of the supernatural*; it is the hour of grace. In it, 'the seemingly uncanny bottomless depth of our existence as experienced by us is the bottomless depth of God communicating himself to us' (Rahner, in McCool, 1975, pp. 197–8).[7]

Plainly, Rahner is not here 'attempting a proof of God's existence, but offering a Christian interpretation of human experience' that recognizes that '*all* human experience is, in varying degrees …, experience in relation to the mystery of God' (Lash, 1988, p. 246–7, italics original). God is thus perceived as 'the infinite horizon of human questioning' or 'the unlimited distance', as we push beyond our experience in reflecting on it. And unlike Proudfoot, Lindbeck and other constructivists (see Chapter 8), for Rahner 'original experience takes a priority over language' and the experience of God to which he points is *prior to* any theological teaching (Kelly, 2002, p. 134).[8]

George Arthur Lindbeck (1923–2018)

Lindbeck was an American Lutheran theologian who extolled a *postliberal theology* that stressed the importance of Christian language and an understanding of the Christian faith as an overarching narrative with its own internal grammar or logic (a '*narrative theology*'). Postliberalism challenges Enlightenment claims about a universal rationality and attacks in particular the prominence given by liberal Christianity to autonomous individuals. Lindbeck criticized liberal (which he called '*experiential-expressive*') theology for locating the core of religion in existential concerns and a common pre-reflective religious experience, and for demoting the status of religion's external features, including its culture, tradition and language. Lindbeck contended that religion is, rather, 'a kind of cultural and/or linguistic framework or medium that shapes the entirety of life and thought'. Christianity should therefore be seen as a *cultural-linguistic system*, with Christian doctrine being the *rules of the grammar* of that system.[9] Becoming Christian was a question of acquiring proficiency in the specific 'Christian language and form of life', and interpreting and experiencing 'one's self and one's world in its terms' (Lindbeck, 1984, pp. 33–4).

Lindbeck claimed that postliberalism 'could also be called' postmodernism' (Lindbeck, 1984, p. 135 n. 1). This seems to be a *moderate form* of postmodernism, which – unlike more radical forms – does not discard notions of truth and reference or make human language the ultimate reality. However, others interpret Lindbeck's understanding (alongside that of

Proudfoot) as rooted in 'an understanding of language that rejects a correspondence between language and external reference', and which understands truths as 'mediated by and *confined* to particular historical and linguistic contexts' (Kelly, 2002, pp. 51, 115, italics original). It is certainly true that Lindbeck acknowledges that human experience is 'shaped, moulded, and in a sense constituted by cultural and linguistic forms' (Lindbeck, 1984, p. 34). Theology, therefore, '*shapes* rather than *is shaped by*, human experiences, including those termed religious or spiritual' (Pope, in Schmidt, 2016b, p. 117, italics original). Together with Proudfoot, this marks Lindbeck as a *constructivist* (see Chapter 8, above).

The influence of postliberalism on many recent trends in Christian, including *radical orthodoxy*, has encouraged contemporary theology's turn away from the Romantic emphasis on feeling, liberal theology's claim that religion is founded on religious experience and perennialist arguments for a common core that underlies the diversity of religious cultures and their linguistic expressions. (See, e.g., Fodor, 2005; Shakespeare, 2007, pp. 32–40.)

David Hay has accepted that Lindbeck's theory poses severe problems for the common core analysis of religious experience, 'because if experience is constructed by language, and thus religious experience by religious language, there is no reason to suppose that the experiences that the adherent of one version of religion has should have any common ground whatsoever with those of adherents of other religions' (Hay, 1988, p. 219). Hay argues, however, among other claims, that:

- 'a very wide range of linguistic or symbolic expression and interpretation can appear in association with what appears to be a common experience';
- religious 'professionals' from widely different cultures do seem to find common ground in their religious and spiritual experiences, the methodology they use to enter into them and their physiological correlates; and
- 'those reporting such experience, at least in Western culture, find that it does not easily fall into the category of subjective production or imaginings and in certain crucial respects is much more like the perception of an "objective" reality' (pp. 222–4).

For other comments and criticisms of Lindbeck, see McGrath, 1997, ch. 2 (pp. 14–34); Kelly, 2002, ch. 3 (pp. 71–89); Fodor, 2005. On postmodernism, see Chapter 19, below.

Exercise: Among the Articles

Read and critically assess the following journal articles:

Katz, Steven T., 1992, 'Mysticism and Ethics in Western Mystical Traditions', *Religious Studies*, 28, 3, pp. 407–23.

Steven Katz's article surveys the theology of a range of Christian mystics and relates this to their understanding of Christian ethics, which in this tradition is deeply theological – indeed, Christological. He writes, 'Christian mystics, in so far as their entire life is an active attempt to emulate and replicate the example of Christ, are intent to the degree that this lies within the realm of human possibility on being paradigms of morality.'

Baumert, Norbert, 2004, '"Charism" and "Spirit-Baptism": Presentation of an Analysis', *Journal of Pentecostal Theology*, 12, 2, pp. 147–79.

The Catholic scholar, Norbert Baumert, offers a biblical and contemporary theology of 'charism' and 'baptism in the Holy Spirit', key terms in Pentecostal and charismatic theology, relating them to wider theological understandings of the work of the Spirit, religious experience and the nature of the Church.

Egan, Harvey D., 2012, 'In Purgatory We Shall All Be Mystics', *Theological Studies*, 73, 4, pp. 870–89.

The contentious theological concept of a purgatory after death is given a new paradigm in this article. The author's sources include the work of some recent theologians, together with classical accounts of religious experience and the notion of a 'purgatorial stage of the consciousness of the mystics, caused by their intense experience of the incompatibility of sin and divine Love'. Harvey Egan's conclusion is an understanding of purgatory, not as a place of torture, but rather as 'an encounter with Jesus Christ, or God, or the Holy Spirit and with the mystical body and the cosmos that purifies and transforms the multidimensional social person that we are'.

> **Brown, David, 2015, 'Realism and Religious Experience',** *Religious Studies*, **51, 4, pp. 497–512.**
>
> In this contribution, the philosophical theologian David Brown takes up the much-discussed parallel between religious experiences and ordinary sense perception (see Chapter 9), responding to its three major philosophical objections (the unusual character of religious experiences' objects, their unusual accompanying conditions and their conflicting contents) by offering a more nuanced and *theologically rooted* response.

Suggestions for Further Reading

Introductory

Holder, Arthur (ed.), 2011, *The Blackwell Companion to Christian Spirituality*, Oxford: Wiley-Blackwell, part IV and ch. 23 (pp. 175–286, 401–16).
Louth, Andrew, 1990, *Discerning the Mystery: An Essay on the Nature of Theology*, Oxford: Oxford University Press.

Advanced

Gavrilyuk, Paul L. and Coakley, Sarah (eds), 2012, *The Spiritual Senses: Perceiving God in Western Christianity*, Cambridge: Cambridge University Press.
Kelly, Thomas M., 2002, *Theology at the Void: The Retrieval of Experience*, Notre Dame, IN: University of Notre Dame Press.
Lash, Nicholas, 2011 [1988], *Easter in Ordinary: Reflections on Human Experience and the Knowledge of God*, London: SCM Press.
Sudduth, Michael, 2009, 'The Contribution of Religious Experience to Dogmatic Theology', in Oliver D. Crisp and Michael C. Rea (eds), *Analytical Theology: New Essays in the Philosophy of Theology*, Oxford: Oxford University Press, ch. 10 (pp. 214–32).

Notes

1 On Schleiermacher, see Barth, 1972 [1952], ch. 11 (pp. 425–73); Kelly, 2002, ch. 1 (pp. 11–49); Theodore Vial, in Oppy and Trakakis, 2009a, ch. 3 (pp. 31–47).

2 This is a powerful feeling of impotent 'creaturehood' and 'general nothingness', which Otto distinguished from the 'consciousness of *createdness*', 'of being conditioned' or of dependence (the mere fact of being created) that he found in Schleiermacher (Otto, 1925, pp. 9–10, 20–1).

3 Otto's reference to the *Confessions* should be to bk xi, 9. This is translated, in Augustine, 1961, p. 260, as 'What is that light whose gentle beams now and again strike through to my heart, causing me to shudder in awe yet firing me with their warmth? I shudder to feel how different I am from it: yet in so far as I am like it, I am aglow with its fire'.

4 *Schematization* involves a concept being 'illustrated' – but not exhaustively or 'conceptually' rendered – by evocative and symbolic 'ideograms' that are rooted in analogous human experiences, such as our 'fear' or 'love' for other people (Otto, 1925, pp. 19–20, 24, 26, 34–5, 48, 144–6).

5 Reasonably accessible studies of Otto include Schlamm, 1991, 1992; Ware, 2007.

6 Rahner may be read as a 'modest postmodernist' (Kerr, 1997, p. 178), who adopted a qualified turn to language and a qualified pluralism that did not reduce theology to its context (Kelly, 2002, pp. 121, 157).

7 See Moser, 2010, pp. 200–9, for an account of how our acquaintance with perfect unselfish love and forgiveness, received as God's non-coercive transformative gift with which in response we can cooperate and express ourselves, may be regarded as 'authoritative direct, first hand evidence of divine reality'.

8 Karl Rahner was an extremely voluminous author, and often a difficult thinker. He is perhaps best approached as an unsystematic theologian (Kerr, 1997, p. 178). A good, brief introduction may be found in Kilby, 2007. On Rahner and religious experience, see Lash, 1988, ch. 15 (pp. 219–53) and Kelly, 2002, ch. 5 (pp. 119–49).

9 For Lindbeck, then, *doctrines are second-order rules* that regulate – 'recommend and exclude certain ranges of' – the belief statements and symbolizing activities of ordinary believers (Lindbeck, 1984, p. 19, cf. 107 and ch. 4). (Doctrines that are interpreted as rules are not *statements*, and so cannot be judged to be either true or false.)

19

The Philosophy of Religious and Spiritual Experience

Interest in the philosophy of religion and philosophical theology has grown considerably since the 1950s, especially in the UK and the USA. Much of this work has been directed to the investigation, criticism and defence of the meaning and coherence of the concepts employed in religious and theological debate, and the validity and strength of the arguments that have been developed both for and against religious beliefs. In a word, it has been *analytical*.

The term 'analytical philosophy' is normally restricted to a particular movement in Western philosophy at the start of the twentieth century, in which the logical analysis of concepts into more simple constituents was used to solve philosophical problems (see Honderich, 1995, pp. 27–30; Blackburn, 1996, pp. 14–15). But, in truth, this is a standard method in – or even understanding of – the academic discipline of philosophy, particularly in its role as a *meta-inquiry*: as 'subject philosophy' or the 'philosophy of' certain phenomena, or a specific field or discipline of study (Passmore, 1967; Flew, 1979, preface; cf. Ward, 1968, pp. 57–8; Williams, 1996).

While different 'schools' or 'traditions' of philosophy may adopt rather different presuppositions and types of argument in relation to religious and spiritual experience, the great majority of recent philosophical publications concerned with the concepts and arguments relating to these forms of experience have been broadly grounded in the analytical tradition (cf. Burhenn, 1995, p. 144).

And most of the more philosophical 'debates' in this book have adopted this perspective: see especially Chapters 1, 8, 9, 10, 11, 12.

Coming to Terms
with the Philosophy of Religious and Spiritual Experiences:

Attributionalists claim that there are only experiences 'deemed to be' religious (by individuals or groups) (e.g. James, Proudfoot, Taves). They are opposed by *inherentists*.

Constructivists or ***Contextualists*** regard the differing situations in which an experience takes place as providing its concepts and interpretations, which cannot be separated from the experiences themselves. The interpreter of a religious experience is thought of as 'constructing' the experience. Opposed by *essentialists*. See Chapter 8.

Doxastic Practice is a socially established way of forming, correcting and evaluating beliefs (e.g. sense experience, memory, mystical experience). See Chapter 9.

Epistemology is the branch of philosophy concerned with claims to knowledge: that is, with what can be known and our ways of securing and justifying knowledge.

Essentialists tend to regard all religious experiences as essentially the same, differing only in how they are interpreted and reported. Opposed by *constructivists/contextualists*. See Chapter 8.

Inherentists accept that there are experiences that are inherently religious or mystical, whose religiousness is 'built into' the experience (e.g. Otto). Opposed by *attributionalists*.

Perennialists are essentialists for whom there is a 'common core' to mysticism or to religious experience that includes certain doctrines: a 'perennial philosophy' underlying its variety. *Contextualists* deny this claim. See Chapter 8.

Postmodernism is a term often used to label a broad movement in philosophy, literature and other forms of artistic expression that developed in the second half of the twentieth century. It is widely regarded as characterizing Western culture today. Postmodernists are opposed to the **'modernism'** of universalist, eighteenth-century Enlightenment notions of the power and significance of human reason, human autonomy, objectivity and social progress. They focus, by contrast, on the particularity and socially conditioned nature of our knowledge and value claims, rejecting grand 'metanarratives'. In practice, postmodernism often embraces – in a 'somewhat abandoned celebration' (Blackburn, 1996, p. 326) – some version of **relativism**, which is the view that truth is somehow relative to the standpoint of those who judge it, whether they be individuals or groups. Postmodernism has been framed in both a radical and a more moderate form.

The radical perspective of **post-structuralism** seeks to 'deconstruct' all texts. The key figure here is the controversial (and obscure) French writer, Jacques Derrida, who seems to argue that meaning does not exist except in and through language, or 'meaningful signification': 'there is nothing [meaning nothing expressible] outside of the text' (Derrida, 1976 [1967], p. 158). Nevertheless, the text itself requires to be **deconstructed** in order to show its inevitable ambiguity and lack of clarity: phenomena that result in a 'play of interpretation' to which there is no end, and therefore no limit. **Difference** determines meaning, for the meaning of a term depends on its difference from other terms and is never fully present in the term by itself. Hence, meaning is never fixed; it is always 'deferred' and, therefore, elusive. Derrida denied that he advocates a total relativism and nihilism, in which there are no thoughts and no facts prior to the language of someone's signification; arguing, rather, that deconstruction is actually an openness towards the other, which incorporates a recognition of the limitation of all such language to describe the other and a recognition of the alienating and exploitative uses of all language. Nevertheless, under this sceptical approach to objectivity an *extreme constructivist* view of religious experience would seem to be the only possible position to take (see Chapter 8).

A more **moderate postmodernism**, while repudiating the idea of an objective knowledge that transcends human language and historicity (and therefore embracing *constructivism*), would reject a deconstructionism for which signs always referred to other signs and exist only in relation to each other, and which was wholly agnostic about any ultimate foundation or centre or extra-linguistic reality corresponding to our language. Some philosophers would therefore say that we *can* attain truths about some thing or system of things, with more or less degrees of accuracy, while denying that truth can only be described in exactly one complete and correct way. Things may thus be said to be 'real' and, therefore, to 'exist' outside language. All the same, here – as in all postmodern understandings of religious experience – learning to designate the true originator of the experience as God is sometimes said to be 'more like learning to use a language than it is like verifying the truth of a particular factual claim' (Lash, 1988, p. 169, cf. 242–3; see also Proudfoot, 1985, pp. 216–27 and Chapter 18, above).

Exercise: Among the Articles

Read and critically assess the following journal article:

Wainwright, William J., 1973, 'Mysticism and Sense Perception', *Religious Studies*, 9, 3, pp. 257–78.

This early paper provides a relatively gentle introduction to philosophical discussion of religious experience, focusing on 'the analogy (or lack of it) between mystical experience and sense experience'. Wainwright defends this analogy against the mid twentieth-century critiques that argue that 'the mystic can legitimately base religious and metaphysical claims on his experience only if he has independent criteria for establishing the existence (or presence) of the supposed object of his experience'.

A wide range of other philosophical articles have been suggested as suitable for exploration in the Exercises in the 'Debates' part of this book.

Focusing on ...

William James (1842–1910)

William James was an American pioneering psychologist and philosopher whose Gifford Lectures of 1901–02, published as *The Varieties of Religious Experience: A Study of Human Nature*, have been very influential in the study of religious experience. This work includes a variety of accounts of religious experience, many of which James drew from the classic empirical study of conversion undertaken by his student, Edwin Diller Starbuck (1866–1947). The accounts were intended to give the reader 'some (albeit indirect) sympathetic acquaintance' with these private experiences (Lash, 1988, p. 29).

For James, as for Schleiermacher (see Chapters 13, 18, above), religion was more a matter of feeling than reasoning, and the status of religious beliefs was regarded as secondary. At the heart of religion, and forming its basis, there lies an inner feeling, and a sense similar to sense experience itself, that are 'almost always the same' and do not vary across religions and cultures, as does their expression in religious thinking. In effect, James 'defined religion in terms of religious experience', but (unlike many) he did not claim that religious experience was *sui generis* and, although he sought to explain it in psychological terms, he left open the possibility 'that it pointed to something more' (Taves, 2009, pp. 4–5). The immediate (non-inferential), authoritative pure experience on which James focuses is something that he regards as a function of one's 'higher self' or 'real being', which a person identifies as she or he 'becomes conscious that this higher part is conterminous[1] and continuous with a MORE of the same quality, which is operative in the universe outside' them. This experienced 'more', for which God is 'the natural appellation', really exists as an active 'higher part of the universe' (James, 1960, pp. 484–5, 491).

Although all human beings possess 'the germ of mysticism' – that is, some capacity for it – James tended to privilege examples of the experience from the mystical elite, who have had the most unusual and extreme experiences (cf. Spohn, 1994). His selection of and concern for the 'varieties of religious experience', and especially for the 'root and centre' of personal religious experience, namely 'mystical states of consciousness', is therefore weighted towards its more dramatic, intense and extraordinary forms (James, 1960, p. 366).

On occasion, James recognizes a monistic core to all unitive mystical experiences (in which individuals 'become one with the Absolute': p. 404); but elsewhere he seems to argue for a dualistic interpretation of this experience. At the time of writing the *Varieties*, James was a theist, although he only acknowledged a finite God (cf. p. 499). A few years later, however, James had moved through a form of pantheism to a belief in God as an impersonal, thoroughly finite, non-creative, 'fundamentally friendly' material object (see Lash, 1988, pp. 78-80).[2]

John Hick (1922-2012)

This British philosopher of religion and liberal Christian theologian adopted a perceptual theory of religious experience, arguing that, for 'the great primary religious figures', belief in God is 'not an explanatory hypothesis ... but a perceptual belief ... [not] an inferred entity but an experienced personal presence' (Hick, 1970, p. 116).[3] He therefore viewed religious faith as 'a form of cognition by acquaintance or cognition in presence' (1973, p. 38), and thus as a 'non-propositional revelation' of the Transcendent itself (1967; 1983, ch. 5; see also Chapter 13, above), which he understood as 'the interpretative element within religious experience, arising from an act of cognitive choice' (1974, p. v).

Hick's epistemology of religion draws on Ludwig Wittgenstein's identification of the phenomenon of 'seeing-as' in seeing a puzzle picture (Wittgenstein, 1968, pp. 193-214),[4] extending this concept to the act of recognizing something as (say) a fork and claiming that 'all seeing is seeing-as' – or (more broadly) 'experiencing-as'. Thus, 'all conscious experiencing involves recognitions which go beyond what is given to the senses' and takes the form of unconscious interpretative activity (Hick, 1974, p. 142; 1985, ch. 2; 2010, p. 65).

As Hick defines distinctively religious experiences (or 'mystical' experiences: 2008, p. 15) very broadly, as 'modifications of consciousness structured by religious concepts', and rejects the view that there is some common raw experience that is interpreted differently according to culturally bound ways (1999, p. 110), he shows himself to be a *constructivist* – that is, he understands the religious interpretation to be already part of the experience (see Hick, 1989b, pp. 142, 295; cf. Stoeber, 1992 and Chapter 8, above). William Alston rejects Hick's view that all experience of objects involves indirect perception via interpretation, on the general grounds that direct awareness is distinguishable from interpretation which is 'something over and above that'. Nevertheless, Alston does allow that, in addition to direct perception of God there may be some *indirect* perception by way of our 'direct awareness of something in creation', for example, God appearing to one as loving or powerful *through* one's sense perception of Nature (Alston, 1991, p. 28).

Hick on Religious Diversity and Truth

Reacting to his own experience of religious diversity, Hick came to embrace a *pluralist(ic) theology of religions*. This regards all great faiths as embodying 'different perception and conceptions of, and correspondingly different responses to, the Real' (Hick, 1989b, p. 240). Hick interprets the religions 'as authentic and valid contexts of salvation/liberation', with each constituting a 'uniquely different (though overlapping) awareness of the ultimately transcendent Reality, as perceived through the "lens" of a particular religious tradition' (Hick, 1993, p. 143). This perception is the work of 'the fifth dimension of our nature, the transcendent within us' (our spiritual nature), which answers and 'inclines us to respond' to the transcendent dimension that lies outside us (1999, pp. 2, 8–9, 167, 247, 253–4; cf. 1985; 1995).

Hick argues that there are *different levels of freedom* in a human being's interpretation of their experience. This is minimal in sensory experience, but at its greatest in religious (or atheistic) interpretation (1974, p. 128; 1989, pp. 160–2; 1999, pp. 167–70). 'The more value laden the meaning the greater our cognitive freedom in relation to it', he writes (2000, p. 272; cf. 1993, p. 31). Thus, people adopt 'the religious mode of apperception' by an 'act of will' or a 'state of willingness or consent' (1973, p. 143). Yet he *also* holds that great religious leaders were subject to such powerful religious experiences that their freedom of belief was in practice much more limited. 'They could no more help believing in the reality of God than in the reality of the material world' (1970, p. 112). As Hick endorses the general epistemological principle of trusting our experiences unless we have some reason to doubt them (2010, p. 57; see also on Swinburne and Kwan in Chapter 9, above), he insists that individuals may rationally trust the veridicality of their own religious experiences, at least if these are powerful enough: 'a sufficiently vivid religious experience' would entitle a person 'to claim to know that God is real' (1974, p. 210). However, this poses a problem. If these people cannot help having the religious experiences (experiences interpreted religiously) that they have, in what sense are these interpretations open to the human will? Hick appears to be distinguishing between (a) coming to an awareness of God, and (b) (afterwards) enjoying that experience. Once people have allowed themselves freely to become conscious of God, 'that experience is, at its top levels of intensity, coercive. It creates the situation of the person who *cannot help* believing in the reality of God' (1970, p. 114). Even so, we might argue that individuals only have *indirect control* over their religious experiences, presumably by freely opening themselves up to the initial religious interpretation.

Hick believes that there are *tests that we may apply to those who claim religious experience*. These include asking ourselves whether we regard them 'as fully sane, sober and rational persons', including whether their claims are 'consistent with our other knowledge' based on 'the rest of our experience' (2008, p. 28). But he came to regard the *key criterion* for distinguishing 'between veridical and delusory religious experiences' (1999, p. 163) to be their *effects in human life* (cf. Chapter 7, above). 'The salvation/liberation which it is the function of religion to facilitate is a human transformation which ... consists, as one of its aspects, in moral goodness' (1989, p. 309) or in spiritual character (1995, p. 77). In this world, the 'soteriological power' of religions is something that can be measured only by these 'human fruits' (1995, p. 111). Essentially, this is a test that may be used by anyone who undergoes a religious experience, so as to authenticate their own experience (2006, pp. 42–3). If our religious experience is of a certain kind, and sufficiently intense, it is likely to change our beliefs and behaviour.

Even some of Hick's Christian critics, however, argue that this does not 'settle the truth question' (Clark Pinnock), in that what is merely 'one *goal* of true religion' has been mistaken 'for a *criterion of truth* in religion' (Douglas Geivett and Gary Phillips). But Hick responds that 'saving truth' is not comparable to other forms of truth, and maintains that a religion's truthfulness '*does* consist in its power to bring people to the ultimate reality we call God, and thereby ... to produce in them the kind of fruit' esteemed by the religions, 'in this present life' (references are in Okholm and Phillips, 1996, pp. 61, 78, 87, 185). (See also Chapter 7, above.) Although this does not *prove* that it is a genuine experience, it may be enough for a person to consider themselves rationally entitled to accept it as such.

> Yet, Hick's position leaves room for agnosticism as well as mystery in religious knowing, for he explicitly acknowledges theological error and 'imaginative projection' (1997, p. 610), in addition to the possibility of delusory religious experiences (2008, pp. 27–8).[5]

Suggestions for Further Reading

Introductory

Burhenn, Herbert, 1995, 'Philosophy and Religious Experience', in Ralph W. Hood, Jr (ed.), *Handbook of Religious Experience*, Birmingham, AL: Religious Education Press, ch. 7 (pp. 144–60).

Davies, Brian, OP, 1993, *An Introduction to the Philosophy of Religion*, Oxford: Oxford University Press, ch. 7 (pp. 120–40).

Gellman, Jerome I., 2005, 'Mysticism and Religious Experience', in William J. Wainwright (ed.), *The Oxford Handbook of Philosophy of Religion*, New York: Oxford University Press, ch. 6 (pp. 138–67).

Griffith-Dickson, Gwen, 2000, *Human and Divine: An Introduction to the Philosophy of Religious Experience*, London: Duckworth, part II (pp. 81–144).

Hick, John, 1973 [1969], 'Religious Faith as Experiencing-As', in John Hick, *God and the Universe of Faiths: Essays in the Philosophy of Religion*, London: Macmillan, ch. 3 (pp. 37–52).

Hick, John, 2008 [1976], 'Mystical Experience as Cognition', in John Hick, *Who or What is God? And Other Investigations*, London: SCM Press, ch. 2 (pp. 14–30).

Peterson, Michael, Hasker, William, Reichenbach, Bruce and Basinger, David, 2013, *Reason and Religious Belief: An Introduction to the Philosophy of Religion*, New York: Oxford University Press, ch. 3 (pp. 33–58).

Advanced

Franks Davis, Caroline, 1999 [1989], *The Evidential Force of Religious Experience*, Oxford: Clarendon.

Swinburne, Richard, 2004, *The Existence of God*, Oxford: Clarendon, ch. 13 (pp. 293–327).

Wainwright, William J., 1981, *Mysticism: A Study of its Nature, Cognitive Value and Moral Implications*, Brighton: Harvester.

Wildman, Wesley J., 2011, *Religious and Spiritual Experiences*, New York: Cambridge University Press, ch. 5 (pp. 144–86).

Notes

1 That is, contiguous, sharing a common boundary.

2 For further material on James, see Lash, 1988, chs 1–8; John E. Smith, 'William James's Account of Mysticism: A Critical Appraisal', in Katz, 1983, pp. 247–79; Richard M. Gale, in Oppy and Trakakis, 2009b, ch. 2 (pp. 13–25).

3 Hick reports on his own religious experiences at Hick, 1999, p. 113; 2002, p. 223; 2010, p. 49.

4 For example, seeing this ambiguous image as either a duck or a rabbit: https://en.wikipedia.org/wiki/Rabbit–duck_illusion.

5 For other criticisms of Hick, see Donovan, 1979, pp. 78–87; Proudfoot, 1985, pp. 171–4; Stoeber, 1992; Heim, 2000; Astley, 2017a.

20

The Anthropology and Sociology of Religious and Spiritual Experience

Historical, cultural and intellectual changes in societies affect the context in which religious and spiritual experiences arise and are assessed. Human beings are greatly influenced by many other people, with their ideas, practices and creations. We all exist, experience and think, not just as individuals, but also as social animals and members of a variety of interconnected social groups (parents and families, peers [persons of the same age, status or ability] and friends, workplace and leisure communities, and on several different levels of *local* belonging). It is to some extent within these different communities that we inherit, learn and are socialized, critically reflect on and adopt or reject many different beliefs, attitudes, values and dispositions to act and experience. 'While psychology hones in on elaborate exploration of the effects of religious experience on the individual, sociology studies the social stage upon which these experiences naturally take place' (Poloma, 1995, p. 177). Both anthropology and sociology are determinedly *social* in their focus.

The sociologist of religion, James Spickard, has argued that 'sociologists have not comprehended religious experiences well' (Spickard, 1993, p. 109). The reason, he claimed at the time, is that William James and others treated experiences as private, thus removing them (unlike James's 'over-beliefs')[1] from the social sphere. In order to progress, Spickard suggested, the sociological study of religious experience should:

- 'acknowledge the role that religious ideas and institutions play in the construction of the experiences themselves' (p. 111), not limiting social influence to ideas alone and not limiting the conceptual component of experience to beliefs alone;
- recognize that people can 'learn to have religious experiences – at least some of them' (p. 116), but also that ideas have little to do with this social formation or learning process, which often occurs as a result of (e.g. meditative) practice 'for which conceptual rules … are next to useless' (p. 117); and
- acknowledge the social dimension of religious practice, in which the 'patterns of inner time' of experience are shared in rituals – so that 'the experiences that people have in religious settings are profoundly social' (p. 119). (He draws the analogy with musical performance.)

The Disciplines

Sociology and anthropology[2] are social sciences that study the behaviour of human beings within their societies. The key difference between the two disciplines is often said to be that, where the focus of study for sociology is *society* and social interactions and institutions, the attention of anthropologists is more directed towards *culture*.[3] While these disciplines overlap in terms of their methods, it is fair to say that sociologists mainly sample a society through interview and questionnaire surveys (see Chapter 3) along with some other methods,[4] whereas anthropologists are more likely to engage in qualitative study of the culture of a community by living within it as 'participant-observers'.[5] Sociological research is usually on a larger scale and tends, if anything, to be more theoretical than is anthropology.

The focus of both disciplines on practice, effects and context means that, in their studies of ritual, worship, healings, etc., it is the *external* expression and evocation of religious and spiritual experiences that is foregrounded, rather than their more internal dimensions. In fact, sociologists do not regard religious and spiritual experiences as internal, immediate, psychological states that are 'separate from, or antecedent to the external social relations of actual human beings within socially interactive moments' (Tite, 2013, p. 10). Rather, a socially based scholarly study of religion regards experience as meaningful 'in light of the actual ritual and political context in which the participant is located' (Fitzgerald, 2000, pp. 129–30). These disciplines, therefore, frequently challenge more individualistic, generalized or abstract accounts, including some psychological, philosophical and theological accounts that may mislead by ignoring the situational features of religious experiences.

The truthfulness of experiential claims are not thought of as relevant to the sociological study of these 'experiential moments', their veridicality being neither affirmed nor denied. However, the methodological neutrality of some anthropological and sociological studies of religious experiences has sometimes worn rather thin, as we shall observe.

Social psychology traditionally bridges the gap between psychology and sociology, being concerned with the way that individuals' attitudes, feelings, beliefs, motivations and behaviour are influenced by society, and how these elements subsequently influence a person's interaction with others. Charles Glock and Rodney Stark (e.g. Stark, 1965: see Chapter 3, above) provided an early sociological taxonomy of religious experience, and the sociologist Andrew Greeley (e.g. Greeley, 1974) did empirical work on peak, paranormal, ecstatic and occult experiences. Empirical studies that quantify the extent of these and other religious and spiritual experiences in societies may be regarded as essentially sociological in nature (also see Chapter 3).

Exercise: Among the Articles

Sociology of Religion

Read and critically assess the following journal articles:

Straus, Roger A., 1981, 'The Social-Psychology of Religious Experience: A Naturalistic Approach', Sociological Analysis, 42, 1, pp. 57–67.

In this article, Roger Straus seeks to resolve the tension between the felt nature of religious experience, as direct and unmediated, and its context-dependent imagery. His approach involves advocating a 'sociological' social psychological approach that differentiates 'conceptual interpretation from perceptual analogizing': identifying the five 'chapters' involved in the 'story' or 'drama' of having a religious experience and noting their social perspectives.

Neitz, Mary Jo and Spickard, James V., 1990, 'Steps toward a Sociology of Religious Experience: The Theories of Mihaly Csikszentmihalyi and Alfred Schutz', *Sociological Analysis*, 51, 1, pp. 15–33.

The next article explores, as a contribution to the sociological study of religious experience, Mihaly Csikszentmihalyi's theory of 'flow' experiences and Alfred Schutz's theory of the tuning-in relationship (as in a musical performance). The authors regard these two theories as offering some useful possibilities for comprehending in social terms the religious experience of 'otherness'.

Yamane, David, 2000, 'Narrative and Religious Experience', *Sociology of Religion*, 61, 2, pp. 171–89.

According to David Yamane, what sociologists study when they study religious experience is not 'phenomenological descriptions' of these experiences, but 'how an experience is made meaningful'. Reviewing previous empirical approaches, Yamane both welcomes and criticizes the work on the nature of experience by Neitz and Spickard (see above), before recommending an alternative, and superior, *narrative approach* to studying the meaning of religious experience. Here, as elsewhere, the primary goal of an interpretive sociology must be 'the hermeneutic recovery of meaning through narrative'.

McRoberts, Omar M., 2004, 'Beyond Mysterium Tremendum: Thoughts toward an Aesthetic Study of Religious Experience', *The Annals of the American Academy of Political and Social Science*, 595, pp. 190–203.

In this contribution, Omar McRoberts addresses the contentious ethnographical issue of the role of empathy in the study of religion, as well as the insistence of Rudolf Otto (and of the phenomenology of religion) that religious experience is solely an ineffable numinous experience that one must experience oneself in order to understand it.

As an alternative way forward, McRoberts proposes 'an aesthetics-oriented method' in the study of religious experience. Through his own ethnographic work with people from many churches, he reports that he 'came to understand beauty as a key part of religious experience and religious communities partly as spaces where people generate and appreciate certain kinds of beauty'. An aesthetic approach is claimed to expand our understanding of religious experience, thereby deepening its sociological consideration.

Coming to Terms
with the Sociology of Religious and Spiritual Experiences

Individualization is a sociological concept particularly sympathetic to a stress on individual experience, rather than tradition. Individualization highlights the autonomy of the individual self and its 'choices' (including 'consumer'-type choices, see below) over against communal values, authority and control. Thus, David Lyon has argued that the therapeutic power of charismatic religious experience, coupled with the Charismatic Movement's deconstruction and deregulation of religion, serve as key elements in its success during the cultural shift from modernity to postmodernity (or 'late modernity') (Lyon, 2000; cf. Wilkinson, 2014, pp. 229–30; on postmodernism, see also Chapter 19, above).

The rational choice (or market) theory in sociology argues that combined behaviour reflects the sum of the choices made by individuals in a society, with each individual choosing in a way that is based on their own preferences and the constraints they face. Thus, subjective individual motivation explains social phenomena. Rational choice theory has been used (e.g. by Stark and Finke) to argue for religious change in 'providers'. For example, in the impact of Pentecostalism where the demand for religion remains high, 'secularization is not the end of religion but only the end of certain providers. Secularization is replaced by religious revival or renewal' (Wilkinson, 2014, p. 224).

> **'Specialness':** The relationship between the exceptional and the everyday is regarded as a key theme in Durkheim and the sociology of religion. Ann Taves employs 'specialness' as a generic term to cover the categories of 'sacred, magical, mystical, superstitious, spiritual, mystical and/or religious' things (Taves, 2009, pp. 26-8, 161-2). The term usefully connects with observable social behaviours – practices of setting apart and forbidding,[6] which are accompanied by certain beliefs. This conceptualization includes, but is not equivalent to, actions and beliefs associated with ascriptions of high positive value. These 'things that someone or some group has granted some sort of special status' (p. 27) include 'ideal things' and absolutes and (surely?) 'values' (such as truth, purity or beauty), but Taves thinks of the category as also embracing 'anomalous' things, agents, places, experiences etc. (pp. 38-46, 163).[7]
>
> **The Thomas Theory:** This sociological theory, formulated in 1928 by William and Dorothy Thomas, is of obvious relevance to the evaluation of religious experiences. It states that if people define situations as real, they are real in their consequences.

Origins of Anthropology

Although anthropology has been lauded for producing the 'best phenomenology', based on direct observation of people's behaviour and accounts of their beliefs that are 'not impaired by religious prejudice' (Staal, 1975, pp. 101-2), at its foundation the science was equally concerned to understand *the origin and development of religion* and, therefore, of the gods/God. These concerns produced the *naturalistic accounts of the invention of religion* that are to be found in the writings of E. B. Tylor (1871) and James Frazer (1950 [1890]). These texts have been very influential in encouraging anthropologists to adopt an *intellectualist approach* that emphasizes human reasoning processes (which were regarded as common across species), and their past errors, in this area. Thus, Tylor treated belief in spiritual beings as rational but mistaken; and for Bronislaw Malinowski such beliefs were purely psychological, being built up by 'observations and by inferences' that produced mistakes that were 'comprehensible in a crude and untutored mind' (Malinowski, 1948, p. 2). By contrast, Durkheim's naturalism focused on social bonding rather than personal and individual beliefs: that is, on the *'social facts'* that a society imposes on its members.

Much contemporary research on the origin and evolution of religion continues this earlier objective, frequently displaying a similar intellectualist perspective on (or prejudice about?) religion. In these studies, religion is regarded primarily as a system of beliefs that is dominated by pre-scientific explanations of natural phenomena, such as our innate tendency to identify patterns; or is explained by applying psychological attribution theory to religious experiences. These studies tend to be multidisciplinary, drawing on evolutionary psychology, neuropsychology and other disciplines, as well as cultural anthropology (e.g. Guthrie, 1995; Boyer, 2001; Atran, 2002; Wolpert, 2006, ch. 8; cf. Barrett, 2004). Fiona Bowie has commented that 'the commonest anthropological approach to the study of religion from the nineteenth century to the present involves steadfastly ignoring or even ridiculing any ontological claims' (Bowie, in Schmidt, 2016b, p. 17).

A New Anthropology?

However, Bowie has also identified 'an alternative anthropological tradition' to the one outlined above, which she labels the 'experiential lineage'. This is the form that the discipline takes when its scholars have undergone some direct personal religious or spiritual experience themselves. Key historical figures in the movement include Lucien Lévy-Bruhl (1949) and Andrew Lang (1898), who regarded beliefs in spirits and in a supreme being as 'different ways of interpreting what are in fact real and universal experiences that occur in all societies' (Bowie, in Schmidt, 2016b, pp. 21–2). Bowie writes of a renaissance in this lineage as a sea change in recent anthropology of religion, precipitated by those with direct personal experience of the transcendent or paranormal – including herself.

Another key figure was Edith Turner (1921–2016), who encouraged anthropologists to take not only their own field experiences seriously, but also the possibility that spiritual beings had a more than symbolic existence. In her brief 1993 article, 'The Reality of Spirits: A Tabooed or Permitted Field of Study?' (see below), Turner challenged the tendency of scholars in her discipline to 'rationalize away the native claim that spirits exist' by treating such assertions as merely symbolic. More radical participant observation, she insists, will question such 'positivistic assumptions' as and when the researcher fully engages in another's rituals to the extent of sharing some of the same spiritual experiences. However, she recommended, 'to reach a peak experience in a ritual it really is necessary to sink oneself fully in it' (Turner, 1993, p. 9). In a later article, Turner writes that 'full religious experience is here to stay in academic anthropology', lambasting 'detached' anthropology for its 'whole sorry cover-up' and insisting that 'there *are* spirits, and we have no business contradicting so many good people around the world' concerning them (Turner, 2006, pp. 46, 50, 51).[8]

Scholars such as these practise an 'openness to the possibility of transcendence'. Bowie herself propounds a methodology that 'requires imagination in order to enter into the world of the other, to "try it on for size"'. While criticized by other anthropologists for 'going native', those who adopt the approach of 'cognitive, empathetic engagement' in their data gathering, employing methods that involve 'an attitude of openness, not rushing to explanation or prematurely looking for closure', claim that they allow for the possibility of the deeper understanding of religious experience that can only come through personal transformation (Bowie, 2013, pp. 707, 711–14; Bowie, in Schmidt, 2016b, pp. 29–31).

This is quite a remarkable position for social scientists to adopt, and one should not exaggerate either its plausibility or its influence. However, it does parallel the long-running debates over the *differences in approach between theology and religious studies* to the same religious texts, beliefs, activities and experiences, which is itself mirrored by the differences between *confessional and non-confessional religious education*, particularly in British educational institutions.[9]

> **Exercise: Among the Articles**
>
> *Anthropology of Religion*
>
> *Read and critically assess the following journal articles:*
>
> **Turner, Edith, 1993, 'The Reality of Spirits: A Tabooed or Permitted Field of Study?',** *Anthropology of Consciousness***, 4, 1, pp. 9–12.**
>
> See comments on this article, above.
>
> **Bowie, Fiona, 2013, 'Building Bridges, Dissolving Boundaries: Toward a Methodology for the Ethnographic Study of the Afterlife, Mediumship, and Spiritual Beings',** *Journal of the American Academy of Religion***, 81, 3, pp. 698–733.**
>
> **Bowie, Fiona, 2016, 'How to Study Religious Experience: Methodological Reflections on the Study of the Paranormal', in Bettina E. Schmidt (ed.),** *The Study of Religious Experience: Approaches and Methodologies***, Sheffield: Equinox, pp. 13–32.**
>
> Fiona Bowie represents the sea change in anthropology of religion that Edith Turner's 1993 article anticipated. In the two articles represented here, Bowie rehearses the reductive anthropological explanations of religion associated with Tylor, Durkheim and their followers, contrasting them with the alternative 'experiential lineage' of those with direct personal experience of the transcendent or paranormal, such as Lang, James, Turner and many others.
>
> See other comments on these articles, above.

Social Power and Social Explanation

One area in which both sociology and social anthropology have made a distinctive contribution to the study of religious and spiritual experiences is the focus on issues of *social power* (discussed as a topic in the sociology of religion by James Beckford, 1983).[10]

Staal (1975, pp. 102–5) had argued that mysticism constitutes only 'a limiting case' within the perspective of the sociology of religion, as it is 'mainly characterized by its asocial or anti-social outlook'. 'Most mystics', he wrote, 'are drop-outs', not social reformers, whose attitude to the world of society is dislike or contempt. But this view is far too sweeping, and even where it does apply, Staal accepted that 'it does not follow that mysticism does not have social implications, even constructive ones'. A more nuanced influence has been the work of the social anthropologist, I. M. Lewis (2003 [1971]).

> The core hypothesis of Lewis's theory is that mysticism serves as a means of access to political and social power or control; and that the employment of mystical strategies … to gain these ends is not random but associated with social contexts that display fairly clear patterns. (Fales, 1996a, p. 149)

> Lewis … finds that mystical experiences occur primarily in two categories of persons, but are used in every case as a strategy for gaining greater access to social or political power. It is employed by disenfranchised, marginalized groups (who are involuntarily possessed by allegedly malignant spirits that through their unwilling hosts may unleash considerable havoc) to recruit or demand attention and concessions from those who oppress them. And, under certain competitive conditions, it is employed by aspirants to high or central status in whom involuntary possession by a central deity can confer authority, sanctity, and the ability to recruit followers. So mystical possession batters at the doors to power, and provides a route to social legitimation. (Fales, 1996b, pp. 297–8)

Although sociological theories may be considered as complementary to philosophical or theological explanations of the origin of RSEs, Evan Fales argues not only that Lewis's theory provides 'a genuine competitor to the theists' view that Christian mystical experiences, at least, are more or less veridical apprehensions of God' (Fales, 1996b, p. 306), but also that theism 'cannot hope to match the explanatory power or empirical backing' of Lewis's theory (Fales, 1996b, pp. 306, 311). Sociology can thus provide naturalistic theories capable of challenging the veridicality of religious experiences (see Chapter 11).

In a related take on mysticism, Don Cupitt – writing of '*the politics of mysticism*' – has proposed that the mystical tradition in religion also 'represents a protest against the legalism of the dogmatic tradition, its obsession with power and control, and its consequent failure – even refusal – to deliver the personal salvation that it seems to promise'. Instead, mysticism offers a deconstruction of 'the dogmatic ideas of God, the human self, and the infinite qualitative difference between them'. Cupitt also argues that this critique is *gendered*: 'Man distinguishes, Woman unites. Man sets up the great distinctions, Woman tends always to undermine them' (cf. above, Chapter 14). Hence, 'mysticism is regarded with horror as undermining due order. It is unclean, improper, and polluting. It is female' (Cupitt, 1988a, pp. 83–4, cf. 86). We need to see mystics, Cupitt urges, in a very different – and entirely sociocultural – way.

> The mystics do not offer us descriptions of language-transcending experiences. If we look at any canonical list of mystics, what one notices straightaway is that these people are *writers*, wordsmiths. Not reporters but *writers*, ... who convey their message, not by pointing to something outside language, but by the way they play games *with* language ... What they write is best interpreted as a slightly mocking and subversive commentary upon the officially approved forms of words for speaking about God. (Cupitt, 1998a, p. 61)

'Mysticism' was one of Ernst Troeltsch's (1865–1923) 'three main types of the sociological development of Christian thought', alongside the church and the sect (Troeltsch, 1919, p. 993). He intended that this categorization should distinguish groups that had 'no permanent form' and were created 'on a purely personal basis' as a result of 'purely personal and inward experience' (p. 994). Such groups tended to depreciate sensual pleasure and worldly power, wealth and knowledge. They also often adopted ascetic forms of life: not as ends in themselves, however, but as a preparation for a mystical union with Christ. In a similar way, Max Weber characterized individual mystics *in terms of their relation to the social order*: thus, 'the contemplative mystic minimizes his activity by resigning himself to the orders within the world as it is, and lives in them incognito, so to speak' (Weber, 1963 [1922], p. 174). The extent to which these descriptions represent 'ideal types',[11] and are categories that can accommodate the wide variety of individuals and groups laying claim to (the wide variety of) mystical experience, is an empirical issue.

Beyond mysticism, the impulse towards the democratization of religion that is implicit in the fact that many forms of religious and spiritual experience are widely shared or transcend social hierarchies can in principle lead to power being more equally shared across religious institutions, as the relationship between the sacred and profane becomes more of a level playing field and is seen less in terms of a vertical hierarchy of authority. (Hence, 'the more entrenched the religious authority, the more hostile toward haphazard inspiration': Lewis, 1971, p. 34.) The alternative vision of power and truth that characterizes much religious and spiritual experience can thus lead to social and public, as well as intellectual and private, changes among members of a religion – including the relatively powerless. Examples of this may include anti-establishment protests, critiques of class/caste,[12] or the creation of intrareligious sects that increase religious choice for a group. And the prophet, shaman, mystic or charismatic may achieve influence and status for him/herself that is quite unrelated to their wealth and worldly power, the usual indicators of these social assets.

> RSEs function both to support the status quo and also to revolutionize it, and thereby often work at cross purposes … [They] are essential power sources for both priestly conservatism and prophetic revolution. Their distinctive usefulness in both applications lies in their ability to structure imaginations and thereby to leverage staggering displays of commitment to cultural and political projects … of both conservative and revolutionary kinds … The practical importance of RSEs … lies less in the putative truth of their cognitive content and more in the way they help to construct, maintain, and transform social realities. (Wildman, 2011, p. 225)

In more spiritual, moral and theological terms, the existence of these experiences and experients challenges many received views (even in religion) about the true nature of true power. Of course, this is not to deny the ways in which both old and new religious movements have also seen religious experiences as a gateway to more secular forms of power – and, hence, often as a gateway that must be guarded and controlled. Nor is it to dismiss the claim that religious experiences may in fact be (what the individuals and religious traditions that recorded, interpreted and transmitted them usually understood them to be) veridical experiences of a greater power (in the case of Christianity, for example, of God's transforming power in and through Jesus: see Johnson, 1998, pp. 184–5; 2010, pp. 91–2).

Social and cultural changes also both influence and are influenced by the *history of ideas* and of different ways of thinking. David Hay and others have identified (in the West, at least) a number of social, cultural and intellectual factors that have produced an *antagonistic attitude to religion* in general, but especially to views about the significance and truthfulness of religious experience. These include:

- the development of Enlightenment ('modernist') views on the autonomy and universality of reason;
- the postmodern move towards individualism and notions of relative truth;
- the rise of natural science and its ideological cousins of naturalism and 'scientism'; and
- the triumph of secular forms of society and the occluding of the role of religion and its institutions and symbols.
(See, e.g., Hay and Morisy, 1985; Hay, 1987, chs 2–4; 1990, pp. 57–9; 2006, chs 9, 10; Batson, Schoenrade and Ventis, 1993, ch. 2.)

Focusing on ...

Max Weber (1864–1920)

Karl Emil Maximilian Weber was a German professor of political economy, who later worked as an independent scholar. In his writings, he sought to identify the subjective meaning of human activities, their intention and context. He argued in *The Protestant Ethic and the Spirit of Capitalism* that the Calvinist doctrine of predestination, including the unknowability of one's election, had eventually led to a capitalist society; for this had its origins in the belief that doing well financially, and saving and using the fruits of one's labour well, was a sign of God's approval. 'The earning of money within the modern economic order is, so long as it is done legally, the result and the expression of virtue and proficiency in a calling' (Weber, 1930 [1904–05], pp. 53–4).

According to Weber, for the sociologist to explain that a certain category of people adheres to a certain belief is to show that these beliefs *make sense to these people*: the reasons for (the 'rationality' of) these beliefs being the meaning they have for people. It is this meaning that is the sociologist's task to reconstruct and render understandable. Religion offers people *soteriological answers* – that is, answers that provide opportunities for salvation, for example, relief from suffering, and reassuring meaning – as well as '*theodicies*' based on the human need to explain puzzling aspects of the world, chiefly the presence of evil in it. On Weber's view, 'charisma' – a form of individual authority rooted in 'affective' (rather than rational or traditional) forms of action – is reflected in prophetic figures and religious founders: people who were considered to be extraordinary and to have exceptional qualities (see Chapter 16, above). In social organizations, however, this charismatic authority is radically changed by 'routinization', mutating into stable, permanent hierarchies.

In his later studies, Weber dealt with the religions of China and India and Ancient Judaism.

Émile Durkheim (1858–1917)

Durkheim has had a major effect on the sociology of religion, and 'his analysis of religions as collective representations of the emotional and moral dynamics of group life ... remains a key influence' (Mellor, in Oppy and Trakakis, 2009a, p. 288). His own views on the essential nature of religion drew on studies of Australian aborigines, whom he had come to believe held religion in its simplest form. Its basis was the *totem*: a symbolic image or emblem that gave identity to a social group, representing its social bond. The totem is something that is *sacred* and therefore demands respect, and (like a god) possesses value and authority and inspires devotion. Durkheim defined a religion as 'a unified system of beliefs and practices relative to sacred things, that is to say, things set apart and forbidden – beliefs and practices which unite into one single moral community called a Church, all those who adhere to it ... by showing that the idea of religion is inseparable from that of the Church, it makes it clear that religion should be an eminently collective thing' (Durkheim, 1915, p. 47). Not only religion, but all social and cultural phenomena, even science, have their origins in these non-rational processes and the formative power and *sui generis* character of society.

Unlike Weber, Durkheim thought that all religions are essentially alike. Durkheim's thought also contrasts markedly with William James's definition of religion in terms of 'the feelings, acts, and experiences' of individuals both 'in their solitude' and insofar as 'they apprehend themselves to stand in relation to whatever they may consider the divine' (James, 1960, p. 50). By contrast, Durkheim's focus was always on the social rather than the individual. Critics have often questioned this focus,[13] as well as his lack of attention to the truth-claims of religion.

Durkheim followed **Ludwig Feuerbach (1804–72)** who, in 'reducing theology to anthropology', argued that 'religion is the dream of the human mind' and God is a 'projection' of the human essence; and reasoned that 'the divine being is nothing else than ... the human nature purified, freed from the limits of the individual' (Feuerbach, 1957 [1841], pp. xxxviii, xxxix, 14). Similarly, Durkheim held that 'religious force is only the sentiment inspired by the group in its members, but projected outside of the consciousnesses that experience them, and objectified ... [by being] fixed upon some object which thus becomes sacred; but any object might fulfil this function' (Durkheim, 1915, p. 229). The totem is 'at once the symbol of the god and of the society', but it is that 'because the god and the society are only one' (p. 206). The reasons with which the faithful justify their rites and myths, Durkheim argues, 'may be, and generally are, erroneous; but the true reasons do not cease to exist and it is the duty of science to discover them.' He insists that 'there are no religions which are false. All are true in their own fashion; all answer, though in different ways, to the given conditions of human existence' (pp. 2–3). Therefore, there is indeed 'an eternal truth that outside of us there exists something greater than us, with which we enter into communion', for 'the god is only a figurative expression of the society'; hence, he can insist, 'the idea of society is the soul of religion' and 'religious forces are therefore human forces, moral forces' (pp. 226, 419).

Despite his thin ontology, Durkheim seems to capture one of the main *goals* of religious spirituality (and, some would say, of religious experience) in his claim that even the believers 'feel that the real function of religion is not to make us think, to enrich our knowledge ..., but rather, it is to make us act, to aid us to live' – to make us *stronger* to resist the trials of existence and the evils of the world (Durkheim, 1915, p. 416; cf. Hardy, 1966, pp. 67–70; 1979, p. 6; Hay, 2011b, pp. 225–6).

Peter Berger (1929–2017)

Berger was an Austrian-born humanistic sociologist of religion and Lutheran theologian, who wrote on socialization, the social construction of reality and issues in religion and society, including secularization (cf. Berger, 1973). In *A Rumour of Angels*, he wrote of 'signals of transcendence', which are 'reiterated acts and experiences that appear to express essential aspects of man's being', such as our propensity for order. People experience them in everyday life as well as in the Church, and they serve as symbols and glimpses that point beyond the empirical domain of natural reality. At times of great joy or evil, in pursuing order against chaos and in the sense of hope, people feel that there exists some supernatural reality beyond that of human existence. Thus when a mother comforts her crying child by saying, 'everything is all right', her reassurance 'transcending the immediately present two individuals and their situation, implies a statement about reality as such' (Berger, 1971, pp. 70, 73).

In *The Heretical Imperative* (1979), in addition to predicting all-encompassing secularization (a view he later retracted, as in Berger, 1999), Berger acknowledged the powerful process of the domestication of dangerous religious experience by the religious tradition and the religious social structures that mediate it.

Suggestions for Further Reading

Introductory

Bowen, John R., 2016, *Religions in Practice: An Approach to the Anthropology of Religion*, Abingdon: Routledge.

Poloma, Margaret M., 1995, 'The Sociological Context of Religious Experience', in Ralph W. Hood, Jr (ed.), *Handbook of Religious Experience*, Birmingham, AL: Religious Education Press, ch. 8 (pp. 161–82).

Schmidt, Bettina E. (ed.), 2016, *The Study of Religious Experience: Approaches and Methodologies*, Sheffield: Equinox, sections 1, 2 (pp. 13–101).

Wilson, Bryan, 1996, 'Religious Experience: A Sociological Perspective', RERC Second Series Occasional Paper 2, Lampeter: Religious Experience Research Centre available at https://repository.uwtsd.ac.uk/355/.

Advanced

Gellman, Jerome, 1998, 'On a Sociological Challenge to the Veridicality of Religious Experience', *Religious Studies*, 34, 3, pp. 235–51.

Taves, Ann, 2009, *Religious Experience Reconsidered: A Building-Block Approach to the Study of Religion and Other Special Things*, Princeton, NJ: Princeton University Press.

Turner, Edith with others, 1992, *Experiencing Ritual: A New Interpretation of African Healing*, Philadelphia: University of Pennsylvania Press.

Young, David E. and Goulet, Jean-Guy (eds), 1994, *Being Changed by Cross-Cultural Encounters: The Anthropology of Extraordinary Experience*, Peterborough, ON: Broadview Press.

Notes

1 This is James's term (used in *The Varieties of Religious Experience*) for a belief held by an individual that requires more evidence than that person presently holds.

2 Strictly 'social and cultural', as distinct from 'biological', anthropology.

3 'Ethnography' is sometimes identified as the branch of anthropology that is engaged in the systematic study of the customs of people and cultures.

4 For example, studying existing data in archival studies or manipulating social situations through experimental work.

5 This involves the anthropologist, as a result of an intensive involvement through 'fieldwork' over an extended period of time, developing a close and intimate familiarity with a group of individuals and noting their behaviour within their 'cultural environment'. In addition to participation in the life of the group, anthropological methods often include informal interviews and group discussions, direct observation studies and studies of life histories.

6 Sociologists of religion also follow Durkheim in recognizing *taboos* as an important aspect of the protection of what is religious, by separating the sacred and the profane.

7 However, it is not clear how wide this net may be cast. The qualifying phrase about being 'granted some sort of special status' may presumably also be used to label works of Art; people deemed to have high social, cultural, intellectual or economic status; and many other objects or attributes that are treated as 'special' rather than 'ordinary' – and sometimes, at least, set apart or forbidden. But often this is *not* in the way that spiritual or religious objects, agents or experiences are perceived and treated.

A *theological* perspective would, perhaps, tend to make more of the valuing dimension; and would try to introduce talk of 'ultimate' and even of 'intrinsic' values. Thus, Frederick Ferré once defined religion as 'an institutionalized way of valuing most comprehensively [in that what is valued is relevant to the whole of life] and intensively [in that this is valued above all things]' (Ferré, 1967, p. 73). And even T. R. Miles regarded 'a concern for cosmic issues' as part of what makes a religious experience 'religious' (Miles, 1972, p 35). Some theological commentators might also baulk at the focus on the special and extraordinary at the expense of 'ordinariness' in spiritual experience (see above, Chapter 5) and its theological significance (cf. Astley, 2002, ch. 3). We must acknowledge, however, that Taves is here articulating a concept of specialness 'as a larger, more encompassing framework' (p. 29) and affirms that 'simple ascriptions of specialness as such are … not *religions* or *spiritualities*, but rather the basic building blocks that people use to construct them' (p. 46, italics original).

8 In this article Turner cites Colin Turnbull, Paul Stoller, Stephen Friedson and Roy Willis as contributors to this sea change in the anthropology of religion.

9 See, e.g., Smart, 1973a, 1973b; Astley and Francis, 1994, sections 2 and 3 (pp. 73–167); Sterk, 2002; Astley, Francis, Sullivan and Walker, 2004; Oliver and Warrier, 2008; Astley, 2012; Ford, 2013, part one.

10 Beckford lists among the range of meanings commonly attributed to 'power', the capacity to produce (and the actual production of intended/foreseen) effects and 'the probability that commands will be obeyed' (p. 29).

11 Essentially, these are hypothetical constructions subjectively formed from real phenomena, but prone to selection, simplification, exaggeration or accentuation of certain characteristics. ('Ideal type' is one of Weber's own key terms.)

12 Thus, Hans Penner argues that 'the significance of Indian mysticism is its relation to caste' (Penner, in Katz, 1983, p. 113).

13 David Hay argued that Durkheim's view was 'incomplete', citing evidence from Hay and Morisy (1985) that 'approximately 70 percent of reported [religious] experience occurred when the person was alone' (Hay and Socha, 2005, p. 595).

Appendix

Religious and Spiritual Experiences and Neuroscience

As explained in the Introduction, this Appendix provides a select bibliography of the neuroscientific perspective on religious and spiritual experiences, including some reports of experiments on drug- and other clinically-induced experiences.

Introductory

Aden, Ross, 2013, *Religion Today: A Critical Thinking Approach to Religious Studies*, Lanham, MD: Rowman & Littlefield, pp. 185–92, 227–39.

Astley, Jeff, 2015, 'Beyond Science and Nature? Reflections on Scientific Reductionism and Mental and Religious Experience', *Journal for the Study of Religious Experience*, 1, 1, 2015, pp. 32–48, available at http://rerc-journal.tsd.ac.uk/index.php/religiousexp/article/view/8/23.

Beauregard, Mario and O'Leary, Denyse, 2007, *The Spiritual Brain: A Neuroscientist's Case for the Existence of the Soul*, New York: HarperCollins.

Brown, Warren S. and Caetano, Carla, 1992, 'Conversion, Cognition, and Neuropsychology', in H. Newton Malony and Samuel Southard (eds), *Handbook of Religious Conversion*, Birmingham, AL: Religious Education Press, ch. 10 (pp. 147–58).

Connolly, Peter, 2019, *Understanding Religious Experience*, Sheffield: Equinox, pp. 123–31.

d'Aquili, Eugene G. and Newberg, Andrew B., 2001, *Why God Won't Go Away: Brain Science and the Biology of Belief*, New York: Ballantine Books.

Dumsday, Travis, 2008, 'Neuroscience and the Evidential Force of Religious Experience', *Philosophia Christi*, 10, 1, pp. 137–63.

Fox, Mark, 2014, *The Fifth Love: Exploring Accounts of the Extraordinary*, Kidderminster: Spirit and Sage (on Kindle), ch. 4.

Gellman, Jerome, 2018 [2004], 'Mysticism', *Stanford Encyclopedia of Philosophy* §8.7.1, available at https://plato.stanford.edu/entries/mysticism/.

Hamer, Dean, 2004, *The God Gene: How Faith is Hardwired into our Genes*, New York: Random House.

Hick, John, 2006, *The New Frontier of Religion and Science: Religious Experience, Neuroscience and the Transcendent*, Basingstoke: Palgrave Macmillan, chs 5–10 (pp. 55–123).

Shushan, Gregory, 2016, 'Cultural-Linguistic Constructivism and the Challenge of Near-Death and Out-of-Body Experiences', in Bettina E. Schmidt (ed.), *The Study of Religious Experience: Approaches and Methodologies*, Sheffield: Equinox, ch. 4 (pp. 71–87).

Wiebe, Phillip H., 1997, *Visions of Jesus: Direct Encounters from the New Testament to Today*, New York: Oxford University Press, ch. 7 (pp. 193–211).

Advanced

Andersen, M. et al., 2014, 'Mystical Experience in the Lab', *Method and Theory in the Study of Religion*, 26, pp. 217–45.

Azari, Nina P. et al., 2001, 'Neural Correlates of Religious Experience', *European Journal of Neuroscience*, 13, pp. 1649–52.

Barrett, Nathaniel F. and Wildman, Wesley J., 2009, 'Seeing Is Believing? How Reinterpreting Perception as Dynamic Engagement Alters the Justificatory Force of Religious Experience', *International Journal for Philosophy of Religion*, 66, 2, pp. 71–86.

Beauregard, Mario and Paquette, Vincent, 2006, 'Neural Correlates of a Mystical Experience in Carmelite Nuns', *Neuroscience Letters*, 405, pp. 186–190.

Beauregard, Mario, 2007, 'Mind does Really Matter: Evidence from Neuroimaging Studies of Emotional Self-Regulation, Psychotherapy, and Placebo Effect', *Progress in Neurobiology*, 81, pp. 218–36.

d'Aquili, Eugene G. and Newberg, Andrew B., 1993, 'Religious and Mystical States: A Neurological Model', *Zygon*, 28, 2, pp. 177–200.

d'Aquili, Eugene G. and Newberg, Andrew B., 1998, 'The Neuropsychological Basis of Religions, Or Why God Won't Go Away', *Zygon*, 33, no. 2, pp. 187–201.

d'Aquili, Eugene G. and Newberg, Andrew B., 1999, *The Mystical Mind: Probing the Biology of Religious Experience*, Minneapolis, MN: Fortress.

Marsh, Michael N., 2010, *Out-of-Body and Near-Death Experiences: Brain-State Phenomena or Glimpses of Immortality?*, Oxford: Oxford University Press.

McNamara, Patrick (ed.), 2006, *Where God and Science Meet: vol. II, The Neurology of Religious Experience*, Westport, CT: Praeger.

McNamara, Patrick, 2009, *The Neuroscience of Religious Experience*, Cambridge: Cambridge University Press.

Persinger, Michael A., 1997, *Neuropsychological Bases of God Beliefs*, New York: Praeger.

Rottschaefer, William A., 1999, 'The Image of God of Neurotheology: Reflections of Culturally Based Religious Commitments or Evolutionary Based Neuroscientific Theories?', *Zygon*, 34, 1, pp. 57–65.

Runehov, Anne L. C., 2007, *Sacred or Neural? The Potential of Neuroscience to Explain Religious Experience*, Göttingen: Vandenhoeck and Ruprecht.

Wildman, Wesley J., 2011, *Religious and Spiritual Experiences*, New York: Cambridge University Press.

Wildman, Wesley J. and Brothers, Leslie A., 1999, 'A Neuropsychological-Semiotic Model of Religious Experiences', in Robert J. Russell, Nancey Murphy, Theo C. Meyering and Michael A. Arbib (eds), *Neuroscience and the Person: Scientific Perspectives on Divine Action*, Vatican State City: Vatican Observatory; Berkeley, CA: Center for Theology and the Natural Sciences, pp. 347–413.

Wildman, Wesley J. and McNamara, Patrick, 2008, 'Challenges Facing the Neurological Study of Religious Behavior, Belief, and Experience', *Method & Theory in the Study of Religion*, 20, 3, pp. 212–42.

References

Aden, Ross, 2013, *Religion Today: A Critical Thinking Approach to Religious Studies*, Lanham, MD: Rowman & Littlefield.
Albrecht, Daniel E. and Howard, Evan B., 2014, 'Pentecostal Spirituality', in Cecil M. Robeck, Jr and Amos Yong (eds), *The Cambridge Companion to Pentecostalism*, New York: Cambridge University Press, ch. 12 (pp. 235–53).
Almond, Philip C., 1982, *Mystical Experience and Religious Doctrine: An Investigation of the Study of Mysticism in World Religions*, New York: Mouton.
Alston, William, 1966, 'Psychoanalytic Theory and Theistic Belief', in John Hick (ed.), *Faith and the Philosophers*, London: Macmillan, pp. 63–102.
Alston, William P., 1986, 'Is Religious Belief Rational?', in Stanley M. Harrison and Richard C. Taylor (eds), *The Life of Religion*, Lanham, MD: University Press of America, pp. 1–15.
Alston, William P., 1991, *Perceiving God: The Epistemology of Religious Experience*, Ithaca, NY: Cornell University Press.
Alston, William P., 1992, 'The Autonomy of Religious Experience', *International Journal for Philosophy of Religion*, 31, 2/3, pp. 67–87.
Alston, William P., 1994a, 'Précis of *Perceiving God*', *Philosophy and Phenomenological Research*, 54, 4, pp. 863–8.
Alston, William P., 1994b, 'Reply to Commentators', *Philosophy and Phenomenological Research*, 54, 4, pp. 891–9.
Alston, William P., 1994c, 'Response to Critics', *Religious Studies*, 30, 2, pp. 171–80.
Alston, William P., 1998, 'God and Religious Experience', in Brian Davies (ed.), *Philosophy of Religion: A Guide to the Subject*, London: Cassell, ch. 2(d) (pp. 65–9).
Alston, William P., 2005, 'Mystical and Perceptual Awareness of God', in William E. Mann (ed.), *The Blackwell Guide to the Philosophy of Religion*, Oxford: Blackwell, ch. 9 (pp. 198–219).

Altmeyer, Stefan and Klein, Constantin et al., 2015, 'Subjective Definitions of Spirituality and Religion: An Exploratory Study in Germany and the US', *International Journal of Corpus Linguistics*, 20, 4, pp. 526–52.

Astley, Jeff, 1981, 'The Idea of God, the Reality of God and Religious Education', *Theology*, 84, 698, pp. 115–20.

Astley, Jeff, 1994, *The Philosophy of Christian Religious Education*, Birmingham, AL: Religious Education Press.

Astley, Jeff, 2002, *Ordinary Theology: Looking, Listening and Learning in Theology*, Aldershot: Ashgate.

Astley, Jeff, 2003, 'Spiritual Learning: Good for Nothing?', in David Carr and John Haldane (eds), *Spirituality, Philosophy and Education*, London: RoutledgeFalmer, ch. 10 (pp. 141–53).

Astley, Jeff, 2004, *Exploring God-Talk: Using Language in Religion*, London: Darton, Longman and Todd.

Astley, Jeff, 2007, *Christ of the Everyday*, London: SPCK.

Astley, Jeff, 2010, *SCM Studyguide to Christian Doctrine*, London: SCM Press.

Astley, Jeff, 2012, 'A Theological Reflection on the Nature of Religious Truth', in Jeff Astley, Leslie J. Francis, Mandy Robbins and Mualla Selçuk (eds), *Teaching Religion, Teaching Truth: Theoretical and Empirical Perspectives*, Bern: Peter Lang, ch. 14 (pp. 241–62).

Astley, Jeff, 2013. 'Ordinary Theology and the Learning Conversation with Academic Theology', in Jeff Astley and Leslie J. Francis (eds), *Exploring Ordinary Theology: Everyday Christian Believing and the Church*, Farnham: Ashgate, ch. 5 (pp. 45–54).

Astley, Jeff, 2017a, 'Conceptual Enquiry and the Experience of "the Transcendent": John Hick's Contribution to the Dialogue', *Mental Health, Religion & Culture*, 20, 4, pp. 311–22.

Astley, Jeff, 2017b, 'Asking Questions and Analysing Answers about Religious Experience: Developing the Greer Tradition', *Mental Health, Religion & Culture*, 20, 4, pp. 348–58.

Astley, Jeff, 2017c, 'Ian Ramsey on Religious Language', *Challenging Religious Issues*, 11, pp. 2–7, available at http://www.st-marys-centre.org.uk/resources/challenging religiousissues/Issue%2011%20Challenging%20Religious%20Issues%20English.pdf.

Astley, Jeff (ed.) 1991, *How Faith Grows: Faith Development and Christian Education*, London: National Society/Church House Publishing.

Astley, Jeff and Francis, Leslie J. (eds), 1994, *Critical Perspectives on Christian Education: A Reader on the Aims, Principles and Philosophy of Christian Education*, Leominster: Gracewing Fowler Wright.

REFERENCES

Astley, Jeff, Francis, Leslie J., Sullivan, John and Walker, Andrew (eds), 2004, *The Idea of a Christian University: Essays on Theology and Higher Education*, Milton Keynes: Paternoster.
Atran, Scott, 2002, *In Gods We Trust: The Evolutionary Landscape of Religion*, Oxford: Oxford University Press.
Audi, Robert (ed.), 1995, *The Cambridge Dictionary of Philosophy*, Cambridge: Cambridge University Press.
Augustine, 1961 [397–8], *Confessions*, ET Harmondsworth: Penguin.
Avis, Paul (ed.), 1997, *Divine Revelation*, London: Darton, Longman and Todd.
Back, K. W and Bourque, L. B., 1970, 'Can Feelings be Enumerated', *Behavioural Science*, 15, pp. 487–96.
Baelz, Peter, 1975, *The Forgotten Dream*, London: Mowbrays.
Bagger, Matthew C., 1999, *Religious Experience, Justification, and History*, Cambridge: Cambridge University Press.
Baillie, John, 1964 [1954], *The Idea of Revelation in Recent Thought*, New York: Columbia University Press.
Barker, Margaret, 2003, 'Isaiah', in James D. G. Dunn and John W. Rogerson (eds), *Eerdmans Commentary on the Bible*, Grand Rapids, MI: Eerdmans, pp. 489–542.
Barnard, G. William, 1992, 'Explaining the Unexplainable: Wayne Proudfoot's "Religious Experience"', *Journal of the American Academy of Religion*, 60, 2, pp. 231–56.
Barrett, C. K., 1971 [1968], *A Commentary on the First Epistle to the Corinthians*, London: Adam & Charles Black.
Barrett, Cyril, 1990, 'The Language of Ecstasy and the Ecstasy of Language', in Martin Warner (ed.), *The Bible as Rhetoric: Studies in Biblical Persuasion and Credibility*, London: Routledge, ch. 11 (pp. 205–21).
Barrett, Justin L., 2004, *Why Would Anyone Believe in God?*, Walnut Creek, CA: Altamira Press.
Barth, Karl, 1957a [1940], *Church Dogmatics*, vol. II, part 1, ET Edinburgh: T. & T. Clark.
Barth, Karl, 1957b [1942], *Church Dogmatics*, vol. II, part 2, ET Edinburgh: T. & T. Clark.
Barth, Karl, 1962 [1959], *Church Dogmatics*, vol. IV, part 3, second half, ET Edinburgh: T. & T. Clark.
Barth, Karl, 1972 [1952], *Protestant Theology in the Nineteenth Century: Its Background and History*, ET London: SCM Press.
Batson, C. Daniel, Schoenrade, Patricia and Ventis, W. Larry, 1993, *Religion and the Individual: A Socio-Psychological Perspective*, New York: Oxford University Press.
Beardsworth, Timothy, 2009 [1977], *A Sense of Presence: The Phenomenology of Certain Kinds of Visionary and Ecstatic Experiences, Based on a Thousand Con-*

temporary First-Hand Accounts, Lampeter: Religious Experience Research Centre [Oxford: Religious Experience Research Unit].

Beckford, James, 1983, 'The Restoration of "Power" to the Sociology of Religion', *Sociological Analysis*, 44, 1, pp. 11–31.

Berger, Klaus, 2003, *Identity and Experience in the New Testament*, ET Minneapolis, MN: Fortress.

Berger, Peter L., 1971 [1969], *A Rumour of Angels: Modern Society and the Rediscovery of the Supernatural*, Harmondsworth: Penguin.

Berger, Peter L., 1973 [1967], *The Social Reality of Religion*, Harmondsworth: Penguin.

Berger, Peter L., 1979, *The Heretical Imperative: Contemporary Possibilities of Religious Affirmation*, Garden City, NY: Anchor.

Berger, Peter L. (ed.), 1999, *The Desecularization of the World: The Resurgence of Religion in World Politics*, Grand Rapids, MI: Eerdmans.

Bettis, Joseph D. (ed.), 1969, *Phenomenology of Religion*, London: SCM Press.

Blackburn, Simon, 1996, *The Oxford Dictionary of Philosophy*, Oxford: Oxford University Press.

Blackburn, Simon, 2005, *Truth: A Guide for the Perplexed*, London; Penguin.

Borg, Marcus J., 2003, *The Heart of Christianity: Rediscovering a Life of Faith*, New York: HarperCollins.

Bowie, Fiona, 2013, 'Building Bridges, Dissolving Boundaries: Toward a Methodology for the Ethnographic Study of the Afterlife, Mediumship, and Spiritual Beings', *Journal of the American Academy of Religion*, 81, 3, pp. 698–733.

Boyatzis, Chris J., 2001, 'A Critique of Models of Religious Experience', *The International Journal for the Psychology of Religion*, 11, 4, pp. 247–58.

Boyer, Pascal, 2001, *Religion Explained: The Evolutionary Origins of Religious Thought*, New York: Basic Books.

Brown, David, 1994, 'Did Revelation Cease?', in Alan G. Padgett (ed.), *Reason and the Christian Religion*, Oxford: Clarendon, ch. 6 (pp. 121–41).

Brown, David, 1999, *Tradition and Imagination: Revelation and Change*, Oxford: Oxford University Press.

Brown, David, 2000, *Discipleship and Imagination: Christian Tradition and Truth*, Oxford: Oxford University Press.

Burhenn, Herbert, 1995, 'Philosophy and Religious Experience', in Ralph W. Hood, Jr (ed.), *Handbook of Religious Experience*, Birmingham, AL: Religious Education Press, ch. 7 (pp. 144–60).

Bush, Stephen S., 2012, 'Concepts and Religious Experiences: Wayne Proudfoot on the Cultural Construction of Experiences', *Religious Studies*, 48, 1, pp. 101–17.

Butler, Cuthbert, OSB, 1967, *Western Mysticism: The Teaching of Augustine, Gregory and Bernard on Contemplation and the Christian Life*, London: Constable.

Cardeña, Etzel, Lynn, Steven Jay and Krippner, Stanley (eds), 2014, *Varieties of Anomalous Experiences: Examining the Scientific Evidence*, Washington, DC: American Psychological Association.

Cardeña, Etzel, Palmer, John and Marcusson-Clavertz, David (eds), 2015, *Parapsychology: A Handbook for the 21st Century*, Jefferson NC: McFarland & Co.

Cartledge, Mark J., 2017, *Narratives and Numbers: Empirical Studies of Charismatic and Pentecostal Christianity*, Leiden: Brill.

Castro, Madeleine, Burrows, Roger and Wooffitt, Robin, 2014, 'The Paranormal is (Still) Normal: The Sociological Implications of a Survey of Paranormal Experiences in Great Britain', *Sociological Research Online*, 19, 3, 16, available at http://www.socresonline.org.uk/19/3/16.html.

Charry, Ellen T., 2007, 'Experience', in John Webster, Kathryn Tanner and Iain Torrance (eds), *The Oxford Handbook of Systematic Theology*, Oxford: Oxford University Press, ch. 23 (pp. 413–31).

Clarke, W. Norris, 1981, 'The Natural Roots of Religious Experience', *Religious Studies*, 17, 4, pp. 511–23.

Coakley, Sarah, 2009, 'Dark Contemplation and Epistemic Transformation: The Analytic Theologian Re-Meets Teresa of Ávila', in Oliver D. Crisp and Michael C. Rea (eds), *Analytic Theology: New Essays in the Philosophy of Theology*, Oxford: Oxford University Press, ch. 14 (pp. 280–312).

Cohen, J. M. and Phipps, J.-F. (eds), 1979, *The Common Experience*, London: Hutchinson.

Corner, Mark, 2005, *Signs of God: Miracles and their Interpretation*, Aldershot: Ashgate.

Connolly, Peter, 1998, *A Psychology of Possession*, Lampeter: Religious Experience Research Centre.

Connolly, Peter, 2019, *Understanding Religious Experience*, Sheffield: Equinox.

Cook, Christopher C. H., 2018, *Hearing Voices, Demonic and Divine: Scientific and Theological Reflections*, London: Routledge.

Cottingham, John, 2003, *On the Meaning of Life*, London: Routledge.

Cottingham, John, 2005, *The Spiritual Dimension: Religion, Philosophy and Human Value*, Cambridge: Cambridge University Press.

Cottingham, John, 2007, 'What Difference Does it Make? The Nature and Significance of Theistic Belief', in John Cottingham (ed.), *The Meaning of Theism*, Oxford: Blackwell, pp. 19–38.

Cottingham, John, 2009, *Why Believe?* London: Continuum.

Cottingham, John, 2014, *Philosophy of Religion: Towards a More Humane Approach*, Cambridge: Cambridge University Press.

Cottingham, John, 2015, *How to Believe*, London: Bloomsbury.

Craig, William Lane and Moreland, J. P. (eds.), 2012, *The Blackwell Companion to Natural Theology*, Oxford: Wiley-Blackwell.

Craighead, Houston A., 1999, 'William James Be Damned: Is It Evidentially Justifiable to Trust Religious Experience?', *Perspectives in Religious Studies*, 26, 4, pp. 405–15.

Cupitt, Don, 1998a, *Mysticism after Modernity*, Oxford: Blackwell.

Cupitt, Don, 1998b, *The Revelation of Being*, London: SCM Press.

Cupitt, Don, 2001, *Emptiness and Brightness*, Santa Rosa, CA: Polebridge Press.

d'Aquili, Eugene G. and Newberg, Andrew B., 1993, 'Religious and Mystical States: A Neurological Model', *Zygon*, 28, 2, pp. 177–200.

d'Aquili, Eugene G. and Newberg, Andrew B., 1999, *The Mystical Mind: Probing the Biology of Religious Experience*, Minneapolis, MN: Fortress.

Daly, Mary, 1973, *Beyond God the Father: Toward a Philosophy of Women's Liberation*, Boston, MA: Beacon Press.

Davis, Stephen T., 1997, *God, Reason and Theistic Proofs*, Grand Rapids, MI: Eerdmans.

Davis, Stephen T., 2009, 'Revelation and Inspiration', in Thomas P. Flint and Michael C. Rea (eds), *The Oxford Handbook of Philosophical Theology*, Oxford: Oxford University Press, ch. 2 (pp. 30–53).

Derrida, Jacques, 1976 [1967], *Of Grammatology*, ET Baltimore, MA: John Hopkins University Press.

Dillistone, F. W., 1983, 'Experience, Religious', in Alan Richardson and John Bowden (eds), *A New Dictionary of Christian Theology*, London, SCM Press, pp. 204–7.

Donovan, Peter, 1998 [1979], *Interpreting Religious Experience*, Oxford: The Religious Experience Research Centre [London: Sheldon].

Dulles, Avery, SJ, 1983, *Models of Revelation*, Dublin: Gill and Macmillan.

Dunn, James D. G., 1970, *Baptism in the Holy Spirit: A Re-examination of the New Testament Teaching on the Gift of the Spirit in Relation to Pentecostalism Today*, London: SCM Press.

Dunn, James D. G., 1975, *Jesus and the Spirit: A Study of the Religious and Charismatic Experience of Jesus and the First Christians as Reflected in the New Testament*, London: SCM Press.

Dunn, James D. G., 2003, *The Theology of Paul the Apostle*, London: T. & T. Clark.

Dupré, Louis and Saliers, Don E. with John Meyendorff (eds), 1990, *Christian Spirituality: Post-Reformation and Modern*, London: SCM Press.

Dupré, Louis and Wiseman, Kames A., OSB (eds), 2001, *Light from Light: An Anthology of Christian Mysticism*, Mahwah, NJ: Paulist Press.

Durkheim, Émile, 1915, *The Elementary Forms of the Religious Life*, ET London: George Allen & Unwin.

Dykstra, Craig, 1981, *Vision and Character*, New York: Paulist Press.

Eck, Diana L., 1993, *Encountering God: A Spiritual Journey from Bozeman to Banaras*, Boston, MA: Beacon Press.

Eddy, Paul R., 2002, *John Hick's Pluralist Philosophy of World Religions*, Eugene, OR: Wipf and Stock.

Edwards, Anthony C. and Lowis, Mike J., 2001, 'The Batson-Schoenrade-Ventis Model of Religious Experience: Critique and Reformulation', *The International Journal for the Psychology of Religion*, 11, 4, pp. 215–58.

Edwards, Jonathan, 1961 [1746], *Select Works of Jonathan Edwards*, vol. III, *Treatise Concerning the Religious Affections*, London: Banner of Truth.

Edwards, Rem B., 1972, *Reason and Religion: An Introduction to the Philosophy of Religion*, New York: Harcourt Brace Jovanovich.

Egan, Harvey D., SJ (ed.), 1996, *An Anthology of Christian Mysticism*, Collegeville, MN: The Liturgical Press.

Eliade, Mircea, 1959 [1957], *The Sacred and the Profane: The Nature of Religion*, ET New York: Harcourt, Brace & World.

Eliade, Mircea, 1968 [1957], *Myths, Dreams, and Mysteries: The Encounter Between Contemporary Faiths and Archaic Realities*, ET London: Fontana.

Ennis, Philip H., 1967, 'Ecstasy and Everyday Life', *Journal for the Scientific Study of Religion*, 6, 1, pp. 40–8.

Evans, C. Stephen, 1985, *Philosophy of Religion: Thinking about Faith*, Downers Grove, IL: InterVarsity Press.

Evans, Donald, 1979, *Struggle and Fulfillment: The Inner Dynamics of Religion and Morality*, Cleveland, OH: Collins.

Evans, Donald, 1989, 'Can Philosophers Limit What Mystics Can Do? A Critique of Steven Katz', *Religious Studies*, 25, 1, pp. 53–60.

Evans, Donald, 1993, *Spirituality and Human Nature*, Albany, NY: State University of New York Press.

Fales, Evan, 1996a, 'Scientific Explanations of Mystical Experiences, Part I: The Case of St. Teresa', *Religious Studies*, 32, 2, pp. 143–63.

Fales, Evan, 1996b, 'Scientific Explanations of Mystical Experiences: II. The Challenge to Theism', *Religious Studies*, 32, 3, pp. 297–313.

Fenwick, Peter and Fenwick, Elizabeth, 1996, *The Truth in the Light: An Investigation of Over 300 Near-Death Experiences*, London: Hodder Headline.

Fenwick, Peter and Fenwick, Elizabeth, 2008, *The Art of Dying: A Journey to Elsewhere*, London: Continuum.

Ferré, Frederick, 1967, *Basic Modern Philosophy of Religion*, London, George Allen & Unwin.

Feuerbach, Ludwig, 1957 [1841], *The Essence of Christianity*, ET New York: Harper & Row.

Firth, Shirley and Wilson, Joanna (eds), 2019, *Death, the Gateway to Life: An Interdisciplinary Exploration of Near-Death Experiences*, Winchester: University of Winchester (available from David.Simpkin@winchester.ac.uk).

Fischer, Roland, 1978, 'Cartography of Conscious States: Integration of East and West', in A. Arthur Sugarman and Ralph E. Tarter (eds), *Expanding Dimensions of Consciousness*, New York: Springer, pp. 24–57.

Fitzgerald, Timothy, 2000, 'Experience', in Willi Braun and Russell T. McCutcheon (eds), *Guide to the Study of Religion*, London: Cassell, ch. 10 (pp. 125–39).

Flew, Antony, 1966, *God and Philosophy*, London: Hutchinson.

Flew, Antony (ed.), 1979, *A Dictionary of Philosophy*, London: Pan.

Fodor, James, 2005, 'Postliberal Theology', in David F. Ford with Rachel Muers (eds), *The Modern Theologians: An Introduction to Christian Theology since 1918*, third edition, Oxford: Blackwell, ch. 14 (pp. 229–48).

Ford, David. F., 2013, *Theology: A Very Short Introduction*, Oxford: Oxford University Press.

Forgie, J. William, 1985, 'Hyper-Kantianism in Recent Discussions of Mystical Experience', *Religious Studies*, 21, 2, pp. 205–18.

Forman, Robert K. C., 1999, *Mysticism, Mind, Consciousness*, Albany, NY: State University of New York Press.

Forman, Robert K. C. (ed.), 1990, *The Problem of Pure Consciousness: Mysticism and Philosophy*, New York: Oxford University Press.

Fowler, James W., 1981, *Stages of Faith: The Psychology of Human Development and the Quest for Meaning*, San Francisco: Harper & Row.

Fox, Mark, 2003, *Through the Valley of the Shadow of Death: Religion, Spirituality and the Near-Death Experience*, London: Routledge.

Fox, Mark, 2008, *Spiritual Encounters with Unusual Light Phenomena: Lightforms*, Cardiff: University of Wales Press.

Fox, Mark, 2014, *The Fifth Love: Exploring Accounts of the Extraordinary*, Kidderminster: Spirit and Sage (on Kindle).

Francis, Leslie J., 2013, 'Mystical Orientation, Mystical Experience, and Mysticism', *Studies in Chinese Religions*, 2, pp. 67–99.

Francis, Leslie J., Ziebertz, Hans-Georg, Robbins, Mandy and Reindl, Marian, 2015, 'Mystical Experience and Psychopathology: A Study among Secular, Christian, and Muslim Youth in Germany', *Pastoral Psychology*, 64, 369–79.

Franke, John R., 2005, *The Character of Theology: An Introduction to Its Nature, Task, and Purpose*, Grand Rapids, MI: Baker Academic.

Franklin, John, 2014, *Exploration into Spirit: A Power Greater Than…*, Lampeter: AHSSE.

Franks Davis, Caroline, 1986, 'The Devotional Experiment', *Religious Studies*, 22, 1, pp. 15–28.

Franks Davis, Caroline, 1999 [1989], *The Evidential Force of Religious Experience*, Oxford: Clarendon.

Frazer, James, 1950 [1922, 1890], *The Golden Bough*, abridged edition, London: Macmillan and Co.

Freud, Sigmund, 1928 [1927], *The Future of an Illusion*, ET London: Hogarth Press.

Freud, Sigmund, 1973 [1933], *New Introductory Lectures on Psychoanalysis*, ET Harmondsworth: Penguin.

Gale, Richard M., 1960, 'Mysticism and Philosophy', *Journal of Philosophy*, 57, 14, pp. 471–81.

Gale, Richard M., 1991, *On the Nature and Existence of God*, Cambridge: Cambridge University Press.

Gale, Richard, 1994a, 'The Overall Argument of Alston's *Perceiving God*', *Religious Studies*, 30, 2, pp. 135–49.

Gale, Richard M., 1994b, 'Swinburne's Argument from Religious Experience', in Alan G. Padgett (ed.), *Reason and the Christian Religion*, Oxford: Clarendon, ch. 4 (pp. 39–63).

Gale, Richard M., 2005, 'On the Cognitivity of Mystical Experiences', *Faith and Philosophy*, 22, 4, pp. 426–41.

Gaskin, J. C. A., 1984, *The Quest for Eternity: An Outline of the Philosophy of Religion*, Harmondsworth: Penguin.

Gavrilyuk, Paul L. and Coakley, Sarah (eds), 2012, *The Spiritual Senses: Perceiving God in Western Christianity*, Cambridge: Cambridge University Press.

Geertz, Clifford, 1993, *The Interpretation of Culture*, London: HarperCollins.

Gellman, Jerome I., 2005, 'Mysticism and Religious Experience', in William J. Wainwright (ed.), *The Oxford Handbook of Philosophy of Religion*, Oxford: Oxford University Press, ch. 6 (pp. 138–67).

Gellman, Jerome, 2018 [2004], 'Mysticism', *Stanford Encyclopedia of Philosophy*, available at https://plato.stanford.edu/entries/mysticism/.

Gimello, Robert M., 1978, 'Mysticism and Meditation', in Steven T. Katz (ed.), *Mysticism and Philosophical Analysis*, New York: Oxford University Press, pp. 170–99.

Gimello, Robert M., 1983, 'Mysticism in its Contexts', in Steven T. Katz (ed.), *Mysticism and Religious Traditions*, New York: Oxford University Press, pp. 61–88.

Glock, Charles Y. and Stark, Rodney, 1965, *Religion and Society in Tension*, Chicago: Rand McNally.

Goleman, Daniel, 1977, *The Varieties of Meditative Experience*, New York: E. P. Dutton.

Goodman, Felicitas D., 2008 [1972], *Speaking in Tongues: A Cross-Cultural Study of Glossolalia*, Eugene, OR: Wipf & Stock.

Gorringe, Timothy, 1989, 'Sacraments', in Robert Morgan (ed.), *The Religion of the Incarnation: Anglican Essays in Commemoration of Lux Mundi*, Bristol: Bristol Classical Press, pp. 158–71.

Greeley, Andrew M., 1974, *Ecstasy: A Way of Knowing*, Englewood Cliffs, NJ: Prentice Hall.

Greer, John E., 1981, 'Religious Experience and Religious Education', *Search*, 4, 1, pp. 23–34.

Greer, John E., 1982, 'The Religious Experience of Northern Irish Pupils', *The Irish Catechist*, 6, 2, pp. 49–58.

Greyson, Bruce, 2012, 'The Psychology of Near-Death Experiences and Spirituality', in Lisa J. Miller (ed.), *The Oxford Handbook of Psychology and Spirituality*, New York: Oxford University Press, ch. 33 (pp. 514–27).

Griffith-Dickson, Gwen, 2000, *Human and Divine: An Introduction to the Philosophy of Religious Experience*, London: Duckworth.

Griffith-Dickson, Gwen, 2005, *The Philosophy of Religion*, London: SCM Press.

Griffith-Dickson, Gwen, 2007, 'Religious Experience', in Chad Meister and Paul Copan (eds), *The Routledge Companion to Philosophy of Religion*, London: Routledge, ch. 63 (pp. 682–91).

Gunton, Colin E., 1995, *A Brief Theology of Revelation*, Edinburgh: T. & T. Clark.

Guthrie, Stewart, 1995, *Faces in the Clouds*, New York: Oxford University Press.

Gutting, Gary, 1982, *Religious Belief and Religious Skepticism*, Notre Dame, IN: University of Notre Dame Press.

Haas, Alois Maria, 1988, 'Schools of late Medieval Mysticism', in Jill Raitt, with Bernard McGinn and John Meyendorff (eds), *Christian Spirituality: High Middle Ages and Reformation*, London: SCM Press, ch. 6 (pp. 140–75).

Hagner, Donald A., 2010, 'Jesus' Self-Understanding', in Craig A. Evans (ed.), *The Routledge Encyclopedia of the Historical Jesus*, New York: Routledge, pp. 324–33.

Happold, F. C., 1970 [1963], *Mysticism: A Study and an Anthology*, Harmondsworth: Penguin.

Halligan, Fredrica R., 1995, 'Jungian Theory and Religious Experience', in Ralph W. Hood, Jr (ed.), *Handbook of Religious Experience*, Birmingham, AL: Religious Education Press, ch. 11 (pp. 231–54).

Hardy, Alister, 1966, *The Divine Flame: An Essay Towards a Natural History of Religion*, London: Collins.

Hardy, Alister, 1975, *The Biology of God: A Scientist's Study of Man the Religious Animal*, London: Jonathan Cape.

Hardy, Alister, 1979, *The Spiritual Nature of Man: A Study of Contemporary Religious Experience*, Oxford: Clarendon.

Harton, F. P., 1933, *The Elements of the Spiritual Life: A Study in Ascetical Theology*, London: SPCK.

Hauerwas, Stanley, with Goldstone, Brian, 2011, 'Disciplined Seeing: Forms of Christianity and Forms of Life', in Stanley Hauerwas (ed.), *Learning to Speak Christian*, London: SCM Press, ch. 3 (pp. 33–60).

Hay, David, 1979, 'Religious Experience Amongst a Group of Post-Graduate Students: A Qualitative Study', *Journal for the Scientific Study of Religion*, 18, 2, pp. 164–82.

Hay, David, 1987 [1982], *Exploring Inner Space: Scientists and Religious Experience*, London: Mowbray.

Hay, David, 1988, 'Asking Questions about Religious Experience', *Religion*, 18, 3, pp. 217–29.

Hay, David, 1990, *Religious Experience Today: Studying the Facts*, London: Mowbray.

Hay, David, 1994, '"The Biology of God": What is the Current Status of Hardy's Hypothesis?', *The International Journal for the Psychology of Religion*, 4, 1, pp. 1–23.

Hay, David, 2006, *Something There: The Biology of the Human Spirit*, London: Darton, Longman and Todd.

Hay, David, 2011a, 'Experience', in Arthur Holder (ed.), *The Blackwell Companion to Christian Spirituality*, Oxford: Wiley-Blackwell, ch. 24 (pp. 419–41).

Hay, David, 2011b, *God's Biologist: A Life of Alister Hardy*, London: Darton, Longman and Todd.

Hay, David and Heald, Gordon, 1987, 'Religion is Good for You', *New Society*, 17 April 1987, pp. 20–2.

Hay, David and Hunt, Kay, 2000, *Understanding the Spirituality of People Who Don't Go to Church*, Nottingham: University of Nottingham.

Hay, David and Morisy, Ann, 1978, 'Reports of Ecstatic, Paranormal, or Religious Experience in Great Britain and the United States: A Comparison of Trends', *Journal for the Scientific Study of Religion*, 17, 3, pp. 255–68.

Hay, David and Morisy, Ann, 1985, 'Religious Meanings: A Contemporary Paradox', *Review of Religious Research*, 26, 3, pp. 213–27.

Hay, David, Reich, Helmut and Utsch, Michael, 2006, 'Spiritual Development: Intersection and Divergence with Religious Development', in Eugene Roehlkepartain, Pamela King, Linda Wagner and Peter Benson (eds), *The Handbook of Spiritual Development in Childhood and Adolescence*, Thousand Oaks, CA: Sage, ch. 4 (pp. 46–59).

Hay, David and Socha, Pawel M., 2005, 'Spirituality as a Natural Phenomenon: Bringing Biological and Psychological Perspectives Together', *Zygon*, 40, 3, pp. 589–612.

Heelas, Paul and Woodhead, Linda et al., 2005, *The Spiritual Revolution: Why Religion is Giving Way to Spirituality*, Oxford: Blackwell.

Heim, S. Mark, 2000, 'Saving the Particulars: Religious Experience and Religious Ends', *Religious Studies*, 36, 4, pp. 435–53.

Helm, Paul, 1997, 'John Calvin's *Sensus Divinitatis*', in *Faith and Understanding*, Edinburgh: Edinburgh University Press, ch. 8 (pp. 177–204).

Hepburn, Ronald W., 1992, 'Religious Imagination', in Michael McGhee (ed.), *Philosophy, Religion and the Spiritual Life*, Cambridge: Cambridge University Press, pp. 127–43.

Hick, John, 1967, 'Revelation', in Paul Edwards, *The Encyclopedia of Philosophy*, vol. 7, London: Collier Macmillan, pp. 189–91.

Hick, John, 1970, *Arguments for the Existence of God*, London: Macmillan.

Hick, John, 1973, *God and the Universe of Faiths: Essays in the Philosophy of Religion*, London: Macmillan.

Hick, John, 1974 [1966], *Faith and Knowledge*, London: Collins.

Hick, John, 1985, *Problems of Religious Pluralism*, Basingstoke: Macmillan.

Hick, John, 1989a [1983, 1973, 1963], *Philosophy of Religion*, Englewood Cliffs, NJ: Prentice Hall.

Hick, John, 1993, *Disputed Questions in Theology and the Philosophy of Religion*, New Haven, CT: Yale University Press.

Hick, John, 1995, *The Rainbow of Faiths: Critical Dialogues on Religious Pluralism*, London: SCM Press.

Hick, John, 1997, 'Religious Pluralism', in Philip L. Quinn and Charles Taliaferro (eds), *A Companion to Philosophy of Religion*, Oxford: Blackwell, ch. 77 (pp. 607–14).

Hick, John, 2000, 'The Religious Meaning of Life', in Joseph Runzo and Nancy M. Martin (eds), *The Meaning of Life in the World Religions*, Oxford: Oneworld, ch. 15 (pp. 269–86).

Hick, John, 2002, *John Hick: An Autobiography*, Oxford: Oneworld.

Hick, John, 2004 [1999], *The Fifth Dimension: An Exploration of the Spiritual Realm*, Oxford Oneworld.

Hick, John, 2004 [1989b], *An Interpretation of Religion: Human Responses to the Transcendent*, London: Macmillan.

Hick, John, 2006, *The New Frontier of Religion and Science: Religious Experience, Neuroscience and the Transcendent*, Basingstoke: Palgrave Macmillan.

Hick, John, 2008, *Who or What is God? And Other Investigations*, London: SCM Press.

Hick, John, 2010, *Between Faith and Doubt: Dialogues on Religion and Reason*, Basingstoke: Palgrave Macmillan.

Hobbes, Thomas, 1914 [1651], *Leviathan*, London: Dent.

Holder, Arthur, 2011, 'Introduction', in Arthur Holder (ed.), *The Blackwell Companion to Christian Spirituality*, Oxford: Wiley-Blackwell, pp. 1–12.

Honderich, Ted (ed.), 1995, *The Oxford Companion to Philosophy*, Oxford: Oxford University Press.

Hood, Ralph W., Jr, 1975, 'The Construction and Preliminary Validation of a Measure of Reported Mystical Experience', *Journal for the Scientific Study of Religion*, 14, 1, pp. 29–41.

Hood, Ralph W., Jr, 1995a, 'The Facilitation of Religious Experience', in Ralph W. Hood, Jr (ed.), *Handbook of Religious Experience*, Birmingham, AL: Religious Education Press, ch. 24 (pp. 568–97).

Hood, Ralph W., Jr (ed.), 1995b, *Handbook of Religious Experience*, Birmingham, AL: Religious Education Press.

Hood, Ralph W., Jr, 2006, 'The Common Core Thesis in the Study of Mysticism', in Patrick H. McNamara (ed.), *Where God and Science Meet: How Brain and Evolution Studies Alter our Understanding of Religion*, vol. III *The Psychology of Religious Experience*, Westport, CT: Praeger, ch. 5 (pp. 119–38).

Hood, Ralph W., Jr and Francis, Leslie J., 2013, 'Mystical Experience: Conceptualizations, Measurement, and Correlates', in Kenneth I. Pargament (ed.), *APA Handbook of Psychology, Religion and Spirituality*, vol. 1, *Context, Theory, and Research*, Washington, DC: American Psychological Association, ch. 21 (pp. 391–405).

Hood, Ralph W., Jr and Hall, James R., 1980, 'Gender Differences in the Description of Erotic and Mystical Experiences', *Review of Religious Research*, 21, 2, pp. 195–207.

Hood, Ralph W., Jr and Williamson, W. Paul, 2000, 'An Empirical Test of the Unity Thesis: The Structure of Mystical Descriptors in Various Faith Samples', *Journal of Psychology and Christianity*, 19, 3, pp. 232–44.

Hood, Ralph W., Jr, Hill, Peter C. and Spilka, Bernard, 2018 [2009], *The Psychology of Religion: Empirical Approaches*, New York: Guilford.

Horwich, Paul, 1992, 'Truth, Theories of', in Jonathan Dancy and Ernest Sosa (eds), *A Companion to Epistemology*, Oxford: Blackwell, pp. 509–15.

Hospers, John, 1967 [1956], *An Introduction to Philosophical Analysis*, second edition, London: Routledge & Kegan Paul.

Hügel, Friedrich von, 1923 [1908], *The Mystical Element of Religion as Studied in Saint Catherine of Genoa and her Friends*, two volumes, London: Dent.

Hunt, Harry T., 2000, 'Experiences of Radical Personal Transformation in Mysticism, Religious Conversion, and Psychosis: A Review of the Varieties, Processes, and Consequences of the Numinous', *The Journal of Mind and Behavior: An Interdisciplinary Journal*, 21, 4, pp. 353–98.

Hunter, Jack and Luke, David (eds), 2014, *Talking with the Spirits: Ethnographies from Between the Worlds*, Brisbane: Daily Grail.

Huxley, Aldous, 1958 [1946], *The Perennial Philosophy*, London: Collins [Chatto & Windus].

Inbody, Tyron, 2005, *The Faith of the Christian Church*, Grand Rapids, MI: Eerdmans.

Iyadurai, Joshua, 2015, *Transformative Religious Experience: A Phenomenological Understanding of Religious Conversion*, Eugene, OR: Wipf and Stock.

James, William, 1912 [1906], *Essays in Radical Empiricism*, New York: Longman Green and Co.

James, William, 1917 [1896], 'The Will to Believe', *Selected Papers in Philosophy*, London: Dent, ch. VII (pp. 99–124).

James, William, 1960 [1902], *The Varieties of Religious Experience: A Study in Human Nature*, London: Collins. (The Random House, New York, 1929 edition is available online at http://web.archive.org/web/20080727010425/http://etext.lib.virginia.edu:80/toc/modeng/public/JamVari.html.)

Jantzen, Grace, 1989, '"Where Two are to Become One": Mysticism and Monism', in Godfrey Vesey, (ed.), *The Philosophy in Christianity*, Cambridge: Cambridge University Press, pp. 147–66.

Jantzen, Grace M., 1994, 'Feminists, Philosophers, and Mystics', *Hypatia*, 9, 4, pp. 186–206.

Johnson, Luke Timothy, 1998, *Religious Experience in Earliest Christianity: A Missing Dimension in New Testament Studies*, Minneapolis, MN: Fortress.

Johnson, Luke Timothy, 2010, *The Writings of the New Testament: An Interpretation*, London: SCM Press.

Johnstone, Brick and Wildman, Wesley J. et al., 2018, 'Affect as a Foundational Psychological Process for Spirituality and Empathy', *Mental Health, Religion & Culture*, 21, 4, pp. 370–79.

Jung, Carl Gustav, 1933, *Modern Man in Search of a Soul*, ET London: Routledge & Kegan Paul.

Jung, Carl Gustav, 1983, *Jung: Selected Writings*, ET London: Fontana.

Katz, Steven T. (ed.), 1978, *Mysticism and Philosophical Analysis*, New York: Oxford University Press.

Katz, Steven T. (ed.), 1983, *Mysticism and Religious Traditions*, New York: Oxford University Press.

Katz, Steven T. (ed.), 2013, *Comparative Mysticism: An Anthology of Original Sources*, New York: Oxford University Press.

Kay, William K., 2009, *Pentecostalism*, London: SCM Press.

Kellenberger, James, 2017, *Religious Epiphanies across Traditions and Cultures*, New York: Palgrave Macmillan.

Kelly, Thomas M., 2002, *Theology at the Void: The Retrieval of Experience*, Notre Dame, IN: University of Notre Dame Press.

REFERENCES

Kelsey, Morton T., 1976, *The Christian and the Supernatural*, London: Search.

Kerr, Fergus, 1997, *Immortal Longings: Versions of Transcending Humanity*, London: SPCK.

Kilby, Karen, 2007, 'Karl Rahner', in David F. Ford with Rachel Muers (eds), *The Modern Theologians: An Introduction to Christian Theology since 1918*, third edition, Oxford: Blackwell, ch. 5 (pp. 92–105).

King, Ursula, 1997, *Christ in All Things: Exploring Spirituality with Teilhard de Chardin*, London: SCM Press.

King, Ursula, 2009, *Ecological and Mystical Spirituality from an Interfaith Perspective*, Lampeter: Religious Experience Research Centre.

Kirkpatrick, Lee A., 1995, 'Attachment Theory and Religious Experience', in Ralph W. Hood, Jr (ed.), *Handbook of Religious Experience*, Birmingham, AL: Religious Education Press, ch. 19 (pp. 446–75).

Knowles, David, OSB, 1979 [1967], *What is Mysticism?*, London: Sheed and Ward.

Kwan, Kai-man, 2011, *The Rainbow of Experiences, Critical Trust, and God: A Defence of Holistic Empiricism*, New York: Bloomsbury.

Kwan, Kai-man, 2012, 'The Argument from Religious Experience', in William Lane Craig and J. P. Moreland (eds), *The Blackwell Companion to Natural Theology*, Oxford: Wiley-Blackwell, ch. 9 (pp. 499–552).

Land, Steven J., 1990, 'Pentecostal Spirituality: Living in the Spirit', in Louis Dupré and Don E. Saliers, with John Meyendorff (eds), *Christian Spirituality: Post-Reformation and Modern*, London: SCM Press, ch. 17 (pp. 479–99).

Lang, Andrew, 1898, *The Making of Religion*, New York: Longmans, Green & Co.

Langford, Michael, 1981, *Providence*, London: SCM Press.

Lash, Nicholas, 1988, *Easter in Ordinary: Reflections on Human Experience and the Knowledge of God*, London: SCM Press.

Laurentin, René, 1977, *Catholic Pentecostalism*, London: Darton, Longman and Todd.

Lévy-Bruhl, Lucien, 1975 [1949], *The Notebooks on Primitive Mentality*, ET Oxford: Blackwell.

Lewis, H. D., 1969, *The Elusive Mind*, London: George Allen & Unwin.

Lewis, H. D., 1970, *Our Experience of God*, London: Fontana.

Lewis, I. M., 2003 [1971], *Ecstatic Religion: A Study of Shamanism and Spirit Possession*, Abingdon: Routledge.

Lindbeck, George A., 1984, *The Nature of Doctrine: Religion and Theology in a Post-liberal Age*, London: SPCK.

Lindblom, J., 1962, *Prophecy in Ancient Israel*, Oxford: Blackwell.

Livingstone, James C., 1971, *Modern Christian Thought: From the Enlightenment to Vatican II*, New York: Macmillan.

Lyon, David, 2000, *Jesus in Disneyland: Religion in Postmodern Times*, Cambridge: Polity Press.

Mackie, J. L., 1982, *The Miracle of Theism: Arguments For and Against the Existence of God*, Oxford: Clarendon.

Macquarrie, John, 2004, *Two Worlds are One: An Introduction to Christian Mysticism*, Minneapolis, MN: Fortress.

Malinar, Angelika and Basu, Helene, 2008, 'Ecstasy', in John Corrigan (ed.), *The Oxford Handbook of Religion and Emotion*, Oxford: Oxford University Press, ch. 13 (pp. 241–58).

Malinowski, Bronislaw, 1948, *Magic, Science, and Religion, and Other Essays*, Boston, MA: Beacon Press.

Malony, H. Newton and Southard, Samuel (eds), 1992, *Handbook of Religious Conversion*, Birmingham, AL: Religious Education Press.

Mariña, Jacqueline, 2008, 'Friedrich Schleiermacher and Rudolf Otto', in John Corrigan (ed.), *The Oxford Handbook of Religion and Emotion*, Oxford: Oxford University Press, ch. 25 (pp. 457–73).

Marsh, Michael N., 2010, *Out-of-Body and Near-Death Experiences: Brain-State Phenomena or Glimpses of Immortality?*, Oxford: Oxford University Press.

Martin, C. B., 1955, 'A Religious Way of Knowing', in Antony Flew and Alasdair MacIntyre (eds), *New Essays in Philosophical Theology*, London: SCM Press, ch. V (pp. 76–95).

Martin, Charles B., 1959, *Religious Belief*, Ithaca, NY: Cornell University Press.

Marx, K. and Engels, F., 1957, *On Religion*, ET Moscow: Progress Publishers.

Maslow, Abraham H., 2014 [1964], *Religions, Values and Peak Experiences*, USA: Stellar Books.

Mavrodes, George I., 1970, *Belief in God: A Study in the Epistemology of Religion*, New York: Random House.

Maxwell, Meg and Tschudin, Verena (eds), 1990, *Seeing the Invisible: Modern Religious and Other Transcendent Experiences*, London: Penguin.

McCool, Gerald A. (ed.), 1975, *A Rahner Reader*, ET London: Darton, Longman and Todd.

McCutcheon, Russell T., 2012, 'Introduction', in Craig Martin and Russell T. McCutcheon (eds), *Religious Experience: A Reader*, Sheffield: Equinox, pp. 1–16.

McGinn, Bernard, 1988, 'The English Mystics', in Jill Raitt, with Bernard McGinn and John Meyendorff (eds), *Christian Spirituality: High Middle Ages and Reformation*, London: SCM Press, ch. 8 (pp. 194–207).

McGinn, Bernard (ed.), 2006, *Essential Writings of Christian Mystics*, New York: Random House.

McGinn, Bernard, 2013, '"The Violent are Taking It by Storm" (Mt. 11.12): Reflections on a Century of Women's Contributions to the Study of Mystical Spirituality', *Spiritus: A Journal of Christian Spirituality*, 13, 1, pp. 17–35.

McGinn, Bernard and Meyendorff, John, with Leclerq, Jean (eds), 1993, *Christian Spirituality: Origins to the Twelfth Century*, New York: Crossroad.

McGrath, Alister E., 1997 [1990], *The Genesis of Doctrine: A Study in the Foundations of Doctrinal Criticism*, Grand Rapids, MI: Eerdmans.

McGuire, Meredith B., 2016, 'Individual Sensory Experiences, Socialized Senses, and Everyday Lived Religion in Practice', *Social Compass*, 63, 2, pp. 152–62.

McIntosh, Mark A., 2008, *Divine Teaching: An Introduction to Christian Theology*, Oxford: Blackwell.

Merton, Thomas, 1948, *The Seven Story Mountain*, New York: Harcourt Brace.

Miles, T. R., 1972, *Religious Experience*, London: Macmillan.

Mitchell, Basil, 1973, *The Justification of Religious Belief*, London: Macmillan.

Moberly, R. W. L., 2006, *Prophecy and Discernment*, Cambridge: Cambridge University Press.

Moore, Peter G., 1973, 'Recent Studies of Mysticism: A Critical Survey', *Religion*, 3, 2, pp. 146–56.

Moser, Paul K., 2010, *The Evidence for God: Religious Knowledge Reexamined*, Cambridge: Cambridge University Press.

Moustakas, Clark, 1994, *Phenomenological Research Methods*, Thousand Oaks, CA: Sage.

Neitz, Mary Jo, 1995, 'Feminist Theory and Religious Experience', in Ralph W. Hood, Jr (ed.), *Handbook of Religious Experience*, Birmingham, AL: Religious Education Press, ch. 22 (pp. 520–34).

Newman, John Henry, 1974 [1845], *An Essay on the Development of Christian Doctrine*, Harmondsworth: Penguin.

Nissinen, Martti, 2017, *Ancient Prophecy: Near Eastern, Biblical, and Greek Perspectives*, Oxford: Oxford University Press.

O'Hear, Anthony, 1984, *Experience, Explanation and Faith: An Introduction to the Philosophy of Religion*, London: Routledge & Kegan Paul.

Okholm, Dennis L. and Phillips, Timothy R. (eds), 1996, *Four Views on Salvation In a Pluralistic World*, Grand Rapids, MI: Zondervan.

Oliver, Simon and Warrier, Maya (eds), 2008, *Theology and Religious Studies: An Exploration of Disciplinary Boundaries*, London: T. & T. Clark.

Oman, Doug, 2013, 'Defining Religion and Spirituality', in Raymond F. Paloutzian and Crystal L. Park (eds), *Handbook of the Psychology of Religion and Spirituality*, second edition, New York: Guilford Press, ch. 2 (pp. 23–47).

Oppy, Graham and Trakakis, N. N. (eds), 2009a, *Nineteenth-Century Philosophy of Religion*, Durham: Acumen.

Oppy, Graham and Trakakis, N. N. (eds), 2009b, *Twentieth-Century Philosophy of Religion*, Durham: Acumen.

Otto, Rudolf, 1925 [1917], *The Idea of the Holy*, ET London: Oxford University Press.

Otto, Rudolf, 1931, *Religious Essays: A Supplement to 'The Idea of the Holy'*, ET London: Oxford University Press.

Otto, Rudolf, 1932 [1926], *Mysticism East and West: A Comparative Analysis of the Nature of Mysticism*, ET New York: Macmillan.

Paffard, Michael, 1973, *Inglorious Wordsworths: A Study of Some Transcendental Experiences in Childhood and Adolescence*, London: Hodder and Stoughton.

Paffard, Michael, 1976, *The Unattended Moment: Excerpts from Autobiographies with Hints and Guesses*, London: SCM Press.

Paloutzian, Raymond, 1981, 'Purpose in Life and Value Changes after Conversion', *Journal of Personality and Social Psychology*, 4, pp. 1153–60.

Parrinder, Geoffrey, 1976, *Mysticism in the World's Religions*, London: Sheldon.

Passmore, John, 1967, 'Philosophy', in Paul Edwards (ed.), *The Encyclopedia of Philosophy*, London: Collier Macmillan, vol. 6, pp. 216–26.

Pendlebury, Michael, 1992, 'Experience, Theories of', in Jonathan Dancy and Ernest Sosa (eds), *A Companion to Epistemology*, Oxford: Blackwell, pp. 125–9.

Penelhum, Terence, 1971, *Problems of Religious Knowledge*, London: Macmillan.

Peterson, Michael, Hasker, William, Reichenbach, Bruce and Basinger, David, 2013 [1991], *Reason and Religious Belief: An Introduction to the Philosophy of Religion*, New York: Oxford University Press.

Pike, James A. with Kennedy, Diane, 1969, *The Other Side: An Account of My Experiences with Psychic Phenomena*, London: W. H. Allen.

Pike, Nelson, 1986, 'John of the Cross on the Epistemic Value of Mystic Visions', in Robert Audi and William J. Wainwright (eds), *Rationality, Religious Belief, and Moral Commitment: New Essays in the Philosophy of Religion*, Ithaca, NY: Cornell University Press, ch. 1 (pp. 15–37).

Pike, Nelson, 1992, *Mystic Union: An Essay in the Phenomenology of Mysticism*, Ithaca, NY: Cornell University Press.

Plantinga, Alvin, 1981, 'Is Belief in God Properly Basic?', *Noûs*, 15, pp. 41–51.

Plantinga, Alvin, 1983, 'Reason and Belief in God', in Alvin Plantinga and Nicholas Wolterstorff (eds), *Faith and Rationality: Reason and Belief in God*, Notre Dame, IN: University of Notre Dame Press, pp. 16–93.

Pojman, Louis, 1986, *Religious Belief and the Will*, London: Routledge & Kegan Paul.

Poloma, Margaret M., 1995, 'The Sociological Context of Religious Experience', in Ralph W. Hood, Jr (ed.), *Handbook of Religious Experience*, Birmingham, AL: Religious Education Press, ch. 8 (pp. 161–82).

Price H. H., 1966, 'Faith and Belief', in John Hick (ed.), *Faith and the Philosophers*, London: Macmillan, pp. 3–25.

Price, H. H., 1969, *Belief*, London: George Allen & Unwin.

Proudfoot, Wayne, 1985, *Religious Experience*, Berkeley, CA: University of California Press.

Proudfoot, Wayne, 2010, 'Attribution and Building Blocks: Comment on Ann Taves's Religious Experience Reconsidered', *Religion*, 40, 4, pp. 308–10.

Proudfoot, Wayne and Shaver, Phillip, 1975, 'Attribution Theory and the Psychology of Religion', *Journal for the Scientific Study of Religion*, 14, 4, pp. 317–30.

Rad, Gerhard von, 1968 [1967], 'The Prophets' Call and Reception of Revelation', in Gerhard von Rad, *The Message of the Prophets*, ET London: SCM Press, pp. 33–49.

Rahner, Karl, 1978 [1976], *Foundations of the Christian Faith: An Introduction to the Idea of Christianity*, ET London: Darton, Longman and Todd.

Raitt, Jill with McGinn, Bernard and Meyendorff, John (eds), 1988, *Christian Spirituality: High Middle Ages and Reformation*, London: SCM Press

Ramsey, Ian T., 1955, 'Review of W. T. Stace: *Religion and the Modern Mind* and *Time and Eternity*', *Mind*, LXIV, 253.

Ramsey, Ian T., 1957, *Religious Language: An Empirical Placing of Theological Phrases*, London: SCM Press.

Ramsey, Ian T., 1965, *Christian Discourse: Some Logical Explorations*, London: Oxford University Press.

Ramsey, Ian T., 1971, *Our Understanding of Prayer*, London: SPCK.

Ramsey, Ian T., 1974, *Christian Empiricism*, London: Sheldon.

Rankin, Marianne, 2008, *An Introduction to Religious and Spiritual Experience*, London: Continuum.

Raphael, Melissa, 1994, 'Feminism, Constructivism, and Numinous Experience', *Religious Studies*, 30, 4, pp. 511–26.

Rawlinson, Andrew, 1997, *The Book of Enlightened Masters: Western Teachers in Eastern Traditions*, Chicago, IL: Open Court.

Rayburn, Carole A., 1995, 'The Body in Religious Experience', in Ralph W. Hood, Jr (ed.), *Handbook of Religious Experience*, Birmingham, AL: Religious Education Press, ch. 20 (pp. 476–94).

Richardson, Alan and Bowden, John, (eds), 1983, *A New Dictionary of Christian Theology*, London: SCM Press.

Robeck, Cecil M. (ed.), 1985, *Charismatic Experiences in History*, Peabody, MA: Hendrickson.

Roberts, Robert C., 2008, 'Emotions Research and Religious Experience', in John Corrigan (ed.), *The Oxford Handbook of Religion and Emotion*, Oxford: Oxford University Press, ch. 27 (pp. 490–506).

Robinson, Edward, 1977a, *The Original Vision: A Study of the Religious Experience of Childhood*, Oxford: The Religious Experience Research Unit.

Robinson, Edward (ed.), 1977b, *This Time-Bound Ladder: Ten Dialogues on Religious Experience*, Oxford: The Religious Experience Research Unit.

Robinson, Edward (ed.), 1978, *Living the Questions: Studies in the Childhood of Religious Experience*, Oxford: The Religious Experience Research Unit.

Russell, Bertrand, 1935, *Religion and Science*, London: Oxford University Press.

Ryle, Gilbert, 1963 [1949], *The Concept of Mind*, Harmondsworth: Penguin.

Sarbacker, Stuart, 2016, 'Rudolf Otto and the Concept of the Numinous', in *Oxford Research Encyclopedia of Religion*, available at http://oxfordindex.oup.com/view/10.1093/acrefore/9780199340378.013.88.

Sartori, Penny, 2014, *The Wisdom of Near-Death Experiences: How Understanding NDEs Can Help Us Live More Fully*, London: Watkins.

Sanders, E. P., 2016, *Paul: The Apostle's Life, Letters, and Thought*, London: SCM Press.

Schlamm, Leon, 1991, 'Rudolf Otto and Mystical Experience', *Religious Studies*, 27, 3, pp. 389–98.

Schlamm, Leon, 1992, 'Numinous Experience and Religious Language', *Religious Studies*, 28, 4, pp. 535–51.

Schleiermacher, Friedrich, 1928 [1830], *The Christian Faith*, ET Edinburgh: T. & T. Clark.

Schleiermacher, Friedrich Daniel Ernst, 1958 [1799], *On Religion: Speeches to its Cultured Despisers*, ET New York: Harper & Row.

Schmidt, Bettina E., 2016a, *Spirit and Trance in Brazil: Anthropology of Religious Experiences*, London: Bloomsbury.

Schmidt, Bettina E. (ed.), 2016b, *The Study of Religious Experience: Approaches and Methodologies*, Sheffield: Equinox.

Schreiner, Susan, 2011, *Are You Alone Wise? The Search for Certainty in the Early Modern Era*, New York: Oxford University Press.

Sears, Robert A., 2017, 'The Nature of Experience: Empirical Considerations and Theological Ramifications', *Perspectives on Science and Christian Faith*, 69, 1, pp. 13–26.

Shafranske, Edward P., 1995, 'Freudian Theory and Religious Experience', in Ralph W. Hood, Jr (ed.), *Handbook of Religious Experience*, Birmingham, AL: Religious Education Press, ch. 10 (pp. 200–30).

Shakespeare, Steven, 2007, *Radical Orthodoxy: A Critical Introduction*, London: SPCK.
Short, Larry, 1995, 'Mysticism, Mediation, and the Non-Linguistic', *Journal of the American Academy of Religion*, 69, 4, pp. 659–75.
Smart, Ninian, 1958, *Reasons and Faiths: An Investigation of Religious Discourse, Christian and Non-Christian*, London: Routledge & Kegan Paul.
Smart, Ninian, 1960, *A Dialogue of Religions*, London: SCM Press.
Smart, Ninian, 1965, 'Interpretation and Mystical Experience', *Religious Studies*, 1, 1, pp. 75–87.
Smart, Ninian, 1969, *Philosophers and Religious Truth*, London: SCM Press.
Smart, Ninian, 1971, *The Religious Experience of Mankind*, London: Fontana.
Smart, Ninian, 1973a, *The Science of Religion and the Sociology of Knowledge: Some Methodological Questions*, Princeton, NJ: Princeton University Press.
Smart, Ninian, 1973b, *The Phenomenon of Religion*, London: Macmillan.
Smart, Ninian, 1978, 'Understanding Religious Experience', in Steven T. Katz (ed.), *Mysticism and Philosophical Analysis*, New York: Oxford University Press, pp. 10–21.
Smart, Ninian, 1979, *The Philosophy of Religion*, London: Sheldon.
Smart, Ninian, 1997, *Dimensions of the Sacred*, London: Fontana.
Smart, Ninian and Konstantine, Steven, 1991, *Christian Systematic Theology in a World Context*, London: Harper Collins.
Smith, Huston, 1992 [1976], *Forgotten Truth: The Common Vision of the World's Religions*, New York: HarperOne.
Smith, John E., 1968, *Experience and God*, London: Oxford University Press.
Soskice, Janet Martin, 1985, *Metaphor and Religious Language*, Oxford: Clarendon.
Spickard, James V., 1993, 'For a Sociology of Religious Experience', in William H. Swatos, Jr (ed.), *A Future for Religion: New Paradigms for Social Analysis*, Newbury Park, CA: Sage, pp. 109–28.
Spilka, Bernard and McIntosh, Daniel N., 1995, 'Attribution Theory and Religious Experience', in Ralph W. Hood, Jr (ed.), *Handbook of Religious Experience*, Birmingham, AL: Religious Education Press, ch. 18 (pp. 421–45).
Spohn, William C., 1994, 'William James on Religious Experience: An Elitist Account?', *American Journal of Theology and Philosophy*, 15, 1, pp. 27–41.
Spohn, William C., 1999, *Go and Do Likewise: Jesus and Ethics*, New York: Continuum.
Staal, Frits, 1975, *Exploring Mysticism*, London: Penguin.
Stace, Walter T. (ed.), 1960, *The Teachings of the Mystics*, New York: Mentor Books.
Stace, Walter T., 1961, *Mysticism and Philosophy*, London: Macmillan.
Stanton, G. N., 2001, 'Galatians', in John Barton and John Muddiman (eds), *The Oxford Bible Commentary*, Oxford: Oxford University Press, ch. 67 (pp. 1152–65).

Stark, Rodney, 1965, 'A Taxonomy of Religious Experience', *Journal for the Scientific Study of Religion*, 5, 1, pp. 97–116.

Stark, Rodney, 1999, 'A Theory of Revelations', *Journal for the Scientific Study of Religion*, 38, 2, pp. 287–308.

Sterk, Andrea (ed.), 2002, *Religion, Scholarship and Higher Education: Perspectives, Models and Future Prospects*, Notre Dame, IN: University of Notre Dame Press.

Stiver, Dan R., 2009, *Life Together in the Way of Jesus Christ: An Introduction to Christian Theology*, Waco, TX: Baylor University Press.

Stoeber, Michael, 1992, 'Constructivist Epistemologies of Mysticism: A Critique and a Revision', *Religious Studies*, 28, 1, pp. 107–16.

Sudduth, Michael, 2009, 'The Contribution of Religious Experience to Dogmatic Theology', in Oliver D. Crisp and Michael C. Rea (eds), *Analytic Theology: New Essays in the Philosophy of Theology*, Oxford: Oxford University Press, ch. 10 (pp. 214–32).

Swinburne, Richard, 1970, *The Concept of Miracle*, London: Macmillan.

Swinburne, Richard, 2004 [1979], *The Existence of God*, Oxford: Clarendon.

Sykes, S. W., 1979, 'Barth on the Centre of Theology', in S. W. Sykes (ed.), *Karl Barth: Studies of his Theological Method*, Oxford: Clarendon, ch. 2 (pp. 17–54).

Taliaferro, Charles, 2012, 'The Project of Natural Theology', in William Lane Craig and J. P. Moreland (eds.), *The Blackwell Companion to Natural Theology*, Oxford: Wiley-Blackwell, ch. 1 (pp. 1–23).

Tamminen, Kalevi, 1994, 'Religious Experiences in Childhood and Adolescence: A Viewpoint of Religious Development Between the Ages of 7 and 20', *The International Journal for the Psychology of Religion*, 4, 2, pp. 61–85.

Tanner, Kathryn, 1997, 'Jesus Christ', in Colin Gunton (ed.), *The Cambridge Companion to Christian Doctrine*, Cambridge: Cambridge University Press, ch. 13 (pp. 245–72).

Taves, Ann, 1999, *Fits, Trances and Visions: Experiencing Religion and Explaining Experience from Wesley to James*, Princeton, NJ: Princeton University Press.

Taves, Ann, 2009, *Religious Experience Reconsidered: A Building-Block Approach to the Study of Religion and Other Special Things*, Princeton, NJ: Princeton University Press.

Taves, Ann, 2010, 'Experience as Site of Contested Meaning and Value: The Attributional Dog and its Special Tail', *Religion*, 40, 4, pp. 317–23.

Taves, Ann, 2016, *Revelatory Events: Three Case Studies of the Emergence of New Spiritual Paths*, Princeton, NJ: Princeton University Press.

Taylor, Charles, 1989, *Sources of the Self: The Making of the Modern Identity*, Cambridge: Cambridge University Press

Taylor, Charles, 2002, *Varieties of Religion Today: William James Revisited*, Cambridge, MA: Harvard University Press.

Thayer, H. S., 1964, 'Pragmatism', in D. J. O'Connor (ed.), *A Critical History of Western Philosophy*, London: Collier Macmillan, ch. 14 (pp. 437–62).

Thiessen, Gerd and Merz, Annette, 1998, *The Historical Jesus: A Comprehensive Guide*, ET London: SCM Press.

Thornton, Martin, 1974, *My God: A Reappraisal of Normal Religious Experience*, London: Hodder & Stoughton.

Thouless, Robert H., 1971, *An Introduction to the Psychology of Religion*, third edition, Cambridge: Cambridge University Press.

Tilley, Terrence W., 1994, 'Religious Pluralism as a Problem for "Practical" Religious Epistemology', *Religious Studies*, 30, 2, pp. 161–9.

Tilley, Terrence W., 2010, *Faith: What It Is and What It Isn't*, Maryknoll, NY: Orbis.

Tite, Philip A., 2013, 'Theoretical Challenges in Studying Religious Experience in Gnosticism: A Prolegomena for Social Analysis', *Bulletin for the Study of Religion*, 42, 1, pp. 8–18.

Troeltsch, Ernst, 2009, 2010 [1919], *The Social Teaching of the Christian Churches*, two volumes, ET Louisville, KY: Westminster John Knox Press.

Tugwell, Simon, OP, 1972, *Did You Receive the Spirit?*, London: Darton, Longman and Todd.

Tugwell, Simon, OP, 1979, 'Faith and Experience V: Religious "Natural History"', *New Blackfriars*, 60, 705, pp. 61–75.

Turner, Edith, 1993, 'The Reality of Spirits: A Tabooed or Permitted Field of Study?', *Anthropology of Consciousness*, 4, 1, pp. 9–12.

Turner, Edith, 2006, 'Advances in the Study of Spirit Experience: Drawing Together Many Threads', *Anthropology of Consciousness*, 17, 2, pp. 33–61.

Tylor, Edward Burnett, 1871, *Primitive Culture*, London: John Murray.

Wach, Joachim, 1958, *The Comparative Study of Religions*, New York: Columbia University Press.

Wainwright, William J., 1981, *Mysticism: A Study of its Nature, Cognitive Value and Moral Implications*, Brighton: Harvester.

Wainwright, William J., 1995, *Reason and the Heart: A Prolegomenon to a Critique of Passional Reason*, Ithaca, NY: Cornell University Press.

Wainwright, William J., 2005, *Religion and Morality*, Aldershot: Ashgate.

Wakefield, Gordon S. (ed.), 1983, *A Dictionary of Christian Spirituality*, London: SCM Press.

Wakefield, Gordon S., 2001, *Groundwork of Christian Spirituality*, Peterborough: Epworth.

Ward, Keith, 1968, *Fifty Key Words in Philosophy*, London: Lutterworth Press.
Ward, Keith, 1990, *Divine Action*, London: Collins.
Ward, Keith, 1994, *Religion and Revelation: A Theology of Revelation in the World's Religions*, Oxford: Oxford University Press.
Ward, Keith, 2005, *Is There a Common Core of Religious Experience?*, Lampeter: Religious Experience Research Centre, available at https://repository.uwtsd.ac.uk/457/.
Ward, Keith, 2008, *The Big Questions in Science and Religion*, West Conshohocken, PA: Templeton Foundation Press.
Ward, Keith, 2014, *The Evidence for God*, London: Darton, Longman and Todd.
Ware, Owen, 2007, 'Rudolph Otto's Idea of the Holy: A Reappraisal', *Heythrop Journal*, 48, pp. 48–60.
Washburn, Michael, 2003, *Embodied Spirituality in a Sacred World*, Albany, NY: State University of New York Press.
Webb, Mark, 2017 [2011], 'Religious Experience', *Stanford Encyclopedia of Philosophy*, available at https://plato.stanford.edu/entries/religious-experience/.
Weber, 1930 [1904–05], *The Protestant Ethic and the Spirit of Capitalism*, ET London: George Allen & Unwin.
Weber, Max, 1963 [1922], *The Sociology of Religion*, ET Boston, MA: Beacon Press.
Wiebe, Phillip H., 1997, *Visions of Jesus: Direct Encounters from the New Testament to Today*, New York: Oxford University Press.
Wilber, Ken, 1993 [1977], *The Spectrum of Consciousness*, Wheaton, IL: Quest.
Wildman, Wesley J., 2011, *Religious and Spiritual Experiences*, New York: Cambridge University Press.
Wildman, Wesley J., 2013, 'Spiritual Experiences: A Quantitative-Phenomenological Approach', *Journal of Empirical Theology*, 26, pp. 139–64.
Wiles, Maurice, 1976, *What is Theology?*, Oxford: Oxford University Press.
Wilkinson, Michael, 2014, 'Sociological Narratives and the Sociology of Pentecostalism', in Cecil M. Robeck, Jr and Amos Yong (eds), *The Cambridge Companion to Pentecostalism*, New York: Cambridge University Press, ch. 11 (pp. 215–34).
Williams, Bernard, 1996, 'Contemporary Philosophy: A Second Look', in Nicholas Bunnin and E. P. Tsui-James (eds), *The Blackwell Companion to Philosophy*, Oxford: Blackwell, pp. 25–37.
Wilson, John Cook, 1926, *Statement and Inference*, vol. II, Oxford: Oxford University Press.
Wittgenstein, Ludwig, 1965, 'Lectures on Ethics', *Philosophical Review*, 74, 1, pp. 3–12.
Wittgenstein, Ludwig, 1968, *Philosophical Investigations*, ET Oxford: Blackwell.
Wolpert, Lewis, 2006, *Six Impossible Things Before Breakfast: The Evolutionary Origins of Belief*, London: Faber and Faber.

Wolterstorff, Nicholas, 1995, *Divine Discourse: Philosophical Reflections on the Claim that God Speaks*, Cambridge: Cambridge University Press.

Woods, Richard (ed.), 1981, *Understanding Mysticism*, London: Athlone.

Wulff, David M., 1995, 'Phenomenological Psychology and Religious Experience', in Ralph W. Hood, Jr (ed.), *Handbook of Religious Experience*, Birmingham, AL: Religious Education Press, ch. 9 (pp. 183–99).

Wulff, David M., 2000, 'Mystical Experience', in Etzel Cardeña, Steven Jay Lynn and Stanley Krippner (eds), *Varieties of Anomalous Experience: Examining the Scientific Evidence*, Washington, DC: American Psychological Association, ch. 13 (pp. 397–440).

Wuthnow, R., 1976, 'Peak Experience: Some Empirical Tests', Mimeographed Paper, Berkeley, California: Survey Research Center (cited in Hay and Morisy, 1978).

Wynn, Mark, 2009, 'Towards a Broadening of the Concept of Religious Experience: Some Phenomenological Considerations', *Religious Studies*, 45, 2, pp. 147–66.

Yandell, Keith E., 1975, 'Some Varieties of Ineffability', *International Journal for Philosophy of Religion*, 6, 3, pp. 167–79.

Yandell, Keith E., 1993, *The Epistemology of Religious Experience*, Cambridge: Cambridge University Press.

Yandell, Keith E., 1997, 'Religious Experience', in Philip L. Quinn and Charles Taliaferro (eds), *A Companion to Philosophy of Religion*, Oxford: Blackwell, ch. 47 (pp. 367–75).

Yandell, Keith E., 1999, *Philosophy of Religion: A Contemporary Introduction*, London: Routledge.

Yao, Xinzhong and Badham, Paul, 2007, *Religious Experience in Contemporary China*, Cardiff: University of Wales Press.

Zaehner, Robert Charles, 1957, *Mysticism, Sacred and Profane: An Inquiry into Some Varieties of Praeternatural Experience*, London: Oxford University Press.

Zaleski, Carol, 1987, *Otherworld Journeys: Accounts of Near-Death Experience in Medieval and Modern Times*, Oxford: Oxford University Press.

Zinnbauer, Brian J. and Pargament, Kenneth I. et al., 1997, 'Unfuzzying the Fuzzy', *Journal for the Scientific Study of Religion*, 36, 4, pp. 549–64.

Index of Subjects

(RSEs = religious and spiritual experiences)

Absolute, the 7, 37, 103, 125, 126, 142, 161n, 179, 221; cf. 198, 208
absorption, experiences of 6–7, 139–40, *see also* monism/identity; mysticism/mystical experiences (narrow sense), monistic
acceptance of beliefs 71, 86, 87, 103, 151, 223, *see also* reception
critical/rational or uncritical *xin*, 71, 73, 103, 107, 110, 111, 114n, 122, 223, 226, see *also* principle of credulity/critical trust; principle of testimony
acceptance, spiritual 48, 152, 206
acquaintance 53n, 92, 96, 115, 221; cf. 220
activity 4, 149; cf. 49, 141, 144
 brain 97, *see also* neuroscience of RSEs
 divine 41, 76, 104, 150–2, 155, 186, 194
 human 4, 149, 158, 236
affect/affections 14n, 22, 33, 62, 82n, 129, 149, 172, 201, 206, *see also* attitudes; dispositions; emotions; feelings

agnosticism 70–2, 137, 218–19, 224
alienation 128, 218
Alister Hardy Archive *xiii*, 7, 21, 23, 26n, 63, 68, 77, 86–7, 94, 152
analogies/metaphors, religious 137–8, 82n, 139, 143–4, 147n, 209, see also analogies/metaphors for RSEs/revelation
 underspecified 124
analogies/metaphors for RSEs/revelation 46, 53n, 124, 137, 142, 143–4, 156–7, 164, 180, 191, 209, 215n
 absorption, *see* absorption, experiences of; drop of water/streamlet
 bee/bird 138–9
 being borne away, clothed, held, possessed, poured onto 77, 180, 182
 creativity 69, 177
 drop of water/streamlet 53n, 139
 God giving birth to God in the soul 199
 journey 102n, 195, 197, 199
 letting be/go 199

sailor seeing lighthouse 118–19
manager's endorsement 161n
music 100, 142, 227, 229
orgasm 165–7, 168n, see also sexual union; cf. 23
poetic inspiration 181
relationship 166–7, see also religious and spiritual experiences/religious experiences, as relationship
sense experience 10, 58, 59, 60–1, 108–9, 112n, 113n, 116, 118–20, 122n, 124, 156–7, 167, 195, 212, 219, 228, see also perception model of religious experience; spiritual vision; cf. 96, 107, 109, 112n
sexual union 53n, 139, 163–4, 168n, see also orgasm; spiritual marriage
tuning-in 229, see also music
analysis
  conceptual xin, 11, 22, 25, 29, 32, 33, 101n, 147n, 155, 161n, 167, 176, 184, 216, 218, 228, 231, see also philosophy, analytical
  non-numerical 27
  phenomenological 20, ch. 2, ch. 3, see also phenomenology of RSEs
  qualitative ch. 2, ch. 3
  quantitative/statistical 27, 31, see also ch. 2, ch. 3
  sociological 228, 239, see also ch. 20
angels 39, 43, 125, 179, 191n, 200
Anglicans 9, 30, 138, 152
  Anglo-Catholics 160
anomalous experiences 47–8, 50–1, 63, 80–1, 179, 231
anthropology of RSEs 9, 20, 21, 29, 34, 43, 99, 171–2, ch. 20
  new anthropology 232–4

Association of Religion Data Archives 26n
'Ātman 38, see also s soul; spirit, human
apocalyptic 188
apparitions, see visions/visual experiences
apprenticeship of the spirit 70, 72, 76, see also experiments, devotional; formation and experience; learning, religious/spiritual; spiritual disciplines
appropriation, see reception
archetypes 173–4
arousal
  physiological 128
  of RSEs 176, see also triggers of RSEs
art 47, 58, 242n, 218
'as if' acting/believing/living 72
asceticism/ascetics 65n, 87, 196, 236
  larger asceticism 54n
ascription 8, 14n, 243n
Association of Religion Data Archives 26n
assurance 6, 46
atheism/anti-theism/non-theism 10, 70, 71, 75, 126, 210, 222, see also God; theism
'Ātman 38, see also s soul; spirit, human
attachment theory 172
attitudes 3, 7, 11, 15n, 48, 60, 62, 72, 77, 82n, 98, 125, 158, 161n, 179, 207–8, 226, 228, 233, 235, 238, see also dispositions
attribution 8, 14n, 82n, 89, see also causation/causes
  attributionalists 217
  theory 14n, 89, 176, 232

INDEX OF SUBJECTS

auditions/auditory experiences 31, 43–5, 51, 53n, 113n, 156, 157, 161n, 180, 181, 182, 195, 203; cf. 79, 140, *see also* revelation, auditory model
authenticity, tests of ch. 7, 183, 222–3, *see also* self-authenticating beliefs/experiences
authorities, religious/spiritual 21, 27, 70; cf. 41, 152–3
auto-description 8, 14n, 84
autonomy 130, 150, 164, 206, 211, 218, 230, 238
awe/ful 25, 40, 49, 53n, 54, 59, 60, 80, 135, 139, 208, 215n

beatific visions 47, 195, 196
behaviour/behaviours ix, 7, 10, 11, 14n, 54n, 62, ch. 7, 171, 174, 183–4, 223, ch. 20, see also practices, religious/spiritual
  moral 61, 62, ch. 7, 106, 165
  religious 11, 61
behaviourism 174
Being, experience of 37, 48
beliefs/believers/believing, *see* cognition; knowledge
  religious 3, 5, 6, 10, 11, 14n, 60, 61, 62, 72, 77, 78, 82n, ch. 8, 103, 107, 108, 109, 110, 111, 112n, 113n, 114n, ch. 10, 123–4, 127, 129, 132, 133n, 134n, 145, 149, 154, 155–6, 158, 159, 172, 179, 182, 183, 191n, 192n, ch. 18, ch. 19, 226, 227, 228, 231, 232, 233, 238–9, 240, 242n
  first-hand/second-hand believers 82n
  freedom of 222–3
  half-believers 72
  moral 78, 209, 213
  properly basic 113n
  as secondary to experience 38, ch. 8, 149, 157–8, 187, 199, 207, 220; cf. 150
belief-system 61, 108, 117, 118, 120, 131, ch. 18, *see also* theism
belief-like stance 72
Bible, *see* Scripture/scriptures
biblical studies *x*, ch. 16
blessedness 39, 69
bliss 38, 43, 48, 49, 54n, 71, 128, 208, *see also* joy
both-and positions 98–9, 118–21
bracketing, *see* epoché
Brahman 7, 38, 85, *see also* Absolute, the; monism/identity
breadth of RSEs 21, ch. 5, 70, 75, *see also* extraordinary cf. ordinary experiences
Buddhism 77, 96, 204n
building blocks (of religions/spiritualities) 243n

call, *see* vocation
Calvinists 6, 154, 238, *see also* Calvin, John
capitalism 238
Carmelites 199–200
caste 243
categorization of religious and spiritual experiences, *see* classification of RSEs
Catholics, Roman 10, 54, 154, 158–9, 160, 194, 210–11, 213, *see also* Carmelites; Dominicans; Jesuits
causation/causes 31, 67–8, 74n, 75, 82, 90, 104–6, 109, 112n, 122n, 130–1, 134n, 166, 174, 198, 202,

207, 213, 215n, *see also* conditions, ch. 9, ch. 10; cf. 50
  attribution of 8, 14n, 82n, 89
  contributory 68, 74n, 166
  and correlation 130, *see also* correlations
  natural/naturalistic, *see* naturalism/naturalistic perspectives
  precipitating 74n
  primary/secondary 130
chambers/dwelling places/mansions 200, *see also* analogies/metaphors for RSEs/revelation, journey; religious and spiritual experiences/religious experiences, stages of
character, God's 79, 80, 149, 155, 156, 179, 181, 191n–192n, *see also* God
character, human
  moral 3, 7, 10, 11, 15n, 22, 59, 60, 70, 71, 76–8, 105, 165, 213, *see also* values/valuing, moral
  spiritual 223, *see also* values/valuing, spiritual
charisma/charismatic authority 185–6, 239; cf. 41
charisma/charismatic gifts/charisms, *see* glossolalia; healings/healing experiences; interpretation, of tongues; prophecy/prophetic experiences; Spirit, divine/Holy Spirit, gifts of
charismatics/charismatic experiences 30, 31, 41, 42–3, 44, 157, 159, 189, 191n–192n, 213, 230, 237, *see also* Pentecostals/pentecostal experiences
checking procedures for RSEs, *see* testing phenomena/theories

chemicals, *see* drugs
childhood experiences 30, 33, 128, 172; cf. 164, 188, 241
Christian/Christianity x, 4, 10, 12, 30, 31, 38, 40, 42, 43, 44,45, 46, 52n–53n, 57, 61–2, 69, 72, 76, 77, 79, 81, 82n, 85, 90, 93, 96, 103, 109–10, 117, 120, 133n, 135, 139, 140, ch. 13, 163, ch. 16, ch. 17, ch. 18, 221, 223, 235, 236, 238, *see also* Catholics, Roman; Orthodoxy, Eastern; Protestants;
Christology 61, *see also* ch. 16
classic/elite experiencers *x*, 21, 27, 63, 76, 77, 157, 168n, 173, ch. 16, ch. 17, 212, 213, 220
classification of RSEs ch. 2, 29, ch. 4, 93, 118, 183
  bottom-up/top-down 21–22
  Hardy's classification 7, 21, 25n–26n, 43, 62–3, 66n, 68, 74n, 77
cognition (as knowing, thinking) 10, 14n, 25, 66n, 71, 92, 93, 105, 121, 122n, 124, 128, 144, 151, 158, 176, 177, 221, 237
  cognitive, empathetic engagement 233
  cognitive freedom 221–3
  cognitive psychology 93, 99, 171
  cognitive resolution 42
  non-cognitive experience 96, *see also* ch. 8 *passim*
cognitive (as fact asserting/denying, factual) 88, 105, 112n, 113n, 125, 147n; cf. 120–1, 138–9, 143
  non-cognitive 124–5, 138–9, 143
cognitive immediacy criterion 120
common core of mysticism/RSEs 32, 83–4, 85, 86, 87, 95, 99, 124,

161n, 165, 209, 212, 217, *see also* perennialism/perennial philosophy
conditions 8, 13n, 67, 69, 71, 78, 86, 99, 102n, 104–5, 109, 113n, 125, 127, 163, 166, 181, 210, 214, 215n, 218, 235
 differential 74n
 necessary 68, 70, 74n, 99, 109, 117, 129, 233
 standing 74n
 sufficient 67–8, 103, 119, 129
confessional/non-confessional religious education 233
consciousness, human *xi*n, 5, 38, 43, 44, 47, 49, 58, 64, 74, 96, 97, 140, 161n, 174, 186
 creature-consciousness 49, 54n, 164, 208, 215n; cf. 199
 false 128
 God-consciousness 149, 191n
 numinous 209, *see also* numinous experiences
 pure 54, 85, 91, 92, 96, 97, 98, 99, 102n, *see also* pure consciousness events (PCEs)
 religious consciousness 206, 207, *see also* piety
 unitary consciousness 38, 41, *see also* identity/identification/undifferentiated union, experiences of; One/oneness; pure consciousness events (PCEs); unitary/unitive states/experiences;
 self-consciousness 182, 185, 207
 super-consciousness 49
consequences, *see* fruits of RSEs
 immediate/long-term, *see* immediate (at once) and long-term consequences of RSEs

conservatives (in theology), *see* theology/theological perspectives on RSEs, conservative theology
conservativism (social) 237
constructivism, social 83, 85–95, 96, 97–100, 101n, 102n, 114n, 120, 161n, 164, 165, 209, 211, 212, 217, 218, 221
 catalytic 90
 hard/complete 90, 94, 95
 'Kantian constructivism' 102n; cf. 88–9
 soft/incomplete/weak 89
contemplation/contemplative experiences 40, 140, 177, 196–7, 201, 209, 236–7
conterminous/contiguous 222, 224n
contextualism, *see* constructivism, social
contingency, experience of 50, 125, *see also* consciousness, human, creature-consciousness
contradiction theory 145
conversions/conversion experiences 30, 42, 46, 53n, 59, 87, 94, 109–10, 174, 176, 177, 184, 186, 195, 220, *see also* self-transformation; spiritual change/transformation
correlations 31, 32, 33, 69, 129, 130, 134n, 150, 212
 and causation 130
creation 49, 114n, 122n, 130–1, 140, 150, 166, 186, 222, *see also* consciousness, creature-consciousness; contingency, experience of; making-creation; preserving/sustaining-creation; cf. 221

continuous 130
creativity 48, 69, 159, 174, 177, 199
criticism/critical openness *xi*n, 73, *see also* acceptance of beliefs, critical/rational or uncritical
culture/cultural
 anthropology 227, 232, 242n, *see also* anthropology of RSEs
 background/context 21, 43, 44, 83, 85, 86, 88, 90, 94, 95, 96, 97–8, 121, 124, 127, 164–5, 172, 184, 188, 211, 212, 218, 226,238, 242, *see also* contextualism
 change 230, 238
 cross-cultural differences/similarities 42, 83–4, 85, 96, 99, 101n, 157, 209, 212, 220, 221
 cultural-linguistic 99, 211–12
 expression 172
 origins 239
 status 242
 study of 28–9, 242n, *see also* ethnography
 values 120
cumulative case, *see* inference, cumulative arguments

darkness, experiences of 44, 141, 197, 198, 199, 200, *see also* soul, dark night of the soul; cf. 82, 173
dead, visions of 39, 43, 125, *see also* ghosts
deconstruction 236
deification 53n, 139
delusions 7, 12, 122–3, 133n, 223, 224, 238, *see also* illusions, ch. 9
demonic quiet 80
demons/Devil 39, 43, 79–80, 162, 208, *see also* spirits, evil

depression 68
depth of experience/truth 29, 54n, 58, 60, 196, 208, 210–11
design, experiences of 50, 125
desire/longing 43, 53n, 62, 80, 135, 201, 202, 208
despair 68
difference 218
direct awareness 6, 10, 91, 92, 99, 102n, 110–11, 115, 116, 117–21, 122n, 139, 143, 182, 196, 206, 207, 215n, 221–2, 228, 232, 234, *see also* acquaintance; intuition/intuitive experiences
direct, 'immediate' experience cf. mediated inferences ch. 8, 115–121, 122n, 206
discernment 138, *see also* intuition/intuitive experiences; religious and spiritual experiences/religious experiences
 of spirits 79, 180, 182
disciplines, academic *vii–viii, ix–x*, part 4
 of anthropology/sociology ch. 20, especially 227–8, 232
 defined *ix*
 cf. fields *ix*
 multidisciplinary approach *ix–x*
 of philosophy 216–7
 of psychology ch. 15
 of theology 205
disciplines, spiritual, *see* spiritual disciplines
disclosure 138, *see also* revelation
dispositions 7, 11, 59, 60, 62, 70, 71, 76, 77, 113n, 226
diversity *vii*, 91, 99, 113n, 123–6, 158, 161n, 165, 212, 222–4; cf. 95

INDEX OF SUBJECTS

divine quiet 80, 138, *see also* prayer, of quiet
doctrines 8, 90, 92, 93, 97, 98, 101, 114n, 119, 124, 139, 148, 149, 153–4, 157, 158, 159, 160, 161n, 205–7, 211, 215n, 217, 238
 as grammar/rules of cultural-linguistic system 211, 215n
Dominicans 153, 199
doxastic practices 107–10, 111, 113n, 114n, 115, 124, 217
drama 68
dread 128, 208, 209, *see also* fear
dreams 43, 113n, 173, 182, 203
drive theory 172
drugs 68–9, 74n, 131, *Appendix*
dualism 38, 39, 52n–53n, 139, 145, 221
duck-rabbit, ambiguous image of 225n, *see also* experiencing-as
dying for death 44

ecstasy/ecstatic experiences 29, 43–5, 48, 49, 62, 74n, 79, 173, 180, 182, 183, 185, 191n, 198, 203, 208, 228
 shamanistic ecstasy 44
ecumenical thesis 83
ego, *see* self
 ego death 204n
egoism, ethical 77
elites, *see* classic/elite experiencers
emic/etic approaches 9, 14n
emotions ix, 3, 6, 7, 43, 68, 125, 128, 135, 149, 176, 179, 186, 191n, 206–8
emptying out, *see* forgetting
encounter experiences 46, 53n, 142, 151, 155, 161n, 179, 188, 190, 195, 206, 209, 213; cf. 38, 96

energy, urgent 40, 208; cf. 186
enlightenment 7, 41, 77, 152
Enlightenment, the/post-Enlightenment 52n, 206, 211, 218–19, 238
enthusiasm 44
epistemic imperialism 108
epistemic transformation 163; cf. 7, 58–9, 60, 71, 76, 105
epistemology 217, *see also* knowledge
 of receptivity and involvement 59–60; cf. 108
epoché 20
erotic experiences/imagery 163–4, 202, *see also* analogies/metaphors for RSEs, orgasm; sexual union
essentialism 83–4, 85, 86, 91, 99, 101n, 161n, 165, 209, 217, see also common core of mysticism/RSEs; perennialism/perennial philosophy; pure consciousness events (PCEs)
etic, see emic/etic approaches
ethnography 20, 28–9, 229, 230, 234, 242n
ethnomethodology 28
evangelicals 31, 128
everyday RSEs/experiencers, see classic/elite experiencers; extraordinary cf. ordinary experiences; ordinary believer/experiencer/ordinary theology; religious and spiritual experiences/religious experiences
evidentialism 122n
evil awareness/presence 30, 45, 80, 125; cf. 208
evolutionary psychology 171, 232
exercises x–xi, 4, 22, 23, 29–31, 32–3,

64, 73, 91, 100, 110, 125, 126, 136, 148–9, 156, 162–3, 173, 175–8, 189–90, 194, 213–4, 219, 228–30, 234
existential significance 10, 47, 57, 64, 69, 164, 177, 211
experience
  character and content of 5
  complexity of 54n, 85, 90, 98, 122n, 133n, 176; cf. 25
  definition of 4–5
  enduring/extended 7, ch. 5, 179
  freedom in 222–3
  gendered 162
experiencer 14n, 49, 85, 86, 94, 105, 106, 142, 143, see also experient
experiencing-as 47, 61–2, 50, 181, 221
experient 5, 14n, 94, 103, 147n, 168n, 237, see also experiencer
experiential-expressive position 99, 211
experientialism 115
experiments 27, 36n, 69, 73, 79, 130, 154, 165, 175, 176, 242n, 244, see also testing phenomena/theories
  devotional 70–4
  experimental faith 71–3
explanation 9, 14, 20, 34, 67, 80, 84, 89, 100, 116–18, 120, 124, 127, 131, 138, 145, 160, 221, 235–6, see also attribution; causation/causes; conditions
  best explanation, see inference, inference to the best explanation; religious experience, best explanation of
  aesthetics-oriented method approach to 230
  naturalistic/reductive/scientific approach to ix, 68, 120, 123, 126–37, 232, 234, Appendix, see also naturalism/naturalistic perspectives; projection theory
  narrative approach to 229
  psychological approach to ch. 3, 45, 127–8, 130, ch. 15, 220, 232
  social approach to 28, 34, 127, 128–9, 162, 172, ch. 16, ch. 20
extraordinary cf. ordinary experiences 9, 10, 21, 26n, ch. 5, 76, 79, 83, 85, 97, 102n, 106, 144, 156, 173, 174, 179, 189, 207–8, 210, 220, 231, 241, 242n–243n, see also breadth of RSEs; ordinary believer/experiencer/ordinary theology; religious and spiritual experiences/religious experiences, dramatic; cf. 14n
extra-sensory perception (ESP) 30, 50–1
Eysenck Personality Questionnaire 33

facilitators of RSEs 61, 62, 152, 202, see also triggers of RSEs
faith 10, 30, 42, 46, 62, 76, 111, 117, 148, 149, 150, 151, 159, 174, 181, 185, 211, 221
  eyes of 188
  human 11
  as *visio* 61, 188
faithfulness 30, 76
faiths, non-Christian/world viii, 32, 70, 82n, 135, 139, 149, 175, 212, 222–4, see also Buddhism, Hinduism, Islam
fear 24, 54n, 80, 127, 163, 215, see also dread

feelings 4, 5, 7, 8, 9, 11, 14n, 23, 28, 39, 40, 42, 50, 51, 53n, 54n, 58, 71, 74n, 77, 134n, 135, 149, 151, 161n, 164, 172, 176, 181, 206, 207–9, 212, 215n, 220, 228, 240, 241, see also emotions
feeling of absolute dependence 54, 149, 206–7
fictions 132, 180, 184
field studies 27
fields of study ix–x, part 4
fifth dimension of human nature/universe 12, 222
figurative language, see imagery, religious; metaphors/models, religious; model, definition of
film 68
flesh 44, 82n, 187
flow 43, 54n, 229
forbidden things 231, 239, 242n, see also taboos
forgetting 96–7, 144, 201
forgiveness 45–6, 116, 117, 210, 215n
formation and experience 5, 59–60, 62, 92, 121, 227, see also learning, religious/spiritual
  Christian 62, 211
foundationalism/non-foundationalism 113n, 218–9
  modest foundationalism 122n
fruits of RSEs 30, ch. 7, 106, 124, 128, 132, 223
  spiritual cf. moral/social 75
fulfilment
  human 12, 153, 186
  prophetic 79, 104
  religious 125, 196
  wish-fulfilment 127, 172
fundamentalism 151, 158

gender ch. 14
general/specific experiences, see breadth of RSEs
generosity 76, 160
gentleness 76
ghosts 39, 43, 209, see also dead, visions of; spirit, human
gift
  God's 45, 151, 158, 201n, 215n, see also God, gift of; grace; Spirit, divine/Holy Spirit, gifts of
  life as 59–60, 61
glossaries viii, 196–7, 217–9, 230–1
glossolalia 30, 42, 53n, 159
God 6, 11, 12, 14n, 15n, 41, 49, 50, 53n, 76, 85, 124, 125, 129–31, 173–4, ch. 16, ch. 17, ch. 18, 222–3, 231, 235, 236, 239, 240, see also grace; theology/theological perspectives on RSEs; theism; transcendence
  absence of 134n, 166–7, 200
  arguments from religious experience/arguments for God 57, 64, ch. 10, 131, 154; cf. ch. 9
  experience of 6, 10, 23, 23, 30, 31, 33, 37–8, 39, 41, 42, 43, 44, 45–7, 49, 50, 52n–53n, 54n, ch. 5, 68, 71–3, 79–80, 85, 89, 96, 99, ch. 9, 115–16, 119–20, 122n, 131, 134n, ch. 12, ch. 13, ch. 16, ch. 17, ch. 18, 221–2, 224, 235
  deconstruction of 236
  finite 221
  gender of 137, 162–4, 168n, 172, 202, 241, see also Freud, Sigmund
  gift of, see gift, God's; grace; Spirit, divine/Holy Spirit, gifts of
  immutable 138
  impassible 138

ineffable, *see* ineffability/ineffable
mercy of 80, 209, *see also* grace
personal 12, 14n, 39, 57, 103, 104, 109, 116, 123, 126, 132, 154, 155, 157, 168, 182, 186, 221, *see also* theism; cf. 167; impersonal transcendent being/reality
presence of, *see* presence, experiences of
as projection 128, 171–2, 224, 240
reduced to/'only a figurative expression of' society 240
God-consciousness 149, 191n
gods/deities 11–12, 14, 15n, 39, 43, 71, 126, 131, 140, 172, 179, 183, 191n, 231, 235, 240, *see also* God
Good Friday Experiment 69
grace 45, 46, 53n–54n, 69, 70, 76–7, 150, 152, 155, 191n, 195, 196, 197, 201–2, 210–11, 215n

happiness 7, 33, 39, 75
harmony 40, 48, 136
 of contrasts 209
healings/healing experiences 30, 42, 47, 128, 186, 189, 191, 227; cf. 11, 61
heart 10, 11, 15n, 42, 43, 140, 142, 186, 187, 195, 200, 215n
heat/warmth, experiences of 44, 53n, 201, 215n
Hebrew Bible, *see* Old Testament
hermeneutics 20, 93, 179, 229, *see also* interpretation
hetero-description 8
high/higher/highest
 bliss 49
 capacities/employment/faculties of the mind/perception 10, 53, 141, 196, 199, 220

part of the universe 220
part of the self, 220; cf. 199
social status 127, 235, 237, 242n; cf. 129, 204, 226, 231, 235, 242n
special status 231, 242n–243n
stages of religious experience 69, 141, 140
highest common factor of experiences 84
Hinduism 43, 53, 77, 85, 103, 130, 140, 204n
 Advaita Vedanta 77, 103
historical context of RSEs ch. 17, 238
historical theology x, ch. 17
holistic empiricism 57; cf. 58
holy/Holy, the 40, 41, 51, 60, 71, 117, 207–9, *see also* numinous experiences
hope 60, 72, 241
 profound 72
horizon of experience 54n, 210
 infinite 211
horror 208–9; cf. 236
humanistic psychology 174
humanistic sociology 241
humility 60, 80, 106, 168n, 199, 202, 203, 208

ideals/ideal things 78, 102, 231
ideal types 25n, 236–7, 243n
identity/identification/ undifferentiated union, experiences of 6–7, 32, 38, 39, 40, 53n, 76, 84, 95, 125, 139–41, 146, 179, 209, see also knowledge, by identity; monism/identity; mysticism, mystical experience; cf. union/unity, experience of; cf. 76, 187

INDEX OF SUBJECTS

absorption in, *see* absorption, experiences of
analogy of drop of water/ streamlet 53n, 139
illness 68, 127, 216
illumination
  faculty of 113n, 210; cf. 49, 177
  illuminative stage 197–8
  God's 197, 198
illusions 104, 112n, 128, 133, *see also* ch. 9; cf. delusions
image of God 12, 172, 199; cf. 43
imagery, religious 53n, 69, 76, 122, 124, ch.12, 161n, 163, 168n, 173, 195, 196, 198, 199, 201, 202, 204n, 228, 239
imagination (positive or negative) 25, 43, 44, 53n, 58, 59, 72, 80, 100, 118, 132, 136, 137, 160, 181, 212, 224, 233
immanence 14n, 164, *see also* transcendence
  ecstatic immanence 48
immediate (at once) and long-term consequences of RSEs 54n, ch. 7, 116
'immediate feeling'/'immediate perception' 206
immediate/non-mediated (non-inferential) RSEs 6, ch. 8, 116, 120, 148, 174, 196, 206, 220, 227, *see also* intuition, intuitive experiences
impersonal transcendent being/ reality 7, 12, 103, 109, 123, 125, 126, 134n, 221, *see also* Absolute, the
impulses 44, 180
index, *see* research/survey instruments
individual cf. social 11, 41, 102, 158, 164, 172, 174, 183, 188, 211, 226, 227–8, 230, 242n, 321–2, 236, 240; cf. 128
individualization 230
ineffability/ineffable 39, 40–1, 69, 126, 135–6, 141–4, 145, 146, 162, 198, 229; cf. 147n
  definitional 142
  degrees of 142
  grammatical/second-order status 142–3
  relative 142–3
inexperienceable, the 85
inference 13, 94, ch. 10, 155, 171, 207, 231, *see also* intuition/intuitive experiences; knowledge, direct cf. inferential
  cumulative arguments 119
  inference to the best explanation 91, 102n, ch. 10, 131
  inferential argument from religious experience, *see* religious experience, as argument/evidence/ grounds/premise for existence of God
infinite, sense and taste for 149, 206
inherent/intrinsic/intrinsically related to 8, 98, 158, 166, 186
inherentists 83, 217
inspiration experiences 41, 42, 79, 113n, 150, 159, 180–4, 186, 191n, 237; cf. 240
  poetic 161n, 181
intellectualist approach 231–2
intense experiences 33, 42, 43, 44, 47–8, 54n, 76, 143, 150–1, 162, 197, 200, 209, 213, 220, 223
intentionality/intentional object 13n, 49, 92, 96

interpretation ix, 8, 20, 24, 32, 38, 47, 52n, 53n, 58, 61, 63, 65n, 68, 82n, ch. 8, 112n, 116–17, 119, 122n, 120, 124, 125, 126, 134n, 138, 143, 151–2, 156, 157, 160, 161n, 163, 166, 172, 174, 176, 179, 181, 183, 207, 211, 212, 217, 218, 221, 222–3, 228–9, 232, 236, 238
cf. description 8–9, 87–9, 95, 124, 127, and ch. 8 *passim*
as conceptualization 8, 38, 39, 49, 85–9, 91, 92–4, 97–8, 102n, 118, 120, 143, 209, 217, 221, 227, 229; cf. 96, 215
as constitutive of experience 9, 88–9, 90, 91, 92, 97–8, 212, and ch. 8 *passim*
as conversation/dialogue 100
degrees of 97; cf. 98
as expression 100
fallible/sinful 106, 151
incorporated 86, 88, 101n
of tongues 30, 42, 159
as translation 100
under-/over-interpretation 122n
interpretive anthropology, *see* ethnography
interpretive experiences 47, 50, 65n; cf. ch. 8, 115
interventionism/non-interventionism 14n, 59, 81, 130, 182–3
interviews 24, 27, 28–31, 34, 36n, 45, 70, 242n, 227
introspection 14n, 38, 107, 108, 109, 114n, 148, 149
intuition/intuitive experiences 37, 41, 47, 109, 116, 138, 149, 151, 206, 207, *see also* beatific visions
invention of religion 231–2, *see*

also Feuerbach, Ludwig; Freud, Sigmund; projection theory
inventory, *see* research/survey instruments
Islam 53, 103, 133n, 149, 204n
Sufism 53, 93

Jesus Christ 12, 43, 61, 75, 76, 82n, 90, 122n, 148, 150, 153, 155, 156, 158, 179, 185–6, 188, 189, 190, 191n–192n, 202, 213, 236, 238
example of 213, 238
quests of the historical Jesus 185
transfiguration of 179, 189
resurrection of 179, 188, 190; cf. 192
visions of ix, 43, 45, 52n, 130
John's Gospel 188
John the Baptist 76
joy 7, 39, 42, 44, 68, 54, 59, 69, 76, 80, 206, 241
Jesuits 210
Judaism x, 53, 79, 93, 159, 183n, 188, 204n
Hasidism 53

kindness 76
kingdom 61
knowledge ix, x, 3, 5, 39, 41, 46, 53, 67, 75, 79, 84, 96, 99, 102n, 103–4, 111, 112n, 116, 117, 122, 124, 130, 134n, 138, 140, 141, 142, 150–1, 154, 155–8, 163, 168n, 181, 182, 185, 193, 196, 198, 200, 201, 207, 217, 210, 218, 222, 223, 224, 236, 240, *see also* beliefs/believers/believing; cognition (as knowing, thinking)
by acquaintance 53n, 92, 96, 115, 221

direct cf. inferential ch. 10, 149, 156, 181, 206, 207, 220, 221, *see also* unknowing
filial 168n
by identity 38, 96, *see also* pure consciousness events (PCEs)
tacit knowledge 149
word of knowledge/wisdom 79

language *xi*, 9, 20, 42
  about the religious/spiritual and RSEs 9, 42, 44, 46, 48, 62, 68–9, 74n, 80, 85, 88, 90, 91, 92, 94, 95, 96, 99, 100, 101n, 102n, 122n, 124–5, ch. 12, 161n, 187, 194, 195, 204, 206–7, 209, 211–12, 215n, 218–19, 236, *see also* analogies/metaphors, religious; analogies/metaphors for RSEs/revelation; imagery, religious; non-cognitive religious language; revelation, propositional/non-propositional
  gendered 163–4, *see also* God, gender of
learning, religious/spiritual 59–62, 98, 191n, 211, 219, 226, 227, *see also* formation and experience; Lindbeck, George Arthur
liberals (in theology) *see* theology/theological perspectives on RSEs, liberal theology
light, experiences of 23, 44, 51, 52n, 53n, 195, 198, 200, 215n; cf. 49, 58–9, 80, 82, 104, 210
lightness/weight, experiences of 43
liquidity, experiences of 44, 53n
literature 58, 218
locutions, *see* auditions/auditory experiences

longing, *see* desire/longing
loss 44, 45, 134n, 163
love, experience/development of 23, 45, 49, 52n–53n, 54n, 76–7, 116, 134n, 139, 142, 155, 195, 196, 198, 201, 202, 209, 210, 215n, *see also* grace
self-love 76
Lutherans 205, 207, 211, 241

making-creation 129–30
market theory 230
Marsh Valley Chapel experiment 69
Mary 43, 99
M-beliefs 119–10
meaning/meaningfulness 3, 7, 9, 11, 15n, 20, 50, 58, 59, 60, 63, 75, 77, 128, 134n, 164, 174, 196, 227–8, 229, 238–9
  disclosures of 59
measure, *see* research/survey instruments
mediated RSEs (mediated through concrete/sensory or abstract/linguistic media, but direct and non-inferential) 47, 50, 58, 64, ch. 8, 122n, 164, 212
unmediated RSEs (direct and non-inferential, but not mediated through concrete or abstract media) 47, ch. 8, 194, 122n, 209
medical materialism 130
meditation/meditative experiences 25, 47–8, 68, 69, 70, 102, 137–8, 144, 146, 196, 201, 227
memory 45, 80, 92, 107, 109, 217
metaphors/models, religious 58, 59, 61, 76, 82n, 113n, 124, 137, 138–9, 143–4, 145, 147n, 180, 191n

underspecified 124
metaphysical beliefs 39, 45, 67, 78, 84, 119, 205–6, 219, see also Absolute, the; atheism/anti-theism/non-theism; monism/identity; naturalism/naturalistic perspectives; theism
Micaiah 191n
middle ways, see both-and positions
miracles 47, 130, 80–1, see also interventionism/non-interventionism; providence
model, definition of 139
modernism/postmodernism 48, 211, 215n, 218–9, 238
monism/identity 38, 40, 52n–53n, 125, 139–40, 145, 163, see also mysticism, mystical experiences (narrow sense), monistic
monotheism 14n, see also God; theism
moral experience/vision 10, 57–60, 64, 82n, 109, 195, 237
moral instincts 54n
moral preparation 87, 105
moral transformation 12, 42, 43, 45, 59–60, 71–2, ch. 7, 87, 106, 159, 168n, 213, 215n, 223, 237, 238, see also spiritual change/transformation
moral values, see values/valuing, moral
more, the 53n, see also transcendence/transcendent reality
Moses/Mosaic 181, 196
music 4, 58, 68, 69, 100, 122, 141–2
Muslims, see Islam
mystery 12, 40, 54n, 64, 90, 102n, 137, 138–9, 140–1, 143–4, 207–8, 210–11, 224
mysterium tremendum et fascinans (dreadful and entrancing Mystery) 40, 207–9, 229
mystery of experience 54n
Mystical Experience Registry 26n
mystical perception/experiences (broad sense, Alston's term) 6, ch. 9, 119–20
Mysticism Scale/M-scale (Hood) 32, 95
mysticism/mystical experiences (narrow sense) 13n, 14n, 28, 32, 33–4, 37–40, 40–1, 48, 52n, 77–8, 82n, 84, 85, 87, 88–90, 94, 95, 98–9, 101n, 127, 131, 141, 144–5, 152, 176, 189, ch. 17, 217, 219, 237, *Appendix*
anthologies of 40
celestial 39
characteristics/marks of 37–40, 83–4, 85, 135, 152, 162–3, 235, 236, see also theistic
cf. church and sect 236
Christian 38, 44, 52n–53n, 76, 93, 96, 139, 163, ch. 17, 213, 235, see also theistic
exclusive/inclusive 54n
extrovertive 38, 39, 93, 95, 103, see also monistic
female 163–5, 168n, see also Teresa of Avila; Julian of Norwich; Margery Kempe; Hildegard of Bingen
gendered ch. 14, 236
intermediate 39
introvertive 38, 39, 95, 96, see also monistic; pure consciousness events (PCEs)

INDEX OF SUBJECTS

infinite 39
monistic 6–7, 38–9, 40, 52n–53n, 125, 126, 133n, 139–41, 221
panenhenic 39, 40
social role/status ch. 20
soul 39
terrestrial 39
theistic 7, 38, 46, 49, 52n–53n, 113n, 125, 133n, 139, 140–1, *see also* Christian
mystical way 70
mystical world 101n
mystics, individual, 79, 93, 96, 102n, 136, 140–1, 163, 190, 194, 195, 198, 199, 203
  Carmelite 44, 53n, 79–80, 135–6, 137–8, 139, 163, 168n, 196, 197, 199–200, 204n
  English 53n–54n, 173, 201–2

natural science perspectives on RSEs 10, 22, 124, 171, 238, *Appendix*
naturalism/naturalistic
  perspectives 57, 68, 120, 126–33, 166, 228–9, 231–2, 236, 238, *Appendix*
  religious 134n; cf. Cupitt, Don
Nature
  mysticism 30, 39, 49, 125, 209
  other experiences of/relationships with 11, 40, 47, 50, 57, 60–1, 122n, 156, 199, 209, 222
near-death experiences (NDEs) 51, 94, 125
neo-Platonism 93, 198, 199
neuroscience of RSEs x, xin, 45, 47, 76, 97, 126, 130–2, 134n, 232, *Appendix*

neurosis 127–8, 172
New Testament 40, 75–6, 79, 126, 155, 157, 179, 180, 182–3, 184–90, 210
Nirvāna/Nibbāna 49, 85, 92, 126, *see also* nothing/nothingness
noetic 39, 153
non-cognitive religious language 124–5, 138–9, 143
non-rational/arational 40, 207, 209, 239
non-realism 48, 147n
non-scientific knowledge 58
nothing/nothingness 49, 299, 218; cf. 215n
novelty 158–60
numinous experiences 5, 40–1, 46, 49, 53n, 54, 69, 84, 113n, 117, 128, 135, 164, 173, 207–10, 229

OBEs, *see* out-of-body experiences
object relations theory 172
objective or subjective experience/RSEs 4–7, 9, 13n, 20, 47, 61, 63–4, 78–9, 88, 87, 93, 97, 99–100, 102n, ch. 9, 115, 118, 123, 129–32, 134n, 138, 145, 149–50, 162–3, 166, 168n, 175, 187, 206–7, 212, 218–19, 221
objectivity of experience/RSEs 63, 79, ch. 9, 118, 123, 129–30, 168n, 218
  criteria of testing for 104–6
Old Testament 40, 126, 155, 157, 179, 180–4, 186, 187, 191n, 192n, 210
One/oneness 38, 39, 53n, 123, 124, 140, 145, 199, 221, *see also* monism/identity; cf. 125, 240
OOBEs, *see* out-of-body experiences

openness 11, 59, 70–3, 134n, 151, 158–60, 187, 218, 233
  critical 73, 79–81
  to dialogue 160
operationalization 32, 32
ophthalmology, spiritual 60–1
ordinary believer/experiencer/ ordinary theology 3, 7, 17, 21, 27, 28, 33, 62, 70, 77, 215n, 220, *see also* classic/elite experiencers
ordinary experience, *see* breadth of RSEs; classic/elite experiencers; extraordinary cf. ordinary experiences; religious and spiritual experiences/religious experiences
Orthodoxy, Eastern 147n, 158–9
orthodoxy, radical 212
orthodoxy, religious 23–4, 47
other faiths/religions, *see* faiths, non-Christian/world
out-of-body experiences 30, 51, 66n, 94
over-beliefs 226, 242n
overrider system of RSEs 107, 108–10, 119, 114n

Pagans 204n
pantheism 221
paradoxes/paradoxicality 39, 69, 144–6
paranormal/parapsychological experiences 50–1, 228, 232, 234
participant observation 27–8, 227, 231, 233, 242n
passivity 39, 41, 42, 74n, 141, 152, 163, 197, *see also* activity; pure consciousness events (PCEs)
passive night of the soul 200
prayer of passive recollection 196

patience 76, 202
pattern/patterning, experiences of 50, 97, 174, 232; cf. 227
Paul, Apostle 42, 44, 75–6, 79, 82n, 130, 157, 173, 182–3, 190, 191n–192n, 196, 198
  as mystic 190
peace 7, 42, 46, 49, 68, 69, 76, 80, 140, 195
peak experiences 48, 54, 125, 128, 174, 228, 233
Pentecostals/pentecostal experiences 30, 41, 42–3, 128, 157, 159, 189, 213, 230, *see also* charismatics/charismatic experiences
perception model of religious experience 5–6, 10, 14n, 38, 41, 49, 50, 53n, 54n, ch. 5, 88, 92–3, 97, 102n, ch. 9, ch. 10, 124, 127, 129–30, 131, 134n, 136, 140, 151, 155, 157, 163, 167, 180, 184, 188, 194–5, 196, 198, 206, 207, 212, 214, 219, 221–2
  indirect perception model 122n, 221–2
perception of God's absence 134n
perception, emotional 206
perennialism/perennial philosophy 84, 86–9, 90, 93, 95, 96, 97–100, 101n, 102n, 209, 212, 217
  neo-/new/psychological perennialists 95, *see also* pure consciousness events (PCEs)
personality 33, 38, 134n, 176, 181
phenomenology of RSEs 19–20, 21, 22, 26n, 46, 47, 64, 84, 97, 102n, 150–1, 187–8, 207, 209–10, 229, 231; cf. 59

INDEX OF SUBJECTS

philosophia perennis 84, *see also* perennialism/perennial philosophy
philosophical perspectives on RSEs ch. 19, *see also* part 3 *passim*
philosophy
  analytical 102n, 216–7
  meta- 216
Pietists 6
piety 149–50, 206–7
pluralistic hypothesis 123, 222–3, *see also* Hick, John
poetry 139, 161n, 180, 181, *see also* literature
politics/political 162, 163, 165, 187, 199, 228, 236, *see also* power, social/political
possession 44, 45, 162, 180, 182, 183, 235, *see also* demons/Devil; spirits
postliberalism 99, 211–12
postmodernism, *see* Enlightenment, the/post-Enlightenment; modernism/postmodernism
power, divine/superior 3, 28, 30, 53n, 61, 80, 152, 173, 181, 185–6, 204n, 208, 223, 230
power, social/political 127, 163–4, 235–8, 239, 243n, *see also* status, social
practice, social 128, 162, 165, 226, 227, 231, 237
practices, religious/spiritual 3, 9, 10, 11, 33, 40, 43, 58, 59, 63, 70, 77, 87, 88, 90n, 92n, 94n, 129, 149, 159, 174, 182, 196, 205, 209, 227, 239
pragmatism/pragmatic theory 78–9, 82n, 106
prayer 7, 25n, 30, 43, 44, 47, 68, 69, 70, 71, 74n, 80, 139, 200, 202
  of active recollection 196
  contemplative/interior/mystical/mental 140, 196, 201; cf. meditation/meditative experiences
  experiment in 70–2
  infused/supernatural 196, 197
  of passive recollection 196
  pray-er 72
  of quiet 196
  of simplicity 196
  of union 196
pre-apprehension of infinite being 210–11
presence, experiences of 3, 6, 14n, 28, 29–30, 42, 45, 46, 59–60, 66n, 89, 103, 117, 155, 156, 161n, 157–8, 166, 179, 207–8, 221
  unnamed presence 46, 207
preserving/sustaining-creation 14n, 50, 106, 130
principalities/powers 126, *see also* gods/deities; spirits
principle of credulity/critical trust 105–6, 107, 111, 113n, 222
principle of non-contradiction 144–6
  cf. contradiction theory 145
principle of testimony 111
principle of unrestricted naturalistic explanation 120
privacy 24, 26n
private/public experience 4–5, 112n–113n, 127, 162, 200, 220, 226–7, 237; cf. 24, 26n
profane 208, 237, 242n, *see also* sacred/sacredness
projection theory 127–8, 129, 171, 224, 240
prophecy/prophetic experiences 30, 40, 41, 42, 44, 75, 79, 117, 136, 157,

159, 161n, 180–4, 186, 191n, 206, 209, 237, 239
  social communication/dimension of 183–4
Protestants 6, 10, 45, 149, 150, 154, 158, 159, 194, 238, *see also* Anglicans, Calvinists, Lutherans
protestant work ethic 238
providence 50, 130, *see also* miracles
providers 230
psi phenomenon, *see* extra-sensory perception (ESP); paranormal/parapsychological experiences
psychic death 204n
psychoanalytic theory 127, 172, 173, 174
psychology/psychological perspectives on RSEs 5, 6, 14n, 22, ch. 3, 44, 45, 48, 59, 69, 73, 77, 79, 82n, 93, 94–5, 102n, 111, 126–9, 130–1, 132, 133n, 141, 149, 150, 162, 166, ch. 15, 182, 185, 188, 189, 204n, 210, 220–1, 226, 227, 228, 231–2, *Appendix*
  empirical psychology 47, 69, 175–7
  rational psychology 175
  transpersonal psychology 174–5
psychosis 33, 82n, 128, 134n
pure consciousness events (PCEs) 38–9, 49, 54n, 85, 91, 92, 95–7, 98, 102, 125, 220, *see also* knowledge, by identity
pure delight 48
pure prayer 140
purgatory 213
  purgative stage 197, 202
purity 201–2

qualitative research ch. 3, 175–7, 227

quantitative research ch. 3, 129, 175–7
questionnaires 26n, 27, 31, 33, 34, 36n, 70, 86–7, 227
questions, survey 14n, 27–8, 29, 30, 31, 32, 36n, 66n, 87, 95
  Bourque question 14n, 28
  Hardy question 14n, 21, 28, 30, 65n–66n, 175
  Greeley question 14, 28
  Greer question 28
  open/closed 27, 31, 36n
  Stark question 28, 29
  Wuthnow question 28

raptures 44
rational choice theory 230
reason/reasoning ix, 41, 64, 107, 108, 111, 115, 118, 129, 141, 150, 163, 171, 175, 218, 220, 231, 238
rebutters 114n, *see also* overrider system of RSEs
reception 150–3, 183–4
reductionism ix, 68, 127, 130–1, *see also* explanation, naturalistic/reductive/scientific approach to
descriptive/explanatory 127
references xi, *References*
Reformed, *see* Protestants, *also* Protestants, Calvinists
regression 127, 172
relativism 142, 218, 238, *see also* truth/truths
reliability, statistical 31
reliability, experience of 50
religion
  characterization of/definition of 3, 6, 7, 11, 58, 111, 127, 128, 139, 149, 153, 172, 173–4, 206, 207, 211, 220, 223, 231–2, 239–40, 242n

INDEX OF SUBJECTS

essence/spirit of 206–7, 220, 242n
foundation in religious
  experiences 3, 5–6
and freedom 222–3
function of 239–40
soteriological power of 223
religious and spiritual experiences/
  religious experiences
accounts of/data of ix, x, 21, part 2,
  ch. 5, 88, 128–9, 134n, 154, part 4
as argument/evidence/grounds/
  premise for existence of God 57–8,
  63–4, 64, 72, ch. 10, 120–1, 122n,
  131, 154, 206, 215n, see also self-
  authenticating beliefs/experiences;
  testing phenomena/theories
best explanation of 88–9, 91, 102n,
  ch. 10, 131
characteristics of 4, 5, 14n, ch. 2, 29,
  ch. 4, 59, 62–3, 64, 69, 83–4, 85, 96,
  135, 146, 152, 162, 165, 214
continuing 63 and ch. 5 *passim*
definition of ch. 1, 29, 54n, 165
direct, *see* direct awareness
dramatic 62, 164, 220, *see also*
  extraordinary cf. ordinary
  experiences
elite experiences 26n, *see also*
  classic/elite experiencers
as envisioning 63
and human evolution 172, 175, 232;
  cf. 158
family resemblances between 26n
as foundational to religion 3, 5–6
function of 75, 132, 237, 240
and freedom 222–3
as gendered ch. 14, 236
indirect and mediated/direct and
  immediate, non-mediated (by
objects, language, concepts) 47,
  50, 58, 64, 88, 92, 102n, 122n,
  194, 211, 212, *see also* direct,
  'immediate' experience
  cf. mediated inferences
inerrancy/infallibility of 124,
  151, 157, *see also* self-
  authenticating beliefs/experiences;
  fundamentalism
and interpretation ch. 8, *see also*
  interpretation
as intuitions, *see* intuition/intuitive
  experiences
as objective/subjective, *see* objective
  or subjective experience/RSEs
as neither objective nor
  subjective 13n, 97, 145, 206–7
objectivity of, *see* objectivity of
  experience/RSEs
as perceptions of God, *see*
  perception model of religious
  experience
pathological/non-pathological 127,
  172
as relationship 12, 39, 49, 103, 116,
  134n, 166–7, 168n, 172
and revelation 149–53
as *revision* 63
spontaneous 69, 70, 80, 94, 173,
  174, 181; cf. 47, 65n
stages of 69, 80, 99, 164, 177, 196,
  197, 198, 200, 213; cf. 172
survival value of 175, *see also* and
  human evolution
and theology 153–8
as union/unity, *see* identity/
  identification/undifferentiated
  union, experiences of; One/
  oneness; union/unity, experience

of union without distinction
unitary/multiple 113n
universality/non-universality
   of 54n, 96, 104–5, 127, 172, 207,
   232
   in USA 28, 29, 30, 50, 151, 161n,
   220, *see also* Association of
   Religion Data Archives
   in UK 23–4, 28, 29–31, 33, 45,
   46, 50, 51, 66n, 82n, 129, *see also*
   Alister Hardy Archive
renewal experiences, *see* conversion
   experiences
research/survey instruments 26n, 31,
   32, 33, 95
   reliability/validity of 31
responsive experiences 29
reticence in reporting RSEs 23–4,
   26n
revelation 7, 29, 41, 43, 44, 45, 48,
   52n, 59, 61, 65n, 79, 80, 104, 114n,
   117, 124, 133n, 138, ch. 13, 179,
   180–4, 191n, 200, 201–2, 206, 221
   accommodation of 124
   as achievement, not task 161n
   auditory model 156, 157, 180,
   182, *see also* auditions/auditory
   experiences
   media of 158–9
   particularity of 161n; cf. 218
   progressive 133n
   propositional/non-propositional
   42–3, 155–8, 161n, 181–3, 200, 221
   and religious experience 149–53
   verbal, *see* propositional/non-
   propositional
   visual model 58, 60, 61, 156, 157,
   see also spiritual ophthalmology;
   spiritual vision

rhetoric 60, 144–6
roots of RSEs 75, 220
routinization 239, *see also* charisma/
   charismatic authority
'RSEs' ix, 12, *see also* religious and
   spiritual experiences/religious
   experiences

sacred/sacredness 3, 28, 38, 39, 64,
   69, 135, 164, 231, 237, 239, 240,
   241, 242n, *see also* profane
sacred places 64
sacred scriptures 21, 27, ch. 16
saints 43, 125, ch. 17
   secular/political saints 75
salvation 11, 14n, 42, 45, 122, 125,
   155, 222–3, 236, 239
sampling 27, 28, 29, 31, 34, 227
sanctification 45–6, *see also* self,
   self-surrender; self-transcendence;
   self-transformation
scale, *see* research/survey instruments
schemas/schematization 209, 215n
scientism 171, *see also* naturalism/
   naturalistic perspectives
Scripture/scriptures 27, 40, 126, 139,
   140, 151, 154, 157, 158, 160, ch. 16,
   205
   authoritativeness of 45
   conformity to/test of 80, 159, 161n
secularization 230, 238, 241
'seems', understanding/use of
   term 19–20, 105, 129, 134n
   epistemic sense of 134n
self 7, 13, 28, 30, 38, 39, 40, 43, 44,
   49, 53n, 57, 145, 172, 174, 181,
   194–5, 220, 230, 236
   fifth dimension of 12, 221
   no-self 49

self-actualization 128, 174
self-authenticating beliefs/experiences 103, 114n, 118, 119, 120–1, 153–4
self-centredness 7, 12, 76, 82n
self-consciousness, religious 207
self-contradiction 144–5
self-control 76
self-discipline 63, 70, 76
self-forgetting, see forgetting
self-formation 59–60
self-induced belief 72, 90; cf. 80, 181, 244
self-knowledge 196, see also self
self-surrender 12, 42, 54, 69, 76, 82n, 163–4, 177, 204n
self-transcendence 7, 48, 49, 76, 174
self-transformation 6, 42, 44, 48, 53, 59, 76, 82n, 128, 139, 168n, 177, 196, 197, 215n, 233, 238, see also ch. 7 *passim*
self-understanding of Jesus 185
Self, absolute 140, 145, see also Absolute, the; Brahman
sense experience/perception 3, 10, 13n, 14n, 38, 43, 53, 58, 63, 65n, 69, 89, 93, 96, 97, 102n, 104–6, 107–9, 111, 112n, 113n, 114n, 116, 118, 122n, 136, 140, 167, 194, 197, 198, 199, 201, 204n, 214, 217, 219, 220, 221, 222
  analogy of religious experience with sense experience 10, 58, 108–9, 112n, 113n, 116, 122n, 124, 156, 157, 167, 219, 118–20, see also perception model of religious experience; spiritual vision; cf. 96, 107
sense, see meaning/meaningfulness
sensus divinitatis 113n
sensus spiritualis 10; cf. 58
separation 41, 53, 124, 145, 164, 227, see also transcendence
set of subject 108, 127
setting apart 231, 239, 242n
setting of subject 127, 188, 227, see also belief-system; constructivism, social; culture/cultural, background/context; historical context of RSEs; society/social; sociological perspectives on RSEs; solitary cf. social
shamanism 44, 237
shewings 202
significance, see meaning/meaningfulness; existential significance; ultimate significance
significance, statistical 27, 31, see also quantitative research
sin 12, 42, 45, 82n, 105, 151, 158, 165, 187, 195, 202, 213
smell, experiences of 105, 195, 204
social cf. individual, see individual cf. social
social science perspectives on RSEs 22, 27–8, 129, ch. 14, ch. 15, 188–9, ch. 20
society/social, see practice, social; sociological perspectives on RSEs
  change/transformation 128, 177, 237, 238
  facts 232
  influence 227
  power, see power, social/political
  pressure 24, 204n
  readjustment 42
  settings of RSEs 227, see also setting of subject
  as soul of religion 240

sociological perspectives on RSEs 9, 25n, ch. 3, 126–9, 131, 162–3, 172, 179, 184, 185, 188, 204n, ch. 20

solitary cf. social 86, 172, 243n, *see also* individual cf. social

soteriology 6, 14n, 223
  soteriological answers 239
  soteriological power 223

soul 37, 38, 39, 44, 45, 52n–53n, 69–70, 80, 84, 135–6, 139, 141, 163, 168n, 171, 173, 174, 180, 182, 186, 192n, 194, 196, 197, 198, 199, 200, 201, 202, 204n, 207–8
  dark night of the soul 136, 137, 197, 200, 204n

special/specialness 231, 242n–243n

Spirit, divine/Holy Spirit 11, 12, 30, 41, 42–3, 45–6, 53n, 76, 79, 140, 141, 150, 152–3, 158, 159, 161n, 164, ch. 16, 210, 213; cf. 199
  baptism in the Spirit 30, 42–3, 184, 186, 213; cf. 198
  as breath/wind 147n, 153, 186; cf. 171
  fruit of 75–6, 82n, *see also* fruits of RSEs
  gifts of 30, 42, 79, 82n, 158, 186, 79, 180, 184, *see also* glossolalia; healings/healing experiences; interpretation, of tongues; prophecy/prophetic experiences
  internal/inward testimony of 45–6, 152

spirit, human 10, 39, 44, 141, 164, 171, 186, 187
  active night of the spirit 196, 200
  continuity with divine Spirit 187
  dark night of the spirit 197, 200, *see also* soul, dark night of the soul

fifth dimension of human nature 12, 222
inner awareness/eyes of the spirit/soul 40, 156, 161, 180, 194–5, 201, 203, 209, 220
passive night of the spirit 200

spirits 39, 79, 186, 191, 232–4, *see also* spirit, human
  evil 45, 79, 125, 186, 191, 235, *see also* demons/Devil

spiritual change/transformation 6, 12, 30, 42, 43–4, 45, 53n, 58–9, 60–4, 69, 70–3, 75–7, 82n, 98, 128, 139, 177, 196, 197, 223, 233

spiritual disciplines 9, 63, 70, 77, 92, 175, 196, *see also* apprenticeship of the spirit; self-discipline

spiritual experiences
  accounts of 5, 7, 9–12, ch. 2, 30, ch. 4, ch. 5, part 4 *passim*, *see also* religious and spiritual experiences/religious experiences
  compare neurosis/psychosis 82n, 128, 174, 175, *see also* neurosis; psychosis
  definition of 9–12

spiritual guru/guide/mentor/teacher 70, *see also* formation and experience; learning, religious and spiritual

spiritual marriage 44, 53n, 137, 168n, 174, 196, 197, 200

spiritual ophthalmology, 60–1, *see also* spiritual vision

spiritual senses, 10, 65n, 188, 198
  doctrine of 10

spiritual values, *see* values/valuing, spiritual

spiritual vision 59–64, 69, 75,

INDEX OF SUBJECTS

164, 177, 237; cf. 58, *see also* epistemic transformation; moral transformation; self, self-transformation; spiritual change/transformation

spirituality 7, 10–12, 14n, 42–3, 59–60, 175, 185, 195, 196, 199–203, 238, 240, 243n, *see also* spiritual change/transformation
  definition of 10–12, 14n
  as fifth dimension of human nature 12, 222
  horizontal/vertical dimensions of 12
  human 12

statistics 28, 31, 34; cf. 29

status
  cultural 242
  social 127, 235, 237, 242n; cf. 129, 204, 226, 231, 235, 242n
  special 231, 242n–243n

sub-conscious 74n, *see also* Freud, Sigmund

super-ego 128, *see also* Freud, Sigmund

super-sensible 11, *see also* transcendence

surveys, *see* interview studies; questions, survey; questionnaires

synchronicity, *see* pattern/patterning, experiences of

taboos 23, 232, 234, 242n

taste, experiences of 53n, 105, 195, 201, 204, 210; cf. 149, 206

taxonomy of RSEs 25n, 29, 30, 228, *see also* classification of RSEs

testimony 104, 110–11, 117, 118, 125, *see also* diversity; principle of testimony

internal testimony of Holy Spirit 45–6, 152

testing phenomena/theories 31, 32, 34, 45, 70–3, ch. 7, 94, ch. 9, 119, 120, 129, 134n, 175, 168n, 207, 219, 223, *see also* experiments

tests of conformity 80, 159, 161n

theism 7, 10, 12, 14n, 28, 38, 46–7, 49, 57, 60, 71, 72, 75, 105, 106, 114n, 116–17, 119, 125, 129–30, 133n, 152, 154, 162, 166, 221, 235–6, *see also* atheism/anti-theism/non-theism; God
  broad 84
  cumulative case for theism 119
  -friendly, -incompatible, -neutral, -unfriendly religious experiences 125–6

theistic arguments 64, *see also* ch. 10

theistic mysticism, *see* mysticism/mystical experiences (narrow sense), theistic

theistic experiences 28, 46–7, 104, 106, 114, 119, 152, *see also* mysticism/mystical experiences (narrow sense), theistic
  as gendered ch. 14

theology/theological perspectives on RSEs x, 5, 6, 9, 10, 22, 48, 61, 63, 65n, 81, 42, 93, 99, 117–20, 125, 126, ch. 12, ch. 13, 162–3, 165, 168n, ch. 16, ch. 17, ch. 18, 216, 221, 224, 228, 233, 235–6, 237–8, 240, 241, 242n–243n, *see also* theism
  apophatic theology 198, 140–1, 201
  cataphatic theology 140
  conservative theology 125, 160

definition 205
downward 150
dogmatic theology 120, 153, 154, 205, 236
experiential-expressive theology 99, 161n, 211
liberal theology 54n, 81, 99, 81, 125, 133, 138, 150, 157–8, 205–7, 211, 212, 221; cf. 111
narrative 211–12
natural theology 120, 150, 154
negative way/theology of negation, see apophatic theology
of obedience 150, 158, 210
philosophical theology 138, 205, 214, 216
postliberal/postmodern theology 99, 113, 215n, 211–12; cf. 218–19, 230
reduced to anthropology 240
and RSEs 153–8
and religious studies 233
and revelation 148–53
subjective/from below up 149
speculative theology 153
systematic theology 61, 153, 154, 205; cf. 199
theology of religions 125, 222–4
theophanies 43, 179
thinking that feels like something 176
Thomas Theory 231
timelessness 39, 134n, 199
tongues, gift of, see glossolalia; interpretation, of tongues
top-down/bottom-up 21–22, 98
totems 172, 239, 240
tradition, Christian/religious/ spiritual 7, 9, 10, 21, 32, 62, 75, 77, 79, 83–4, 86, 89, 92, 94, 95, 98, 109, 121, 123–6, 150, 152, 154, 156, 157, 158–9, 160, 161n, 185, 179, 187, 188, ch. 17, 205, 206, 209, 211, 213, 222, 230, 236, 241
local 43
philosophical 93, 216
trances/ecstatic trances 43–5, 128, 174, 182, 183
tranquillity 44, 80
transcendence 3, 6–7, 11–12, 14n, 15n, 30, 37, 40–1, 42, 44, 48, 49, 50, 53n, 57, 59, 63–4, 71, 104, 134n, 135, 138, 141, 143, 150, 174, 179
transcendent/transcendental reality 40, 57, 59, 63–4, 68, 84, 104, 105, 123, 125, 135, 138, 141, 143, 150, 153, 161n, 196, 197, 221–2, 232, 234
fifth dimension of human nature/ universe 12, 222
signals of 241
transcendental
argument 63
orientation 210
transformation, see epistemic transformation; moral transformation; self-transformation; society/social, change/transformation; spiritual change/transformation; ch. 7 passim
inner 6, 14n, 30, 59, 76
transience 39
translation metaphor 20, 100, 142
transports 44, 208
triggers of RSEs 25n, ch. 6, 87, 131, 176
truth/truths 5, 7, 20, 30, 43, 46,

INDEX OF SUBJECTS

58–9, 61, 78–9, 84, 87, 100, 101n, 103, 104–6, 117, 125, 149–50, 153–4, 155–8, 171, 183, 191n, 196, 211, 212, 218–9, 222–3, 228, 231, 237, 238, 240, *see also* veridical experiences/veridicality and ch. 9 *passim*
- eternal 240
- saving 223
- subjective 47, 61, 78, 93, ch. 9, ch. 10, *see also* objective or subjective experience/RSEs

truthful experiences, *see* veridical experiences/veridicality

typology of RSEs 25n, 84, 93, 99, 236–7, 243n, *see also* classification of RSEs; ideal types

ultimacy experiences 10, 47–8
ultimate reality/realities 11, 12, 38, 39, 49, 50, 53n, 54n, 71, 85, 89, 102n, 104, 119, 123, 126, 131, 134n, 138, 142, 143, 198, 211, 223
ultimate significance 10, 11–12, 47, 54n, 121, 242n
uncanny 209, 210–11
unconscious 44, 94, 97, 98, 133n, 147n, 221, *see also* Freud, Sigmund; Jung, Carl Gustav
- collective unconscious 173
uncritical, *see* criticism/critical openness
underminers 114n, *see also* overrider system of RSEs
uninterpreted experience 85, 88, *see also* essentialism; constructivism, social; pure consciousness events (PCEs)
union without distinction,

see identity/identification/ undifferentiated union, experiences of; One/oneness

union/unity, experience of 6–7, 32, 37, 38, 39, 44, 49, 53n, 69, 76, 93, 95, 103, 124, 125, 139, 163, 168n, 172, 174, 179, 190, 196, 197, 198, 199, 200, 201, 204n, 209, 236, *see also* mysticism/mystical experiences (narrow sense), theistic; cf. 146
- analogy of sexual union 53, 163–4, 168n; cf. 165–7, *see also* spiritual marriage
- communion with God/Christ 38, 202; cf. 240
- degrees of union 201
- distinguished from monism/ identity 38, 53n, 139, *cf. also* union without distinction,
- intimate contact/union 32, 37, 136, 139–41, 150–1, 164, 204n; cf. 134, 164

unitary/unitive states/ experiences 14n, 37, 38, 41, 197, 221, *see also* identity/identification/ undifferentiated union, experiences of; One/oneness; pure consciousness events (PCEs); union/unity, experience of

unitive stage 197
universalism 83, 84, 218
unknowing 137, 141, 142, 201
unknowing union 198
unseen, the 53n, 67n

validity
- statistical 31
- universal 103–4

value-laden experiences 121, 222
values/valuing 3, 7, 11–12, 15n, 17, 20, 21, 40, 44, 58, 59, 60, 70, 75, 77, 78, 82n, 89, 90, 103–4, 105, 117, 120, 121, 134, 143, 153, 159, 175, 183, 200, 210, 218, 222, 226, 230, 231, 242n–243n, 253, *see also* meaning/meaningfulness
  communal/social 230
  intrinsic 58, 242
  lasting 63
  moral 3, 7, 15n, 41, 59, 70, 77, 82, 210
  spiritual 11–12, 15n, 58, 59, 60, 70–1, 210, 231
variables 27, 31, 36n
variety *vii*, 7, 32, 41, 43, 84, 95, 100, 101n, 124n, 158–60, 164, 176, 209, 217, 220, 237, *see also* diversity
veridical experiences/veridicality 5, 63–4, ch. 9, 115, 119, 120–1, 122n, 123, 124, 126, 130–1, 145, 184, 222–3, 228, 235–8
via negativa 147, *see also* theology/theological perspectives on RSEs, apophatic theology
virtues 12, 75–7, 80, 82n, 106, 197, 238, *see also* character, human; fruits of RSEs; values/valuing

visions/visual experiences 23, 30, 40, 43–5, 51, 53n, 63, 65n, 79, 80, 113n, 138, 153, 161n, 173, 179, 180–2, 184, 186, 188, 191n, 195, 200, 202, 203, 209, *see also* Christ, visions of
  corporeal/bodily cf. imaginative/intellectual 43
  visions of God 47, 139, 195, *see also* beatific visions; theophanies
  visual model of revelation, *see* revelation, visual model
vitality 48
vivid experiences 47–8, 49, 110, 222
vocation 41, 182
Vorgriff 210–11

well-being 7, *see also* happiness
  moral 42, 82n
  spiritual 42
wholly other 40, 41, 141, 207, 209
will to believe 72
wonder 25n, 40, 50, 54n, 59, 139, 209
worship 15n, 41, 42, 46, 62, 68, 70, 74n, 139, 186, 207, 227; cf. 178n

Yahweh/the LORD 180–1, 191n, *see also* God
  court of Yahweh 126

Index of Names

Abraham 188
Abraham, William 151–2, 161n
Aden, Ross 13, 22, 28, 84, 101, 165, 172, 244
Albrecht, Daniel E. 11, 41, 42, 43
Alister Hardy Religious Experience Research Centre *xiii*
Alister Hardy Trust *xiii*
Almond, Philip C. 101n
Alston, William 6, 14n, 92–3, 103, 105, 107–10, 111, 112, 113n, 114n, 115, 116, 119–20, 122n, 124, 129, 132, 221–2
Altmeyer, Stefan 11
American Psychological Association 175
Andersen, M. 245
Arbib, Michael A. 246
Argyle, Michael 33, 176, 177
Aristotle 82n, 144
Ashton, John 189
Astley, J. 11, 12, 14n, 20, 24, 26n, 47, 60, 62, 63, 65, 73, 90, 113n, 125, 134n, 143, 146, 158, 225n, 243n, 244
Atran, Scott 232
Audi, Robert 115
Augustine of Hippo 43, 142, 194–5, 209, 215n

Avis, Paul 151–2, 157, 160, 167, 181, 182
Azari, Nina P. 176, 245

Back K. W 14n, 36n
Badham, Paul 21
Baelz, Peter 72, 73, 74n
Bagger, Matthew C. 80, 86, 89, 93, 94, 102n, 113n, 115, 120, 122n, 131, 168n, 193, 200, 204n
Baillie, John 155
Barker, Margaret 182
Barnard, G. William 82n, 102n
Barrett, C. K. 79
Barrett, Cyril 161n
Barrett, Justin L. 232
Barrett, Nathaniel F. 245
Barth, Karl 150, 154, 215n
Basinger, David 118, 133, 244
Basu, Helene 43
Batluck, Mark 190
Batson, C. Daniel 69, 164, 177, 238
Baumert, Norbert 213
Beardsworth, Timothy 21, 34
Beauregard, Mario 244, 245
Beckford, James 235, 243n
Beckman, Patricia Z. 203
Berger, Klaus 61, 184, 191

Berger, Peter L. 241
Bettis, Joseph D. 20
Birnbacher, Dieter 176
Blackburn, Simon 5, 78, 216, 218
Blum, Jason 147
Bondi, Roberta 141
Bonner, Gerald 195
Borg, Marcus J. 61
Bourque, L. B. 14n, 28, 36n
Bowden, John 141
Bowen, John R. 241
Bowie, Fiona 232–4
Bowlby, John 172
Boyatzis, Chris J. 177
Boyer, Pascal 232
Brothers, Leslie A. 246
Brown, David 159, 160, 214
Brown, Warren S. 244
Burhenn, Herbert 216, 224
Burrows, Roger 51
Bush, Stephen S. 91, 98, 102n
Butler, Bishop Joseph 152, 161n
Butler, Cuthbert, OSB 40

Caetano, Carla 244
Calvin, John 113n, 152
Cardeña, Etzel 51
Cartledge, Mark J. 30, 42
Castro, Madeleine 51
Charry, Ellen T. 22, 161n
Clarke, W. Norris 152
Cloud of Unknowing 173, 201; cf. 137, 142
Coakley, Sarah 10, 22, 147n, 163, 167, 194, 214
Cohen, J. M. 22
Connolly, Peter 5, 21, 25, 44, 45, 132, 244
Cook, Christopher J. 31, 45

Corner, Mark 134n
Cottingham, John 7, 58–60, 65
Craig, William Lane 25, 64
Craighead, Houston A. 23, 24, 25, 112, 168n
Crystal L. Park 177
Csikszentmihalyi, Mihaly 54n, 228
Cupitt, Don 48, 147n, 236
Currie, Raymond 29, 32

d'Aquili, Eugene G. 76, 77, 97, 244, 245, 246
Davies, Brian, OP 224
Davis, Stephen T. 8, 119, 133n, 155, 157, 160
Dein, Simon 31
Denys/Pseudo-Dionysius 140–1, 198, 200
Derrida, Jacques 218
Dillistone, F. W. 9
Donovan, Peter 22, 65n, 113n, 116, 117, 121, 122n, 225n
Dulles, Avery, SJ 160, 161n
Dumsday, Travis 244
Dunn, James D. G. 82n, 181, 182, 184, 185–6, 187, 191, 191n–192n
Dupré, Louis 40, 160, 204
Durkheim, Émile 231–2, 234, 239–40, 242n
Dykstra, Craig 59

Eck, Diana L. 11, 14n
Eckhart, Meister Johannes 96, 163, 199
Eddy, Paul R. 102n
Edwards, Anthony C. 177
Edwards, Jonathan 10, 22, 82n
Edwards, Rem B. 13n
Egan, Harvey D., SJ 40, 213

Eliade, Mircea 84, 210
Engels, F. 128
Ennis, Philip H. 44
Erricker, Clive 25
Evans, C. Stephen 41, 113n, 122n
Evans, Donald 12, 15n, 91, 92, 98–9, 102n
Experientia Project 189

Fales, Evan 130, 235–6
Farges, Albert 116
Farmer, Lorelie J. 30
Fenwick, Elizabeth 51, 77
Fenwick, Peter 51, 77
Ferré, Frederick 242n
Feuerbach, Ludwig 171, 240
Firth, Shirley 51
Fischer, Roland 22
Flew, Antony 4, 216
Fodor, James 160, 212
Ford, David. F. 243n
Forgie, J. William 102n
Forman, Robert K. C. 38, 49, 84, 88, 89, 90, 93–4, 95–6, 98, 144
Fowler, James W. 11
Fox, George 130
Fox, Mark 21, 34, 51, 52n, 77, 94, 245
Francis, Leslie J. 28, 33, 35, 129, 134n, 152, 243n
Franke, John R. 160
Franklin, John 36n
Franks Davis, Caroline 4, 8, 14n, 22, 41, 42, 52, 65n, 71, 73, 84, 94, 98, 105, 113n, 116, 119, 121, 122n, 124, 127, 132, 133, 224
Frazer, James 231
Freud, Sigmund 127–8, 129, 133n, 171–2, 173, 174
Friedson, Stephen 243n

Gale, Richard M. 72, 78, 79, 105, 107, 108, 109, 110, 112n, 127, 143, 168n, 225n
Gaskin, J. C. A. 5, 115, 121
Gavrilyuk, Paul L. 10, 22, 194, 214
Geertz, Clifford 20
Geivett, Douglas 223
Gellman, Jerome 9, 13, 14n, 40, 53n, 89, 90, 96–7, 102n, 109–10, 144, 146, 162, 224, 242, 245
Gimello, Robert M. 90
Glock, Charles Y. 22, 36n, 228
Goldstone, Brian 62
Goleman, Daniel 21
Gorringe, Timothy 152
Goulet, Jean-Guy 242
Greeley, Andrew M. 28, 36n, 44, 228
Greer, John E. 14n, 24, 28, 36n
Greyson, Bruce 51
Griffith-Dickson, Gwen 26n, 63, 89, 94, 97, 100, 101, 103–4, 108, 111, 112, 119, 131, 165–7, 168n, 224
Grünbaum, Adolf 133n
Gunton, Colin E. 157–8, 160
Guthrie, Stewart 232
Gutting, Gary 106, 168n

Haas, Alois Maria 199
Hagner, Donald A. 185
Halligan, Fredrica R. 174
Hamer, Dean 245
Happold, F. C. 39, 40, 138, 139
Hardy, Alister 7, 14n, 21, 24, 25n, 28, 36n, 42, 43, 52, 62–3, 65n–66n, 68, 71, 74n, 77, 81, 82n, 87, 152, 153, 175, 240
Harton, F. P. 196
Hasker, William 115, 118, 122n, 133, 244

Hauerwas, Stanley 62
Hay, David 8, 14n, 21, 23–4, 26n, 28, 29–30, 35, 36n, 45, 46, 50, 66n, 76, 77, 81, 82n, 129, 133, 175, 212, 238, 240, 243n
Heald, Gordon 23, 26n
Heelas, Paul 11
Heim, S. Mark 125, 225n
Helm, Paul 113n
Hepburn, Ronald W. 78
Hick, John 12, 22, 47, 63, 65n, 74n, 75, 81, 82n, 86, 110, 123, 132, 133, 155, 221–4, 225n, 245
Hildegard of Bingen 79, 203
Hill, Peter C. 28, 35, 178
Hills, Peter 33
Hilton, Walter 53n–54n, 197, 201–2
Hobbes, Thomas 113n
Holder, Arthur 9, 190, 203, 214
Hollywood, Amy 203
Honderich, Ted 216
Hood, Ralph W., Jr ix, 28, 32, 33, 35, 39, 52n, 68–9, 82n, 87, 95, 102n, 129, 131, 134, 152, 163, 176, 178, 178n, 224, 241
Horwich, Paul 78
Hospers, John 67, 74n
Howard, Evan B. 11, 41, 42, 43
Hume, David 74n
Hunt, Harry T. 5, 6, 44, 82n, 128
Hunt, Kay 28
Hunter, Jack 44
Hurtado, L. W. 189
Huxley, Aldous 84

Inbody, Tyron 151
Isaiah 136, 188
Iyadurai, Joshua 42

Jacobs, Janet Liebman 167
James, William 6, 8, 21, 22, 25, 39, 41, 46, 52, 53n, 72, 73, 75, 78, 79, 82n, 84, 102n, 110, 112, 114n, 122n, 130, 141–2, 152, 162, 176, 177, 217, 220–1, 225n, 226, 234, 240, 242n
Jantzen, Grace M. 53n, 162–3
John of the Cross 53, 135–6, 163, 168n, 197, 199, 200
Johnson, Luke Timothy 22, 42, 54n, 187–8, 191, 238
Johnstone, Brick 14n
Julian of Norwich, Mother/Lady/Dame 202
Jung, Carl Gustav 173–4, 210

Kant, Immanuel 102n
Katz, Steven T. 13n, 26n, 40, 52n, 76, 85, 86, 87, 89, 90, 91, 94, 96, 98, 99, 101n, 138, 143, 146, 213, 225n, 243n
Kay, William K. 42
Kellenberger, James 45
Kelly, Thomas M. 90, 206, 207, 211, 212, 214, 215n
Kelsey, Morton T. 44
Kempe, Margery 202
Kennedy, Diane 51
Kerr, Fergus 215n
Kilby, Karen 210
King, Ursula 11
Kirkpatrick, Lee A. 172
Klein, Constantin 11
Klug, Leo F. 29, 32
Knowles, David, OSB 44, 53n, 70, 76–7, 142, 196, 197
Konstantine, Steven 205
Kourie, Celia, 190

INDEX OF NAMES

Krippner, Stanley 51
Kwan, Kai-man 13n, 21, 22, 25, 38–9, 46–47, 58, 63–4, 65n, 82n, 105, 109, 113n, 116, 124, 125–6, 130, 144, 154, 222

Land, Steven J. 43, 160
Lang, Andrew 232, 234
Langford, Michael 134n
Lash, Nicholas 75, 86, 92, 211, 214, 215n, 219, 220, 221, 225n
Laurentin, René 42
Leclerq, Jean 11, 204
Leibniz, Gottfried Wilhelm 84
Lévy-Bruhl, Lucien 232
Lewis, H. D. 53, 116, 146
Lewis, I. M. 43, 44, 235–6, 237
Lindbeck, George A. 99, 161n, 211–12, 215n
Lindblom, Johannes 44, 65n, 180–1, 186
Livingstone, James C. 149
Lootens, Matthew R. 194
Louden, Stephen H. 35
Louth, Andrew 52n, 198, 214
Lowis, Mike J. 177
Luke, David 45
Lynn, Steven Jay 51
Lyon, David 230

Mackie, John L. 71
Malinar, Angelika 43
Malinowski, Bronislaw 231
Malony, H. Newton 42, 46, 244
Marcusson-Clavertz, David 51
Mariña, Jacqueline 63, 205, 208
Marsh, Michael N. 51, 245, 246
Martin, C. B. 109
Marx, Karl 128, 129

Maslow, Abraham H. 48, 84, 174
Mavrodes, George I. 13n, 104, 113n, 116, 118, 122n, 151
Maxwell, Meg 21, 34, 152
McCombs, Charles R. 29, 32
McCool, Gerald A. 211
McCutcheon, Russell T. 86
McGinn, Bernard 11, 40, 165, 194, 202, 204
McGrath, Alister E. 157, 203, 212
McGuire, Meredith B. 63
McInroy, Mark J. 10
McIntosh, Daniel N. 14n, 52n
McIntosh, Mark A. 61
McNamara, Patrick 246
McRoberts, Omar M. 229–30
Meissner, W. W. 173, 178
Merton, Thomas 161n
Merz, Annette 185
Meyendorff, John 11, 160, 204
Meyering, Theo C. 246
Miles, T. R. 4, 13n, 73, 131, 138, 242n
Mill, John Stuart 67
Mitchell, Basil 118–19, 121
Moberly, R. W. L. 180, 182–3, 191
Mooney, Raymond 51
Moore, Peter G. 26n, 86, 98, 146
Moreland, J. P. 25, 64
Morisy, Ann 14n, 24, 28, 129, 238, 243n
Moser, Paul K. 168n, 215n
Moustakas, Clark 20
Murphy, Nancey 246

Nash, Tristan 75
Neitz, Mary Jo 164, 229
Newberg, Andrew B. 76, 77, 97, 244, 245, 246
Newman, John Henry 160

Nissinen, Martti 183

O'Hear, Anthony 106
O'Leary, Denyse 244
Okholm, Dennis L. 223
Oliver, Simon 243n
Oman, Doug 11
Oppy, Graham 72, 78, 79, 133n, 215n, 225n, 239
Otto, Rudolf 40, 84, 94, 102n, 164, 206, 207–10, 215n, 217, 229
Owen, H. P. 86

Paffard, Michael 21, 22, 49
Pahnke, W. N. 69
Palmer, John 51
Paloutzian, Raymond 42, 117
Paquette, Vincent 245
Paramaartha 96
Pargament, Kenneth I. 10, 33
Parrinder, Geoffrey 38, 40
Passmore, John 216
Pendlebury, Michael 5
Penelhum, Terence 155
Penner, Hans 52n, 96, 101n, 243n
Perovich, Anthony 102n
Persinger, Michael A. 246
Peterson, Michael 118, 133, 244
Phillips, Gary 223
Phillips, Timothy R. 223
Phipps, J.-F. 22
Pike, James A. 51
Pike, Nelson, 53n, 93, 200, 204n
Pinnock, Clark 223
Plantinga, Alvin 113n
Pojman, Louis 72, 73, 74
Poloma, Margaret M. 101n, 226, 241
Pope, Robert 148–9, 150, 212
Price Henry H. 71–2, 74, 74n

'Prudence' 165–6
Proudfoot, Wayne 4, 8–9, 14n, 22, 68, 82n, 86, 87–8, 89, 90, 91, 92, 93, 101, 101n, 102n, 110–11, 114n, 115, 127, 142, 146, 209, 211, 212, 217, 219, 225n
Pseudo-Dionysius, *see* Denys

Rahner, Karl 10, 210–11, 215n
Raitt, Jill 204
Ramsey, Ian T. 90, 122n, 138–9, 145–6, 147n
Rankin, Marianne 9
Raphael, Melissa 164
Rawlinson, Andrew 21
Rayburn, Carole A. 163
Reed, Esther 167
Reginald, Brother 153
Reich, Helmut 76
Reichenbach, Bruce 118, 133, 244
Richardson, Alan 141
Robeck, Cecil M. 42
Roberts, Robert C. *ix*
Robinson, Edward 21, 36n, 63
Rottschaefer, William A. 246
Runehov, Anne L. C. 246
Russell, Bertrand 126–7
Russell, Robert J. 246
Ryle, Gilbert 161n

Saliers, Don E. 160, 204
Sanders, E. P. 44, 82n
Sarbacker, Stuart 210, 215n
Sartori, Penny 51
Schlamm, Leon 215n
Schleiermacher, Friedrich 6, 22, 81, 149–51, 158, 161n, 185, 191n, 205–7, 215n, 220
Schmidt, Bettina E. *ix*, 45, 51, 75, 84,

94, 148, 150, 188, 190, 212, 232, 233, 234, 241, 245
Schoenrade, Patricia 69, 164, 177, 238
Schutz, Alfred 229
Sears, Robert A. 99
Shafranske, Edward P. 172
Shakespeare, Steven 212
Shaver, Phillip 14n
Short, Larry 143
Shushan, Gregory 51, 245
Sjørup, Lene 167
Smart, Ninian 5, 6, 38, 40, 76, 84, 97, 99, 101n, 133n, 143, 146, 147n, 151, 205, 210, 243n
Smith, Huston 38, 39
Smith, John E. 87, 122, 146, 151, 225
Smith, Margaret 37
Soskice, Janet Martin 137, 147
Southard, Samuel 42, 46, 244
Spickard, James V. 226–7, 229
Spilka, Bernard 14n, 28, 35, 52n, 176, 178
Spohn, William C. 61, 220
Staal, Frits x, 5, 20, 70, 131, 231, 235
Stace, Walter T. 32, 38, 39, 40, 52n, 84, 95, 144–6
Stanton, G. N. 82n
Starbuck, Edwin Diller 21, 220
Stark, Rodney 22, 28, 29, 32, 36n, 150–1, 228, 230
Sterk, Andrea 243n
Stiver, Dan R. 113, 155
Stoeber, Michael 94, 98, 101, 133n, 221, 225n
Stoller, Paul 243n
Straus, Roger A. 228–9
Streng, Frederick 138

Sudduth, Michael 115, 116, 120, 154, 214
Sullivan, John 243n
Sushan, Gregory 51, 245
Swinburne, Richard 6, 13, 22, 64, 105–6, 107, 111, 112, 116, 122n, 124, 129, 130, 134n, 222, 225
Sykes, Stephen W. 150

Taliaferro, Charles 120, 154
Tamminen, Kalevi 177
Tanner, Kathyrn 151
Taves, Ann 8, 9, 14n, 44, 63, 90, 98, 217, 220, 231, 242, 243n
Taylor, Charles 15n, 92, 102n
Teresa of Ávila (Teresa of Jesus) 44, 53n, 79–80, 137–8, 139, 163, 196, 197, 199, 200, 204n
Thayer, H. S. 78
Thiessen, Gerd 185
Thomas Aquinas 147n, 153
Thomas, Dorothy 231
Thomas, William 231
Thompson, Colin 200
Thornton, Martin 65n
Thouless, Robert H. 204n
Tilley, Terrence W. 15n, 110
Tippett, Alan 46
Tite, Philip A. 57, 188–9, 227
Trakakis, N. N. 72, 78, 79, 133n, 215n, 225n, 239
Trethowan, Illtyd 54n
Troeltsch, Ernst 236
Tschudin, Verena 21, 34, 152
Tugwell, Simon, OP 42, 153
Turnbull, Colin 243n
Turner, Edith 232–3, 234, 242, 243n
Tylor, Edward Burnett 231, 234

Underhill, Evelyn 84
Upanishads, the 140
Utsch, Michael 76

Ventis, W. Larry 69, 164, 177, 238
Vial, Theodore 215
von Balthasar, Hans Urs 10
von Hügel, Friedrich 49, 54n
von Rad, Gerhard 182, 183, 190, 191n

Wach, Joachim 54n
Wainwright, William J. 14n, 26n, 37, 38, 40–1, 64, 69, 72–3, 77–8, 87, 88, 106, 108, 109, 113n, 116, 130, 145, 219, 224, 225
Wakefield, Gordon S. 11, 52n, 185, 187, 195, 198, 200, 204n
Walker, Andrew 243n
Walker, Michael 86
Ward, Keith 5, 58, 65, 65n, 75, 80, 82n, 84, 124, 134n, 157, 160, 216
Ware, Kallistos 63
Ware, Owen 215n
Warrier, Maya 243n
Washburn, Michael 175
Webb, Mark 13
Weber, Max 185, 236–7, 238–9, 240, 243n
Wesley, John 10, 45, 161n
Wiebe, Phillip H. ix, 34, 43, 45, 52n, 112n, 190, 203, 245
Wilber, Ken 22, 175
Wildman, Wesley J. 5, 9, 10, 12, 13, 14n, 21, 39, 47–8, 50–1, 53, 54n, 57, 63, 75, 81, 82n, 107, 120–1, 132, 133, 134n, 224, 237, 245, 246
Wiles, Maurice 141, 157
Wilkinson, Michael 230
Williams, Bernard 216
Williams, Catrin H. 188, 190
Williams, Rowan 294n
Williamson, W. Paul 32, 87, 95
Willis, Roy 243n
Wilson, Bryan 241
Wilson, Joanna 51
Wilson, John Cook 116
Winkelman, Michael 84
Wiseman, Kames A., OSB 40
Wittgenstein, Ludwig 26n, 50, 221
Wolpert, Lewis 232
Wolterstorff, Nicholas 161n
Woodhead, Linda 11
Woods, Richard 37, 40
Wooffitt, Robin 51
Wordsworth, William 40, 49
Wulff, David M. 20, 127, 178
Wuthnow, R. 28, 36n
Wynn, Mark 63, 64

Yamane, David 229–30
Yandell, Keith E. 6, 19–20, 22, 92, 98, 111, 114n, 115, 116, 142
Yao, Xinzhong 21
Young, David E. 242

Zaehner, Robert Charles 39, 43, 52n–53n, 139
Zaleski, Carol 51
Zinnbauer, Brian J. 10

www.ingramcontent.com/pod-product-compliance
Lightning Source LLC
Chambersburg PA
CBHW051147290426
44108CB00019B/2632